History as Rhetoric

Studies in Rhetoric/Communication
Thomas W. Benson, General Editor

History
as
Rhetoric

Style, Narrative, and Persuasion

Ronald H. Carpenter

University of South Carolina Press

Published in Columbia, South Carolina, by the
University of South Carolina Press

Manufactured in the United States of America

Library of Congress Cataloging-in-Publication Data

Carpenter, Ronald H., 1933–
   History as Rhetoric : Style, Narrative, and Persuasion /
Ronald H. Carpenter.
    p. cm. — (Studies in rhetoric/communication)
   Includes bibliographical references and index.
   ISBN 1–57003–032–4
   1. Narration (Rhetoric) 2. Style, Literary. 3. History—
Methodology. 4. Historiography. I. Title. II. Series.
   PN203.C36 1995   94-18749
   808–dc20

Contents

History as Rhetoric

Chapter One

On Style and Narrative in History
A *Rhetorical* Perspective

History can persuade. Discourse approached, read, and accepted by most people as historical writing embodies certain elements that allow it to shape attitudes and actions. Perhaps the most immediately apparent of these qualities is credibility. For readers of history, "both the structure of the narrative and its details are representations of past actuality"; and scholars of the philosophy of history acknowledge that the "claim to be a true representation is understood by both writer and reader."[1] Surely a subtle but long-term impress of such credibility may be in our schools. In *America Revised,* a work that analyzes some of the most widely used history textbooks from which children "get their first and most lasting idea of what the United States is all about," Frances FitzGerald describes a preparatory mind set with which such discourse often is read and studied:

> Those of us who grew up in the fifties believed in the permanence of our American-history textbooks. To us as children, those texts were the truth of things: they were American history. It was not just that we read them before we understood that not everything that is printed is the truth, or the whole truth. It was that they, much more than other books, had the demeanor and trappings of authority. They were weighty volumes. They spoke in measured cadences: imperturbable, humorless, and as distant as Chinese emperors. Our teachers treated them with respect, and we paid them abject homage by memorizing a chapter a week.[2]

With that credibility, historical writing about the past acquires the status of being among the most persuasive discourse to influence attitudes and actions for the future.[3]

People often read history for its lessons about life. The great nineteenth-century historians were read, as John Clive attests, "because they saw themselves as prophets as well as historians, firmly believing that their role carried with it the obligation to say what they thought about society and politics of the present and the future as well as the past; because they usually said this with a confidence made evident in the cadence of their prose; because, along with the specific view of that segment of the past with which each of them was concerned, they also communicated a general view of the world."[4] Subsequent historians wrote with similar obligations and impress; still other writers of history likely will do so in the future. But what happens when their inherently credible medium of communication is characterized as well by its authors' *rhetorical* prowess, particularly in works read widely among the general public as well as people empowered to make crucial decisions in the world of practical affairs? The answer to that question is the raison d'être of this book.

"Rhetoric" is not a pejorative word. In a characteristic—but unfortunate—usage, "rhetoric" too often is preceded by the adjective "empty" to characterize what "other" people say ostensibly as empty promises or groundless, emotional appeals in stark contrast to discourse which presumably "tells it like it is." Or in another meaning (at least for some historians), "rhetoric" refers but to "Structures and Writing Techniques Essential to Successful Publication in the Field of History"; with that subtitle, Savoie Lottinville restricts *The Rhetoric of History* to mechanical matters such as bibliographies and edited documents, continuity, the avoidance of clichés, opening scenes, and methods of citation (with brief commentary about effective portraiture of heroes and villains).[5] Essentially a primer for graduate students who aspire to scholarly publication, Lottinville's book largely ignores the cumulative body of knowledge generated from the fourth century B.C. to the present, all with the goal of making people more effective in using language to influence others: rhetorical theory. For in a general but meaningful definition, rhetoric is "the rationale of informative and suasory discourse" whose "central" function is *"adjusting ideas to people and people to ideas."*[6]

Because of their reliance upon words, writers of history—whatever their degrees of objectivity, professional stature, or historiographical prowess—cannot escape potential rhetorical elements and effects that accrue simply from two discrete and significant facets of their process of composition: style and narrative. Therefore, as an introduction to the chapters in the present study which document facets of persuasiveness by which historical writing influences attitudes and actions, the following rhetorical perspective briefly will (1) define style and narrative, as well as (2) explain opinion leadership as the pertinent frame of reference for examining writers of history in their suasory role in society.

I

Style is the confounding canon of rhetoric. Over the centuries, confusing rules and principles have evolved due in part to the cumbersome Greek and Latin terminology that has been used to designate techniques of achieving style. In the English Renaissance, for instance, diligent students learned nearly two hundred arcane names for schemes and tropes, such as *brachiepia* and *epizeuxis* and *sinathrismus,* and other esoteric (but nevertheless precise) terminology to describe a "garden of eloquence" deemed appropriate (including *polysyndeton,* the way this sentence repeats its conjunction).[7] Successful students mastered those stylistic techniques then because an ideally educated gentleman was as deft with a pen as with a sword. Shakespeare was a product of that educational system, and Sister Miriam Joseph demonstrated how the Bard incorporated virtually all of those stylistic features at various places throughout his writing and thereby undoubtedly enhanced its impressiveness.[8] Renaissance students also were confronted, though, with imprecise if not nebulous ways of describing the instrumental qualities of their style, such as "elegance" or "vivacity" or "sublimity" or "forcefulness." So I. A. Richards's observation is pertinent: "the interesting question is surely NOT whether Shakespeare uses a given figure, but what *that* variation from flat writing does for him and for us just there."[9] Answers to that question inescapably address that central rhetorical function of "adjusting ideas to people and people to ideas."

To cast sentences in discourse, a writer has the essential tasks of choosing words (lexicon) and arranging them in appropriate orders (syntax). Word choices and their arrangements typically are constrained, however, to yield customary conformations to the common idiom. Language usage nevertheless embodies *"hierarchies of alternatives"* whereby "at both lexical and structural choice points, to the extent that there *is* choice, certain alternatives will be most probable, others less probable, and others very improbable." When grammatical syntax and lexicon nevertheless reflect an *"individual's deviations"* from more normative language usage, the resultant statement reflects that person's style, or in

Charles Osgood's view, "*how* a person talks about something rather than *what* he talks about."[10] Or as other commentary asserts, "underlying the very notion of style is a postulate of *independence of matter from manner*."[11] Although that contemporary view suggests a dichotomy between stylistic form and ideational substance, what people comprehend as the content of discourse may be influenced by its manner of presentation. For example, writers of English normatively make actor-action sentences wherein subjects of sentences occur before predicates, and objects follow predicates. If the King James Bible had conformed to those constraints, the Ephesians should have been made to say "Diana is great" when praising their admired goddess; but in "Great is Diana," customary placement is syntactically inverted in a "scheme" known generically in rhetoric handbooks as *anastrophe* (with variations known as *prozeugma*, *mezozeugma*, or *hypozeugma*, depending upon the exact location to which a word is inverted). With the *anastrophe*, Diana does seem more impressive. And like other communicators, writers of history may acquire rhetorical advantage expressed in this classical axiom: "A main difference between poet and poet, orator and orator, really does lie in the aptness with which they arrange their words."[12]

Admittedly, some stylistic choices in history serve succinctness, accuracy, or both. While writing *The Ordeal of the Union*, for instance, Allan Nevins characteristically reduced sentence lengths 20% in successive drafts. An early draft had twenty-five words: "We can now see that in political sagacity, adherence to principle, and vision of the national future, Lincoln rose superior to any of his contemporaries." With one revision, the sentence reached its published length of twenty words: "In political sagacity, adherence to principle, and vision of the national future, Lincoln rose superior to any of his contemporaries." Intermediate drafts sometimes were required, though. One early sentence used twenty-one words: "The story of the treatment of prisoners of war on both sides was becoming a story of callous neglect and cruelty." A second draft had eighteen words: "The treatment of prisoners of war on both sides was becoming a story of callous neglect and cruelty." And the final, published version contained fifteen words: "The treatment of prisoners of war on both sides was often a story of neglect."[13] As a journalist from 1913 to 1931 (at the *New York Evening Post, New York Sun,* and *New York World*), Nevins wrote—in his "spare time"—sufficient history worthy enough for him to be appointed De Witt Clinton Professor at Columbia University.[14] Journalists compose quickly with a physical eye on the clock to meet deadlines and an internal eye on the column inches in the final copy. And as Huntington Library research associate, Nevins still composed and typed drafts of history exceptionally fast.[15] After a stroke impaired his physical dexterity, Nevins dictated manuscript drafts at home to his secretary Lillian Bean, who remembered he would "edit a chapter and go into the other part of the house and back again within ten minutes, expecting that 60 pages were already typed, corrected, footnoted, and ready for the publisher."[16]

But impulses for succinct style did not undermine accuracy. Even in failing health, Nevins's editorial eye found phrasings more faithful to the reality of perceptual and cognitive processes. An early draft said, "How rich with new experiences of nature was this war. Many a Yankee or Western lad thought he knew all about nature. Nevertheless . . . he saw with clearer eyes than ever before the light of the sunshine, the beauty of the dawn." Longhand revisions say the lad "fancied" he knew about nature and "saw with sharper vision than before the beauty of the dawn." Similarly, Southerners had not "predicted" the war would "soon end" but "boasted" it "would end within weeks." After his death in 1971, the Huntington Library honored Nevins's memory with an exhibit including a three-shelved library cart holding eighty-three books written or edited by him; but in Ray Billington's estimate, he "was certainly the author of more than fifty books, edited at least seventy-five more, and published fully a thousand articles and reviews."[17] That quantity of writing was matched by its quality. No less a wordsmith than Adlai Stevenson sought the historian's help in drafting "even a few paragraphs" for a speech.[18] When Nevins retired from Columbia University in 1958, Alfred Knopf lauded him with the assertion that the historian was, "bar[ring] perhaps two of three of his colleagues, the only scholar of his time who is writing history in the grand manner."[19] And when deviations from normative syntax or lexicon yield sentences in a "grand manner," they also may attain style with *rhetorical* impress.

Ultimate products of style in historical writing are narratives. For in its efforts to evince "particular actuality," this discourse cannot escape a quality of narration which evolves simply from the writer's "succession of events—with the study of how one event is superseded by another."[20] Admittedly, some novels or plays that comprise epic fiction also are "true" in that, in Peter Munz's words, the "universals they contain have actuality, even though none or hardly any of the particular events in them can be said to have actually taken place." But as Munz observes further, historical narratives are accepted as "true in the sense that all the particular events they contain can be said to have actually happened . . . although we must recognize that . . . they are not portraits or mirror images or reports of what actually happened, but stories as seen and understood by somebody."[21] Narration thereby poses problems among historians, for the profession at times has deemed the creation of "simpler tales" merely "a strategy by which historians could win back the lost popular audience."[22] Nevertheless, because of the nature of their discourse, writers of history cannot avoid attaining some degree of narrativity which is another basis of potential persuasive impact upon readers.

In a seminal essay for appreciating the rhetorical implications of writing history, Walter Fisher defines "narration" not as "fictive composition" but rather as "symbolic actions—words and / or deeds—that have sequence and meaning for those who live, create, or interpret them." Undergirding this "narrative paradigm" is an axiom that "humans are essentially storytellers," and therefore "rationality is determined by the nature of persons as narrative beings—their inherent awareness of *narrative probability,* what constitutes a coherent story, and their constant habit of testing *narrative fidelity,* whether the stories they experience ring true with the stories they know to be true in their lives." In the world of pragmatic affairs, when "rival stories" confront people, several factors help endow discourse with its rhetorical potency:

> Any story, any rhetorical form of communication, not only says something about the world, it also implies an audience, persons who conceive of themselves in very specific ways. If a story denies a person's self-conception, it does not matter what it says about the world. . . . There are several reasons why this should be true. First, narration comes closer to capturing the experience of the world, and simultaneously appealing to the various senses, to reason and emotion, to intellect and imagination, and to fact and value. It does not presume intellectual contact only. Second, one does not have to be taught narrative probability and narrative fidelity; one culturally acquires them through a universal faculty and experience.[23]

The rhetorical view of narration resonates favorably with those historians who seek insights into how their discourse affects readers. Although the concept of narrative has been "increasingly subjected to sophisticated analysis, and with less than satisfactory results," Louis Mink nevertheless agrees that "story-telling is the most ubiquitous of human activities, and in any culture it is the form of complex discourse that is earliest accessible to children and by which they are largely acculturated."[24] Like style, narration thereby is an indispensable element when accounting for persuasiveness of historical writing.

II

In order to appreciate more fully the potential rhetoric of style and narrative in historical writing, a truism about communication and persuasion requires restatement: attributing persuasive effect to any particular discourse is rash. Attitudes and actions are molded by a matrix of message inputs, many of which are, as Samuel Becker has said, "unorganized" and "overlaid" to form a complex communication "mosaic" which "consists of an immense number of fragments or bits of information on an immense number of topics . . . scattered over time and space and modes of communication. Each individual must grasp from this mosaic those bits which serve his needs, must group them into message sets which are relevant for him at any given time . . . and close the gaps between them in order to arrive at a coherent picture of the world to which he can respond." Therefore, critics of discourse and its effects also should acknowledge Becker's corollary observation that persuasion to attitudes or actions rarely results from "any one communication encounter, or even a series of encounters by a single speaker or writer."[25] Still, some discourse may be particularly salient for exerting influence at a given point in time because of another phenomenon identified in research about communication and persuasion: opinion leadership. For another truism warrants repetition: "when people are exposed to information which they believe is important, they will generally turn to additional sources to verify or supplement what they got from the original source."[26] Historical writing often is that pivotal, influential source.

In an early effort to explain a "two-step flow of communication," Joseph Klapper found that people often are "more crucially influenced in many matters" by individuals perceived as "opinion leaders" amidst a matrix of what is read or heard as discourse.[27] Several factors conduce to individuals' achieving opinion leadership. Because these communicators and the people whom they influence "are very much alike and typically belong to the same primary groups," one criterion for achieving opinion leadership often is similarity; but because a group's opinion leader typically is deemed to be better informed about the matter at hand than the group itself is, another significant criterion is pertinent knowledge.[28] In many instances of their influence, opinion leaders provide reinforcement through face-to-face, oral communication. Nevertheless, a writer may exercise such influence when perceived to be what Klapper calls "a super representative" of a group because of his or her being "characteristically more competent," with "access to wider sources of pertinent information." Furthermore, when "found to be 'like everyone else, only slightly moreso' in reference to group norms," an opinion leader's "influence is related . . . to the *personification of certain values* of the group to which leader and follower belong" and "for a considerable number of individuals as well." Although many studies of this phenomenon sought to measure "the leader's role in producing change," the effect more often ascertained was "influence in favor of constancy and reinforcement"; and this guidance from opinion leaders "seems to be sought or accepted in specific areas partly—or perhaps largely—because it provides . . . followers with the sort of satisfactions they seek in those areas."[29] When it offers guidance and reinforcement, historical writing—and rhetorical elements therein—can be viewed profitably from this pertinent frame of reference known as opinion leadership.

Although they may not attribute their influence to rhetorical elements of style and narrative, some writers of history admit they reinforce or corroborate already extant values which in turn guide behavior. As president of the American Historical Association in 1931, Carl Becker articulated his pragmatic view that "we do not impose our version of the human story on Mr. Everyman; in the end it is rather Mr. Everyman who imposes his version on us." For Becker, the "proper function" of historians was "not to repeat the past but to make use of it, to correct and rationalize for common use Mr. Everyman's mythological adaptation of what happened." He therefore concluded that "the secret of our success in the long run is in conforming to the temper of Mr. Everyman, which we seem to guide only because we are so sure, eventually, to follow it."[30] Barbara Tuchman subsequently reminded the AHA that "since the outbreak of World War II the statistics of the book trade reflect the growing appetite of the public for biography, autobiography, science, sociology and history—especially contemporary history." Moreover, public interest in the "literature of actuality" more than novels, poetry, and drama is pragmatic in origin; for "in a time of widening uncertainty and chronic stress the historian's voice is the most needed, the moreso as the others seem inadequate, often absurd. . . . the opportunity, I think, is plain for the historian to become the major interpreter in literary experience of man's role in society. The task is to provide both the matter to satisfy the public interest and those insights into the human condition without which any reading matter is vapid."[31]

Across a spectrum of society, people approach historical discourse precisely for such reinforcement. A student wrote to express appreciation for Merle Curti's ability to express well "some of the vital lessons of life," particularly "as we grow older and tend to become conservative and intolerant."[32] After listening to Curti's radio lectures in the 1940s from the University of Wisconsin, a woman voiced this request:

> Because we live in a household quite divided by the merits of the New Deal, I hung with tenacity on every word of your lecture this morning. You mentioned another course in basic history in which economic and political issues of the New Deal were analyzed in greater detail. Is there a reference list in that course for readings on the Depression and New Deal? I should deeply appreciate suggestive reading. As a mother I feel the contribution I might make to a busy husband and to the meeting of a demand for facts, from children reaching maturity when arguments wax warm.[33]

The United States Air Force asked Curti to fulfill a similar role at the Air War College during the Cold War:

> One of the initial studies in the curriculum, "Problem Solving," has the objective of stimulating constructive and analytical thinking. The study integrates the discussion method with problem solving and emphasizes contextual analysis. As a means to better understanding of the effects of American tradition and culture on our habits of thinking, we plan to cover the historical, social, political and economic concepts which influence our attempts to solve problems. We believe this coverage can best be attained if the students can listen to particularly qualified individuals speak on appropriate subjects. We should be most appreciative if you would consent to give us a lecture covering "The Federal System and Political Parties."[34]

Curti also was invited to coauthor an *academic* book with clearly suasory objectives:

> As we all know, recent years have stimulated many statements of the need for a lucid account of a faith that all opponents of Soviet despotism can adhere to. . . . a firm yet adaptable set of beliefs that can enlist all possible opposition to the reactionary ideology that glowers at us from Russia. What is direly needed is a counter-ideology that can coalesce all opponents of Soviet tyranny into an iron resistance, a set of intellectual postulates with yet an emotional glow which might lift the West from its confusion, disunity, and dull, shaken malaise that verges on cynicism and indifference. Our military forces and their civilian springboards must have ideals to fight for if they are to combat the savage fanaticism of thoroughly indoctrinated Communist troops. . . . Today the world, stalled in a political impasse of indeterminate span, hangs in nervous suspense and dread of an impending holocaust. There is therefore increasing urgency for us to develop potent ideological weapons to lessen the likelihood of our having to resort to the use of weapons of physical destruction.

Moreover, this "noteworthy" book should have "the glory and thrill of a mythology, yet the simultaneous wisdom and simplicity of Lincolnian phraseology; it should have not localized origin or applicability, but should reflect a real cosmopolitanism, unfettered by national, ethnical, or class prejudices or patriotisms; it should assume the more noble aspects but not the irrefutable dogmatism of Holy Scripture." Because his "deeper studies into human affairs and motivation" have provided him with "a richer insight than many of us have," Curti was a likely participant in the project.[35]

More poignant evidence of the historian as opinion leader is this letter to Allan Nevins from a woman in Garfield Heights, Ohio, a blue-collar, working-class suburb of Cleveland:

> I sincerely hope I'm not imposing on you, but I'll use as justification a very deep love of history which I'm sure you can understand. During the past several months I have been increasingly interested in two very wonderful people who did so much for our country—Colonel John C. Fremont and his wife Jessie. It all started with a biographical novel by Irving Stone "Immortal Wife." I'm in my early 20's, Mr.

Nevins, and as yet not married. Jessie Benton Fremont thought and felt as I do about so many things. I couldn't help but love her. Perhaps one day I too can be the kind of wife and woman she was in my own way. Mr. Stone's bibliography lists your book "Fremont, Pathfinder of the West" and I finally managed to obtain a copy published in the American Classics series. I am nearly finished with it. As with all really good books, it ends too soon. Somehow you begin to feel you know these people personally and you don't want to lose them. So again I've checked your bibliography and have written to 10 different bookstores in an effort to locate at least a copy of Colonel Fremont's own book on his explorations. . . . By any chance do you know where I can find a copy of Colonel Fremont's book? Thank you Mr. Nevins for taking the time to read my letter, and thank you sincerely for all your wonderful books. Thank you especially for bringing to life the very heart and soul of Colonel Fremont.[36]

These words of a Ms. Everyman illustrate precisely the role of historians as opinion leaders, for she sought out the "literature of actuality" to find further guidance or reinforcement for ideas and values acquired first from other sources in the vast communication mosaic of society.

III

The goal of this book is to explicate rhetorical roles of style and narrative as they conduce to writers achieving opinion leadership in pragmatic affairs. To pursue such an aim, however, is *not* to raise the specter of objectivity or lack of it in that discourse. Although their writing may aspire to the "noble dream" of objectivity which impresses professional peers, Peter Novick demonstrated how the writing of historians "is closely tied to changing social, political, cultural, and professional contexts."[37] Obviously, "the idea and ideal of 'objectivity' . . . has been the key term in defining progress in historical scholarship" when seeking "truth about the past," yet recent work in the history, philosophy, and sociology of science "has made us increasingly aware of the influence of external and social factors in theory choice, in deciding what is 'a fact,' and even in defining 'rationality.'"[38] Nor will explication of rhetoric in history evoke another specter of whether its writers indeed are professional historians whose discourse is intended for scholarly readers or are those other authors whose efforts are directed at "best-seller-dom in history." For to some extent in the academic world, "providing history for the general reading public" has been deemed the province of "amateurs like Walter Lord, Cornelius Ryan, William L. Shirer, John Toland, and Barbara Tuchman, whom most professional historians, justly or unjustly, regarded as the equivalent of chiropractors and naturopaths."[39] The important criterion is that their discourse indeed was approached and accepted as "history" by readers who often were in positions to make decisions of substantial import.

In Part I of the present study, "Historians as Rhetorical Stylists," a chapter on Frederick Jackson Turner identifies elements of style contributing to the long-term, rhetorical impact of the Frontier Thesis. Carl Becker's style then is examined for its overt contributions to his rhetorical impress as an essayist, a propagandist in World War I, and author of an eminently successful textbook, *Modern History*. An analysis of Alfred Thayer Mahan's writing suggests how the rhetoric of style created a subtle paramessage to complement the manifest content of *The Influence of Sea Power Upon History*. In each case, chapters in Part I identify what each influential writer hoped to accomplish rhetorically, the stylistic means which each employed on behalf of those objectives, and when or why each initially acquired those predilections for language and subsequently applied them in discourse. Moreover, rhetorical influence of that style is delineated in terms of what the general public or people in public affairs have identified as persuasive, and evidence of that effect often is found in primary-source collections of letters to historians in which readers themselves account for how and why they were persuaded and to what specific attitudes or actions.

In Part II, "The Rhetoric of Narrative in History," the influence of *The Guns of August* upon President John Kennedy during the Cuban Missile Crisis is explained using correspondence between Barbara Tuchman and her editor during the writing of that book—all suggestive of how the work embodies emplotment modes identified by Hayden White as instrumental in narration. Another chapter explicates narrative fidelity of historical writing when consonant with readers' prior knowledge and experience, and primary-source materials help explain how historical writings of Alfred Thayer Mahan influenced Japanese naval officers when they were formulating their strategic goal for the Pearl Harbor attack as well as implementing tactics during the raid. Because "rival stories" may prevent writers from achieving intended persuasion, the historian unsuccessful as a would-be rhetor merits attention. Thus, rhetorical efforts of Frank L. Owsley on behalf of agrarianism are contrasted with influential historical writing such as that from Woodrow Wilson and Charles A. Beard on behalf of industrialism and economic success.

But suasory roles of style and narrative in historical writing may transcend efforts of any one writer or chronological parameters of any well-defined rhetorical situation. Richard Neustadt and Ernest May offer the reminder that "the majority of mankind" acquires historical knowledge and resultant attitudes in a "stream of time," learning from "pieced-together stories" gleaned from a wide range of communication to which people are exposed in their lifetimes.[40] Thus, Part III is a concluding chapter which traces Americans' frontier metaphors to describe their twentieth-century combat, in the "stream of time" from early corroboration by historians as opinion leaders through evolution into an archetype influencing contemporary society. And because this book begins by referring to rhetoric in American history textbooks, so too does it conclude with speculation about future obligations of those who write history. For with its potential for rhetorical impress, the history we read is capable of being among our most persuasive discourse.

Notes

1. Louis O. Mink, "Narrative Form as Cognitive Instrument," in *The Writing of History: Literary Form and Historical Understanding,* ed. Robert H. Canary and Henry Kozicki (Madison: University of Wisconsin Press, 1978), 130.

2. Frances FitzGerald, *America Revised: History Schoolbooks in the Twentieth Century* (Boston: Little, Brown, 1979), 7.

3. I have explored the rhetoric of history in several shorter essays which constitute bases of my more detailed discussion in this present volume. See my "Rhetorical Genesis of Style in the 'Frontier Hypothesis' of Frederick Jackson Turner," *Southern Speech Journal* 36 (Spring 1972): 233–48; "Alfred Thayer Mahan's Style on Sea Power: A Paramessage Conducing to *Ethos," Speech Monographs* 42 (August 1975): 190–202; "Style in Discourse as an Index of Frederick Jackson Turner's Historical Creativity," *Huntington Library Quarterly* 40 (May 1977): 269–77; "Frederick Jackson Turner and the Rhetorical Impact of the Frontier Thesis," *Quarterly Journal of Speech* 63 (april 1977): 117–29; "The Historical Jeremiad as Rhetorical Genre," in *Form and Genre: Shaping Rhetorical Action,* ed. Karlyn Campbell and Kathleen Jamieson (Falls Church, Va.: Speech Communication Association, 1977), 103–17; "Carl Becker and the Epigrammatic Force of Style in

History," *Communication Monographs* 48 (December 1981): 318–39; *The Eloquence of Frederick Jackson Turner* (San Marino, Calif.: Huntington Library, 1983); "America's Opinion Leader Historians on Behalf of Success," *Quarterly Journal of Speech* 69 (May 1983): 111–26; "On American History Textbooks and Integration in the South: Woodrow Wilson and the Rhetoric of Division and Reunion 1829–1889," *Southern Speech Communication Journal* 51 (Fall 1985): 1–23; and "Admiral Mahan, 'Narrative Fidelity,' and the Japanese Attack on Pearl Harbor," *Quarterly Journal of Speech* 72 (August 1986): 290–305; repr. in *Naval History: The Seventh Symposium of the U.S. Naval Academy,* ed. William B. Cogar (Wilmington, Del.: Scholarly Resources, 1988), 195–211.

4. John Clive, *Not by Fact Alone: Essays on the Writing and Reading of History* (New York: Alfred A. Knopf, 1989), 34.

5. Savoie Lottinville, *The Rhetoric of History: A Critical Examination of the Structures and Writing Techniques Essential to Successful Publication in the Field of History* (Norman: University of Oklahoma Press, 1976).

6. Donald C. Bryant, *Rhetorical Dimensions in Criticism* (Baton Rouge: Louisiana State University Press, 1973), 11, 19. Bryant's earlier expression of this definition was in "Rhetoric: Its Functions and Its Scope," *Quarterly Journal of Speech* 39 (December 1953): 401–24.

7. Still available for reading now are Renaissance handbooks teaching rhetoric primarily as stylistic skills, such as Henry Peacham's *Garden of Eloquence* (1593), in a facsimile reproduction with an introduction by William G. Crane (Gainesville, Fla.: Scholars' Facsimiles and Reprints, 1954); Richard Sherry's *Treatise of Schemes and Tropes* (1550), in a facsimile reproduction with introduction and index by Herbert Hildebrandt (Gainesville, Fla.: Scholars' Facsimiles and Reprints, 1961); and George Puttenham's *Arte of English Poesie* (1589), edited by Gladys Willcock and Alice Walker (Cambridge: Cambridge University Press, 1936). The appeal of stylistic rhetorics in the Renaissance is discussed in Wilbur Samuel Howell, *Logic and Rhetoric in England, 1500–1700* (New York: Russell and Russell Reprints, 1961). For tabular classification of these syntactical options detailing their various names, as well as an explanation of why they deviate from the common idiom for English, see my "The Essential Schemes of Syntax: An Analysis of Rhetorical Theory's Recommendations for Uncommon Syntax," *Quarterly Journal of Speech* 55 (April 1969): 161–68.

8. Sister Miriam Joseph, *Shakespeare's Use of the Arts of Language* (New York: Columbia University Press, 1947).

9. I. A. Richards, *Speculative Instruments* (Chicago: University of Chicago Press, 1955), 158.

10. Charles Osgood, "Some Effects of Motivation on Style of Encoding," in *Style in Language,* ed. Thomas A. Sebeok (New York: John Wiley and Sons, 1960), 293–96.

11. Rulon Wells, "Nominal and Verbal Style," in *Style in Language,* 215.

12. Dionysius of Halicarnassus, *On Literary Composition* 3, trans. W. Rhys Roberts (London: Macmillan, 1910), 73.

13. See the successive drafts of chapter 3, "Cement of the Union," for *The Organized War to Victory 1864–1865,* and those of chapter 13, "New Crises in Foreign Relations," for *The Organized War 1863–1864,* in Box 37, Allan Nevins Collection, Henry E. Huntington Library, San Marino, Calif.

14. Allan Nevins, "Some Elementary Lessons on Life and Scholarship" (1967), in Box 41, Allan Nevins Collection. Nevins wrote as well for *Collier's Weekly, Saturday Evening Post,* and the *New York Times Sunday Magazine.* See also Ray A. Billington, *Billington on Nevins: A Talk Given before the Zamorano Club* (San Marino. Calif.: n.p., 1980), 5–6. One hundred and seventy-five copies were printed; my copy was given to me by Daniel Woodward, head librarian at the Huntington. Nevins retired from Columbia at the compulsory age of sixty-eight, when he was invited to the Huntington Library as senior research associate, serving until his death in 1971.

15. I met Allan Nevins and Ray Billington during my first visit to the Huntington Library in 1970, participating (mostly by listening) in their luncheon conversations and in their favorite post-lunch activities: well-known walking tours in the Huntington gardens and lawn bowling on the expanse of grass adjoining the "Readers'" entrance to the library. For a brief description of Nevins as a fast typist when he was writing history, see also Billington, *Billington on Nevins,* 13.

16. Lillian K. Bean to William Q. Maxwell, 8 February 1970, in Box 45, Allan Nevins Collection. Nevins dictated volumes 7 and 8 of *The Ordeal of the Union* to Lillian Bean. Not without problems in the process, that dictation at one point had the secretary hearing a reference to De Tocqueville's "bastardly" book— which Nevins thankfully caught and changed to "masterly." In the last stages of writing *The Ordeal of the Union,* Nevins was "too ill to work on the proofs," so his wife had someone "correcting the sentences." As Mrs. Nevins said, "I don't like others knowing that Allan's writing needed improvement but perhaps it is better than having poorly constructed sentences appear" (Mary Nevins to Lillian Bean, 9 January 1971, in Box 45, Allan Nevins Collection).

17. Billington, *Billington on Nevins,* 9–11.

18. Adlai E. Stevenson to Allan Nevins, 7 December 1963, in Box 44, Allan Nevins Collection.

19. Alfred A. Knopf, in *Lines of Tribute to Allan Nevins from Several of His Friends on the Occasion of His Retirement from the Faculty of Columbia University in the City of New York* (San Francisco: Peregrine Press, 1958). Thirty-one copies were printed; the copy at the Huntington Library is Rare Book No. 383474.

20. Peter Munz, *The Shapes of Time: A New Look at the Philosophy of History* (Middletown, Conn.: Wesleyan University Press, 1977), 22–23.

21. *The Shapes of Time,* 217–18.

16 History as Rhetoric

22. Peter Novick, *That Noble Dream: The "Objectivity Question" and the American Historical Profession* (Cambridge: Cambridge University Press, 1988), 622–23.

23. See Walter R. Fisher, "Narration as a Human Communication Paradigm: The Case of Public Moral Argument," *Communication Monographs* 51 (March 1984): 1–22. See in particular 14–15.

24. Mink, "Narrative Form as Cognitive Instrument," in *The Writing of History* 133.

25. Samuel Becker, "Rhetorical Studies for the Contemporary World," in *The Prospect of Rhetoric*, ed. Lloyd Bitzer and Edwin Black (Englewood Cliffs, N.J.: Prentice-Hall, 1971), 22–25, 33.

26. "Rhetorical Studies for the Contemporary World," in *The Prospect of Rhetoric*, 35.

27. Joseph T. Klapper, *The Effects of Mass Communication* (New York: Free Press, 1960), 51. This process was delineated originally during the presidential campaigns of 1940 and 1948 by Lazarsfeld, Berelson, and Gaudet, who observed then that "ideas often flow *from* radio and print *to* the opinion leaders and *from* them to the less active sections of the population." See *The People's Choice* (New York: Columbia University Press, 1948), 151.

28. See Elihu Katz, "The Two-Step Flow of Communication: An Up-To-Date Report on an Hypothesis," *Public Opinion Quarterly* 21 (Spring 1957): 63, 77; Elihu Katz and Paul F. Lazarsfeld, *Personal Influence: The Part Played by People in the Flow of Mass Communication* (Glencoe: Free Press, 1955), 286; and Bernard Berelson and Gary Steiner, *Human Behavior: An Inventory of Scientific Findings* (New York: Harcourt, Brace, and World, 1964), 550.

29. Klapper, *The Effects of Mass Communication*, 34–36, 51. For another overview and critique of research about opinion leadership and the "two-step flow of communication," see Frederick C. Whitney, *Mass Media and Mass Communication in Society* (Dubuque: William C. Brown, 1975), 56–58, 412–15, and 446–47.

30. "Everyman His Own Historian" was Carl Becker's presidential address delivered before the American Historical Association Convention in Minneapolis on 29 December 1931; it is published in Becker, *Everyman His Own Historian: Essays on History and Politics* (New York: Appleton-Century-Crofts, 1935), 233–55; see esp. 253. For one analysis of Becker's orientation, see Cushing Strout, *The Pragmatic Revolt in American History: Carl Becker and Charles Beard* (New Haven: Yale University Press, 1958).

31. Barbara Tuchman, "The Historian's Opportunity," address to the American Historical Association, December 1966; repr. in *Saturday Review*, 25 February 1967, 27–31; and in Tuchman, *Practicing History: Selected Essays* (New York: Alfred A. Knopf, 1981), 51–64. See in particular 51–52.

32. William Cleveland to Curti, 25 June 1922, in Box 7, File 32, Merle Curti Papers, State Historical Society of Wisconsin, Madison, Wis.

33. Mrs. Rudolf Furrer to Curti, 2 May 1945, in Box 16, File 1, Curti Papers.

34. Major General O. A. Anderson, USAF, Commandant, Air War College, to Curti, 15 August 1949, in Box 1, File 8, Curti Papers.

35. John J. Harter, General Studies Dept., University of Southern California, to Curti, 12 February 1951, in Box 18, File 15, Curti Papers.

36. Diane C. Bastic to Allan Nevins, 15 March 1970, in Box 43, Allan Nevins Collection.

37. Novick, *That Noble Dream*, 17, 628.

38. *That Noble Dream*, 1, 10.

39. *That Noble Dream*, 372.

40. Richard Neustadt and Ernest May, *Thinking in Time: The Uses of History for Decision Makers* (New York: Free Press, 1986), 15, 263–64.

Part I

Historians as Rhetorical Stylists

A main difference between poet and poet, orator and orator, really
does lie in the aptness with which they arrange their words.
                    Dionysius of Halicarnassus, *On Literary Composition*

Chapter Two

Frederick Jackson Turner and the Oratorical Origins of Persuasive Style in the Frontier Thesis

Young Fred Turner was impressed. His scrapbook as a University of Wisconsin freshman provides the proof.[1] In 1879, an event inextricably molded Frederick Jackson Turner's outlook toward style in discourse and thereby his subsequent writing of history: the oratorical triumph of upperclassman Robert M. La Follette. As a University of Wisconsin senior that year, La Follette won in April a contest at the Madison campus with an oration titled "Iago," a state championship with it in May, and an interstate contest in Iowa City a week later, defeating contestants from six states. His notable success warranted a hero's welcome in the assembly chamber of the state capitol, where he was congratulated formally by University of Wisconsin regents as well as leading citizens of Madison.[2] La Follette was elected eighteen months later as district attorney of Dane County (wherein Madison and the University of Wisconsin are located); and thus an illustrious political career was virtually founded on a single speech.[3] In 1879 Turner, the impressionable freshman, was awed by that speech. On the evening of La Follette's triumphant return to Madison after winning the state championship at Beloit, Wisconsin, Turner was in the crowd of students waiting at the telegraph office for news of the contest result; he marched in that group, with a band, to the railroad station to await the winner's 2:25 A.M. train home; and he then participated in the victory parade back to campus—all described with élan in the account he wrote for his father's newspaper in Portage, the *Wisconsin State Register*:

At half past one we fell in on the campus, with two drums—Loomis and Anderson—Capt Cole presiding over the piccolo with his usual grace and dignity, and Curtis, a scientific "fresh" on the cornet. We whooped her right up all the way downtown, the police keeping out of sight in a most gentlemanly manner. Got down to the depot, and Capt Cole took command and dressed them into line. Then the train came in. There were about sixty boys on the train, and when the two crowds saw each other, maybe we didn't yell! We nabbed on to La Follette, and took him home to the inspiring strains of "The Brannigans' Band." When we got to the house, the band played "When Johnnie Comes Marching Home Again," in a touching manner. John Anderson, one of the defeated contestants at the home contest, made a handsome speech, welcoming La F. home. Bob then replied. His voice trembled a little when he thanked the boys for the splendid manner in which they greeted him. He then bade us good night, and we ended off by giving three rousing cheers for Bob, and three more for the Beloit boys who took a whipping like gentlemen. We then marched part way up to the University and disbanded, every one enthusiastic, and not a *drop* of liquor in the whole crowd.

Down at Beloit, the boys kept patting Bob on the back before he went on, and he went on and stood facing the audience for about ten seconds and began. He took the audience by storm. He held their attention all the time, and when he sat down there was a perfect roar of applause. His subject is Iago, one of the characters in Othello. His gestures are elegant, articulation simply wonderful, and his power of language is enormous. When the decision of the judges was read, every University boy jumped to his feet and went for Bob, got him on their shoulders and rushed into the street, cheered and cheered again, and sent us the news.

I haven't got over my enthuse yet—that's why I have so much to say about it. I didn't get in till long after 3 A.M., and not to sleep till 4. The boys have never shown any college feeling before, and when it did come out, it came. If Bob carries the interstate contest, how we will everlastingly make things hum.

Yours truly,
F.

That newspaper account of La Follette's victory is pasted in Turner's scrapbook with a text of "Iago" on the adjoining page. Oratory whose "power of language is enormous" left an indelible imprint. Turner's style in history was shaped by this event, and he recognized that what he had learned in 1879 as a University of Wisconsin freshman became a pivotal factor in the writing that brought him to the pinnacle of his profession, a paper in 1893 called "The Significance of the Frontier in American History" or, as subsequently known, the Frontier Thesis. On the evening of 24 May 1924, the Harvard History Club hosted a dinner honoring Turner upon his retirement from that university. The guest of honor offered an address starting with a carefully worded prologue stating an intention to describe "some of the forces that have influenced my career" and "how far the little things as well as clearly obvious circumstances affect one's academic life." Although discussion of his family background was written out in four pages of complete sentences, Turner's longhand manuscript then became but an outline list of topics he would cover in the speech, such as graduate and undergraduate courses and professors at Johns Hopkins and the University of Wisconsin. Also prominent on that list—forty-five years after the event—was the notation "La Follette—Iago."[4] Thus, to close his career, this historian who had made a significant impact upon his profession—as well as the general public—included among factors affecting his "academic life" an oration he heard in 1879 as a freshman at Wisconsin. That oratorical event (1) corroborated Turner's inclinations as a high-school student, (2) molded his personal sense of style in college, (3) helped shape a conception later known as the Frontier Thesis, and (4) ultimately contributed to the rhetorical impact of that document upon readers.

I

Portage, Wisconsin, is thirty-seven miles from Madison and the University of Wisconsin. Yet in another sense, Turner's boyhood home was quite a great distance from that cosmopolitan environment. During the formative years of his youth, he observed many facets of frontier life: a hunting party tracking a vicious wolf pack, covered wagons moving through Portage bound for free lands farther west, Indians in town to trade pelts for goods, vigilantes recruited by the sheriff to capture a horse thief, a shootout on the main street of town, and a lynching. Portage had significance in the frontier, for the town developed at the place where fur traders carried their canoes (*portage*) between the Fox River emptying into the Great Lakes and the Wisconsin River leading to the

Mississippi. To a boy whose reading included adventure stories about the far West, accounts of Indian uprisings, and the massacre of Custer and his men at the Little Bighorn River, "the frontier was" as Ray A. Billington puts it, "near and meaningful. . . ." Indeed, the ultimate content of the document Turner called "The Significance of the Frontier in American History" had some of its conceptual roots in observations which, as Billington goes on to affirm, "placed an indelible stamp on him, and played a role in interesting him in the frontier as a molding force."[5] Early life in Portage also shaped within Turner an emergent sense of style for discourse.

For all its frontier facets, Portage was no cultural or literary wasteland in the last quarter of the nineteenth century. Although entertainment often came from traveling troupes of actors and musical artists, a cornerstone of culture was rhetorical. In the latter part of the nineteenth century, Americans appreciated oratory. Whether through Chautauqua lectures or spontaneous debates in various meetings large and small, people heard and often participated in discourse not only as a means of disseminating ideas but also as a mode of influencing attitudes and exhorting others to action.[6] Portage was no different from other small towns. On the Fourth of July, young Fred listened to readings of the Declaration of Independence as well as the orations which climaxed parades that ended at the courthouse. At age fourteen, he was involved in debates and oratorical activities in the Young Men's Lyceum, and if he wanted to read examples of artistic style in language, his home held a respectable library.[7] The household was literate because the father, Andrew Jackson Turner, made his livelihood with language. Having purchased in 1861 a small newspaper, the *Portage Record,* for which he worked initially as a typesetter, Jack Turner ultimately merged that outlet with another rival newspaper he bought, and the resultant *Wisconsin State Register* was published weekly. Although he also invested in timber and a small railroad company, Jack Turner's prominence in Portage rested upon his position as publisher of a newspaper. And with that role as a community opinion leader came a concomitant: political activity that often was rhetorical. He spoke regularly on behalf of Republican candidates, was appointed by a Republican governor to the Wisconsin Railroad Commission, and in 1881 was elected mayor of Portage, serving four terms (two as the voters' unanimous choice). The workings of rhetoric became known to young Fred during dinner-table conversations at home as well as opportunities to observe his father as a speaker and persuader in pragmatic affairs.[8] From his youth in Portage, Fred Turner knew rhetoric worked.

While in Portage, Turner began developing a sense of rhetorical style by collecting excerpts of eloquence which he pasted in his scrapbook. Although initial items therein favor quotations from Ralph Waldo Emerson, other orators and literary figures subsequently came to his attention when he started contributing a "Pencils and Scissors" column for his father's newspaper. Six issues of that column, from January and February 1878, appear in his scrapbook. And although Billington used "Pencils and Scissors" excerpts to suggest the "catholicity of reading interest of a scholar," those quotations also are indices of style that strikes young Fred's eye.[9] Besides Emerson, the authors and orators represented include Goethe, Disraeli, Harriet Beecher Stowe, Thomas Carlyle, Victor Hugo, Rousseau, Daniel Webster, and Robert G. Ingersoll. Stylistic trends are evident. In shorter quotations beginning each column, antitheses prevail—often in neatly turned epigrams such as "Art is long, life short"; "Love swells like Solway, but ebbs like its tide"; or "We should esteem virtue, though in a foe; and abhor vice, though in a friend." Longer quotations often employ rhetorical parallelism, repeating the same word or phrase at beginnings of successive phrases or sentences (known traditionally as *anaphora* or *epanaphora*), as in "Every candid acknowledgement, every conquest . . ."; "Doubt springs from difficulty. Doubt is the recoil of the mind"; or "It is a building of character. It is a building that must stand."

While collecting these quotations, Turner had opportunities in high school to try creating that rhetorical style himself. Although he participated in Memorial Day declamations his last two years of high school, his more significant experience was on 28 June 1878 with a commencement oration, "The Power of the Press," which won first prize—a copy of Macaulay's *History of England*—and this favorable review in the *Wisconsin State Register*: "His thought was original, his style clear and forcible, and his manner self possessed and very earnest. He richly deserved the prize, which was afterward awarded him."[10] Unlike declamations, wherein speakers memorize and deliver speeches written by others, orations are original compositions in which personal prowess with rhetoric is displayed. For young Turner, ideational content was a paean to the newspaper and its role in society; in stylistic form, his oration displays efforts to produce personally the eloquence contributed to the "Pencils and Scissors" column.

"The Power of the Press" experiments with several sources of rhetorical style. Parallel repetitions for the beginnings of successive sentences occur, as in "It was conceived just as the world was emerging. . . . It rose from that darkness like the sun . . ."; or "What king's court can boast such company? What school of philosophy such wisdom?" Turner works in patterns of two, however, rather than three parallel beginnings known traditionally as the tricolon. Alliteration also appears, as in "sweetest songs" and "words of wisdom." He is capable, too, of stylistic inversions (*anastrophe*) of customary syntax, as in his opening sentence: "About four centuries ago was born in the brain of John Guttenberg [*sic*], an idea destined to be the propagator of learning, of Christianity, and of civilization, and thus to sway the future of the world" (normative syntax has subject-predicate order, or "an idea was born." But note, as well, the alliteration, parallel repetition, and climax order known as *klimax, scala,* or *gradatio*). Also present are attempts to achieve antitheses by placing opposites close together in a sentence. Some of those syntactical appositions are overt, as in "risen and decayed" or "the past became the present." In the main, however, the high-school efforts do not embody the balance necessary for epigrams. The constructions are less antonymical, as in "of the ignorant, by the ignorant" or "not only a possibility, but even a probability." Other attempts at antitheses are too wordy, a quality undermining their epigrammatic potential, as in "The more despotic a monarch, the greater the restrictions does he place upon the utterances of the Newspaper; while on the other hand, as the freedom of the Press increases, so does the freedom of the people." Nevertheless, the experience suggested to Turner how antitheses could be made artistically, for the first prize—Macaulay's *History of England*— offers salient examples of antithetical style to sharpen historical portraiture. Although sometimes criticized for stylistic excesses, Macaulay is known for epigrammatic antitheses, as in characterizing King James II: "To bend and break the spirits of men gave him pleasure, and to part with his money gave him pain. What he had not the generosity to do at his own expense he determined to do at the expense of others."[11] Turner's prize in his first oratorical triumph was another piece in a pattern of experiences leading to a sense of style for writing history.

Winning first prize for his high-school commencement address was deeply gratifying. Oratorical contests are emotional experiences of considerable magnitude. Intense psychological involvement occurs while one is creating and polishing the oration to a finished product. Nuances of voice and bodily movement are on display when one is delivering that product to the public. And after many hours of memorization and rehearsal, one's emotions and expectations for success are heightened. Even with prior experience in Memorial Day declamations, Turner—who was at an age when young men often feel awkward or self-conscious—must have felt some uncertainty, if not stage fright. Yet his emotions were controlled enough to earn him praise for performing in a "manner self possessed and very earnest," and his experiments with personal style in discourse were lauded as both "clear and forcible." For any uncertainty about future success in college, the young man learned his likely arena for achievement might be participation in oratorical endeavors in his new environment.

II

For students entering the University of Wisconsin in 1878, an avenue to fame was forensic abilities generally and oratorical prowess specifically. The "big man on campus" then likely was its prize-winning orator. Rhetoric was a significant aspect of higher education in the latter part of the nineteenth century, particularly in land-grant universities whose academic programs in rhetoric and oratory would make Midwesterners as articulate as Easterners with access to New England private schools. The University of Wisconsin then had a required "Rhetoricals" program wherein freshmen and sophomores prepared six essays and six public declamations a year, and they attended exercises in which juniors and seniors delivered chapel-stage orations and in which some underclassmen delivered declamations of special merit.[12] As might be expected (considering his previous successes), Turner's freshman and sophomore "Rhetoricals" grades were 90 and 93 percent.[13] His sophomore rendition of Mark Antony's "Address to the Romans" at the April 1881 College Rhetoricals was judged "the finest declamation and the best rendered that has been heard from the Assembly Hall stage" (Turner had been stricken with spinal meningitis in 1879 at the end of his freshman year and did not return to the University until 1881, shortly before the Rhetoricals).[14] That academic program also included both Greek and Latin, in which students read speeches of Demosthenes and Cicero.

Although exposure to rhetorical discourse from the classics contributed to that sense of style evolving from his "Pencils and Scissors" column, Turner also heard prominent speakers with similar style, particularly during the 1881–82 school year. According to his Commonplace Book list, Madison and the University of Wisconsin were on the itineraries of Bayard Taylor, John Fiske, Edwin Meade, Matthew Arnold, Henry Ward Beecher, and Robert G. Ingersoll.[15] Of these, Ingersoll seemed to be of special interest to Turner. As a result of his nominating speech for James G. Blaine in the Republican Convention of 1876, Ingersoll achieved national fame. He was in constant demand for campaign oratory on behalf of Republican candidates, one of the most listened-to lecturers in the country, and frequently called upon to give addresses on national holidays such as Decoration Day (now Memorial Day). Listeners in Madison might have reacted as Hamlin Garland did at age sixteen when hearing Ingersoll: "I enjoyed the beauty of his phrasing and the almost unequaled magic of his voice. . . . He . . . electrified us. At times his eloquence held us silent as images and then some witty turn, some humorous phrase, brought roars of applause. At times we cheered almost every sentence like delegates at a political convention. At other moments we rose in our seats and yelled. There was something hypnotic in his rhythm as well as in his marvelous lines like a Saxon minstrel. His power over his auditors was absolute." Or as Henry Ward Beecher said when he introduced Ingersoll to a Brooklyn audience in 1880, here was "a man who—and I say it not flatteringly—is the most brilliant speaker of the English tongue of all men on this globe."[16] For a young man seeking still other models for emulation of eloquence, Ingersoll was a likely complement to La Follette.

An early page of the 1881–1882 Commonplace Book has this entry: "Read Plato, Emerson, Green, Ingersoll, Carlyle, More, Milton's Areopagitica." From the context, the tense is not clear. Either Turner had read Ingersoll that academic year, or he was reminding himself to do so. Considering his father's staunch Republicanism, Turner likely was familiar already with the "Plumed Knight" nominating speech of Blaine in 1876. Nor was the reference likely to Ingersoll's popular lecture "The Liberty of Man, Woman, and Child" (first delivered in 1877), for "Pencils and Scissors" had already included a quotation from this address: "Laughter should make dimples of joy enough in the cheeks of the world to catch and hold and glorify the tears of grief." If he were to have read Ingersoll's speech again, however, the speech would have offered Turner salient examples of stylized repeated sentence beginnings (*anaphora*): "I believe in the fireside. I believe in the democracy of the home. I believe in the republicanism of the family. I believe in liberty, equality, and love." Antitheses also are prominent in it: "I hate dictation. I love liberty"; "Our fathers worshipped the golden calf. The worst you can say of an American now is, he worships the gold of the calf."[17] Turner also could see how Ingersoll combined *anaphora* (or *epanaphora*) with a heaping of particulars about several facets of the subject being discussed, a technique known in classical treatises on style as *frequentatio, symphoresis, synonimia,* or *sinathrismus*:[18]

> A little while ago I saw models of nearly everything that man has made. I saw models of all the water craft, from the rude dug-out in which floated a naked savage . . . up to a man-of war, that carries a hundred guns and miles of canvas—from that dug-out to the steamship that turns its brave prow from the port of New York, with a compass like a conscience, crossing three thousand miles of billows without missing a throb or beat of its mighty iron heart. . . . I saw at the same time the weapons. . . . I saw, too, the armor. . . . I saw at the same time their musical instruments. . . . I saw . . . I saw . . . I saw their implements of agriculture, from a crooked stick that was attached to the horn of an ox by some twisted straw, to the agricultural implements of this generation.

Or he might have read Ingersoll's Decoration Day address, delivered in 1882 with neatly balanced antitheses such as "a brazen falsehood and a timid truth," "the coffin of honor and the cradle of war," "cheers for the living; tears for the dead," or the long sequence in "Liberty and slavery—the right and wrong—the joy and grief—the day and night—the glory and the gloom of all the years."[19]

For all his interest in Ingersoll and other orators he heard while in college, Turner nevertheless was impressed most by a student peer, Robert La Follette. *The* convincing evidence of that impact is twofold: the scrapbook story about the senior's oratorical triumph with a text of "Iago" on the adjoining page as well as Turner's admitting upon retirement from Harvard that "La Follette—Iago" was among the "forces that have influenced my career." The rewards La Follette reaped for his oratorical prowess motivated Turner—the freshman from Portage—to strive for similar success by emulating a rhetorical style whose "power of language is enormous." Before coming to Madison, he had shown predilections for such style in his "Pencils and Scissors" column as well as in his winning oration in high school, "The Power of the Press." When one admires and seeks to emulate another on the basis of some common ground between them, one often goes on to imitate that person's behavior in other areas. And when one values the rewards that such a model is receiving, one's motivation to imitate that person's behavior increases. This process of psychological identification likely accounts for Turner's efforts to master La Follette's style and perhaps attain equally impressive acclaim.[20] As an exemplar for emulation, "Iago" was endowed with easily identifiable stylistic characteristics.

In thematic content, La Follette's "Iago" is portraiture with language as the medium of expression identifying facets of Iago's character. In its stylized form, "Iago" corroborates Turner's emerging sense of style. Parallel repetitions for clause or sentence beginnings occur frequently: "Whatever is most mean, whatever is most hard, whatever is vilely atrocious"; "All its artful cunning, all its devilish cruelty"; "He is hardly human. . . . He is wanting in ethical parts. . . . He is a fraction. . . . He is a paradox." The oration abounds with alliteration: "noble nature," "cursed cunning," "hypocritical and heartless," "passionate, powerful," "cynical, sly," "somber mingling of a smile and a sneer." The preeminent feature of La Follette's style, however, is antithesis. One hundred and twenty sentences of "Iago" incorporate sixty-five antitheses! With neat balance and sharp apposition, La Follette achieves epigrammatic style about Iago's "poverty of sentiment and wealth of intellect" or "a twisted body and a majestic mind." To amplify the idea of the character of Iago as a "union of opposites," the oration extends the theme antithetically: "Richard III is more humanely terrible; Iago more devilishly perfect. Richard loves nothing human; Iago hates everything good. . . . Richard is fire; Iago, ice. Richard III is more objective; Iago more subjective. . . . Richard III mounts the throne of England on a score of dead bodies; Iago wins the throne of Hell in three strides." Other antitheses are created when two antonymical words are juxtaposed (*oxymoron*): Iago is "sublimely hideous" and "devilishly perfect."

Attempts to perfect that oratorical style are evident in Turner's 1881–82 Commonplace Book. In addition to his required text that year, Adams Sherman Hill's *Principles of Rhetoric,* he also read Herbert Spencer's "Philosophy of Style."[21] Several drafts of an oration called "The Imaginativeness of the Present" in Turner's Commonplace Book show his efforts to create Spencerian inversions of syntax (*anastrophe*) such as "lament not. . . . Weep not. . . ." Drafts of that oration also contain alliteration; and parallel repetitions are consistently at beginnings of clauses or sentences: "He only predicts . . . he only shows. . . ."; "Imagination respects the cause. . . . Imagination is a perception. . . ." A more refined ability to achieve balanced antitheses now is evident in sharper juxta-positions of opposites: "the past dreamed—the present acts." And attempting to equal style in La Follette's "Iago," Turner uses sequential antitheses for amplification: "The useful arts are gradually becoming merged with the fine arts. Instead of erecting a monument to Vulcan we build a locomotive. Our shrine to Neptune is found in an ocean propel-ler. In place of dramatic poetry we now have imaginative philosophy which speculates and experiments with an end in view. The man who in the past would have written on the parchment rolls an ode to Liberty, now writes an article for the daily press and the multitude read it." Turner is still learning, however; some antitheses are poorly balanced, disre-garding the criterion for epigrammatic quality whereby one element offsets another in contextual meaning as well as number of words, as in "Plato wrote his Atlantis, Moore [sic] his Utopia—But the Americans erected a republic based on the great progressive possibilities of a free people and our faith in humanity."

The sense of style evolving in Turner's Commonplace Book is consonant with how rhetoric was taught during the latter part of the nineteenth century. As Boylston Professor of Rhetoric at Harvard, Adams Sherman Hill helped set in motion a trend which viewed rhetoric as the study of style for persuasive writing.[22] As the text at the University of Wisconsin, Hill's *Principles of Rhetoric* largely excluded the classical canons of *inventio* and *dispositio*— respectively, the faculties for finding appropriate arguments or motivational appeals and then arranging them in an apt order—for rhetoric, as the book's introduction proclaims, "does not undertake to furnish a person with something to say; but it does undertake to tell him how best to say that with which he has provided himself."[23] So young Fred studied the art of achieving grammatical purity through the avoidance of barbarisms, solecisms, and improprieties as well as through the choice and arrangement of words for "clearness, force, and elegance." Although Hill had relatively short chapters on argumentative composition, including suggestions about propositions and proof, the pragmatic subject of "persuasion" was reduced essen-tially to considerations of style.

In addition to showing attempts to master such style, Turner's Com-monplace Book demonstrates a tendency that was becoming ingrained in him during his years as a student orator at the University of Wisconsin: his "cannibalizing" excerpts from his earlier discourses for use in his later ones. For instance, segments of "The Imaginativeness of the Present" are basically reworded from Turner's high school oration, "The Power of the Press."[24] In turn, 1881–82 drafts of "The Imaginativeness of the Present" furnish ideas, if not intact passages, for the next rhetorical milestone in his life: winning the undergraduate Burrows Prize at the Junior Exhibition on 18 May 1883 with an oration entitled "The Poet of the Future." Although portions of the speech were drafted much earlier in his Commonplace Book, he still worked hard in anticipation of the event. In a letter from home a full month before the contest, Turner's father was "glad that you have your oration completed. Now that you have got it in form you will be able to reconstruct sentences and add some ideas that will suggest themselves without giving you much labor."[25] By expecting diligence with style from his son, the elder Turner reinforced the importance of the Burrows Prize contest. The student who won the senior Lewis Prize graduated and left campus soon thereafter, and any accolades that were forthcoming had to wait for those rare occasions when he encountered his former professors or classmates. The junior Burrows Prize orator, however, had a full year to remain on campus and bask in the glow of his victory.

In polished style, "The Poet of the Future" clearly emulates "Iago." Stylistic prowess is discernible in alliterations such as "lisping lines," "cold, critical," and "proclaims the progress." Parallel repetition occurs idiosyncratically by now in twos (rather than tricolons) at beginnings of successive clauses and sentences: "Beneath every literature there is a philosophy. Beneath every work of art there is an idea of nature and life." Almost a self-fulfilling prophecy, "The Poet of the Future" also has antitheses: "He will unite the logic of the present and the dream of the past" and "He will reflect all the past and prophesy the future." With other antitheses such as "The reign of aristocracy is passing; that of humanity begins," the orator shows himself a stylistic equal of La Follette. The Madison newspaper observed that "The verdict of the audience was in perfect accord with the judges. There was no possibility of doubt regarding the justice of the award. To the audience Mr. Turner's oration was the superior one of the evening in all the essential points of thought, composition, and delivery."[26] And the campus newspaper reported, "Mr. Turner, as predicted, had an excellent production. . . . As was expected, the judges decided in favor of Mr. Turner of Adelphia."[27] Rhetorically, Turner had arrived.

Another oration was necessary from Turner, however, for the senior Lewis Prize competition which was to take place at commencement 18 June 1884. With an antithesis drawn from his 1881–82 Commonplace Book, "Architecture Through Oppression" described how "the history of humanity has been a romance and a tragedy." Antitheses abound: "Millions groaned that one might laugh, servile tillers of the soil, sweating that others might dream; drinking the logwood of life while their masters quaffed its nectar. Many are the historians who have painted the glories of the past; few there are that tell the lamentation and the ancient tale of wrong."[28] With inevitable alliteration and parallel repetitions for clause or sentence beginnings, Turner's La Follettesque style helped him win the Lewis Prize; and with junior and senior "Rhetoricals" grades of 96 percent and 98 percent, Turner was to become known as the "remarkable boy orator" of Wisconsin.[29] With that reputation, he later secured his first academic employment: teaching rhetoric to University of Wisconsin freshmen. In the 1885–86 and 1886–87 issues of the University Catalogue, he is listed among "Instructors and Assistants" in rhetoric and oratory; in the 1887–88 catalogue, he is designated as "Instructor in History and Oratory." Although now committed to a career as historian, Turner continued to teach rhetoric in the program headed by the esteemed David B. Frankenburger.[30]

Another aspect of Turner's undergraduate experience merits attention. For all it taught him about style of persuasive discourse, Hill's rhetoric textbook embodied a practical wisdom that Turner later related to writing history. While advantageous for the persuader, stylistic prowess is not an end in itself, Hill maintained. Audiences aware of and thereby wary of a communicator's skill with style are less likely to be persuaded: "A reputation for eloquence, on the contrary, is an obstacle to success in Persuasion. It procures clients, but it puts juries on their guard. It attracts large audiences, but it deepens the hostility of those who disagree with the speaker. So long as the audience are thinking about an orator's eloquence or his reputation for eloquence, so long he is not eloquent, so far as they are concerned. Until his eloquence makes them forget his reputation for eloquence, he is unsuccessful." To illustrate stylistic "excesses," Hill took two historians—Gibbon and Macaulay—to task about antitheses "which add little or nothing to the sense and which have been compared to the false handles and keyholes with which furniture is decorated, that serve no other purpose than to correspond to the real ones." Hill also taught that sometimes the fault of

the writer "consists in so frequent a use of Antitheses as to give the composition an artificial air," often forcing stylists to "exaggeration" rather
than "*real* antitheses, corresponding to a real opposition between ideas."[31]
Young Fred's Commonplace Book for the 1881–82 school year indicates
he viewed antitheses not as "artificial" but as "*real . . .* corresponding to
a real opposition between ideas." Among longhand directives to himself therein, one says, "show that the practical is needed now in raising
the masses toward the ideal." And in planning a passage about Americans perceiving aesthetic value in what is practical, Turner reminds himself to "show that it is filled with . . . beauty and grandeur of art but to us
looking at it from the near position . . . it cannot be appreciated, seems
rough and harsh." His antitheses, then, are less studied artifices imposed
afterward upon statements and more likely indices of his conceptualiz-
ing in mutually exclusive dichotomies between opposites. That tendency
had subtle influences upon Turner's early efforts to write history.

III

After his earning his bachelor's degree, Turner worked a year as a
newspaper reporter but returned to the University of Wisconsin as a
graduate student in history.[32] Turner's attraction to a career as historian
evolved partly from the satisfaction an undergraduate class project had
afforded him. Professor William F. Allen received a request from Herbert
Baxter Adams at Johns Hopkins for information on early land holdings
in Wisconsin (for a book Adams was writing). As a junior, Fred was one
of six students participating in the project to supply that information.
Working through friends of his father's and examining records and diaries of early Wisconsin settlers, Turner developed a monograph titled
"The History of the 'Grignon Tract' on the Portage of the Fox and Wisconsin Rivers," published in 1883.[33] Thus as an undergraduate, his
discourse was in print and in the public eye—in the form of historical
writing instead of orations. Again reflecting the influence of La Follette's
stylized portraiture in "Iago" during his University of Wisconsin graduate work, Turner tried characterization in an 1887 review of *Franklin in
France,* by Edward E. Hale and Edward E. Hale, Jr. Answering the question "Who was the first great American?" he there previewed a Frontier
Thesis portrayal:

If we accept as necessary conditions of this title that the recipient must be preeminently the representative of the leading tendencies of the nation, original as it is original, and that he must have won and held the admiration of the world, whom can we find to fulfill the requirements before Benjamin Franklin, and who has better satisfied them? His greatness lay in his ability to apply to the world a shrewd understanding that disclosed in the ordinary things about him potent forces for helpfulness. His life is the story of American common sense in its highest form, applied to business, to politics, to science, to diplomacy, to religion, to philanthropy. Surely this self-made man, the apostle of the practical and the useful, is by the verdict of his own country and of Europe entitled to the distinction of being the first great American.[34]

That theme of character Turner pursued in a later speech: "The question has sometimes been asked 'Who was the first great American?' I suppose that this means 'great' in the sense of having achieved recognition beyond the confines of one's own nation—great in the recognition of the world; and to be the great American, one must be representatively great—great in the qualities which characterize Americans at their best."[35] While the theme is the same as that in praise of Franklin, Turner is here lauding Lincoln.

During the 1888 American Historical Association Convention, Turner concluded that suasory characterization was necessary for historians. Writing to Professor Allen after the meeting, he observed that "the papers were good, but many of them, especially of the younger men . . . were too much in the nature of detailed research—facts not *illuminated*— not of the most interesting character for a spoken address."[36] That perception was given sharper focus in 1889, after Turner had read Theodore Roosevelt's *Winning of the West* and underlined passages about "individual initiative" and the hunters as "peculiar heroes of the frontier." In 1890, Turner began a file folder labeled "The Hunter Type"— men who "found too little elbowroom in town life" and "loved to hear the crack of their long rifles, and the blows of the ax in the forest."[37] An interest in characterization of the frontiersman was reinforced when Roosevelt wrote letters to Turner and explained that "my aim is especially to show who the frontiersmen were and what they did, as they gradually conquered the west. . . . I have always been more interested in the men themselves than in the institutions through and under which they worked."[38] Turner's retirement speech outline at Harvard in 1924 included "Roosevelt's writings" and "my admiration for him," for he agreed with Corrine Roosevelt Robinson's assessment that her brother Theodore was an *"all around American"* who embodied frontier ideals because he had *"lived* the West, as well as studied it."[39] A predilection for characterization in history is conspicuous throughout Turner's life. Impressed by lines in Dante's *Inferno* (36.112), depicting those "who through a hundred thousand perils have come unto the West," he translated the episode into English and amassed other translations in a file folder which includes a heavily marked copy of Rudyard Kipling's "The Foreloper" (also variously titled "The Pioneer" and "The Explorer"):

> His neighbors' smoke shall vex his eyes, their voices break his rest;
> He shall go forth till south is north, sullen and dispossessed;
> He shall desire loneliness, and his desire shall bring
> Hard on his heels, a thousand wheels, a people and a king.
> He shall come back on his own track, and by his scarce cool camp,
> There shall he meet the roaring street, the derrick and the stamp;
> For he must blaze a nation's way, with hatchet and with brand,
> Till on his last won wilderness an empire's bulwarks stand.[40]

Upon Turner's death, his daughter recalled how this particular verse had itself "always been father to me." [41]

An impulse to achieve characterization cannot be ignored in Turner's concept of historical writing. In the mid 1890s, he lauded Woodrow Wilson's *Division and Reunion* as the "wedding of a good literary form to historical writing" to achieve "flesh and blood" vitality, and in turn editors pressed Turner to write "real, definite, human pictures of pioneer life" as well as "vivid character sketches of the men, mingling biography, interpretation of achievement and dramatic presentation of important episodes in their lives."[42] Although he often promised publishers to write such accounts and to infuse them with the "vitality" of his "proper literary presentation," the over-committed academician could not deliver the manuscripts.[43] Turner also was extolled portraiture in his eulogy of Reuben Gold Thwaites, superintendent of the State Historical Society of Wisconsin for twenty-seven years: Thwaites "saw his characters . . . vividly and dramatically as real people. He had . . . a knack for keen but kindly characterization. . . . He never read or penned a note that he did not see the picturesque, the human scene behind the bare record. . . . The

history of institutions, or industrial development of laws and governments, appealed to him less than the history of individual achievement."[44]
Students working with Turner knew his appreciation for rhetorical composition generally and for characterization specifically. He advised one
student writing a thesis to relieve "the dryness of the subject, as well as
to give it its element of personality and human interest"; another he told
to "make your leaders *live,* by clothing them in reality" to create "a picture that can be seen and appreciated."[45] Yet another student of Turner's
recalled how her teacher's "was never an abstract frontier, never an
abstract section that he was describing—it was toiling, thinking, loving,
hating human beings of whom he was thinking."[46] Turner firmly believed that characterization as historical content should be articulated
in a form that evinces rhetorical style. After reflecting about papers that
had been delivered at the 1888 American Historical Association convention, his 1891 essay "The Significance of History" argued that although
attempts to "force dull facts into vivacity" could result in distortion, he
would "gladly admit that in itself an interesting style, even a picturesque manner of presentation, is not to be condemned, provided that
truthfulness of substance rather than vivacity of style be the end
sought."[47] That rhetorical predilection exerted a subtle influence upon
Turner's historical writing early in 1891 when he was adapting a paper
on "American Colonization" for a speech he was to deliver to the
Madison Literary Club on 9 February 1891.

In doing the research for *The Genesis of the Frontier Thesis,* Ray
Billington decided that Turner "arrived at most of his conclusions by
January 1891" and that the "hypothetical timetable" describing
conceptualization of the Frontier Thesis used a psychological model of
creative thinking which might ascertain "the leap forward" or "moment
of illumination, when the significant idea, the defined hypothesis, the
brilliant solution suddenly presents itself." But Billington studied what
Turner read from 1885 to 1893 and examined his correspondence,
published essays, and mass of three-by-five note cards—only *indirect*
evidence from which to infer the workings of a mind. A more direct
index of that "leap forward" and "moment of illumination" is attained
by close stylistic analysis of longhand revisions and marginal notes in
Turner's address on "American Colonization" to the Madison Literary
Club. Those crossed-out words and phrases as well as their substitu-
tions are direct evidence of intellectual progress toward the Frontier
Thesis *at the very moments Turner was engaged in creative efforts.* Although

Billington agrees that "American Colonization" brought Turner "well along the road" and "anticipated most of the concepts made famous by his 1893 essay on the significance of the frontier," that assessment is founded upon "American Colonization" statements which in final form were articulated later in the Frontier Thesis.[48] The overlooked but important factor is their *initial* form and what happened psychologically as the author polished them stylistically for the Madison Literary Club.

The first page of "American Colonization" reflects a rhetorical predilection for introductory impact upon audiences. To describe ancient impulses to colonize, Turner uses two antitheses: "The *völkerwanderung* had hardly resulted in the downfall of Rome and the rise of the feudal system, when the crusades followed, and the last scene in the crusades was the first scene in the exploration of the New World" (this latter antithesis was moved to the first page from the fourth page of an earlier draft in the same file folder). He also uses characteristic alliteration and parallel repetition: "From island to island, and from cape to cape, these traders planted their posts in the Mediterranean, bringing arts and the alphabet to Greece and sowing the seeds of civilization in Carthage and in Spain." Crucial for historical creativity, however, are subtle stylistic changes preceding these statements. In his first sentence, "The colonizing spirit is one form of the nomadic instinct," the original word "migratory" (which might apply to all animal life) was crossed out and replaced with "nomadic," which pertains to human activity. Indeed, an earlier draft appended to that first sentence a reference to "instinct that sends the bird to the new skies," but deleting the idea of avian instincts and substituting "nomadic" for "migratory" focuses attention upon human activity as opposed to animal or even broad racial impulses (as suggested by subsequent deletion of "stocks" in favor of "tribes"). However subtle, those changes are consonant with a rhetorical predilection for characterization.

The focus upon activities of humans is implied on that first page another way. After "Phoenicia was the first great colonizing power," Turner deleted "Her ships and caravans were the shuttles that wove together the fabric of oriental civilization, and into her ports came the riches of the East." He proceeded instead directly to "traders" who brought arts and the alphabet to Greece. By deleting references to inanimate ships and impersonal caravans, he came closer conceptually to a position articulated on the fifth and sixth pages: "American history . . . is the history of the application of men and ideas to these physical conditions." The manuscript at that point begins repudiating an accepted belief that American institutions evolved from English institutions and earlier "germs" in medieval German forests (to historians of that generation, this was logically true because their comparisons revealed unmistakable similarities with ancient Teutonic practices that proved common origins).[49] Repudiation of that "germ" theory is established more firmly several pages later with this synthesizing statement:

> The colonization of the central region resulted in the formation of middle colonies in every respect. As mixed in its nationality as any of the existing states; with a variety of social divisions, the middle class preponderating; varied in its industries, being agricultural like the South, and commercial like New England, possessing the mixed town and county form of local government, heterogeneous in its religious sects; characteristically western in the west and in the east a typically eastern colony; it was, in a word, a mediating region—a region which interpreted New England to the South and the East to the West. It was also a pivotal region, a fighting ground for ideas and social forms.

To some extent, this passage embodies antithetical appositions between the South and New England as well as "western in the west and in the east a typically eastern colony." And in its margin, a sharp vertical line is drawn next to "mediating region" and a "fighting ground for ideas and social forms"—accompanied by an underlined, longhand conclusion: "typical of U.S." From striving for style, Turner foregrounded in his own mind a concept that uniquely American factors were major determinants of our history.

Turner's repudiation of the germ theory was not complete at this point, however. He still equivocated, saying in "American Colonization" that New England towns were "products of three forces: the congregational polity, the revival of the old English town organization, and the peculiar local conditions." Although acknowledging "peculiar local conditions," he does not discount "the revival of the old English town organization." Equivocation also appears on the next page with "There are too many analogies between the New England town and the 'tun' of our German forefathers to be overlooked. Placed again in the wilderness environment, the descendants of the Anglo-Saxon reproduced many of the characteristics of the early towns." Still, that sentence is followed by the reiteration that "we must not neglect the local conditions as fac-

tors in producing the New England town." Other evidence of equivocation is in terminology reflecting a then-popular conception of biological
environmentalism in the realm of human society.[50] The congregational
form of church organization, for instance, "being a self governed body
. . . was sufficient unto itself, and like some forms of animal life it was
capable of subdivision without destroying the life of the parts." Nevertheless, after several more pages contrasting Puritan colonies with French
and Spanish colonization, Turner makes *the* crucial synthesis:

> Indeed, it is only in the present that the colonizing era is coming to
> a close. I do not hesitate to say that this fact is the key to American
> history. As the occupation of the New World transformed Europe so
> the occupation of the Great West has determined the flow of American
> energies, been the underlying explanation of political history, and has
> had profound reactive effects upon the social and economic life of the
> East. What first the Mediterranean Sea, and later the New World, were
> to the Aryan peoples, breaking the bond of custom, and creating new
> activities to meet new conditions, that the undeveloped West has been
> to the American descendants of these Aryans.

In focusing on "the Great West," he found "the key to American history." For in the margin next to this sentence of his draft, the historian
wrote in longhand, "need of studying this." His frontier "thesis" thereby
was isolated, and "American Colonization" bears this out another
way. In seven remaining pages, the manuscript identifies specific facets of the American experience which should be studied: "We can never
understand our country properly until we know the materials out of
which our Western States have been constructed. We need students
who shall neglect Pocahontas and the question of the first white child in
Brown County, in order that they may study where and by what means
the characteristics and population of western states like Kansas, California and Wisconsin were produced. . . ." By arguing in 1891 that "we do
not understand ourselves," Turner set the tone for 1893 and "The Significance of the Frontier in American History," which identifies fourteen facets of the American frontier to be studied.

A final indication of importance of the "key to American history" is
in the Frontier Thesis itself. Just as Turner adapted introductions for
rhetorical impact, he concluded his discourses with compelling perora-
tions. Admittedly, the Madison Literary Club manuscript has no strong

conclusion, merely asking whether the United States should imitate German colonial policy. The audience is left hanging (considering his propensities, however, the concluding pages of this address likely were moved from that file to another speech). But the 1893 address to the American Historical Association does conclude with a strong rhetorical tone in its final two sentences: "What the Mediterranean Sea was to the Greeks, breaking the bond of custom, offering new experiences, calling out new institutions and activities, that, and more, the ever retreating frontier has been to the United States directly, and to the nations of Europe more remotely. And now, four centuries from the discovery of America, at the end of a hundred years of life under the Constitution, the frontier has gone, and with its going has closed the first period of American history."[51] To achieve ultimate, persuasive form for his Frontier Thesis of 1893, Turner chose that synthesizing statement of 1891 that led him to conclude "need of studying this."[52]

A version of that concept was published by Turner before 1893. His "Problems in American History" appeared in a November 1892 issue of *Aegis*, a University of Wisconsin undergraduate newspaper. He had been invited to submit a paper on some aspect of Wisconsin's early history but "delayed preparing his essay until the last moment, as was his custom."[53] The deadline was met instead with a paper about "the key to American history" from Turner's "American Colonization" address; for considering his own directive about a "need of studying this," a statement along the lines of the ideas he presented in "Problems in American History" must have been evolving in his mind.[54] In broad outline, this 1892 article presents almost the same points in the same sequence as in 1893 for "The Significance of the Frontier in American History," whose first footnote acknowledges its "foundation" in the *Aegis* publication rather than in "American Colonization" (Turner likely sensed the professional appropriateness of citing a published paper rather than a speech as the conceptual antecedent).[55] "Problems in American History" proved important for another reason. Among those who responded to reprints sent around the country to Turner's professional peers, Albion Small at the University of Chicago expressed delight and suggested the publication deserved "a more prominent place than the columns of a college newspaper."[56] More important for Turner's professional development, Herbert Baxter Adams at Johns Hopkins read the article and invited him to present it in longer form at an American Historical Association meeting scheduled for Chicago on 12 July 1893. Turner accepted.

And Turner procrastinated. On 16 July 1893, he apologized to Woodrow Wilson for not corresponding earlier because of being in the "final agonies of getting out a belated paper for the American Historical Association."[57] As usual when preparing speeches or articles, he waited until the last minute, even for as professionally important an event as this. Although nominally a paper for historian peers, the Chicago presentation had the added aura of being part of a "World's Congress of Historians and Historical Students" held in conjunction with the "World's Columbian Exposition." While some sophisticates deplored an AHA role amid amusements of a world's fair, an ambitious historian from a midwestern university might perceive opportunity to prove that prairies produced more than corn and Populists, but Billington suggests that the essay, as it was delivered, likely was written "in the few weeks—or days, or hours—before it was due."[58] Probably on the train from Madison and in his University of Chicago room, the young academician prepared under pressure—which invariably exerts influence upon style of discourse through a heightened state that Charles E. Osgood explains this way:

> the generalized, energizing effects of drive may be identified with arousal of a neural system in the brainstem from which there is diffuse, nonspecific projection into the cortex, these impulses having a facilitative, "tuning-up" function. Assuming . . . a multiplicative relation between habit strength and drive in producing reaction potential, the effect of increased drive, including encoding behavior, should become more *stereotyped*—the alternatives selected at all choice points should tend to be the most familiar, the most often practiced, the most expected.[59]

As a result of his successes in rhetorical endeavors, Turner had a stereotyped style for oral presentations.

Turner's presentation that night in Chicago was a response to a "rhetorical situation" that Lloyd Bitzer characterizes as an *"exigency"* potentially capable of "modification through discourse."[60] On 12 July 1893, the American Historical Association was an audience "almost solidly behind the 'germ' theory to explain the genesis of their nation's institutions." If any of those historians were interested in American factors, they had likely investigated the "slavery" thesis of Hermann von Holst and James Ford Rhodes, for any other view of American historiography "flew in the face of tradition, logic, and common sense."[61] The Wisconsin historian's different view led him to seek a specific response from his immediate audience and the profession at large: more research about frontier factors that influenced national history. After a brief reference to the census of 1890, that theme is stated emphatically in the introductory remarks and then repeated fourteen times in references to specific facets of the frontier to be studied. In an autobiographical statement twenty-nine years later, Turner said that in retrospect, his 1893 paper was "a protest against eastern neglect, at the time, of institutional study of the West"; and as he also admitted around the same time, "the truth is that I found it necessary to hammer pretty hard and pretty steadily in the frontier idea to 'get it in.'"[62]

Little acclaim was forthcoming for Turner that evening. After hearing five lengthy addresses on the program that hot July night in Chicago, the 200 or so historians responded only with what Billington calls "the bored indifference normally shown a young instructor from a backwater college reading his first professional paper"; and according to one person in the audience, the paper provoked no discussion whatsoever.[63] Accustomed to success in oral discourse and to the praise he subsequently received, Turner must have been disappointed. Admittedly, we do not know for certain what, specifically, he said on the evening of 12 July 1893. Fifth on the program, his paper followed George Kriehn's "English Popular Uprisings of the Middle Ages," George P. Fisher's "The Social Compact and Mr. Jefferson's Adoption of It," Jesse Macy's "The Relation of History to Politics," and Reuben Gold Thwaites's "Early Lead Mining in Illinois and Wisconsin." Turner certainly could not have read all thirty-eight pages known now as the Frontier Thesis. Considering the heat, hour, and length of the program, he likely offered only excerpts. Although the *Chicago Tribune* described papers in this session as "interesting," the reporter covering the event deemed only George Kriehn's worthy of being summarized in two paragraphs; other speakers and topics were mentioned just by name (with Turner's incorrect). The man accustomed to rave reviews for rhetoric had to be content with "Prof. J. F. Turner concluded the evening's program with a paper entitled 'The Significance of the Frontier in American History.'"[64]

During the following months, Turner found no comfort in other reactions to his efforts that night. The official report of the Congress for the *Dial* and the *Independent* did not mention "The Significance of the Frontier in American History" (although Thwaites's discussion of lead mining in Wisconsin was praised). University of Wisconsin President Charles Kendall Adams likely attended that night but was not motivated to mention Turner's paper five days later when writing a letter about the historian's qualifications. In a newspaper account of the trip to Chicago two days after the event, Turner's father described his son as an admirable guide to the fair—but did not mention the paper. Back at the University of Wisconsin, the student newspaper analyzed effects of the Columbian Exposition on historical writing but did not mention the Frontier Thesis. Turner also presented the paper in December 1893 to the annual meeting of the State Historical Society of Wisconsin, which published the essay in its 1894 proceedings. In 1894, the American Historical Association also published the essay, but reprints sent far and wide among the profession prompted little positive return. After assessing this trend, Billington epitomizes those early reactions in the main as "less-than-enthusiastic." [65]

All this changed, however. Initial negative response in and after Chicago contrasted sharply with ultimate positive reaction nationally. After its first publications in 1894, "The Significance of the Frontier in American History" appeared over the years in several anthologies and then as chapter 1 of Turner's 1920 book, *The Frontier in American History.*[66] In 1921, Charles A. Beard lauded its "immense and salutary" influence, saying "In the literature of American History there is perhaps no essay or article more often cited or quoted than Professor Turner's."[67] With ever-increasing numbers of disciples between 1910 and the Great Depression of the 1930s, the Frontier Thesis "dominated the profession so completely that the American Historical Association was branded one great Turner-verein."[68] But other people read the Frontier Thesis. In its many reprintings and as the first chapter of his 1920 book, the statement came before college students and people in public life, businessmen and housewives—a mass public readership whose attitudes are always the bases of a national psychology; and the reactions of those readers are pertinent when "The Significance of the Frontier in American History" is viewed as oratory.

IV

The Frontier Thesis is replete with language behaviors which are not nearly the scientific or epistemological usages expected to predominate in scholarly writing but more the hortatory or evocative elements typical of discourse with suasory intent.[69] That rhetorical tone causes consternation among some historians. Richard Hofstadter deplores its "vagueness," "imprecision," "overstatement," "obsessive grandeur," and "disposition to illustrate but not define"; and reacting to Turner's "lack of caution in defining terms or stating principles," Billington agrees that his "assertions were too positive, his generalizations too sweeping, to convince historians who regarded themselves as exact scientists."[70] Considering, however, Turner's record of success when using such statements in his prize-winning college orations, a similar oratorical tone might be expected in a document prepared under pressure, for oral presentation when rhetorical impress upon an audience was important. Close reading of the Frontier Thesis reveals its La Follettesque style. The essay lapses easily into alliteration such as "traders and trappers," "flocks or furs," "ideas and institutions," and "decade to decade distinct advances." Turner also uses repeated alliterative pairings of "savagery" and "civilization," perhaps reflecting his father's continued editorial condemnation in the *Wisconsin State Register* of the Indian "savages" who massacred settlers and the drunken "worthless savages" who alarmed women and generally menaced life and property in Portage (as an impressionable twelve year old, Turner saw troops arrive in Portage in 1873 to remove forcibly nearby "savages" to a Nebraska reservation). Rhetorical parallelism is prominent, too, at beginnings of successive phrases or short sentences (and often in twos): "to the changes of an expanding people . . . to the changes involved in crossing a continent"; "Stand at Cumberland Gap. . . . Stand at South Pass . . ."; "The exploitation of the beasts . . . the exploitation of the grasses . . . the exploitation of the virgin soil . . ."; and "It was western New York. . . . It was western Virginia. . . ." Further evidence of Turner's tendency to use extracts from previous manuscripts is the fact that several of these sequences are carried over intact from his "Problems in American History" of 1892.

Antitheses are a salient stylistic method in the Frontier Thesis. Consistently, they phrase thematic statements or amplify ideas: "Too exclusive attention has been paid by institutional students to the Germanic origins, too little to the American factors," for example. The frontier's impact upon the arriving European then is immediately illustrated with two antitheses: "It takes him from the railroad car and puts him in the birch canoe. It strips off the garments of civilization and arrays him in the hunting shirt and the moccasin." Similarly, "the West was not content with bringing the farm to the factory . . . tariffs were passed, with the cry of bringing the factory to the farm." Forty-seven antitheses develop juxtapositions like those between "slender paths of aboriginal intercourse" and "complex mazes of modern commercial lines," "good" and "evil," "dangers" and "benefits," "primitive" and "developed," "bonds of custom" and "unrestraint," as well as the repeated antithesis "savagery" and "civilization." Even while quoting others, the essay favors the well-turned antithetical epigram, such as that from the nineteenth-century Southern spokesperson Lucius Q. Lamar: "In 1789 the states were the creators of the federal government; in 1861 the federal government was the creator of a large majority of the states." Turner also uses Abraham Lincoln's antitheses from the "House Divided" address to the Republican State Convention, Springfield, Illinois, 16 June 1858: "this government cannot endure permanently half slave and half free. It will become all of one thing, or all of the other" as well as an extended illustration about differences "between a talking and a working politician."

The La Follettesque style emulated in 1879 is evident in 1893—and remained unchanged throughout many reprintings of the Frontier Thesis, including its incorporation as the first chapter of *The Frontier in American History*. As Charles Beard's book review aptly characterized the Frontier Thesis chapter, "of its thirty-eight pages fully one-half are narrative and descriptive, and bear on the main theme only by way of illustration." But that evocative or hortatory tone complements its introduction and conclusion. The address begins with timeliness (if not urgency) by delineating an epochal moment: "In a recent bulletin of the superintendent of the census for 1890 appear these significant words: 'Up to and including 1880 the country had a frontier of settlement, but at present the unsettled area has been so broken into by isolated bodies of settlement that there can hardly be said to be a frontier line. In the discussion of its extent, its westward movement, *etc.*, it cannot, therefore, any longer have a place in the census reports.' This brief official statement marks the closing of a great historic movement." Similarly, the final sentence of Turner's peroration emphasizes that same pivotal point: "And now, four centuries from the discovery of America, at the end of a hundred years of life under the Constitution, the frontier has gone, and with its going has closed the first period of American history."

Reacting in retrospect to Turner's rhetorical tone, historians perceived in the Frontier Thesis a variety of implications for its readers. Daniel Boorstin acknowledged Turner's "historical skill and poetic imagination" but pronounced his statement "more an autopsy than an anatomy of our institutions." For while Boorstin saw the Frontier Thesis as "a declaration of the uniqueness of the American past," he felt it "equally a prophecy of a lack of uniqueness in the American future" because the critical factor making the United States different from Europe was then "ceasing to exist." To justify that pessimistic reading, Boorstin quotes Turner's last sentence: "And now, four centuries from the discovery of America, at the end of a hundred years of life under the Constitution, the frontier has gone, and with its going has closed the first period of American history."[71] Similarly, David Noble called Turner a "Jeremiah" who, like earlier Puritan theologians, "accepted the burden of warning the people" who would stray from the "purity and simplicity" of their better life in the New World and thereby return this society to the "alien forces" and tragic vicissitudes of life characterizing Europe of the old World.[72] Billington, however, suggested "the outstanding feature of the frontier thesis was optimism" and its "rose-tinted view of the future."[73] So Turner's Frontier Thesis became more than a statement about historiography. Compelling evidence about attitudes shaped by the discourse does not emerge clearly, however, from historians' interpretations (although they sometimes offer valuable perspectives). Rather, the vivid indices of the public's focus are to be found in correspondence to Turner from lay readers and students in his own time, in extensive newspaper reviews and editorials, and in obituaries and letters to the family after the historian's death, wherein individuals explain what the Frontier Thesis meant to them personally.

A trend in these responses is unmistakable. Over and over, people identified one specific thematic element and pinpointed the precise two-sentence passage in which it is articulated: a characterization founded rhetorically upon a stylistic heaping of particulars about the frontiersman (that *frequentatio, symphoresis, synonimia, or sinathrismus* characteristic of La Follette's "Iago"). Those two sentences read as follows: "To the frontier the American intellect owes its striking characteristics. That coarseness and strength combined with acuteness and inquisitiveness; that practical, inventive turn of mind, quick to find expedients; that masterful grasp of material things, lacking in the artistic but powerful to effect great ends; that restless, nervous energy, that dominant individualism, working for good and for evil, and withal that buoyancy and exuberance which comes with freedom—these are traits of the frontier, or traits called out elsewhere because of the existence of the frontier." In one review of Turner's *Frontier in American History*, this crucial passage in the book's first chapter—itself the original Frontier Thesis address—was singled out this way: "The author's thesis is set forth in the following extract, which also shows something of the quality of his writing."[74] Other reviewers also quoted these lines as epitomizing the Frontier Thesis for Americans. And for overtly commercial objectives, a five-page promotional statement from the National Book Buyers' Service used this exact passage as one of two direct quotations from the book.[75]

Stylistically, this passage incorporates several language variables which deviate from the common idiom and evince eloquence. Although better balanced antitheses appear elsewhere in the Frontier Thesis, this portrayal has those between "good" and "evil," "lacking" and "powerful," as well as "coarseness and strength combined with acuteness and inquisitiveness." Although more idiomatic syntax likely would utilize subject-predicate-object order and state "The American intellect owes its striking characteristics to the frontier," Turner inverts the normative sequence (*anastrophe*) to place "to the frontier" first in the sentence—a variation suggestive of the disruptive syntactical patterns of an individual in a more impassioned state. More prominent is repetition in clausal beginnings (*anaphora, epanaphora*): "that coarseness and strength . . . that practical inventive turn of mind . . . that masterful grasp . . . that dominant individualism . . . and withal that buoyancy and exuberance. . . ." In utilizing the syntax of "traits of the frontier, or traits called out elsewhere because of the existence of the frontier," Turner also achieves a repetition of clausal endings (*antistrophe* or *epistrophe*) and thereby through such parallelism achieves additional salience for his crucial word, "frontier."

From early discussions of rhetorical theory on style to more contemporary research in psycholinguistics, stylistic repetition *is* understood to be functional. In Aristotle's *Rhetoric* (1414a), the effect of schematic repetition is illustrated with a passage from Homer's *Iliad*: "Nireus from Syme brought three curved ships; Nireus, son of Aglaia and of Charopus; Nireus, most beautiful of all the Greeks who came to Troy, saving Achilles only." Aristotle advises that "if a good many things are said about a person, his name will have to be mentioned pretty often; accordingly, if his name is often mentioned, one has the impression that a good deal has been said about him. By the use of this fallacy, Homer, who mentions Nireus only in this single passage, makes him important, and has preserved his memory, though in the rest of the poem he says never a

word more about him."[76] Or, as the Greek critic Demetrius observes in
On Style, "Nireus is not himself important in the *Iliad,* and his contribution is even less so, three ships an a few men, but Homer makes him
appear important and his contribution great. . . . although Nireus is
mentioned only once in the action, we remember him. . . . If Homer had
said: 'Nireus, the son of Aglaia brought three ships from Syme,' he might
as well not have mentioned him."[77] Potentially, stylistic repetition can
perform similar pragmatic functions of emphasis in contemporary discourse. Time-honored research attests to the communicative values of
"the added strength given to the stimulus by repeating it and in the
consequent increase of our sensitivity to the stimulus"; and axiomatically, "repetition of a stimulus, up to a certain point, may have a greater
effect than a single stimulus, even if the latter is fairly strong."[78] For
people responding to style in language specifically, the probability of
their recalling a repeated word "is just about twice the probability of
recalling a unique word"; and that effect occurs not only while one is
listening but also while reading, because "thresholds vary inversely with
frequency of prior usage" in the discourse being heard or read (and not
to the relative frequency with which these verbal stimuli appear in counts
of more probable words generally).[79]

Parallel repetition of "that" is functional rhetorically, too, for the word
is used by Turner virtually as a conjunction linking items in the series
together. According to traditional rhetorical theory, an impressive "mul-
tiplicity of the circumstances" is conveyed by adding the conjunction
between each item in series (*polysyndeton*), for, as the eighteenth-century
Scottish rhetorician George Campbell put it, with "a deliberate attention to every circumstance, as being of importance. . . . much additional
weight and distinctness are given to each particular by the repetition of
the conjunction."[80] Or, as Campbell's contemporary Hugh Blair viewed
the matter, conjunctions are "multiplied" so that the objects in between
"should appear as distinct from one another as possible, and that the
mind should rest, for a moment, on each object by itself"; and if the
communicator's intention is "to show in how many places the enemy
seemed to be at one time," the conjunction is "very happily redoubled, in
order to paint more strongly the distinction of these several places."[81]

The pivotal eighty-six-word portrait of the frontiersman in the Frontier Thesis also embodies another, influential source of eloquent style.
Syntactical formats which postpone sentence elements for later-than-
customary appearance impose a strain on composers' memory; and

rather than exert additional effort, writers are apt to avoid such suspensions. One way to achieve uncommon suspension is to withhold words with the greatest semantic signification until the end of a sentence; and as recommended in traditional rhetorical theory, this climax order (*klimax, scala, gradatio, auxesis,* or *incrementum*) is a step-by-step progression suggesting the increasing importance of the items listed.[82] In the passage often quoted from the Frontier Thesis, Turner proceeds from attributes which are passive ("acuteness and inquisitiveness") or practical ("inventive . . . quick to find expedients") to those suggesting activity ("restless, nervous energy") and power ("masterful grasp," "powerful to effect great ends," and "dominant individualism"). He ends with an attribute suggestive of the greatest importance in this context: "and withal that buoyancy and exuberance which comes from freedom" (with the alliterative quality from repetition of *fr* and the initial and medial *b*). The Frontier Thesis thus embodies much of the stylistic quality that Alan Nevins achieved while writing about the Civil War—that "grand" or "impressive" mode of syntax and lexicon lauded by classical Greek rhetoricians, whereby events are endowed with enhanced epic scope or significance because the language itself has the "grandeur" that complements appropriately such subject matter as "a great and notable battle on land or sea, or when there is talk of the heavens, or of the earth."[83] In the Aristotelian paradigm of style, specifically, rhetorical effect well may be derived from syntax and lexicon that is "impressive" because that *onkos* as form enhances the impression of significance of content thereby phrased.[84] *Onkos* signifies "bulk, mass, or swelling," but as a descriptor of style, the term designates the quality of impressiveness whereby the subject matter being treated is endowed with added "elevation," "dignity," or "expansiveness."[85] When delineating various aspects of the advancing frontier, Turner uses repetition in sentence beginnings (*anaphora*), all suggesting the scope or breadth of the frontier geographically and therefore the impressiveness of the experiences it offered: "to the changes of an expanding people . . . to the changes involved in crossing a continent"; "Stand at Cumberland Gap. . . . Stand at South Pass . . ."; "The exploitation of the beasts . . . the exploitation of the grasses . . . the exploitation of the virgin soil . . ."; and "It was western New York. . . . It was western Virginia. . . ." Against that backdrop of expansiveness, the frontiersman was all the more impressive in his attributes.

Suppose the character portrayal in that pivotal passage of eighty-six words were phrased in a mode less oratorical and more typical of "scholarly" prose likely favored by historians who eschew "rhetoric" in their writing. The passage might read this way: "The American intellect owes many of its striking characteristics to the frontier. These character traits include, most importantly, that buoyancy and exuberance which comes with freedom. Other such characteristics include (1) coarseness and strength combined with acuteness and inquisitiveness, (2) a practical, inventive turn of mind, quick to find expedients, (3) a masterful grasp of material things, lacking in the artistic but powerful to effect great ends, (4) a restless, nervous energy, and (5) dominant individualism, working for good and for evil. These are traits which often are called out and applied elsewhere because of the existence of the frontier." Not as many readers likely would respond favorably to the passage, for it lacks style long proclaimed as a potential source of emphasis. Undergirding its discussion of persuasive style in discourse, Aristotle's *Rhetoric* (1404b) observes that "words are like men; as we feel a difference between people from afar and our fellow townsmen, so it is with our feeling for language. And hence it is well to give the ordinary idiom an air of remoteness; the hearers are struck by what is out of the way, and like what strikes them." Or as another translator has rendered this passage: "to alter or vary language in this way invests it with a higher dignity; for we feel towards language just as we feel towards men; 'familiarity breeds contempt' for the words we are constantly meeting in everyday intercourse, whist 'strangers' assume a higher importance and dignity in our eyes. Hence we are to aim at a 'strange' i.e. unusual, not familiar, novel, out of the common way diction" because with "uncommon" style which "strikes one as singular," communicators can attain a statement which "forces itself upon the attention."[86]

At any given moment, a welter of stimuli are presented to people who must select those to which they will respond in some coherent way, and what they respond to is the result of attention, the active, selective aspect of perception, involving the preparation and orientation of the individual to perceive a particular stimulus pattern—with consequent inhibition of all others.[87] Psychologists know novelty is one of those factors that determine the stimuli to which an individual will react, and its capability to do so evolves from a "*discrepancy* between the individual's expectancy about the stimulus and his present perception of that stimulus."[88] We expect the letter "S" to be printed correctly on sign saying "SALE" in a store window. "S" printed in reverse does not accord with our expectations and hence embodies for us that novelty which, in the psychology of communication, is one of those "factors of advantage" or "stimulus attributes commanding priority" in our minds.[89] Substantial research demonstrates "that unfamiliar stimulus objects are approached, explored, and manipulated," and that attention occurs because a nervous system "filter" has a "bias" towards novel stimuli.[90] Because readers and listeners expect the common idiom, the same factor of advantage can be operative in discrepant language usages at subtle levels of syntax and lexicon. In the psychology of communication, "the best omnibus word to describe this principle in operation is *emphasis*, the special stress or weight given to . . . particular stimulus units (whole arguments, propositional sentences, key words) by presenting them with special potency."[91] Familiar ways of achieving emphasis are increases in volume for oral discourse or larger print for written discourse, but style also can achieve saliency for ideas.[92] In the parlance of stylistics, this phenomenon is known as "foregrounding" through uncommon syntax and lexicon rather than "automized" language behavior characterizing communication in conventional forms.[93]

Foregrounding is a pragmatic function of style not completely alien to the historical profession. Reaffirming "the rhetorical function of literary style in the writing of history," some historians believe with Lionel Gossman that "the function of style . . . is to capture and hold the reader's attention, to convey ideas as effectively as possible, and, in the end, to confirm the pact that unites writer and reader in a common universe of meanings. . . . For the historian, in sum, rhetorical rather than poetic considerations remain paramount."[94] In Turner's case, that functional factor was influential for readers. His stylized portraiture made his discussion of the frontier "a human sort of thing, rather than just a chronicle of events which happened on certain remote dates, hazy even in the imagination"; and by infusing "real life into the dead bodies of a good deal of evidence which is coming to be heard," the Frontier Thesis "touched not merely on the historical, is not merely scientific in treatment and value, but has its element of romance as well."[95] Another critic saw Turner's discussion of the frontiersman as "an admirable account of the types of settlers in the various districts at various periods" in which "no incident seems to be too small to escape his scrutiny."[96] Some responses to the portrayal were as glowing as one which said the "able discussions of men . . . had the flavor of Attic Salt and the grace of English from the well undefiled."[97] Whether in newspaper reviews, public statements, or correspondence about the Frontier Thesis, readers were reminded of other pioneer attributes such as cooperativeness, optimism, individualism, self-reliance, resiliency, steadfastness, neighborliness, confidence, wholesomeness, enthusiasm, calmness of purpose, or spirit of adventure.[98] One reaction to Turner's writing emphasized the virility of the frontiersman as portrayed in the Frontier Thesis:

> Far from the tumult of the elder world,
> Long hidden in the mists of untried seas,
> Waited the western lady untamed and fair.
> Then came each European breed to woo her.
> Smiling she reached her open arms;
> But like a beast, with tooth and claw
> She rent and tore and gnashed, and laughed
> To see her weakling lovers falter and recoil.
> Rose then the elemental man,
> Stripped of his European rags,
> Naked and stark. And with bare hands
> He seized her, spread over her broad bosom,
> Clutched mountain, plain, and valley, wood and stream.[99]

Even an academically oriented review of *The Frontier in American History* lauded the "virile" democracy of Turner's frontier (a passage which the historian marked off in longhand in his personal copy).[100] Still another trait impressing readers was initiative, flowing from the frontiersman's "unbounded confidence in his ability to make his dream come true."[101] In reviewing Turner's book, Carl Becker quoted the same two-sentence passage and repeated "initiative" in a positive context seven times![102]

Admittedly, not all responses were positive. Some people altered this portrayal to reflect peculiar biases. When a Milwaukee reviewer restated that crucial characterizing passage originally of eighty-six words length, one word was omitted: "coarseness."[103] While Midwesterners might identify with all other attributes, some did not see themselves as coarse. A Bostonian saw the frontiersman as one who took "civilized ways with him into the wilds" and then "relapsed toward barbarianism."[104] After grading final examinations for the course Turner taught at Harvard called "The History of the West," a graduate assistant quoted for the professor some of his students' answers about how pioneer life produced "virtually anarchic individualism" and how "the dangers of

Indian warfare brought the frontiersman to the verge of communism—
and a little beyond it"; and in another student's notebook for the same
course, the frontiersman "goes to his end without scruples leaving out
more and more the moral phase and with a certain increasing element
of coarseness."[105] In these instances, prior stereotypes helped evoke
meanings not consonant with Turner's goals.

Despite some variant interpretations, the pioneer portrayal in the
Frontier Thesis was sufficiently persuasive to become what Edwin Black
has called a "beckoning archetype." People often "look to the discourse
they are attending for cues that tell them how they are to view the world,
even beyond the expressed concerns, the overt propositional sense, of
the discourse." Often projected by that message is "the image of a man"
who as a rhetorical "second persona" becomes "a model of what the
rhetor would have his real auditor become."[106] Sometimes, the image is
hazy or ill-defined. Although he thought Turner "put into definite shape
a good deal of thought which has been floating around rather loosely,"
Theodore Roosevelt, for instance, did not state the possible implications
of pioneer attributes.[107] Other readers only sensed generally that the Frontier Thesis was "uplifting and timely," providing a "clearer view" of
"the ideals of the true American"; and for 1896, the historian had "done
the country a great service in publishing it at this time."[108] Several
decades later, some of Turner's admirers still believed that the pioneers'
attributes he described were pertinent in times of "stress and strain"
and that the Frontier Thesis portrayal had meaning not only "for the life
of his own time" but for the "present and future life of America" as
well.[109] But as more readers and listeners over the years projected pioneer attributes into their own personal lives, they eschewed a general
rose-tinted optimism and drew instead pragmatic conclusions about
specific, practical applications.

Stylized portraiture served as a vehicle by which Turner achieved a
basic objective of discourse: identification. Several critics have written
at length about persuasive dimensions of identification as it functions
across a wide spectrum of discourse. From a literary and dramatistic
perspective, Kenneth Burke asserts that rhetorical effectiveness in
essence is a function of identification which produces an "*acting together*"
or "consubstantiality" between author and audience; for in the broadest
sense, "you persuade a man only insofar as you can talk his language by
speech, gesture, tonality, order, image, attitude, idea, *identifying* your
ways with his."[110] As persuasion theorists write about identification from

an empirical perspective, modeled behavior is its outcome. For an effect of identification is that in which "some of the characteristics of a model belonged to the individual and the individual behaved as if some of the characteristics and affective states of the model belonged to him"; and in coming to act as if "the goal states of the model belonged to him, a person strives to imitate aspects of the model's behavior."[111] Furthermore, modeled behavior can become a pattern extending over a relatively long time.[112] Successful persuaders often present portraits of personae whose behavior is rewarded and thereby depicted as worthy of emulation by readers. As Walter Weiss has put it axiomatically, "sentiment toward a character is at the root of identification." And if portrayed as prosperous or important, for instance, that character becomes a model for others who desire to achieve the same satisfying state: "If a person perceives that his own behavior and personality are exhibited by an identificand who is successful," Weiss continues, "the 'match' can serve as confirmation or reinforcement. . . . One incentive for identification is the perception that the model commands or attains a rewarding or satisfying state. Psycho-logic may lead the identifier to conclude that, if he possessed the characteristics of the identificand, he too would achieve desired goals."[113] Turner might not have appreciated the jargon of "psycho-logic," but he sensed the value of portraying what some psychologists refer to as "attractiveness" of some person after whom readers might model their own behavior, even if the emulation was an "unconscious inference" from exposure to discourse.[114] And that rhetorical role of a beckoning archetype is exemplified in readers' responses to the Frontier Thesis portrayal of the pioneer.

Whether in the 1890s or the 1930s or in between, many Americans who read the Frontier Thesis or heard Turner lecture in class saw pioneer attributes as model behaviors directly applicable in a variety of situations in their lives. Even if they had neither read nor heard Turner, other Americans nevertheless emulated that same, mythic frontier hero. And that appeal persists. In an editorial commentary about James Fenimore Cooper's *Last of the Mohicans*, the most recent film version released in 1992 was extolled for its epic portrayal of Cooper's fictional "hero, Natty Bumppo, better known by his nicknames: Deerslayer, Hawkeye, Pathfinder, Leatherstocking"; for residing in this characterization of the frontiersman "was a new myth for a new world, a character whose prowess would suit him for Homer or the Round Table. . . . His particular fascination is that however many unnecessary words

Cooper may stuff into his mouth, Natty is laconic in action. He never fails to act when he must, and never acts when he doesn't need to. He is a man without anxiety—'what Adam might have been . . . before the fall,' as Cooper puts it."[115] Whether in the literature of popular culture or in what they learned from the discourse called history, Americans had ample opportunities to appreciate frontier attributes—and to emulate them.

Differentiating between "*discursive logic*" and "*creative imagination,*" Ernest Bormann argues that "*language,* man's prime instrument of reason reflects his mythmaking tendency more than his rationalizing tendency." To explain how people might overlook Turner's argument about historiography, that viewpoint deems the more potent elements of discourse to be those which contribute to a group's "rhetorical vision" serving to sustain "members' sense of community, to impel them strongly to action . . . and to provide them with a social reality filled with heroes, villains, emotions, and attitudes."[116] Turner's role in that process was unique, however, for he corroborated popular culture authoritatively through the credible medium of historical writing. Henry Nash Smith offers this pertinent explanation of why the Frontier Thesis was prepotent to achieve opinion leadership:

> Brilliant and persuasive as Turner was, his contention that the frontier and the West had dominated American development could hardly have attained such universal acceptance if it had not found an echo in ideas and attitudes already current. Since enormous currency of the theory proves that it voices a massive and deeply-held conviction, the recent debate over what Turner actually meant and over the truth or falsity of his hypothesis is much more than a mere academic quibble. It concerns the image of themselves which many—perhaps most—Americans of the present day cherish, an image that defines what Americans think of their past, and therefore what they propose to make of themselves in the future.[117]

Reinforcing what people had already learned through their popular culture—from the literary endeavors of James Fenimore Cooper in the Leatherstocking Tales to the myriad dime novels about other frontiersmen—the salient rhetorical vehicle in the Frontier Thesis is portraiture in a stylized passage that comprises two sentences. And if Turner is an exemplar of the historian as opinion leader, still another factor appropriately might be added to the list of qualities conducing to this mode of influence. In addition to having "similarity" with the group to be persuaded but yet being "characteristically more competent" with "access to wider sources of pertinent information," this "super representative" also may derive opinion leadership from stylistic prowess and the resultant capability to phrase well those values and sentiments that a public holds in high esteem.

People "knew" already that for virtually any problem facing Americans, the best solution was emulation of pioneers' ways, and Frontier Thesis readers recognized its reinforcement of those attitudinal inclinations. In the face of the "present political unrest" in the 1890s, readers appreciated Western ideals as "new forces" worthy of being the desirable "trend of the times"; in the 1920s, people saw Turnerian models as alternatives to those "essentially communistic in their intent"; and pioneer attributes were applicable in the spring of 1933 to the "great national emergencies, such as we have been going through during the past few weeks."[118] Turner's students who later taught history often found his treatment of the "fundamentally social and economic nature of our politics to be clarifying and stimulating" for their own students.[119] After going on to "responsible offices in government, business, and other affairs," some of those former students, as August C. Krey recalled, still "dropped in on him for advice on their problems."[120] After World War I, frontier ideals became sources of arguments about internationalism and the League of Nations. Facing the problem of building an equitable and enduring peace, some Americans were alarmed about selling "our frontier ideals, all for a mess of pottage, in order to follow in the path marked by men who cannot really understand America"; and for them, the "conquest of a continent was certainly a healthier occupation for Americans than the social struggles and international entanglements of the present."[121] Conversely, a New York City bank vice president believed the national character shaped by the frontier might counteract "the gentlemen who are trying to convince us that present-day Americanism calls for a forsaking of all international cooperation and that it is almost un-American to favor the League of Nations." And as he epitomized application of Turner's characterization of the frontiersman, "the American type and American ideal" were rallying points behind which "we can muster a united nation in these days of international problems."[122] For advocates on either side of an issue, Turner was an opinion leader who provided guidance or reinforcement.

Turner's frontiersman model therefore was ubiquitous for emulation by readers who sensed their own need, in the bank vice president's words, to "apply the old spirit to modern life." For, as another respondent attested, almost anyone could utilize pioneer attributes in "much of his contacts with people all his life."[123] The historian was asked repeatedly to make the Frontier Thesis easily available to audiences other than students and professional peers. Perceiving frontier attributes as ones they themselves possessed or hoped to possess, people thought the concept should be published in outlets reaching a wider readership than that of "technical journals."[124] In this way, the Frontier Thesis helped its readers become what Michael C. McGee has called a "people" with a "social unity and collective identity," for in this mode of rhetorical transaction, "the audience, essentially a group of individuals, reacts with a desire to participate in that dramatic vision, to *become* 'the people' described by the advocate." That participation was unique, however. In more likely instances of providing "not a description of *reality*, but rather a *political myth*," the creator of discourse "warrants his argument with abundant examples."[125] This was not the case in the Frontier Thesis, though, which did not specify discursively what readers could or should do in their own lives. Rather, abundant examples of personal applications were created in the minds of Turner's respondents!

What remains is only to suggest further the compelling quality of Turner's stylized characterization evolving from imitating Robert La Follette oration, "Iago." Consider but one more person's feeling that children should have a "thorough appreciation of the great strength of the Americans of the past," for, as it was expressed to Turner, "our boys and girls are growing up possessing wealth which their fathers and mothers did not. With this wealth has come false ideals. Your great work, it seems to me, has been to impress upon our young people here the great work which their fathers accomplished. You gave them an insight into the true greatness of America and the true greatness of the West, which I believe no other man can do."[126] No archetype is more beckoning than that which people hold up for their children to emulate. And the archetype which Turner portrayed persuasively in the Frontier Thesis was "foregrounded" and made impressive by rhetorical style he learned and mastered as a prize-winning, student orator at the University of Wisconsin.

Notes

1. Frederick Jackson Turner's scrapbook, initially dated 1876, is in Box 62 of the Frederick Jackson Turner Collection, Henry E. Huntington Library, San Marino, Calif.(HEH, TU). Unless specified otherwise, correspondence and primary source materials used in chapter 2 are from this collection. Turner's scrapbook and other primary-source materials in the Huntington's Turner Collection figure prominently in my previous volume, *The Eloquence of Frederick Jackson Turner* (San Marino, Calif.: Huntington Library, 1983).

2. Gordon F. Hostettler, "The Political Speaking of Robert M. La Follette," in *American Public Address: Studies in Honor of Albert Craig Baird*, ed. Loren Reid (Columbia: University of Missouri Press, 1961), 15–16.

3. See Hostettler, "The Political Speaking of Robert M. La Follette," in *American Public Address*; and Carroll P. Lahman, "Robert M. La Follette," in *A History and Criticism of American Public Address*, ed. William Norwood Brigance (New York: McGraw-Hill, 1943), 2:945.

4. Turner's notes for his retirement speech are in Box 56.

5. See Ray A. Billington, *Frederick Jackson Turner: Historian, Scholar, Teacher* (New York: Oxford University Press, 1973), 15–16; and Billington, *The Genesis of the Frontier Thesis* (San Marino, Calif.: Huntington Library, 1971), 4–5.

6. I have commented at length elsewhere about how those oratorical impulses diminished as Americans increasingly accepted a role of reticence, becoming members in good standing of what President Richard Nixon called (with positive, political results) the "Great Silent Majority." See my "The Symbolic Substance of Style in Presidential Discourse," *Style* 16 (Winter 1982): 38–49.

7. Billington, *Frederick Jackson Turner*, 9–10.

8. *Frederick Jackson Turner*, 6–7, 13–14.

9. *Frederick Jackson Turner*, 10.

10. *Wisconsin State Register*, 26 May 1877, 1 June 1878, 22 June 1878, 6 July 1878. Turner's scrapbook also contains his text of "The Power of the Press" and the newspaper account of the event.

11. For discussion of Macaulay's "affection for Ciceronian antithesis and Augustinian balance," see Peter Gay, *Style in History* (New York: McGraw-Hill, 1974), 97–99, 106–14.

12. *Catalogue of the University of Wisconsin 1881–1882*, 55. The 1883–1884 catalogue offers the same description of the "Rhetoricals" program.

13. Turner's University of Wisconsin transcript is in Box 53, HEH, TU.

14. *Wisconsin State Register*, 30 April 1881, and the *University Press* of the same date.

15. The "F. J. Turner 1881 Commonplace Book" is identified as "Vol. 3" in the Turner Collection at the Huntington Library.

16. Cited in Wayland Maxfield Parrish and Alfred Dwight Huston, "Robert G. Ingersoll," in *A History and Criticism of American Public Address,* ed. William Norwood Brigance (New York: McGraw-Hill, 1943), 1:364, 368–69.

17. For a text of "The Liberty of Man, Woman, and Child" and another appraisal of Ingersoll, see *American Speeches,* ed. Wayland Maxfield Parrish and Marie Hochmuth (New York: Longmans, Green, 1954), 409–46; see esp. 415–16, 420, and 422.

18. For a listing and discussion of the syntactical sources of style, see my "The Essential Schemes of Syntax: An Analysis of Rhetorical Theory's Recommendations for Uncommon Syntax," *Quarterly Journal of Speech* 55 (April 1969): 161–68.

19. Robert G. Ingersoll, "Decoration Day Address," in *American Public Address 1740–1952,* ed. A. Craig Baird (New York: McGraw-Hill, 1956), 172–77. This particular published draft is as delivered in New York City on 30 May 1888; but as Baird notes (169), Ingersoll wrote an earlier version in 1882. Or Turner might have wanted to read Ingersoll's noted eulogy upon the death of his brother, 2 June 1879 (in Baird, ed., *American Public Address,* 177–79).

20. For detailed discussion of the psychological process of identification, see my "The Stylistic Identification of Frederick Jackson Turner with Robert M. La Follette: A Psychologically Oriented Analysis of Language Behavior," *Transactions of the Wisconsin Academy of Sciences, Arts and Letters* 63 (1975): 102–15.

21. The Commonplace Book lists all books read by Turner that year as well as in 1880–81.

22. See John P. Hoshor, "American Contributions to Rhetorical Theory and Homiletics," in *History of Speech Education in America,* ed. Karl Wallace (New York: Appleton-Century-Crofts, 1954), 142; and Ronald F. Reid, "The Boylston Professorship of Rhetoric and Oratory, 1806–1904," *Quarterly Journal of Speech* 45 (October 1959): 239–57.

23. Adams Sherman Hill, *The Principles of Rhetoric* (New York: Harper and Brothers, 1878), iv.

24. A text of "The Power of the Press" is included in my volume *The Eloquence of Frederick Jackson Turner,* 117–20; for examples of Turner's tendency to "cannibalize" from one oration to another, see 116.

25. Andrew Jackson Turner (Turner's father) to Turner, 19 April 1883, in Box A.

26. *Wisconsin State Journal,* 19 May 1883.

27. *University Press,* 19 May 1883. The text of the oration was published in the *University Press,* 26 May 1883, and I include that text in *The Eloquence of Frederick Jackson Turner,* 121–24. "Adelphia" was the name of the small and relatively new literary society at the University of Wisconsin, its more prestigious and longer-established societies being Athena and Hesperin. See the *University Press,* 17 May 1881, about the establishment if Adelphia.

28. Turner's oration "Architecture Through Oppression," initially published in the *University Press*, 21 June 1884, also appears in *The Eloquence of Frederick Jackson Turner*, 125–26.

29. Joseph Schaefer, "The Author of the 'Frontier Thesis,'" *Wisconsin Magazine of History* 15 (September 1931): 86–89.

30. Turner's admiration for Frankenburger is evinced in his eulogy in 1906 upon the death of his teacher. See my *The Eloquence of Frederick Jackson Turner*, 26 and 132 (Turner's longhand text is in Box 55). For discussion of Turner as a teacher of oratory, see Goodwin R. Berquist, Jr., "The Rhetorical Heritage of Frederick Jackson Turner," *Transactions of the Wisconsin Academy of Sciences, Arts and Letters* 59 (1971): 28–30.

31. Hill, *The Principles of Rhetoric*, 131, 242.

32. Newspaper experience is not uncommon for historians. As noted in chapter 1 above, Allan Nevins was a practicing journalist for nearly twenty years (starting in 1913 as a *New York Post* editorial writer, then as *New York Sun* literary editor, and finally between 1925 and 1931 as a *New York World* staff writer). He wrote as well for *Collier's Weekly*, the *Saturday Evening Post*, and the *New York Times Sunday Magazine*. At the outset of World War II, Nevins's journalistic skills were sufficiently known to Elmer Davis, who headed the Office of War Information. Nevins was enlisted for public information duties in Australia and ultimately moved on to become Chief Public Affairs Officer in the American Embassy in London. See Allan Nevins, "Some Elementary Lessons on Life and Scholarship," 1967, in Box 41, Allan Nevins Collection, Henry E. Huntington Library, San Marino, Calif. See also Ray Billington, *Billington on Nevins: A Talk Given before the Zamorano Club* (San Marino, Calif.: n.p., 1980), 5–6. If memory serves me correctly about my conversations with Billington in the early 1970s, he too had newspaper experience with the *Detroit Free Press*.

33. *Wisconsin State Register*, 23 June 1883.

34. *Dial* 8 (May 1887): 7–10.

35. Turner, "Notes for an Address before the Lincoln Centennial Association," File Drawer 14A.

36. Turner to William F. Allen, 31 December 1888, in Box 1.

37. Turner's personal copy of *Winning of the West* is the Huntington Library Rare Book 139455; "The Hunter Type" folder is in File Drawer 15B, HEH, TU.

38. Theodore Roosevelt to Turner, 10 and 26 April 1895, in Box 2.

39. Turner's underlining occurs in his copy of "Impressions of Theodore Roosevelt as a little boy and young man, by his sister Corrine Roosevelt Robinson," ca. 1920, in Box 56.

40. "Notes on Dante," File Drawer 15B.

41. Dorothy Kinsley (Turner) Main to Max Farrand, 21 March 1933, in Box 50. For other indices of Turner's enchantment with this verse, see the *London Sunday Times*, 25 March 1923; Joseph Schafer to Max Farrand, 29 June 1933, in

Box 50A; and Max Farrand, "Frederick Jackson Turner at the Huntington Library: A Memorial," typescript, in Box 49.

42. Tuner to Wilson, 24 December 1894, in Box 1; S. S. McClure, of *McClure's Magazine,* to Turner, 19 October 1986; and John S. Phillips of *McClure's Magazine,* to Turner, 9 October 1896, in Box 2.

43. See Turner's description of a projected book about George Rogers Clark, in his letter to Houghton Mifflin, 21 January 1901, in Box 3.

44. Frederick Jackson Turner, *Reuben Gold Thwaites: A Memorial Address* (Madison: State Historical Society of Wisconsin, 1914), 41–43.

45. Turner to Kenneth Colgrove, 1 June 1915, in Box 25; and Turner to Arthur H. Buffington, 15 February 1917, in Box 27.

46. Grace Lee Nute, "Frederick Jackson Turner," *Minnesota History* 13 (June 1932): 159–61.

47. Frederick Jackson Turner, "The Significance of History," in *The Early Writings of Frederick Jackson Turner,* ed. Fulmer Mood (Freeport, N.Y.: Books for Libraries Press, 1969), 44.

48. See Billington, *Genesis,* 53–56; and Billington, *Frederick Jackson Turner,* 99–103. I include a text of "American Colonization" in *The Eloquence of Frederick Jackson Turner;* Turner's typescript draft is in File Drawer 15A.

49. *Genesis,* 3.

50. For additional discussion of Turner's metaphors, see William Coleman, "Science and Symbol in the Turner Frontier Hypothesis," *American Historical Review* 72 (October 1966): 22–49.

51. This excerpt from the Frontier Thesis, and all others utilized herein, are from the version which appeared originally in the *Proceedings of the State Historical Society of Wisconsin* (Madison, 1894); repr. in Mood, *Early Writings,* 185–219.

52. For further analysis of the Madison Literary Club address, see my "Style in Discourse as an Index of Frederick Jackson Turner's Historical Creativity: Conceptual Antecedents of the Frontier Thesis in His 'American Colonization,'" *Huntington Library Quarterly* 40 (May 1977): 269–77; or *The Eloquence of Frederick Jackson Turner,* 32–41.

53. Billington, *Genesis,* 56. Billington agrees the *Aegis* essay was cannibalized from earlier lectures.

54. "Problems in American History" is reprinted in Mood, *Early Writings,* 71–83.

55. See the reprinting in Mood, *Early Writings,* 185.

56. Albion Small to Turner, 9 November 1892, in Box 1.

57. Turner to Woodrow Wilson, 16 July 1893, in Box 1.

58. See Billington, *Genesis,* 160–63; or Billington, "Frederick Jackson Turner: Non-Western Historian," *Transactions of the Wisconsin Academy of Sciences, Arts and Letters* 59 (1971): 9–10.

59. Charles E. Osgood, "Some Effects of Motivation on Style of Encoding," in *Style in Language,* ed. Thomas A. Sebeok (Cambridge: M.I.T. Press, 1966), 296–97.

60. See Lloyd F. Bitzer, "The Rhetorical Situation," *Philosophy and Rhetoric* 1 (Winter 1968): 1–14.

61. Billington, *Genesis,* 3, 170.

62. Turner's autobiographical letter to Constance L. Skinner, 15 March 1922, is MS E902 in the Frederick Jackson Turner Collection, State Historical Society of Wisconsin, Madison, Wis. See also Turner to Arthur M. Schlesinger, 18 April 1922, in Box 31A.

63. Billington, *Genesis,* 166–67.

64. These reactions, including the newspaper reporter's misspelling of Turner's initials, are in Billington's note, *Genesis,* 167.

65. See Billington, *Genesis,* 171–74. See also the description of early reactions to the address in Mood's introductory essay, "Turner's Formative Period," in *Early Writings,* 39.

66. For an annotated bibliography of Turner's publications, see *The Early Writings,* 233–37.

67. Charles A. Beard, "A Review of *The Frontier in American History,*" *New Republic* 25 (16 February 1921): 349.

68. Billington, *Genesis,* 3–4. See also Billington, *Frederick Jackson Turner,* 186–87; Harvey Wish, *Contemporary America,* rev. ed. (New York: Harper, 1955), 46–47, 517; Max Lerner, *America as a Civilization* (New York: Simon and Schuster, 1957), 34; and Richard Hofstadter, *The Progressive Historians* (New York: Alfred A. Knopf, 1969), 47–164. For bibliographies of studies about Turner, see Billington, *Frederick Jackson Turner,* 565–69; and Wilbur R. Jacobs, *The Historical World of Frederick Jackson Turner* (New Haven: Yale University Press, 1968), 262–74.

69. See C. K. Ogden and I. A. Richards, *The Meaning of Meaning* (New York: Harcourt Brace, 1923), 123–26, 149, 158–59.

70. Hofstadter, *The Progressive Historians,* 84, 119–20, 126; Billington, *Genesis,* 174–75.

71. Daniel J. Boorstin, *The Genius of American Politics* (Chicago: University of Chicago Press, 1953), 163–64.

72. David Noble, *Historians against History: The Frontier Thesis and the National Covenant in American Historical Writing since 1830* (Minneapolis: University of Minnesota Press, 1965), 3–4, 16.

73. Billington, *Frederick Jackson Turner,* 185–86.

74. *Washington Star,* 24 March 1923. This and other newspaper reactions cited herein are among extensive clippings in File Drawer 15D.

75. See *Detroit Saturday Night,* 8 January 1921; and Carl Becker, review of *The Frontier in American History,* by Frederick Jackson Turner, *Nation* 3 (10 November 1920): 536. Dated 1920, the promotional announcement is in File Drawer 15D, HEH, TU.

76. Aristotle, *Rhetoric* 3.12, trans. Lane Cooper (New York: Appleton-Century-Crofts, 1932), 218.

77. Demetrius, *On Style* 61, trans. G. M. A. Grube (Toronto: Toronto University Press, 1961), 76.

78. Jon Eisenson, J. Jeffery Auer, and John Irwin, *The Psychology of Communication* (New York: Appleton-Century-Crofts, 1963), 239; Giles W. Gray and Claude M. Wise, *The Bases of Speech*, 3d ed. (New York: Harper and Row, 1959), 416.

79. See Nancy C. Waugh, "Immediate Memory as a Function of Repetition," *Journal of Verbal Learning and Verbal Behavior* 2 (1963): 109; and Richard L. Solomon and Leo Postman, "Frequency of Usage as a Determinant of Recognition Threshold for Words," *Journal of Experimental Psychology* 43 (1952): 198. Nevertheless, the threshold of recognition also is more efficient according to "the relative frequency with which that word occurs in the Thorndike-Lorge word counts"; see Davis Howes and Richard L. Solomon, "Visual Duration Threshold as a Function of Word-Probability," *Journal of Experimental Psychology* 41 (1951): 410.

80. George Campbell, *The Philosophy of Rhetoric*, ed. Lloyd F. Bitzer (Carbondale: Southern Illinois University Press, 1963), 368.

81. Hugh Blair, *Lectures on Rhetoric and Belles Lettres*, vol. 1, 3d ed. (London, 1787), 292–93.

82. For complete discussion of these principles, see my "The Essential Schemes of Syntax," *Quarterly Journal of Speech* 55 (April 1969): 161–68.

83. Demetrius, *On Style* 75, trans. G. M. A. Grube (Toronto: University of Toronto Press, 1961), 80.

84. Aristotle, *Rhetoric* 3.6, in the Cooper translation.

85. See the commentary by George A. Kennedy in *Aristotle on Rhetoric: A Theory of Civic Discourse*, trans. and ed. Kennedy (New York: Oxford University Press, 1991), 233–34.

86. Aristotle, *Rhetoric* 3.2, in the Cooper translation; and *Rhetoric* 3.2, trans. E. M. Cope, in Cope, *An Introduction to Aristotle's Rhetoric* (London: Macmillan, 1867), 283–84.

87. My generalization here reflects the following discussions: Edwin G. Boring, Herbert S. Langfeld, and Henry Porter Weld, *Foundations of Psychology* (New York: John Wiley and Sons, 1948), 218; Bernard Berelson and Gary A. Steiner, *Human Behavior: An Inventory of Scientific Findings* (New York: Harcourt, Brace, and World, 1964), 100; Karl U. Smith and William M. Smith, *The Behavior of Man* (New York: Henry Holt, 1958), 233; George A. Miller, *Psychology: The Science of Mental Life* (New York: Harper and Row, 1962), 346; Ernest Hilgard, *Introduction to Psychology* (New York: Harcourt, Brace, 1953), 295; Robert Woodworth and Harold Schlosberg, *Experimental Psychology* (New York: Holt, Rinehart, and Winston, 1954), 72; D. O. Hebb, *The Organization of Behavior* (New York: Science Editions, 1961), 4.

88. William N. Dember, *The Psychology of Perception* (New York: Holt, Rinehart and Winston, 1960), 348.

89. Eisenson, Auer, and Irwin, *The Psychology of Communication*, 239.

90. My generalization here reflects the following discussions: D. E. Berlyne, "Novelty and Curiosity as Determinants of Exploratory Behavior," *British Journal of Psychology* 40 (1949): 68–80; Norman L. Munn, *Psychology: The Fundamentals of Human Adjustment,* 3d ed. (Boston: Houghton Mifflin, 1956), 319; Judson S. Brown, *The Motivation of Behavior* (New York: McGraw-Hill, 1961), 330; and Donald E. Broadbent, *Perception and Communication* (London: Pergamon Press, 1958), 85–86.

91. Eisenson, Auer, and Irwin, *The Psychology of Communication,* 250.

92. For my early overview of this pragmatic notion about style, see "Style and Emphasis in Debate," *Journal of the American Forensic Association* 6 (Winter 1969): 27–31.

93. M. H. Short, "Some Thoughts on Foregrounding and Interpretation," *Language and Style* 6 (Spring 1973): 97; Irene R. Fairley, "Syntactic Deviation and Cohesion," *Language and Style* 6 (Summer 1973): 216.

94. Lionel Gossman, "History and Literature," in *The Writing of History: Literary Form and Historical Understanding,* ed. Robert H. Canary and Henry Kozicki (Madison: University of Wisconsin Press, 1978), 39.

95. Helen Wengler to Turner, 10 March 1921, in Box 31; and Charles Andrews to Turner, 6 February 1894, in Box 1.

96. *London Times Literary Supplement,* 25 August 1921.

97. W. H. Shepherd to Turner (n.d.), in "Vol. 1, Red Book," a collection of letters to Turner from students and friends upon his leaving the University of Wisconsin to teach at Harvard.

98. *Boston Transcript,* 19 November 1920; *New York Churchman,* 2 April 1921; *Pacific Christian Advocate,* 5 January 1921; *New York Times,* 17 March 1932; commencement address at Bradley Polytechnic Institute by Christian C. Kohlsaat, 24 June 1898, cited in the *Peoria Journal* of that date. See also Arthur Buffington to Turner, 30 December 1920, in Box 30; and Lewis Stilwell to Charles Edwards, 26 April 1924, in "Vol. 2, Blue Book," a collection of letters written upon the occasion of Turner's retirement from Harvard.

99. Poem by Homer C. Hockett, in "Vol. 2, Blue Book."

100. Review of *The Frontier in American History,* by Frederick Jackson Turner, *Harvard Alumni Bulletin* 23 (16 December 1920): 267.

101. Review of *The Frontier in American History,* by Frederick Jackson Turner, "Bookshelf" supplement, *Atlantic* 127 (January 1921): 4–6. In some recent bound volumes of the *Atlantic,* this supplement is excluded. Turner's copy, however, is in File Drawer 15D.

102. Becker, review of *The Frontier in American History,* by Frederick Jackson Turner, *Nation* 3 (10 November 1920): 536.

103. Review of *The Frontier in American History,* by Frederick Jackson Turner, *Milwaukee Sentinel,* 30 January 1921.

104. Review of *The Frontier in American History,* by Frederick Jackson Turner, *Boston Post,* 18 December 1920.

105. Arthur P. Whitaker to Turner, 27 October 1921, in Box 31; and George W. Bell, notebook for History 17 ("The History of the West"), 1910–11, in File Drawer 14D.

106. Edwin Black, "The Second Persona," *Quarterly Journal of Speech* 56 (April 1970): 112–13, 119.

107. Theodore Roosevelt to Turner, 10 February 1894, in Box 1, HEH, TU.

108. James A. James to Lawrence Larson, 22 May 1910; and William V. Pooley to Turner, 12 May 1910, in "Vol. 1, Red Book"; George W. Stone to Turner, 4 February 1921, in Box 31; and David Kinley to Turner, 24 August 1896, in Box 2.

109. *St. Louis Post Dispatch,* 2 April 1935; and Phillip F. La Follette to Joseph Schafer, 12 August 1933, in Box 50A.

110. Kenneth Burke, *A Rhetoric of Motives* (New York: George Braziller, 1955), 21, 55.

111. Jerome Kagan, "The Concept of Identification," *Psychological Review* 65 (1958): 304.

112. See Eleanor E. MacCoby and William C. Wilson, "Identification and Observational Learning from Films," *Journal of Abnormal and Social Psychology* 55 (1957): 76–87; or Albert Bandura and Althea Huston, "Identification as a Process of Incidental Learning," *Journal of Abnormal and Social Psychology* 63 (1961): 311–18. See also my "The Stylistic Identification of Frederick Jackson Turner with Robert M. La Follette," and my *The Eloquence of Frederick Jackson Turner,* 30–31, 100.

113. Walter Weiss, "Effects of the Mass Media of Communication," in *Handbook of Social Psychology,* vol. 5, 2d ed., ed. Gardner Lindzey and Elliot Aronson (Reading, Mass.: Addison-Wesley, 1969), 5:98–100.

114. See William J. McGuire, "The Nature of Attitudes and Attitude Change," *Handbook of Social Psychology,* 2d ed., ed. Gardner Lindzey and Elliot Aronson (Reading, Mass.: Addison-Wesley, 1969), 3:180, 187; and W. W. Meissner, "Notes on Identification," *Psychoanalytic Quarterly* 39 (October 1970): 565.

115. Richard Brookhiser, "Deerslayer Helped Define Us All," *Time,* 9 November 1992, 92.

116. Ernest G. Bormann, "Fantasy and Rhetorical Vision: The Rhetorical Criticism of Social Reality," *Quarterly Journal of Speech* 58 (December 1972): 398, 405.

117. Henry Nash Smith, *Virgin Land: The American West as Symbol and Myth* (Cambridge: Harvard University Press, 1970), 4.

118. *Chicago Tribune,* 30 August 1896; *Boston Herald,* 22 August 1896; *Times* (Lowell, Mass.), 7 September 1896. Although reacting to Turner's "The Problem of the West," in the September 1896 *Atlantic Monthly,* they still reflect the Frontier Thesis conceptualization that permeating this essay as well. See also the *New York Evening Post,* 4 December 1920; and Lloyd William Brooke to Caroline Mae Turner, 13 March 1933, in Box 50.

119. Theodore C. Smith, History Dept., Williams College, to Turner, June 1910; see also a similar letter from and Rosa M. Perdue to Turner, 23 April 1910; both in "Vol. 1, Red Book."

120. Typed copy of "Reminiscences of F. J. Turner by August C. Krey," prepared for Ray A. Billington, 18 April 1960, in Box 52.

121. Edgar E. Robinson to Turner, 27 April 1918, in Box 28; and Arthur H. Buffington to Turner, 13 December 1920, in Box 30.

122. Guy Emerson to Turner, 29 September 1919 and 2 January 1919, in Box 29.

123. Guy Emerson to Turner, 23 June 1920; and Lois Rosenberry to Turner, 7 November 1920, in Box 30, HEH, TU.

124. Box 30 of the Turner Collection in the Huntington Library contains over a dozen such letters to Turner. See esp. those from A. Lawrence Lowell (18 October 1920), Frederick Merk (23 June 1920), and Ulrich B. Phillips (16 December 1920). See also the plea in *Historical Outlook* 10 (March 1919): 156.

125. Michael C. McGee, "In Search of 'The People': A Rhetorical Alternative," *Quarterly Journal of Speech* 61 (October 1975): 239–41, 247.

126. Charles McCarthy to Turner, 23 June 1910, in "Vol. 1, Red Book."

Chapter Three

Carl Becker and the Epigrammatic Force of Style in Epideictic History:
An Overt Impact

Carl Becker wrote well. Prowess with words made him prominent among historians in twentieth-century America. In 1913, this "master of style" was said to possess "distinction . . . granted to few men"; by 1915, he was called "the greatest master of historical writing in our country today."[1] Yale University Press received Becker's draft of *The Eve of the Revolution* in January 1918. And with a decision that would make virtually any scholar today envious, the editor "feeling confident" it needed "very little revision . . . sent it straight to the printers to be set in galley-proofs, without taking the usual precaution of reading the manuscript sentence by sentence."[2] William Dodd commended that book for "unsurpassed style," and in 1931, Becker was told by a reader that he evinced "what English style could be made, or allowed, to do."[3] Responding in 1933 to Becker's *The Heavenly City of the Eighteenth-Century Philosophers*, Harold Laski lauded its style as "pure magic"; and Henry Steele Commager voiced to Becker an appreciation for the "singular felicity of your style" in the work.[4] Other people less well known extolled Becker's "facile pen," "lucid style," and "literary artistry without a peer at present in America."[5] In short, Carl Becker's history was deemed eloquent, and the salient source of his renown was style in discourse.

In some studies of style in historical writing, scholars identify facets of language in discourse, sometimes focusing on them within the context of the age, but almost always saying something as well about the historian as a person.[6] To justify examining "management of sentences" or "use of rhetorical devices," Peter Gay argues that "to unriddle the style, therefore, is to unriddle the man"; for "characteristic and habitual" language tendencies are "signposts to larger, deeper matters . . . a network of clues to one another, and, together, to the man—to the historian at work."[7] But *the* work of many historians with eloquent style is rhetorical. Cushing Strout observed that Carl Becker's readers responded to his discourse "not only as a mode of understanding but also as a final destiny," accepting "the concrete world of human history as a source of ultimate values and fulfillment."[8] Admittedly, attributing such effectiveness to historical discourse is difficult, for a central problem is that of ascertaining effects of any one message amid the influence of other messages at that point in time. The problem is compounded when the critical focus is language prowess *per se*, for the endeavor must demonstrate discrete functions of style as supplements to substance, form as complement to content. For Becker, however, that focus is appropriate. In the context of a precept adapted from organizational communication for rhetorical criticism of non-oratorical works, this historian's style itself *is*, by all accounts, "*exceptional*—either qualitatively or quantitatively— in producing . . . desired effects."[9] With evidence as rich as several decades of readers' correspondence to Becker, a case can be made for effectiveness of style in history—without shortcomings of some attempts by historians to assess their own rhetoric.

Analyzing American historical writing since 1830, David Noble included Becker among historians who as "Jeremiahs" took on "the burden of warning the people when they stray from the purity and simplicity" of the New World. In a cultural tradition descended from New England Puritanism, he was a "theologian and political theorist" who demonstrated to this "chosen people . . . that which is real and American and that which is artificial and alien." Moreover, that influence was attributed to "magnificently lucid prose" in works such as Becker's doctoral dissertation at the University of Wisconsin, "The History of Political Parties in the Province of New York 1760–1776."[10] Max Farrand held that thesis up to Yale students as an exemplar; and when the work was republished in 1960, Arthur Schlesinger's foreword declared it "a minor classic of historical literature."[11] Yet few general readers saw that dissertation—or, indeed, most of the other discourse characterized as such by Noble—as Jeremianic. Admittedly, some concepts may chain out from small groups and contribute to a "rhetorical vision" of a larger public, even exerting influence among people who neither read nor heard their original statement.[12] But Noble's analysis was predicated upon *his* meanings read out of—or into—Becker's writing as published. Although that discourse at times has wordings consonant with notions of a "New World

Eden," few explicit statements "warn" readers about dire consequences of straying from "real" ideals; nor are atoning actions in practical affairs specified. Therefore, Becker's rhetoric of style in history is documented here with primary-source reactions largely from readers in the general public who identify discrete facets of style they found persuasive and indicate in their own words attitudinal inferences drawn from what they indeed read, sometimes even quoting back to the author his more persuasive sentences. Furthermore, Becker's rhetorical role as a stylist is not examined on the basis of his more overtly scholarly writings, such as *The Heavenly City of the Eighteenth Century Philosophers*, which have received ample attention. Of primary interest here, rather, is Becker's popular history, when he was (1) emerging as an epigrammatist in a polemic essay in 1910, "Kansas," which vectored his career course, (2) then writing propaganda in World War I, and (3) finally reaching a vast readership with an eloquent and eminently successful high school textbook, *Modern History*.

I

Carl Becker often wrote at odds with himself. He was at once the historian concerned with considerations of research, evidence, synthesis, and accurate interpretation as well as the stylistic craftsman impelled to produce writing with literary merit. At age sixty-eight, while speaking on "The Art of Writing," Becker described his literary and stylistic imperatives as "the most persistent and absorbing interest of my life." Starting "at the early age of eleven," in Waterloo, Iowa, he wanted to be "a writer of novels . . . good literature—as good as *Anna Karenina*"; and thus "it was inevitable then that, as a freshman bound to be a writer of good literature, the course in English composition, or Rhetoric as it was then called, should interest me more than any other."[13] His composition textbook at the University of Wisconsin in 1893 was John F. Genung's *Practical Elements of Rhetoric*, so we know that the future historian did study a rhetoric of style. Although 191 of 474 pages therein treated content, those precepts "applied to literary undertakings." Genung's definition of "discourse" was "any coherent literary production, whether spoken or written." The "written" predominated, however, in discussion of introductions and conclusions of literary works, principles of amplification, paraphrasing, translation, description, portrayal, and narration in literature as well as applications of style in prose and poetry (Genung had one chapter on argumentation, but persuasion in practical affairs was treated in twenty-seven pages as a last chapter if not an afterthought). That textbook described at length various "figures of speech," those "intentional" deviations from the "plain and ordinary mode of speaking, for the sake of greater effect"; and its readers learned from Genung that clearness and concreteness could be derived from metaphor and emphasis from traditional, syntactical figures such as climax and antithesis.[14] And in his reminiscing about how he learned to write, Becker admitted he took "from the library and read with equal care all the other Rhetorics to be found there—a feat which I like to think must be unique in the experience of college freshmen." Yet "they did not after all help me very much. . . . the Rhetorics gave me the run around. I asked for method, they gave me a definition," but Genung's text nevertheless was characterized by Becker as "not at all a bad book." From the outset, this historian was predisposed to achieving a style of literary worth.

Becker's choice of history as a profession was due to Frederick Jackson Turner, whose presence at the University of Wisconsin had been partly responsible for Becker's decision to enroll there. As Becker later recounted in a paean to his teacher: "on the faculty of that University there was a man whom a young lawyer in my town had lauded and bragged about, and familiarly referred to as 'old Freddie Turner,'" so "I went to the University of Wisconsin clear about one thing—I would take a course with old Freddie Turner." He did more, however. Having succumbed to Turner's "indefinable *charm*" (which the paean does define admirably), Becker set his vocational goal in his junior year: "Who would not like to study history as Turner studied it? And write about it as he would write about it? Not possible to do it with his brilliant competence, not a chance; but still there was something to try for, a standard set, an ideal. And so in this eventful junior year I brought out my tiny little wagon and fumblingly hitched it to that bright particular star."[15] A somewhat shy and retiring person like Becker would doubtless find such emulation unrealistic if it included the effort to embody Turner's strong, outgoing personality. Certainly, Becker must have realized he could never be as dynamic a lecturer and orator as his mentor. Yet even if he were disinclined to attempt to outdo Turner in the vocal aspects of effective rhetoric, he does seem to have been inspired not only to equal but to exceed, in his words, his teacher's "brilliant competence" as a writer. For indeed, as Charlotte Watkins Smith has affirmed, "probably no more stimulating atmosphere could have been found at any American university in the 1890s than that at the growing University of Wisconsin."[16] Becker was an undergraduate from 1893 to 1896 and a graduate student until 1898.

Turner tried to curb Becker's literary impulses, however. Times had changed for historians. The earlier nineteenth century was an apogee of "literary historians" like William Hickling Prescott and Francis Parkman. Coming from Boston families of wealth, such men led leisurely lives of study and writing in plying the historical "profession," but as the twentieth century began, historians were earning their livings by teaching.[17] Turner knew this and cautioned his beginning graduate student: "Regarding your minor: the old union between history and literature is now broken in all the growing colleges. So, if you consider the probable demand for instructors, I should not advise you to make a *first* minor of literature. I am not sure that there will not be a reaction and a return to the combination sometime. You might very well make a *second* minor in literature. For a first I would take either Economics or Political Science. You will find a good general knowledge of both essential to historical study, if your work is not to become dilettante."[18] For an idol like Turner, Becker could forego "dilettante" interests in literature, but his emergent style pleased Turner. When his student sought a teaching position, Turner's recommendations praised his "powers of literary expression" and "good literary taste."[19] After all, Becker's dissertation— completed under Turner in 1907—demonstrated mastery of antitheses that his teacher had deemed worthy of emulation in La Follette's style years earlier. In writing about the Stamp Act and the economic crisis of 1768–1770, for instance, Becker gave his antitheses an epigrammatic quality, complementing their *brevitas* through *asyndeton* (the omission of conjunctions between related clauses):

> The first alternative constituted a legitimate and peaceable method of resistance; the second involved a kind of violence inasmuch as it necessitated a violation of law.

> If they were weak in numbers, they might find strength in a further unity of purpose and or organization; failing to receive general approval at home, the society sought for support in other colonies.

> Thus early the two-fold weakness of the non-importation policy was manifest: if sufficiently comprehensive, it gave a monopoly to

those who inaugurated it; if limited to England, it enriched the smuggler.[20]

Indeed, so impressed had Turner been with Becker's eloquence that, seriously ill and hospitalized in 1917, he asked his former student to be ready to write his obituary: "if it's to be done sometime I don't know of anyone I'd sooner trust to do the job than you."[21] Similarly, Charles Haskins (under whom Becker had also taken a considerable number of courses) commended his "exceptional proficiency in English," "considerable power of literary expression," and "power of happy, lucid statement far and above that of the ordinary advanced student."[22] Becker left Wisconsin with the ability to write history with style. But for several years he wrote no history at all.

Becker followed his course work at Wisconsin with a one-year fellowship at Columbia and then with instructorships at Pennsylvania State College in 1899 and at Dartmouth in 1901. In 1902—reflecting the fact that he had taken graduate courses under professors other than Turner—Becker became assistant professor of European history at the University of Kansas.[23] There his career lay fallow. His dissertation, finished under Turner in 1907, evinces an epigrammatic quality. His developing sense of style in history is more evident, however, in the book reviews he was writing at the time for the *Nation*.[24] Although Becker acknowledges in one such review that historians may have a style which, "without being brilliant, is clear and expressive," he prefers writing in which the use of language is artistic rather than "somewhat above the level of 'dissertation English.'"[25] In others of these reviews, the "biting epigram" is praised, as well as "the brilliant or striking phrase," but historical writing is found wanting if there is "no special excellence," "no great literary skill," "no literary 'art' here," or if "the story is told in a style that is clear, but without distinctive merit of any kind."[26] For Becker, history must have more than "the air of saying: 'This is what happened in this place, at this time, to these people; interpret as you please.'"[27]

Also evolving in this period was Becker's complementary view of purpose in history. His essay in 1910, "Detachment and the Writing of History," took issue with "modern" historians "not given to generalization," who would find out and record "exactly what happened."[28] He refuted "a favorite phrase, familiar to every seminary fledgling, that is supposed to point the way: one must cultivate complete *mental detachment*." He argued instead the psychological improbability of an ideal "that it is the business of the historian to 'get the facts.'" For "our objective man, so detached and indifferent" still rejects some data and selects other "facts" which "he considers most important to be known" and groups them around a "concept derived from the practical or intellectual interests that concern him." Moreover, functioning with values and motives, the historian's "reality is whatever relates to his interests, whatever coordinates with his dream world" because "there is, in every age, a certain response in the world of thought to dominant social forces. . . . In an age of political revolution there is perhaps a growing agreement that 'history is past politics.' In an age when industrial problems are pressing for solution the 'economic interpretation' of history is the thing"; and for 1910, that "synthesis by modern historians may very likely have its uses."[29] And in 1910 Becker wrote "Kansas."

"Kansas" is anomalous as historical writing. The essay was Becker's contribution as a former student to a *festschrift* in 1910 honoring his teacher's presidency of the American Historical Association, *Essays in American History Dedicated to Frederick Jackson Turner*.[30] To demonstrate scholarship worthy of Turner's stature, the other nine contributors documented extensively. "Footnotes bottom every page with chapter and verse for all statements," observed a reviewer; and if "some fault" were to be found, "our essayists dive deep and stay under long, and find all that needs to be found. . . . Presumably the writers are young; but there is no sign of the natural exuberance of youth."[31] Except for Becker! Sometimes humorous, often anecdotal, and in the main oratorical, "Kansas" is no scholarly endeavor for a *festschrift*. As editor of a comprehensive collection of Becker's correspondence, Michael Kammen concluded that such a "light" contribution to a *festschrift* would have "shocked" most scholarly minded historians.[32] But the piece was, as one of Becker's former students suggested, a "turning point in Becker's career"; for "as you doubtless know, he was made by his essay on 'Kansas.' That essay did almost as much for Becker as Turner's essay on the Significance of the Frontier did for him."[33] Epigrammatic style in "Kansas," and the persuasive message thereby emphasized, caught readers' attention and opened the way for a role as writer of popular history for the masses.

The essay opens anecdotally, describing two young women returning by rail to Kansas. As their train leaves the "dreary yards" and enters open country, the sight of sunflowers and cornfields prompts from one of them "the fervid expression, 'Dear old Kansas.'" Then, to explain why "Dear old Kansas" reflects "no mere geographical expression, but a 'state of mind,' a religion, and a philosophy in one," Becker discusses Americanism, "pure and undefiled," under three discrete headings: individualism, idealism, and equality. Nowhere in "Kansas" is a rhetorical motif more explicit, however, than in its concluding eight sentences as peroration:

> The Kansas spirit is the American spirit double distilled. It is a new grafted product of American individualism, American idealism, American intolerance. Kansas is America in microcosm: as America conceives itself in respect to Europe, so Kansas conceives itself in respect to America. Within its borders, Americanism, pure and undefiled, has a new lease on life. It is the mission of this self-selected people to see to it that it does not perish from on the earth. The light on the altar, however neglected elsewhere, must ever be replenished in Kansas. If this is provincialism, it is the provincialism of faith rather than of the province. The devotion to the state is devotion to an ideal, not to a territory, and men can say "dear old Kansas!" because the name symbolizes for them what the motto of the state so well expresses, *ad astra per aspera*.[34]

To characterize these "self-selected people" at the outset, though, Becker quotes his idol and the *same* passage from the Frontier Thesis singled out so favorably by other readers or reviewers: "To the frontier, Professor Turner has said, the American intellect owes its striking characteristics. That coarseness and strength combined with acuteness and inquisitiveness; that practical, inventive turn of mind, quick to find expedients; that masterful grasp of material things, lacking in the artistic but powerful to effect great ends; that restless nervous energy; that dominant individualism, working for good and evil, and withal that buoyancy and exuberance that comes from freedom." To support his historical synthesis about Kansans, Becker accompanies that testimony from Turner with a brief quotation from "a recent commencement address" by "Mr. Henry King" (not footnoted) and a longer quotation about "years of struggle of a typical farmer" from "Mrs. McCormick's little book of personal experience and observation" (not footnoted). A quotation from "Mr. E. H. Abbott" is representative of Becker's humor: "It is the quality of piety in Kansas . . . to thank God that you are not as other men are, beer-drinkers, shiftless, habitual lynchers, or even as these Missourians." The bulk of the essay is anecdote and epigram. The former entertains; the latter emphasizes.

That Kansans and thereby Americans are individualistic in a praise-worthy way is an assertion Becker does not prove but, rather, re-articulates antithetically. For example, "the individualism of the frontier is one of achievement, not of eccentricity, an individualism of fact rising from a sense of power to overcome obstacles, rather than one of theory growing out of weakness in the face of oppression." Explaining American ideals, he synthesized materialism favorably: "The American cares for material things because they represent the substance of things hoped for. He cares less for money than making money: a fortune is valued, not because it represents ease, but because it represents struggle, achievement, progress." Economic motives also are worthy, though, for "the Kansas emigrant may have thought he was going to Kansas to resist oppression, but in reality he went to take up a farm." The "passion for equality in Kansas" Becker epitomizes epigrammatically as "an altruistic motive aiming not so much to level all men down as to level all men up. The Kansan's sense of individual worth enables him to believe that no one can be better than he is, while his confident idealism encourages him to hope that none need be worse." And in extolling equality, "Kansas" hints at promulgation of our democracy abroad: "Certainly it is characteristic of Americans to know that they are right. Certainly they are conscious of having a mission in the world and of having been faithful to it. They have solved great problems hitherto unsolved, have realized utopias dreamed of but never realized by Europe. They are therefore in the van of civilization, quite sure of the direction, triumphantly leading the march towards the ultimate goal." The historian later admitted reservations about that hortatory in the essay: "You might well have said of it that it was written too hurriedly and not enough review. It should have been laid away for a year, and then given a good trimming down to take a certain cocky air and jingle out of it."[35] Those fears were unfounded; the essay was effective.

"Kansas" struck responsive chords among people who read it in the original *festschrift* or after a reprinting in 1935. Recognizing a need for "the regeneration of the desires and passions of the mass of the people," a reader in 1913 felt that "the limitless hope, or rather faith" synthesized in "Kansas" seemed "a perpetually fascinating aspect of our western civilization—a thing of exciting possibilities." For another reader in 1936, the essay "set our thinking a little straight on the new political ideas." During World War II, a naval officer wrote to Becker about "Kansas," saying he "used to enjoy most reading that"; his letter was prompted by the recent marriage of a WAVE officer from Kansas to a navy flyer, an event which had reminded the writer of "Dear old Kansas" and caused him to recount Becker's opening anecdote almost word for word.[36] One reader sent a copy of the essay to the governor of Kansas. Another saw it as "so extraordinary a piece of writing that I very much wish to show it to two older friends here" and urged Becker to plan "a book or books that will give the larger public the same sort of delight and instruction which your essay has given me."[37] "Kansas" became required reading in freshman English at the University of Kansas, and a high-school teacher asked Becker for copies to use in her classes.[38] As reprinted in *Everyman His Own Historian* in 1935, Becker's essay did "much to put that volume on the out-of-print and rare list."[39] The essays in it were declared to be worthy of "reading and rereading" for the "second or third time" and the volume itself to be among "our most precious treasures."[40]

In content, "Kansas" reminded Americans how to respond to adversity and to triumph. The essay thereby provided (like Turner's Frontier Thesis portrayal of the pioneer) a rhetorical "second persona" or model after whom people might pattern their lives.[41] Charles A. Beard thought "Kansas" and other essays in *Everyman* would "provide the young generation with ideas that are sadly needed," and two anthologists asked Becker to grant permission for "Kansas" to be reprinted in books for college readers.[42] Louis B. Wright, who in 1940 was planning an anthology "to show the sound qualities" of American life" voiced his rationale for wanting to reprint Becker's essay: "We hope to appeal to the college generation, and we frankly want to counteract some of the anti-American propaganda that has found its way into college reading, though we do not wish to make a chauvinistic, flag-waving book."[43] That "sound" model of what we should be in the face of new, impending adversity would not have been so influential, however, without Becker's stylistic prowess. People read "Kansas"—and urged others to do so—*because* the "charming" and "splendidly written" paper could be read "and enjoyed" and then reread with "much pleasure," "the greatest pleasure," "much interest," and "real joy from the opening sentences."[44] Here was "delightful" discourse read with "interest and avidity."[45] The president of Cornell University bought *Everyman His Own Historian* after reading but "a few pages of Kansas"; and a woman wrote to tell the author that "mother is going to be a Becker fan too when she reads the essay."[46] If indeed we are persuaded by what we attend to, "Kansas" had advantage because the essay was read with close, favorable attention.

Reacting in 1910 to both "Kansas" and "Detachment and the Writing of History," a professional peer summed up Becker's emergent role: "You not only said there, a lot of things that I believe to be profoundly true, but you said them in a way that gave me immense amusement. . . . If you are not very careful you will make a reputation as an epigrammatist."[47] Although that observer added, "whether that is desirable for a professor of European history, may be doubtful," the perceptive conclusion was that such style was "highly desirable for a producer of literature, and perhaps that category is what you are seeking to qualify for." Turner, on the other hand, saw "Kansas" as a "bully essay" which displayed "critical power that is exceptional" and an ability on the part of its author to "win out" against a "literary instinct."[48] So Becker the stylist had the approval of his mentor Turner as well as that of other professionals. He welcomed that reputation—a fact suggested in the tone of his subsequent reviews of histories his peers had published. For example, in praising the work of James Breck Perkins, Becker called it "a story interestingly told in simple, lucid English that is not without its undercurrent of humor, and which, although often diffuse, has frequently an epigrammatic terseness."[49] After "Kansas," Becker was confident enough in reviews of certain books to suggest specific stylistic revisions by their authors, advising one of them to "turn this epigram a little differently"; honing his own sense of style, he also lauded such qualities in their writing as "excellent descriptions of the leading men and women of the time," "a kindly sort of satirical humor," "verve . . . with an occasional irrepressible sardonic sideswipe at anything smug that turns up by the way," and "brilliance" which is "chiefly that of a witty and allusive style."[50]

Becker was invited to write more of "Kansas" caliber. Furthermore, he was asked for *American* history although he taught and should have been doing research and publishing in *European* history. The *Cambridge History of English Literature* asked for three chapters on American historians; another invitation came for a volume on the American Revolution written with style free from the "toils of conventional methods of presentation."[51] Consistently requested was American history "designed as much for the general reader as for the college student" and with "more art in presentation than preliminary research."[52] A "gentleman of means" indicated his "willingness to give whatever financial backing might be necessary" for Becker and some other historians to produce a series covering "the whole field of American history" with books of "literary quality."[53]

The emergent epigrammatist was perceived as a popularizer, too. Agreeing to write a mass-market book, Becker nevertheless admitted to peers as well as to his prospective publisher that, "I am very rusty on American history"; "I have not been teaching American history for a good many years." In his career, in fact, he had taught it only "once or twice."[54] Indeed, in 1935, he refused to be considered for the Harmsworth Professorship of American History at Oxford "because I have never taught American History, and really know very little about it in those matters of detail that a teacher has to know at all times."[55] Nevertheless, the book that Becker started in 1912 was to become *The Beginnings of the American People* for Houghton Mifflin's Riverside History series under the editorship of William E. Dodd. While drafting the third chapter in 1913, however, the historian still harbored fears of "many errors of detail" although Dodd lauded chapter drafts as he read them.[56] Similarly, Turner was shown preliminary drafts and (as might be expected) liked the writing "all too well."[57] Becker understood, though, that he was appealing to the "general reader."[58] As a published piece, the book was declared by one reader to be a "literary essay with a minimum of factual material": "whatever else this volume might be, it was not a textbook."[59] Professional peers at the time, however, regarded the final product as "first rank among books of its kind," "out of the ordinary," and "the most notable piece of historical writing I have seen in this country for some time."[60] Still, only 24,000 copies were sold.[61] Becker nevertheless seemed to forsake the role of scholar in European history, and a causal factor in part may have been economic. One of his peers suggested that "Mrs. Becker was a woman who was not clever and knew nothing about the value of money, and who kept Becker strapped, always strapped. Hence the textbooks. . . . He was devoted to his wife . . . but she kept him poor and driven. . . . Becker had no money to go study history in the MSS., hence he was more or less driven to philosophy of history" as a focal point of his writing.[62] As an eloquent stylist in that realm as well as in textbooks, Becker increased his potential for renown and reward as he wrote for a readership wider than the members of his profession. World War I provided that broader audience.

II

In 1916, Becker published an article entitled "German Historians and the Great War."[63] Writers of German history had plied their craft rhetorically but in "devious ways," Becker argued, to develop in the people of that country an intense, nationalistic feeling of being "destined to a position of material and moral supremacy." Moreover, "Germans today, by dint of applying the lessons of their historians not wisely but too well" had decided to accomplish their goals "if by peaceable means, well and good; if not by peaceable means, then in 'shining armor' and with the good sword." As written by Leopold von Ranke in particular, German history had a rhetorical role: "Most Germans turned to history, seeking the meaning of the present and a guide to the future in the actual historical process, a process which came to be regarded as the true revelation of the divine purpose, or as an embodiment of universal reason in contradistinction to analytical thought or any individual's rationalization of experience. The history of each nation could thus be counted on to furnish the guarantee for its own law and custom, as well as to justify its right to maintain them against any other nation." After America entered the war in 1917, Becker was able to use history rhetorically in the same way: first, by justifying our intervention as consonant with the Monroe Doctrine, and then, by writing propaganda pamphlets for George Creel's Committee on Public Information. If von Ranke justified Germany's "law and custom" and "the right to maintain them against any other nation," Becker performed a similar rhetorical function on behalf of "the true revelation of the divine purpose" of American democracy.

In the spring of 1917, Becker was teaching at the University of Minnesota (he spent a year there after leaving Kansas and before moving to Cornell for the remainder of his career). Professional peers appreciated his growing sense of frustration. Charles Haskins wrote: "I sympathize with your feelings of uselessness at the present moment, for those who cannot serve actively in the present war nor live on the memories of past military prowess."[64] As Becker formally stated his feeling, "we were only professors, but the world was still young, and we wanted to do something to beat the Hun and make the world safe for democracy."[65] His ensuing essay for the *Minnesota Historical Society Bulletin*, "The Monroe Doctrine and the War," was almost as hortatory in its peroration as "Kansas" had been.

For a hundred years we have asked, and not in vain, that Europe should leave America free to try the great experiment in free government. Now that the better part of Europe is engaged in a desperate and uncertain struggle for the preservation of the very ideal of which we have been hitherto the professed champion, it is the part of wisdom as well as highly fitting that we should have our share in making the world safe for democracy. I cannot think that in pledging our lives and our fortunes to bring about that fortunate event, the people of the United States, whose country was "conceived in liberty and dedicated to the proposition that all men are created equal," can be in serious danger of departing from their profoundest traditions.[66]

For "Kansas" of 1910, an American "mission in the world" was to be "in the van of civilization, quite sure of the direction, triumphantly leading the march towards the ultimate goal" of a democratic utopia for Europe too. In 1917, the national mission in World War I was "not really renouncing but only extending the Monroe doctrine" and thereby creating a democracy "peculiarly American." Although Charles Hull agreed generally with the point of view in the essay, he nevertheless warned that its argument might serve "only to provoke general derision."[67] But for other readers, the statement was persuasive. After urging Becker to "reprint this article in some weekly of more general circulation," a reader expressed agreement: "There are many sincere persons, who as you suggest, are seriously disturbed over an apparent repudiation of the Monroe Doctrine. Reading your article will enable them to appreciate the real intent of it, and to understand its accord with our present status."[68] Nevertheless, although aware that the piece was reprinted in the September 1917 *History Teacher's Magazine,* that same reader expressed "regret that it had appeared in a periodical of such limited circulation." Indeed, comparatively few people read Becker in 1917; a larger audience materialized only after his involvement with George Creel's Committee on Public Information and the National Board for Historical Service.

A few weeks after America declared war, a conference of "history men" met in Washington, D.C., "to see what such persons can do for their country in time of war." The resultant National Board for Historical Service would furnish "material useful to Americans in determining their decisions in the great issues which now confront them."[69] Although those writers were cautioned "to avoid the printing of anything which twenty years from now will be subject to discount or looked upon by us with regret," the rhetorical objective was "some articles which, while sound history, furnish information directly serviceable to the informing of the public mind in the present crisis."[70] Becker's writing was published under dual auspices of the National Board for Historical Service and the Creel Committee's War Information Series. The first pamphlet, *German Attempts to Divide Belgium*—its author identified as "Professor of modern European history, Cornell University"—describes Belgium's "living death" at the hands of Germany:

> Upon this unoffending people the German Empire laid its heavy hand. . . . In Belgium the German army has made manifest in deeds the Fatherland's "ritual of envy and broken faith and rapine." . . . As a necessary part of attaining their military ends, the Germans instituted in Belgium a reign of terror such as has not been known among civilized nations. Nothing was omitted that might serve to break the spirit of the people. The record of senseless crimes and cruelties, of bestial acts, of nameless obscenities and revolting savagery which must be charged to the account of the German army in Belgium recalls those deeds by which "the Huns, under their king Atilla, a thousand years ago, made a name for themselves which is still mighty in tradition and story."[71]

A subsequent critic saw such statements as "uncharitable," revealing "the underside of Becker's involvement in the war, the way in which even his good judgments were canceled out by anti-German passions."[72] But in 1917, Americans likely would not fault that pamphlet (after the extensive propaganda to which they had been exposed already).

Becker's second pamphlet, *America's War Aims and Peace Program*, was intended in part for "War Aims" courses in college S.A.T.C. (Student Army Training Corps) programs and for the indoctrination of troops training to fight in France. These materials would bring "adequate and accurate information to the masses" about the "meaning of the struggle"; and to "give these men the torch of the frontiersman," historians would "narrate to them how it has been that this government has come to stand for the things that it does; to show that American ideals have meant something in our way of life."[73] Moreover, the historian was advised to write for a "nonacademic audience."[74] A sophisticated Cornell student recalled S.A.T.C. War Aims courses as "nothing more than an ex parte apologia for the Western Powers."[75] Correspondence responding specifically to *America's War Aims and Peace Program* is conspicuously absent in the Becker Papers, but troops departing for overseas are not likely to write to the author of their training manual—even if persuaded to its point of view. The "masses," though, might accept as "history" what was compiled in the fifty-two pages of a pamphlet written by a "Professor in Cornell University." It reached readers in 700,000 copies![76]

A writer renowned for style, Becker probably disliked his compositional role in *America's War Aims and Peace Program*. The pamphlet mainly compiles quotations. Some are excerpts from German diplomatic notes. Although commentary between quotations is dispassionate, the German government appears perfidious. More quotations are from Woodrow Wilson. Indeed, the "meaning of the struggle" is articulated virtually *all* in Wilson's words—in diplomatic notes; in addresses to Congress of 22 January 1917, 11 February 1918, 4 July 1918, and 27 September 1918; and in all "Fourteen Points" presented to Congress on 8 January 1918.[77] Reacting to a draft of Becker's pamphlet before publication, Wilson said, "I have taken some liberties here and there with this, but send it back with my unhesitating approval" (although a longhand postscript said, "I suggest holding this until after the election").[78] Wilson would give "unhesitating approval" easily because the words were, for the most part, his. As president during World War I, Wilson did not hesitate to correct, amend, and rewrite stylistically, the words of others. For example, as chairman of the Committee on Public Information, George Creel often gave speeches himself—and respectfully submitted advance copies of what he would say to Wilson. The president characteristically polished Creel's drafts stylistically, endowing those drafts with longhand emendations that provided more alliteration, antitheses, rhetorical parallelism in like endings and beginnings for clauses, as well as *scala* or *klimax* constructions. Because of their "large historical interest," Creel saved all the drafts that were returned to him.[79] Perhaps not wishing to risk having his own eloquence emended, Becker the eminent stylist seemed content to use in *America's War Aims and Peace Program* a wealth of quotations from someone else. And just as he had extolled epigrams in reviews after "Kansas," in a review he wrote after the publication of this pamphlet, Becker lauded history "clearly told with a wealth of quotation."[80] When his rhetorical situations changed, this historian changed his conception of rhetoric.

Wilson's Fourteen Points, though, *were* consonant in spirit with the "Americanism, pure and undefiled" advocated for the world in

"Kansas." If "America in microcosm" was based on equality, idealism, and individuality, these attributes could be promulgated abroad. Several of the Fourteen Points would transplant American democracy, whether as "political and economic independence" or "absolutely unmolested opportunity for autonomous development" for Turks, Serbs, Poles, and other European nationalities as well as colonial populations (with success presumably guaranteed ultimately through Point XIV, whereby a "general association of nations must be formed, under specific covenants"). So although the words in the main were Wilson's, American war aims and peace program in 1918 were Becker's. No wonder the historian succumbed to pessimism in 1920, when final peace and the Treaty of Versailles did not bring to Europe and the world that utopia of American democracy. He admitted, "American politics is at a pretty low stage. . . . The world is in that state of confusion, frustration, and disillusionment which always follows great revolutions or great wars."[81] Despairing in detail to Dodd, Becker voiced bitterness toward Wilson for betraying in Paris the lofty idealism which, as testimony, constituted the core of Becker's *War Aims and Peace Program*:

> That he got something at Paris I will admit. But to say that the Peace conforms with the 14 points is either the result of dishonesty or an egoism that enables him to see black as white. . . . The man has no humor, no objectivity, no abiding sense of or contact with reality. . . . To go on talking about the Peace of Versailles as embodying the principles which he proclaimed while fighting the war—this is ridiculous to the point of sublimity. . . . If anything ever comes of the League, Woodrow will have the credit of having launched the experiment and that will have been much, but future generations will never exalt him for having handicapped the new experiment with such a millstone as the Peace of Versailles.[82]

In reply, Dodd lamented "some subtle influence operating in your psychology" which might cause Becker to "retire from the world, become a twentieth century monk and have no part in the life around you."[83]

Becker did not retire. By 1923, he knew his bitterness toward Wilson was unwarranted: "I realized that what I was angry with was myself; I was angry to think that having studied history for twenty-five years I was still so stupid as not to have foreseen that after such a war the Peace of Versailles was precisely what one might have expected. I had a moment of optimism, had experienced a faint hope that Wilson might do what he wished to do. When he failed, I was angry because I had failed to see that he must fail; but took it out on Wilson. But that is all over."[84] A similar letter to Henry Holt admitted "what I really was sore at was myself . . . an old student of history should have known that the Peace, after such a war, could not be the expression of brotherly love."[85] Furthermore, Becker's pessimism was being displaced by a more refined sense of rhetorical purpose for writing history. Correspondence and other statements in the 1920s clearly reveal his abhorrence of war. Although World War I might be explained later "in terms of sequences of events, or the conflict of interests, or the excited state of the public mind," only this assertion was warranted in 1920: "In itself the war is inexplicable on any ground of reason, or common sense, or decent aspiration, or even of intelligent self interest; on the contrary it was as a whole the most futile and aimless, the most desolating and repulsive exhibition of human power and cruelty without compensatory advantage that has ever been on earth."[86] Or as he attested to Merle Curti, "during the war all Europe devoted itself with great energy to killing as many people as possible with the most ruthless methods; lies and deception were the order of the day. Yet how everyone talked of brotherhood, as making the world safe for democracy, and all to destroy it."[87] Becker's decision in 1926 was that "it is no longer possible to lay upon Germany the responsibility for the war"; and rather than allow Americans to think of French and British leaders as "decent high minded gentlemen who were doing their duty to their countries and therefore to the human race," Becker wanted to "jar people loose and make them think a little."[88] That intention was consistent with an earlier, more formal statement about the war: "Let us at least dwell on the past for the purpose of searching out, and correcting if we can, the general conditions, for which we are all in our different measures responsible, which made the misery and sin possible."[89] If ever an event revitalized a sense of rhetorical purpose in the writing of history, World War I did so for Becker.

Becker published *The Eve of the Revolution* in 1918, *The United States: An Experiment in Democracy* in 1920, *The Declaration of Independence* in 1922, and *The Heavenly City of the Eighteenth Century Philosophers* in 1931. These efforts brought him professional prominence, the presidency of the American Historical Association in 1931, and the occasion to present the address "Everyman His Own Historian" to his colleagues in that organization. Articulated therein was a practical moral about the historian's very pragmatic role in helping people cope with the future in "the performance of the simplest acts of daily life."

The extent to which the specious present may be enlarged and enriched will depend upon knowledge, the artificial extension of memory, the memory of things said and done in the past and distant places. But not upon knowledge alone; rather upon knowledge directed by purpose. The specious present is an unstable pattern of thought, incessantly changing in response to our immediate perceptions and the purposes that arise therefrom. At any given moment each one of us (professional historian no less than Mr. Everyman) weaves into this unstable pattern such actual or artificial memories as may be necessary to orient us in our little world of endeavor. But to be oriented in our little world of endeavor we must be prepared for what is coming to us (the payment of a coal bill, the delivery of a presidential address, the establishment of a League of Nations, or whatever); and to be prepared for what is coming to us it is necessary not only to recall certain past events, but to anticipate (note I do not say predict) the future.[90]

Then, as in 1910 when he wrote both about purpose in history *and* "Kansas," Becker in 1931 made another formal statement about purpose—and published *Modern History*.

III

Modern History was an eminently successful textbook for high-school students. With several editions from 1931 on, it was used widely for well over a decade after the historian's death in 1945 (the publishers continued bringing out updated editions). Although a history of Europe since 1600, an opening statement "To Those Who Read This Book" acknowledged its pertinence for young Americans:

We have to remember many things said and done in order to live our lives intelligently; and so far as we remember things said and done we have a knowledge of history, for that is what historical knowledge is—*memory of things said and done*. Thus everyone has some knowledge of history, and it is quite essential that every one should have, since it is only by remembering something of the past that we can anticipate something of the future. Please note that I do not say *predict* the future. We cannot predict the future, but we can *anticipate* it—we can look forward to it and in some sense prepare for it. . . . The more we remember of things said and done (if they be the right things for our purpose), the better we can manage our affairs today, and the more intelligently we can prepare for what is coming to us tomorrow and next year and all our lives.[91]

Here was an echo of "Everyman" about the function of history. But *Modern History* was far more effective than many other textbooks in the field. A teacher said that "many of my pupils who had thought history a bore and a chore, found it alive and stimulating through your exposition." Another extolled it as "a really truly *interesting* book written to *attract* as well as instruct children," and yet another declared the material "so interestingly presented that the pupils welcome it." One teacher with twenty years of experience described her class to Becker: "boys who don't like and often 'ain't interested in English or history,' and yet they almost never leave a course in which they make the acquaintance of your book, without being more intelligent and alert citizens."[92] For similar reasons, the book was adopted by some colleges and universities as well as the Armed Forces Institute for extension courses during World War II.[93] Students praised the book, too. One of them wrote to Becker to tell him the volume made "the study of history more enjoyable than ever."One student "had never wanted to study history but this was different"; another avowed it was "the best book that I have ever read." A fifteen-year-old called it "a great work—I love to read it."[94] The author was asked for autographs, snapshots, and signed photographs.[95] Admitting that he carried one of Becker's books in a sixty-five-pound field pack on a thirty-one-mile march, a World War II infantryman attested: "ever since I read your 'Modern History' back in high school I've admired you and your works very much."[96]

Widespread adoptions led the publisher to plan a long series of updated editions. For instance, the Minneapolis Board of Education adopted *Modern History* in 1932 by "unanimous vote"; in 1933, the book was used in twenty-two of forty-five high schools in New York City; North Carolina adopted it in 1934 for "exclusive use" for five years in the state's high schools; Milwaukee teachers "voted 100 per cent" for its adoption in 1937; and in 1940, Texas renewed an earlier adoption for three more years.[97] When Madison, Wisconsin, considered the textbook for adoption in 1933, "competitors clubbed together" and one "went so far as to hire a teacher of history from the University of Minnesota to prepare a criticism." The volume ultimately won out—although, as Becker had been informed, "competition is very active, and all of it is fighting our book."[98] By 1937, over 124,000 copies had been sold—a number which, according to Irene Gibson of the Silver Burdett Company, represented for sales to public schools"nearly one half of the total enr ollment in medieval and modern history (270,653)." The publisher considered the book "the leader in the field as far as active use is concerned."[99] Sales "generally exceeded our estimates," wrote Gibson, advising Becker that he should consider the "last ten or twelve pages of *Modern History*" as being in "a state of flux," to be "rewritten or changed once a year so as to bring in certain recent happenings" in order to "keep the book up to date."[100] This was a successful text.

Such success was largely a function of style in language. Consistently, respondents said form complemented content to make *Modern History* particularly appealing to readers young *and* old. Carl Sandburg praised "solid content which you wrap with a style . . . that makes it good reading"; Merle Curti lauded style which left "nothing at all to be desired. . . . I had no idea that it was possible for anyone to write such a book as this."[101] Written for high school use specifically, the book had "excellence of style," "exceptional form of presentation," "unusual clarity of style," "well chosen phrases," and "simplicity of language"—all conducing to "impress the most profound student, yet as well and so easily written that it should prove an invaluable text easily understood by any high school pupil."[102] This historical discourse was "vital and interesting," "clearly even entertainingly written," and capable of causing a teacher to go around "reading extracts to other teachers in the building."[103]

Epigrams, particularly derived from antitheses, are prominent in that style—for most chapter titles or for syntheses in the text. Some titles in bold print evince wry humor: "The Second Empire in France: How Louis Napoleon Became a Great Man by Virtue of Being the Nephew of His Uncle" or "How the English Made a Revolution, Were Not Well Pleased with It, and Made Another More to Their Liking." Other titles more consistently utilize balanced antitheses: "How the French People Started Out to Make a Small Revolution and Ended by Making a Great One" or "How the Revolution Was Accomplished in Men's Minds Before They Made It the Work if Their Hands." Upon occasion, an antithesis is not balanced well, as in "How Louis XIV Governed France as He Pleased, Won Much Glory While He Lived, and Was Little Mourned When He Died"; or an antithesis was wryly humorous too, as in "How Napoleon Set France Right Side Up and Turned Europe Upside Down; and How Europe Retaliated by Sending Napoleon Off to St. Helena." Becker's most prominent antitheses achieve balance by retaining but reversing the order of key words in successive halves, an AB-BA format known in traditional rhetorics as *urbanitas, chiasmus, commutatio,* or *antimetabole:* "The French People in the Eighteenth Century: How the Few Lived Well Without Working and How the Many Worked without Living Well" or "Alliances and Armaments: How the Great Powers Prepared for War in Time of Peace, and How the War Came Because the Great Powers Were So Well Prepared for It."

The potential saliency of such statements for quotability and memorability is evident in the success of such lines as John F. Kennedy's "Ask not what your country can do for you—ask what you can do for your country." Contrast the epigrammatic quality of that line from Kennedy's inaugural address with his more idiomatic statement in Detroit during the presidential campaign of 1960: "The New Frontier is not what I promise I am going to do for you. The New Frontier is what I am going to ask you to do for your country." The arrangement in its early, campaign form is both banal and idiomatic, yet that statement as an argument has essentially the same content as his most quoted line from the inaugural address in 1961. Form in the latter version embodies style, a fact which accounts for its effectiveness. Well-balanced, epigrammatic antitheses are not in the common idiom and require both compositional effort and stylistic prowess to construct.[104] In their normative language behaviors, writers and speakers typically reflect a preference for affirmative rather than negative information, often omitting obverse portions of such statements as "to be not a curse but a blessing." Moreover, idiomatic arrangement favors contiguous placement of words associated by similarity of meaning rather than opposition. For instance, after using the words "devil" and "sinister" in a sentence, one would tend to complete that sentence with words similar in meaning to "dark" rather than with those antithetical it, such as "light" or "blessed." These contextual associations operate unconsciously upon syntactical placements and thereby must be deliberately overcome to create antitheses. In his doctoral dissertation, Becker made those antitheses (quoted earlier) by syntactically juxtaposing in the same sentences "a legitimate and peaceable method of resistance" with "a kind of violence"; "weak in numbers" with "strength in a further unity of purpose"; and "if sufficiently comprehensive, it gave a monopoly to those who inaugurated it; if limited to England, it enriched the smuggler." In *Modern History*, such opposites are uncommonly juxtaposed: "small revolution" with "a great one," "much glory" with "little mourned," and "right side up" with "upside down." Because of the greater psychological effort required to create them, well-balanced antitheses are not in the common idiom; and when they do occur in writing or speaking, their novelty as a factor of attention bestows emphasis on statements so phrased.

Of all species of antitheses cast by a writer, that neatly balanced format of the AB-BA construction may be the most likely to attract the favorable attention of a reader or listener, as in John Kennedy's "Ask not what your country [A] can do for you [B] —ask what you [B] can do for your country [A]" or "Let us never negotiate [A] out of fear [B] but let us never fear [B] to negotiate [A]." Becker achieves essentially the same uncommon conformations in *Modern History* when he reverses in the second half of the antithesis the positions of key words: "lived well [A] without working [B]" becomes "worked [B] without living well [A]"; "great powers prepared [A] for war [B]" becomes "war [B] came because the great powers were so well prepared [A]." These *are* the lines of an epigrammatist. The rhetoric textbook Becker used in college had recommended these antithetical conformations as sources of emphasis for ideas. But perhaps the most cogent reason for him to apply them in his own chapter headings came to him in 1917 from a fellow historian, Clarence W. Alvord, who advocated "catchy" statements whereby "the average reader" would be encouraged to "read further" in the text: "First of all let me point out that a book has to be begun somehow and the choosing of an opening sentence is a perplexing problem. For a serious work . . . which must catch the public attention in some way, it is well if an opening paragraph can be written that will attract the attention of the casual reader. A 'firecracker' makes a noise and will generally cause the passer-by to turn his head."[105] So style studied in freshman composition and mastered in "Kansas" with ensuing acclaim was to have a pragmatic function in *Modern History*.

No other specific feature of style in that book consistently received as much positive response as its antithetical epigrams, particularly as chapter titles. Whether in student reactions, book reviews, or teacher evaluations, the trend is unmistakable. The epigrams as chapter headings were hailed as "splendid," "in places positively intriguing," as indications of "the charming style and compelling interest of the book," and as sources of an "altogether successful attempt to talk to the reader." One reviewer spoke for the readership at large: "the chapter headings captivate us at once."[106] Another reader testified that "every time I glance over the table of contents of the book, I am thrilled anew by the chapter titles. They have that kind of perfection that looks so easy but which one knows has been the result of much time and thought."[107] From his omnivorous reading of rhetoric textbooks, Becker acquired the kind of stylistic skill lauded by classical rhetoricians. Cicero, for example, extols a persuasive style "marked by a certain artistry and polish" that evokes "applause and admiration": "although we hope to win a 'Bravo, capital!' as often as possible, the actual ejaculation 'Couldn't be better!' is the one I should like to hear frequently."[108] The rationale is pragmatic: "when a citizen hears an able orator, he readily credits what is said," because, as Cicero goes on to explain, "he imagines everything to be true, he believes and relishes the force of it; and, in short, the persuasive language of the speaker wins his absolute, his hearty assent."[109] Furthermore, in the Ciceronian perception, that effect of style operates not only upon learned people, sophisticated in the nuances of achieving eloquence, but also upon "the unlearned crowd when it forms the audience," because "everybody is able to discriminate between what is right and wrong in matters of art and proportion by a sort of subconscious instinct, without having any theory of art or proportion of their own."[110] In the realm of American presidential discourse, for example, the effectiveness of such style is easy enough to illustrate.[111] But a critic interested in the rhetoric of style in historical writing must do more than acknowledge the appeal of epigrams generally. The rhetorical effectiveness of Becker's epigrammatic style for emphasis also can be demonstrated by identifying which specific ideas were salient in readers' minds after encounters with myriad dates, events, places, and people mentioned in Modern History." A decade of responses reveals parameters of that impact. Impressed in particular by Becker's treatment of the causes of World War I, many readers seemed to infer a pragmatic application as America approached World War II, and they tended as well to rearticulate the specific epigram they learned to epitomize their attitude.

According to the clear trend in reader responses, the most persuasive and thereby "exceptional" chapter of Modern History was "Alliances and Armaments: How the Great Powers Prepared for War in Time of Peace, and How the War Came Because the Great Powers Were So Well

Prepared for It." Teachers found Becker to have treated the causes of the World War "objectively," describing his analysis as "especially fine" and "one of the best bits of peace propaganda I know."[112] One individual saw Becker's discussions of "the responsibility and justification of the Great War" as "superlative examples of the richness of content throughout," and another was "especially pleased with your account of the World War and its causes."[113] Although some readers spoke in general terms— one saying that she saw "straight for the first time internationally"; another, that he appreciated the book "for its treatment of international relationships"—other responses were quite specific: "We, teachers and students, appreciate most of all your unbiased (if such exists) presentation of facts concerning World War Number I. So few texts recognize the fact that France and England deserve to share the responsibility for the war and its results."[114] Thus, as he hoped in the 1920s, Becker did "jar people loose" to believe as another now did: "At present we are studying the World War, and I was quite surprised to discover that each country had a great deal to do with its beginning. I had always been under the impression that the blame was shouldered by Germany and due to her."[115] Surely some readers found corroboration for feelings already taking shape. As his American Historical Association presidential address had proclaimed, historians "do not impose our version of the human story on Mr. Everyman; in the end it is rather Mr. Everyman who imposes his version on us." And with ultimate pragmatism, he admitted "our success in the long run is in conforming to the temper of Mr. Everyman, which we seem to guide only because we are so sure, eventually, to follow it."[116] Nevertheless, whether simply reinforced or newly shaped, attitudes were influenced by *Modern History* and its chapter and opening epigram on the causes of World War I.

One dimension of attitudinal effect was Becker's reinforcement or corroboration for a belief that French, British, and other European leaders were not only as responsible as German leadership for the war but equally as villainous. Relatively dispassionately (but also quoting Becker's chapter title), a reviewer described "the discussion of World War origins and responsibility" as teaching "by inspiration" in its "most stimulating form" that "even today, the personal decisions of the highly placed are often prime movers of mass actions."[117] In more of a diatribe, another reader depicted Europe's leaders as "plotting and planning prime ministers risking the calamity of world war, and millions from all climes marching and maneuvering into position to get a death grip on

one another."[118] Even junior high-school students perceived those leaders unfavorably. The chapter in *Modern History* about causes of the war
contains a paragraph stylized with a rhetorical format called *auxesis* or
incrementum: "Thus up to July 28 the situation seemed to be shaping up
as follows. Austria was determined to make war on Serbia. If Austria
made war on Serbia, Russia was determined to make war on Austria. If
Russia made war on Austria, Germany was determined to make war on
Russia. If Germany made war on Russia, France was determined to make
war on Germany. In this event what was the British government determined to do?"[119] A teacher sent Becker her junior-high students' cartoons "inspired" by that particular paragraph, including one wherein
European countries were caricatured as children threatening one another with snowballs, all suggestive of senseless escalation. Finding
Modern History "indispensable" for "background of the World War," the
teacher too lauded "the peculiar charm of that style that belongs to you
alone, and especially in the headings of chapters."[120] An older reader
thought Becker did not "put sufficient responsibility for the war upon
the German military leaders."[121] But a wide spectrum of readers tended
to see European leaders, if not the peoples themselves, as unworthy of
the idealism with which Americans went to war in 1917.

Another dimension of attitude that Becker's *Modern History* likely
reinforced or corroborated was an inference, drawn from the recent past,
about how America as a nation should conduct itself in the future (or, as
Becker put it in 1920, our recalling "the past for the purpose of searching
out, and correcting if we can, the general conditions, for which we are
all in our different measures responsible"). Many readers took their cue
from one of the book's epigrams—"How the Great Powers Prepared for
War in Time of Peace, And How the War Came Because The Great Powers Were So Well Prepared for It"—and concluded that for the future,
America must avoid armaments and preparations for war. War, they
reasoned, could come again to us simply because we were so well prepared for it. Indeed, "a careful reading" of *Modern History* would, as one
reviewer maintained, "blast the ardor of the military mind," for Becker
does *not* "raise one's estimation of the military system still in vogue
with modern nations."[122] Similarly, William Dodd felt that the textbook
"if adopted in European high schools, would do more to prevent future
wars than meetings of disarmament conferences."[123] In 1939, Becker's
History was declared be a reader to be "never . . . more applicable than it
is today"; and another affirmed: "at the outbreak of the present war I

and my family became interested in reviewing the past history of the nations involved, and I accordingly got out your volume on *Modern History*."[124] In view of his stated purpose for history, Becker surely found satisfaction in these uses of his book to allow "the memory of things said and done in the past and distant places" to make us "prepared for what is coming to us." Other evidence suggests that younger readers indeed might have been developing an attitude against military preparedness. In 1940, someone in the principal's office at New Haven Commercial High School cut out page 632 of Becker's acclaimed chapter and marked a line of text: "and the war came in the end *because* the great powers were so well prepared for it." Sent to the book's publisher, the single page had this reaction typed in the margin: "After all, a text book shouldn't make such a bald statement about preparedness. Many, many people believe and know that such is the only safe way. How about Norway, the most peaceful and unprepared. War came to *that* nation! The writer might suggest that, in his opinion, preparedness causes wars, but even that is questionable in a *text* book."[125] Thus, by taking issue with that book's position regarding armaments, a proponent of preparedness acknowledged indirectly the suasory potency for younger readers of its epigram against preparing for war. For *Modern History* was reinforcing, through a credible medium, an attitude held dear by substantial segments of the American public.

The following account will suggest the communication mosaic in which Becker's epigrams in *Modern History* were read. The U.S. Army Air Corps understood how Americans generally were adverse to military preparedness. In the mid 1930s, the Boeing aircraft company developed the B-17 "Flying Fortress" as a strategic bomber, with bristling armaments and a range that made it capable of offensive attacks against an enemy's industrial and armament centers hundreds of miles away (as the aircraft ultimately did in World War II, flying from bases in England against German cities). To secure funding and public support for manufacturing in quantity an improved version of the bomber during peacetime, the Army Air Corps created a "transparent justification" of its "utility in guarding the sea approaches to the nation." The climax of these "headline-grabbing episodes came in a stunt" whereby a young proponent of strategic, long-range offensive bombing, Curtis LeMay, led a flight of three B-17s in 1938 to find and "intercept" the Italian liner *Rex* in the Atlantic Ocean en route to New York. The Air Corps "pulled out all the stops in securing newspaper and live coast-to-coast radio coverage." Accompanied by dramatic photographs, a *New York Herald Tribune* article, for example, proclaimed the familiar defensive theme with the headline, "Flying Forts, 630 Miles Out, Spot Enemy Troop Ship." By dropping a message on the deck of the liner, the B-17s presumably demonstrated they could "drop a bomb into a pickle barrel from 18,000 feet up" as "an instrument of defense against invasion." The event would remind many people of how General Billy Mitchell sank the "unsinkable" German battleship *Ostfriesland* in 1921 by aerial bombardment in less than twenty-two minutes. No wonder a congressman concluded in 1939 that the B-17 gave America "the ability to strike the enemy over the only two ways in which he can approach the United States, and that is over the Atlantic or Pacific Ocean." For many Americans in the 1930s, the only justifiable military preparedness was that which could be viewed solely as defensive.[126]

For a decade leading up to World War II, many readers of *Modern History*—students and adults alike—phrased responses suggestive of their inference that America should reject the military preparedness which had caused European turmoil and thence our involvement in World War I. An idea rendered salient through Becker's style attained for some readers an effect consonant with the author's purpose for the book and his own feelings about war: "The more we remember of things said and done (if they be the right things for our purpose), the better we can manage our affairs today, and the more intelligently we can prepare for what is coming to us tomorrow and next year and all our lives." As a rhetorical historian, Becker did his part to put this process into motion— a fact epitomized in a report by a college student who, as a practice teacher, evaluated *Modern History* for use as a high-school textbook. Praising the book's style as "an added help to the student," the future educator described how one of Becker's sentences "clings to my memory." After averring how "no one, for example, could express the subject matter in these chapters better than Carl Becker," the student quoted that memorable sentence: "Alliances and Armaments: How the Great Powers Prepared for War in Time of Peace, And How the War Came Because the Great Powers Were So Well Prepared for It."[127]

Earlier in his career as historian, Becker had harbored a reservation that a work might be "too interesting to be a good textbook—students become so interested in reading that they forget to study their lessons."[128] By most accounts, *Modern History* was not "too interesting" as a textbook, for substantial numbers of students studied and remembered its intended "lessons" made salient by style. In the final analysis, though, considering the communication mosaic in which Becker functioned as an opinion leader—for both *Modern History* as well as the earlier essay on "Kansas"—the historian's writing must be regarded as epideictic in its essential nature. For in this mode of discourse, persuaders primarily demonstrate their abilities to articulate well the values and sentiments to which their audiences in large degree already adhere (hence, in traditional rhetorical theory, the genre of epideictic oratory also is known as demonstrative oratory). Epideictic history therefore is a likely place in which to find evidence of the fact that, as Dionysius asserts, "a main difference between poet and poet, orator and orator, really does lie in the aptness with which they arrange their words." If a writer is not preoccupied with marshalling evidence to support arguments with which readers might disagree, he or she can apply a greater measure of rhetorical artistry on behalf of a style which articulates aptly, if not eloquently, an audience's values and sentiments. The likely rhetorical effect becomes one of reinforcement. Like his mentor Turner, Becker is another exemplar of the historian as opinion leader, and eloquent style *per se* again seems to be a quality which may be added to the list of attributes underlying this mode of leadership.

Epigrammatic antitheses can create salience, emphasizing ideas in a way that makes them noticed and remembered. Millions of Americans recall what Neil Armstrong said when he stepped onto the moon, "One small step for a man—one giant leap for mankind," just as they also know John Kennedy's "Ask not what your country can do for you—ask what you can do for your country."[129] Albeit on a smaller scale, Carl Becker achieved similar rhetorical effectiveness through the epigrammatic force of his style in epideictic history. With "Kansas" and with *Modern History*, the historian achieved and fulfilled the role of opinion leadership when his exact antitheses reinforcing values and attitudes were remembered and repeated by readers. Becker's opinion leadership also was evidenced whenever writers of other American history textbooks quoted his epigrammatic antitheses to make their interpretations emphatic. For example, to emphasize their point that the American War of Independence was one of people "without the ballot against the ruling aristocracy," Harold Faulkner and Tyler Kepner concluded a chapter this way: "In this connection it should also be pointed out, as Professor Becker has done, that the 'Revolution was not merely a question of home rule; it was also a question of who should rule at home.'"[130]

Writing about historical writing, Merle Curti offered an observation about Allan Nevins and historians with rhetorical flair: "I cannot share Nevins's faith that history, if written accurately, dramatically, and vividly, and if widely read, would be an important factor in achieving beneficial results now and in the future."[131] Curti and others might reconsider Carl Becker—and the overt impact of his epigrammatic style in history.

Becker ultimately changed his mind about military preparedness. The course of world events motivated him to do so. In the fall of 1941, before Pearl Harbor drew America completely into World War II, his review of William Shirer's *Berlin Diary* ended with this statement of conviction:

> The "Berlin Diary" is so sound and so illuminating that it should be read by every American. It will, of course, do nothing to dispel Mr. Lindbergh's illusions of grandeur, to abate Senator Wheeler's vindictive hatred of Roosevelt, or provide their deluded admirers with intelligence. But in no book that I know of will open-minded Americans get a better idea of Hitler and the Nazis, of what they have done and what they aim to do; in no book will they find more convincing reasons for believing that the United States can best defend its peace and safety by giving all aid, *and not merely all aid short of war*, to Great Britain in freeing Europe from German domination.[132]

In the advent of Pearl Harbor, the formerly disillusioned propagandist was an ardent interventionist again. And during World War II, he contributed (as in World War I) to the American war effort. The historian whose name was linked with the word "detachment" was asked to advise the Pentagon about whether or not to accept "grandiose Air Corps claims that their bombing would break German morale."[133] But Becker never amended his pacifist epigram about alliances and armaments. He once admitted to his former teacher Frederick Jackson Turner, "the literary fellow I have still with me; but I try to keep him in his place, and I hope I succeed passably."[134] A final assessment is that he did not "succeed passably." In Homer C. Hockett's view, Becker was "above all a political philosopher and essayist; his interest in literary form sometimes exceeded his concern with subject matter."[135] The historian could change his mind about substance; the consummate craftsman with style could not change his form. For that history had a permanence as if its epigrams truly had been set in stone.

Notes

1. Wallace Notestein to Becker, 6 November 1913; and William E. Dodd to Becker, 14 August 1915, in Box 7, Carl L. Becker Papers, Olin Library, Cornell University, Ithaca, N.Y. (CBCU). Unless specified otherwise all correspondence cited in chapter 3 is from the Becker Papers at Cornell.

2. To Becker, 14 January 1918, in Box 7. The signature is an illegible scrawl.

3. William Dodd to Becker, 23 January 1919, in Box 7; and T. V. Smith to Becker, 21 August 1931, in Box 8.

4. Harold J. Laski to Becker, 21 January 1933, in Box 9; and Henry Steele Commager to Becker, 15 April 1936, in Box 11.

5. Sergei S. Zlinkoff to Becker, 25 August 1942, in Box 15; and W. Stull Holt to Mrs. Becker, 23 March 1936, in Box 11.

6. For one overview of such studies, see James R. Bennett, Ronald H. Carpenter, Samuel Hornsby, and Ann Garbett, "History as Art: An Annotated Bibliography," *Style* 13 (Winter 1979): 5–36.

7. Peter Gay, *Style in History* (New York: Basic Books, 1974), 7–10.

8. Cushing Strout, *The Pragmatic Revolt in American History: Carl Becker and Charles Beard* (New Haven: Yale University Press, 1958), 1.

9. Phillip K. Tompkins, "The Rhetorical Criticism of Non-Oratorical Works," *Quarterly Journal of Speech* 55 (December 1969): 432, 438.

10. David Noble, *Historians against History: The Frontier Thesis and the National Covenant in American Historical Writing since 1830* (Minneapolis: University of Minnesota Press, 1965), 4, 16–17, 76, 78. For discussion of Becker's perceived role as Jeremiah, see *Historians against History*, 76–97 and 139–56. For other discussion of this role, see my "The Historical Jeremiad as Rhetorical Genre," in *Form and Genre: Shaping Rhetorical Action,* ed. Karlyn Campbell and Kathleen Jamieson (Falls Church, Va.: Speech Communication Association, 1977), 103–17.

11. Max Farrand to Becker, 22 December 1909, in Box 7. Arthur M. Schlesinger, Jr., foreword to *The History of Political Parties in the Province of New York 1760–1776,* by Carl Becker (Madison: University of Wisconsin Press, 1960), iii. The dissertation was published originally as bulletin no. 286, *University of Wisconsin History Series,* vol. 2, no. 1.

12. See Ernest G. Bormann, "Fantasy and Rhetorical Vision: The Rhetorical Criticism of Social Reality," *Quarterly Journal of Speech* 58 (December 1972): 396–407. For instance, in a persuasion campaign in Taiwan about birth control, "three out of four acceptors of the advocated method . . . had had no contact with the official communicators (or field workers) and, by the end of the year in which the campaign occurred, a fourth of the acceptors came from areas not even reached directly by the formal campaign." See Samuel Becker, "Rhetorical Studies for the Contemporary World," in *The Prospect of Rhetoric,* ed. Lloyd Bitzer and Edwin Black (Englewood Cliffs, N.J.: Prentice-Hall, 1971), 25–26.

13. Becker delivered the speech at Wells College in 1941 and at Smith College

in early 1942; the final draft is published in *Detachment and the Writing of History: Essays and Letters of Carl L. Becker,* ed. Phil L. Snyder (Ithaca: Cornell University Press, 1958), 121–44. Extensive quotations from the address are bases of analysis in Charlotte Watkins Smith, "Carl Becker: The Historian as Literary Craftsman," *William and Mary Quarterly* 9 (July 1952): 291–316. This latter essay also is published as chapter 4 of Smith's *Carl Becker: On History and the Climate of Opinion* (Carbondale: Southern Illinois University Press, 1956), 131–66. Becker's draft, with longhand revisions and inserts, is in Box 1, CBCU. In themselves, the revisions reveal the evolution of a style for a particular purpose and audience. I first utilized such progressions of form as they shape content in "Style in Discourse as an Index of Frederick Jackson Turner's Historical Creativity: Conceptual Antecedents of the Frontier Thesis in His 'American Colonization.'" See also chapter 2 above.

14. John F. Genung, *The Practical Elements of Rhetoric,* 2d ed. (Boston: Ginn, 1896), 1, 85, 96–107, 217. For discussion of the focus on style at this time in rhetorical training, see John P. Hoshor, "American Contributions to Rhetorical Theory and Homiletics," in *A History of Speech Education in America,* ed. Karl R. Wallace (New York: Appleton-Century-Crofts, 1954), 142; and Ronald F. Reid, "The Boylston Professorship of Rhetoric and Oratory, 1806–1904: A Case Study of Changing Concepts of Rhetoric and Pedagogy," *Quarterly Journal of Speech* 45 (October 1959): 239–57. For a discussion of why these syntactically derived figures are deviations from psycholinguistic norms, see my "The Essential Schemes of Syntax: An Analysis of Rhetorical Theory's Recommendations for Uncommon Syntax," *Quarterly Journal of Speech* 55 (April 1969): 161–68. I describe their functional effects in "Stylistic Redundancy and Function in Discourse," *Language and Style* 3 (Winter 1970): 62–68; "The Stylistic Basis of Burkeian Identification," *Communication Quarterly* 20 (Winter 1972): 19–23; "The Ubiquitous Antithesis: A Functional Source of Style in Political Discourse," *Style* 10 (Fall 1976): 426–41; "The Symbolic Substance of Style in Presidential Discourse," *Style* 16 (Winter 1982): 38–49; "The Impotent Style of Ronald Reagan," *Speaker and Gavel* 24 (Spring 1987): 53–59; and "The Statistical Profile of Language Behavior with Machiavellian Intent or While Experiencing Caution and Avoiding Self-Incrimination," in *The Language Scientist as Expert in the Legal Setting,* ed. Robert W. Rieber and William A. Stewart (New York: New York Academy of Sciences, 1990), 5–17.

15. Carl Becker, "Frederick Jackson Turner," in *American Masters of Social Science,* ed. Howard W. Odum (New York: Henry Holt, 1927), 273–318; repr. in Becker's anthology, *Everyman His Own Historian: Essays on History and Politics* (New York: Appleton-Century-Crofts, 1935), 191–232.

16. Charlotte Watkins Smith, *Carl Becker: On History and the Climate of Opinion,* 5–6. See also Burleigh Taylor Wilkins, *Carl Becker: A Biographical Study in American Intellectual History* (Cambridge: M.I.T. Press, 1961), 17–21, 49–68. Becker spent the 1892–93 academic year at Cornell College, a Methodist school in Mount

Vernon, Iowa, and not far from Waterloo. Although his grades were high in Greek, Latin, algebra, and trigonometry, his first-year transcript shows his having started and dropped several science courses, including astronomy and freshman engineering. He did not return for a second year. In addition to poor academic performance, the death of his cousin and classmate, Leonard Sarvay, may have made continuing at Cornell College too painful for Becker. The University of Wisconsin did not transfer credits from Cornell, so he started anew as a freshman.

17. See Charlotte Watkins Smith, *Carl Becker*, 132–33; or her essay "Carl Becker: The Historian as Literary Craftsman," *William and Mary Quarterly* 9 (1952): 292.

18. Frederick Jackson Turner to Becker, 3 July 1896, in Box 7.

19. Turner to A. B. Hart, 5 March 1897; and Turner to Seth Low, 23 February 1898, both in Box 7. Becker's picture in the University of Wisconsin yearbook for 1897 is accompanied by the caption, "Rare is the worthiness of authorship." See also Phil L. Snyder to E. Roy Burgess, 23 January 1956, in Box 17.

20. Carl Becker, *The History of Political Parties in the Province of New York 1760–1776* (Madison: University of Wisconsin Press, 1960), 35, 45, 63.

21. Turner to Becker, 13 June 1917, in Box 7.

22. Charles Haskins to Seth Low, 23 February 1898; Haskins to Charles Eliot, 12 March 1897; and Haskins to John Bach McMaster, 7 March 1899, in Box 7.

23. For discussion of this period in Becker's life, see Burleigh Taylor Wilkins, *Carl Becker: A Biographical Study in American Intellectual History* (Cambridge: M.I.T. Press, 1961), 49–73.

24. David Freeman Hawke provides an extensive bibliography of Becker's reviews and other publications in "Carl Becker" (master's thesis, University of Wisconsin, 1950), 1–29. For another bibliography, see Wilkins, *Carl Becker*, 231–35.

25. Carl Becker, review of *American History and Its Geographic Conditions*, by Ellen Churchill Semple, *Nation* 77 (31 December 1903): 534–35; and review of *The Loyalists in the American Revolution*, by Claude H. Van Tyne, *Nation* 76 (4 June 1903): 461–62.

26. Carl Becker, review of *A History of the United States, Vol. I, 1000–1600*, by Edward Channing, *Nation* 81 (13 July 1905): 40; review of *Jacksonian Democracy 1829–1837*, by William MacDonald, *Nation* 83 (26 July 1906): 81–82; review of *The Life and Times of Thomas Smith*, by Burton Alva Konkle, *Nation* 79 (18 August 1904): 146–47; review of *The Life of Nathaniel Macon*, by William E. Dodd, *Nation* 78 (12 May 1904): 378; review of *The Black Hawk War*, by Frank E. Stevens, *Nation* 77 (8 October 1903): 289–90; and review of *Iowa: The First Free State in the Louisiana Purchase*, by William Salter, *Nation* 81 (20 July 1905): 64.

27. Becker, review of *A History of the United States, Vol. II, 1660–1760*, by Edward Channing, *Nation* 87 (5 November 1908): 440–41.

28. See Becker, "Detachment and the Writing of History," *The Atlantic Monthly* 106 (October 1910): 524–36; repr. in Snyder, ed., *Detachment and the Writing of History: Essays and Letters of Carl L. Becker*, 3–28.

29. See "Detachment and the Writing of History," in *Detachment and the Writing of History*, 5–7, 9–11, 14–15, 22–23, 27–28. Becker suggests very strongly here his growing conception of history as a rhetorical medium.

30. "Kansas" is reprinted as the first essay in Becker's *Everyman*, 1–28.

31. Review of *Essays in American History Dedicated to Frederick Jackson Turner*, *Nation* 92 (23 March 1911): 293.

32. Michael Kammen, conversation with author at Cornell University, 26 July 1976. For a brief but insightful overview of Becker's career, see introduction to *What Is the Good of History?: Selected Letters of Carl L. Becker 1900–1945*, ed. Kammen (Ithaca: Cornell University Press, 1973), xv–xxix.

33. Frank J. Klingberg to Phil L. Snyder, 10 November 1955, in Box 17.

34. Becker, "Kansas," in Becker, *Everyman*, 27–28; all subsequent citations from "Kansas" are taken from this reprinting.

35. Becker to C. H. Van Tyne, 25 March 1912, in Box 7.

36. Stewart P. Sherman to Becker, 16 May 1913, in Box 7; Marie P. Sealy to Becker, 3 February 1936, in Box 11; and Lt. Frederick A. Morse to Becker, 19 March 1945, in Box 17.

37. Ed T. Hackney to Becker, 10 April 1914; and J. Franklin Jameson to Becker, 18 January 1911, in Box 7.

38. Allen S. Wilbur, of Appleton-Century-Crofts, to Phil L. Snyder, 14 December 1955, in Box 17; Christine Whinery to Becker, 27 May 1941, in Box 14.

39. Review of *Everyman His Own Historian*, by Carl Becker, *Minnesota History: A Quarterly Magazine* 17 (March 1936): 73. Several reviews of *Everyman* are collected in Box 19.

40. Wilma J. Pugh to Becker, 14 March 1935; George Hedger to Becker, 12 March 1935; and Olaf M. Braumer to Becker, 30 October 1935, in Box 10. Box 10 also contains letters of praise from Merle Curti, Malcolm Cowley, and Carl Van Doren.

41. Edwin Black, "The Second Persona," *Quarterly Journal of Speech* 56 (April 1970): 112–13, 119.

42. Charles A. Beard to Becker, 17 October 1935, in Box 10; Claude M. Simpson to Becker, 27 February 1941, in Box 14; and John T. Flanagan to Becker, 7 May 1944, in Box 16.

43. Louis B. Wright to Becker, 19 September 1940, in Box 14.

44. Henry Adams to J. Franklin Jameson, 22 March 1911; James T. Shotwell to Becker, 7 April 1911; F. M. Fling to Becker, 13 April 1911; Charles Haskins to Becker, 24 January 1911; E. D. Adams to Becker, 22 March 1911; and Cleo Hearn to Becker, 16 January 1916, in Box 7.

45. Oswald G. Villard to Becker, 11 December 1917, in Box 7. The "delight" of readers also is expressed in Eleanor Draper to Becker, 19 March 1916, in Box 7; and Robert Palmer to Becker, 28 March 1935, in Box 10.

46. Albert W. Smith, president of Cornell University, wrote those words on the flyleaf of his copy, 29 June 1937; this information was passed on to Becker in a letter from David Darrin, 13 October 1937 (in Box 12). See also Katherine Hogle to Becker, 8 July 1935, in Box 10.

47. William A. Dunning to Becker, 7 March 1911, in Box 7.

48. Turner to Becker, 21 January 1911; and Turner to Claude H. Van Tyne, 24 February 1911; cited in Wilbur Jacobs, *The Historical World of Frederick Jackson Turner* (New Haven: Yale University Press 1968), 134–35, 209–10.

49. Carl Becker, review of *France in the American Revolution,* by James Breck Perkins, *Nation* 92 (15 June 1911): 604–5.

50. Becker, review of *The Life and Times of Cavour,* by William R. Thayer, *Dial* 51 (16 November 1911): 389–92; review of *Republican France 1870–1912,* by Ernest A. Vizetelly, *Nation* 96 (24 April 1913): 416–17; review of *The Fall of the Dutch Republic,* by Hendrik W. Van Loon, *Nation* 97 (14 August 1913): 145–46; review of *The Rise of American Civilization,* by Charles A. Beard and Mary R. Beard, *Nation* 120 (18 May 1927): 559–60; and review of *The Second Empire,* by Phillip Guedalla, *New Republic* 33 (27 December 1922): 125.

51. John Erskine to Becker, 14 March 1914; and Allen Johnson to Becker, 18 March 1917, in Box 7.

52. Charles Haskins to Becker, 23 April 1917; and Allen Johnson to Becker, 20 April 1916, both in Box 7.

53. W. B. Munro to Becker, 19 July 1915, in Box 7.

54. Becker to William E. Dodd, 23 April 1912; Becker to J. Franklin Jameson, 30 January 1912; and Becker to the Houghton Mifflin Company, 26 June 1912, in Box 7.

55. Becker to Felix Frankfurter, 10 January 1935, in Box 10.

56. Becker to William E. Dodd, 12 November 1913; and Dodd to Becker, 10 April 1914 and 12 December 1914, in Box 7.

57. Turner to Becker, 5 November 1914, in Box 7.

58. Becker to Dodd, 1 November 1914, in Box 7.

59. Homer C. Hockett to Phil L. Snyder, 6 January 1956, in Box 17.

60. Claude H. Van Tyne to Becker, 6 August 1915; Raymond G. Taylor to Becker, 12 May 1915; and Charles Haskins to Becker, 1 July 1915, in Box 7.

61. Houghton Mifflin Company to David Hawke, 31 January 1950; cited in Wilkins, *Carl Becker,* 86.

62. Wallace Notestein to Merle Curti, 26 December 1949, in Box 18, File 15, Merle Curti Papers, State Historical Society of Wisconsin, Madison, Wis.

63. Carl Becker, "German Historians and the Great War," *Dial* 60 (17 February 1916): 160–64. The piece actually is a review of *Modern Germany and Her Historians,* by Antoine Guilland, and of *History of Germany in the Nineteenth Century,* by Heinrich von Treitschke.

64. Charles Haskins to Becker, 5 May 1917, in Box 7.

65. Carl Becker, review of *A History of France from the Earliest Times to the Treaty of Versailles,* by William S. Davis, *New Republic* 22 (14 July 1920): 207.

66. Carl Becker, "The Monroe Doctrine and the War," *Minnesota Historical Society Bulletin* 2 (1917): 61–68. See in particular p. 68.

67. Charles Hull to Becker, 23 May 1917, in Box 7.

68. M. L. Bonham to Becker, 20 September 1917, in Box 7.

69. J. Franklin Jameson to Becker, 2 May 1917; and Turner to Becker, 11 May 1917, in Box 7. For an account of the National Board for Historical Service, see George T. Blakey, *Historians on the Homefront: American Propagandists for the Great War* (Lexington: University Press of Kentucky, 1970). See also Carol S. Gruber, *Mars and Minerva: World War I and the Uses of the Higher Learning in America* (Baton Rouge: Louisiana State University Press, 1975).

70. Jameson to Becker, 2 May 1917, in Box 7.

71. The Committee on Public Information announced this particular pamphlet as published by a "World Peace Foundation" in collaboration with the National Board for Historical Service.

72. Wilkins, *Carl Becker,* 128.

73. Edgar E. Robinson to Frederick Jackson Turner, 27 April 1918, in Box 28, Frederick Jackson Turner Collection, Henry E. Huntington Library, San Marino, Calif.

74. A. L. P. Dennis to Becker, 22 December 1917, in Box 7.

75. Russell N. Chase to Phil L. Snyder, 16 February 1956, in Box 17.

76. Wilkins, *Carl Becker,* 129.

77. Becker's *America's War Aims and Peace Program* is no. 21 (November 1918) in the War Information Series.

78. Woodrow Wilson to George Creel, 26 October 1918, in Box 7. The original copy of this letter is in the Becker Papers in the Olin Library at Cornell University, so Creel must have passed it on to the historian.

79. See my "Woodrow Wilson as Speechwriter for George Creel: Presidential Style in Discourse as an Index of Personality," *Presidential Studies Quarterly* 19 (Winter 1989): 117–26. Drafts of those edited speeches are in a folio of documents presented by Creel to his son in 1931, in the Creel Papers, Library of Congress, Washington, D.C.

80. See Carl Becker, review of *German Social Democracy During the War,* by Edward Bevan, *Nation* 109 (13 December 1919): 768.

81. Becker to Richard Newhall, 24 March 1920, in Box 7, CBCU.

82. Becker to Dodd, ca. 10–12 June 1920, in Box 7, CBCU. This letter is reprinted in *What Is the Good of History?: Selected Letters of Carl L. Becker 1900–1945,* ed. Kammen; it and other letters of this period are bases of analysis in Phil L. Snyder, "Carl L. Becker and the Great War: A Crisis for a Humane Intelligence," *Western Political Quarterly* 9 (1956): 1–10.

83. Dodd to Becker, 15 June 1920, in Box 7.

84. Becker to Dodd, 26 February 1923, in Box 8.

85. Becker to Holt, 1923, in Box 8.

86. Becker to Dodd, 17 June 1920, in Box 7.

87. Becker to Merle Curti, not dated but likely August or September 1928, in Box 5, File 4, Curti Papers.

88. Becker to H. E. Barnes, 21 February 1926, in Box 8.

89. Carl Becker, "The Way of a War," review of *Before the War,* by Viscount Haldane, *Nation* 110 (22 May 1920): 693.

90. The address is published in Becker, *Everyman,* 233–55. See particularly p. 241.

91. Carl Becker, *Modern History* (Morristown, N.J.: Silver Burdett, 1958), v–vi. The 1958 edition was updated about post-World War II Europe by Becker's son, Frederick Carl Becker.

92. W. Seward Salisbury to Becker, 11 November 1941, in Box 14; Mabel Perry to Becker, 29 June 1932, in Box 8; Burr Phillips to Becker, 26 April 1933, in Box 9; and Sadie B. Mandelstein to Becker, 10 February 1936, in Box 11.

93. E.G. Schwiebert, Valparaiso University, to Becker, 16 December 1931, in Box 8; Donald C. McKay, Harvard University, to Becker, 30 July 1934, in Box 9; A. T. Volwiler, Ohio University, to Becker, 31 August, in Box 13; Eugene Pfaff, University of North Carolina, to Becker, 12 December 1938, in Box 13; Helen Anderson, National Park College , to Becker, 10 February 1942, in Box 15; and Earl E. Welch to Becker, 10 January 1943, in Box 16.

94. Joseph J. Berg to Becker, 23 October 1940, in Box 14; Isabel Ann Ballou to Becker, 19 November 1931; and Robert D. Williamson, of the Silver Burdett Company (reporting the student's comment), to Becker, 12 December 1931, in Box 8; Wilson Hawkins to Robert D. Williamson, 3 February 1934, in Box 9.

95. J. Gordon Jeffries to Becker, 8 July 1935, in Box 10; and Annabelle Witt to Becker, April 1934, in Box 10. Elaine Guerber to Becker, 8 December 1933; Sol Pekholtz to Becker, 5 April 1933; and Elizabeth Flynn to Becker, 20 January 1933. All in Box 10.

96. Corporal James R. Murphy to Becker, 20 August 1944, in Box 17.

97. John A. Shoemaker to Becker, 30 April 1932, in Box 8; R. D. Williamson to Becker, 22 September 1933 and 14 May 1934, in Box 9; and Irene Gibson, of the Silver Burdett Company, to Becker, 7 May 1937, in Box 12, and 18 September 1940, in Box 14.

98. R. D. Williamson to Becker, 1 June 1933 and 1 April 1933, in Box 9.

99. Irene Gibson to Becker, 4 May 1937, in Box 12, CBCU. In this letter, Gibson indicated that 45,000 copies were sold in 1935; but she suggested the following fall that although several thousand copies of the 1935 edition were still available, a new edition should be ready for 1939, 5 October 1938, in Box 13.

100. Gibson to Becker, 15 January 1935, in Box 10, and 11 October 1933, in Box 9.

101. Carl Sandburg to Becker, 5 November 1937, in Box 12; Merle Curti to Becker, 20 May 1931, in Box 8.

102. P. J. Treat to Becker, 24 May 1931; S. L. Eby to the Silver Burdett Company, 20 October 1931; Ralph W. Penniman to the Silver Burdett Company, 16 May 1931; Robert Seybold to the Silver Burdett Company, 1 June 1931; Ernest Hicks to Becker, 22 June 1931; and R. F. Schraedly to Becker, 21 March 1932, in Box 8.

103. Guy S. Ford to Becker, 3 August 1931; and Arthur J. May to Becker, 22 August 1931, in Box 8; Eleanor Draper to Becker, 21 May 1933, in Box 9.

104. For discussion of this point, including traditional commentary as well as contemporary research in psycholinguistics, see my "The Essential Schemes of Syntax," *Quarterly Journal of Speech* 55 (April 1969): 161–68; or my "The Ubiquitous Antithesis," *Style* 10 (Fall 1976): 426–41.

105. Clarence W. Alvord to Becker, 23 April 1917, in Box 7.

106. Box 19 contains many reviews of Becker's writing as well as teacher evaluations of his textbook. Cited in the text are a letter from Henry Grimshaw to Becker, 8 May 1934; and the following reviews of *Modern History*: Val Larwin, December 1931 (periodical unidentified); Mark Rich, *Christian Century*, 5 October 1932; Edgar Bruce Wesley (typescript, n.d.); and E. M. Edmondson (typescript, n.d.).

107. Alys F. Conkling to Becker, 4 February 1944, in Box 16.

108. Cicero, *De Oratore* 1.12.50, 1.33.152, 3.26.101, trans. H. Rackham, Loeb Classical Library (Cambridge: Harvard University Press, 1948), I: 39, 105; II: 81.

109. Cicero, *Brutus* 14 and 50, in *Cicero on Oratory and Orators*, trans. and ed. J. S. Watson (London: George Bell and Sons, 1909), 455.

110. Cicero, *De Oratore* 3.50.195, trans. H. Rackham, Loeb Classical Library, II: 105.

111. See, for instance, my "The Symbolic Substance of Style in Presidential Discourse," *Style* 16 (Winter 1982): 38–49.

112. Irma Costello to the Silver Burdett Company, 13 August 1932; Helen Marshall to the Silver Burdett Company, 15 June 1931; and Helen E. Hart to Becker, 26 April 1937, in Box 19.

113. E. M. Edmondson, in a typescript compilation of teacher responses (n.d.), in Box 19; Harry Barnes to Becker, 21 May 1931, in Box 3.

114. Florence G. Nasmyth to Becker, 1 January 1933, in Box 9; Earl Cranston to the Silver Burdett Company, 3 July 1931, in Box 3; Bonnie K. Barnes to Becker, 22 November 1941, in Box 14.

115. Sylvia Lois Willner to Becker, 23 April 1937, in Box 12.

116. Carl Becker, "Everyman His Own Historian," in Becker, *Everyman*, 253.

117. Val Larwin, review of *Modern History*, by Carl Becker, December 1931 (the periodical cannot be identified from the copy in the Cornell holdings), in Box 19.

118. C. C. Janzen to the Silver Burdett Company, 20 July 1931, in Box 19.

119. Becker, *Modern History*, 664.

120. Margaret Rauth to Becker (n.d.), in Box 18.

121. R. D. Williamson, of the Silver Burdett Company (reporting the reader's comment), to Becker, 14 April 1932, in Box 8.

122. Mark Rich, review of *Modern History*, by Carl Becker, *Christian Century*, 5 October 1932, in Box 19.

123. Dodd to R. D. Williamson, 28 November 1933, in Box 9.

124. Amy G. Edmunds to Becker, 29 November 1939; and Thora Morse to Becker, 15 October 1939, in Box 13.

125. Enclosed in a letter from Irene Gibson, of the Silver Burdett Company, to Becker, 14 May 1940, in Box 14.

126. Michael S. Sherry, *The Rise of American Air Power: The Creation of Armageddon* (New Haven: Yale University Press, 1987), 52, 61–62. Earlier, B-10 aircraft were promoted in 1934 by a highly publicized 7,360-mile round-trip flight from Washington, D.C., to Alaska and back to demonstrate emergency defense of our territory. Similarly, in 1937, the press reported a test in which an aircraft squadron located a battleship in fog hundreds of miles off the West Coast—the "greatest happenstance in the world," Curtis LeMay admitted—and "sank" it in a mock attack. See Martin Caiden, *Air Force: A Pictorial History of American Air Power* (New York: Bramhall House, 1957), 42–45, 66–67, 82–83; and Gene Gurney, *The War in the Air* (New York: Bonanza Books, 1962), 10–11, 18, 27.

127. Winston Brown, "Participation Report" for Education 84 (n.d.), in Box 19.

128. Carl Becker, review of *A Brief History of Europe from 1789 to 1815,* by Lucius Henry Holt and Alexander Wheeler Chilton, *New Republic* 22 (5 May 1920): 322.

129. For further discussion of the pragmatic effects of this technique or style, see my "The Ubiquitous Antithesis," *Style* 10 (Fall 1976): 428.

130. See Harold Underwood Faulkner and Tyler Kepner, *America: Its History and People,* 5th ed. (New York: McGraw-Hill, 1950), 76.

131. Merle Curti, review of *Allan Nevins on History,* ed. Ray A. Billington, *Pacific Historical Review* 45 (1976): 278.

132. Italics are mine. Becker's review of *Berlin Diary,* by William Shirer, first appeared in the autumn 1941 issue of the *Yale Review* and was reprinted as an advertisement for the book in *Time,* 27 October 1941, 103. Robert E. Brown characterizes Becker as "a man who changed his mind." See Brown, *Carl Becker in History and the American Revolution* (East Lansing: Spartan Press, 1970), v.

133. Cited in Peter Novick, *That Noble Dream: The "Objectivity Question" and the American Historical Profession* (Cambridge: Cambridge University Press, 1988), 303.

134. Becker to Turner, 24 October 1920, Frederick Jackson Turner Collection, Henry E. Huntington Library, San Marino, Calif., Box 30. The letter also is reprinted in Kammen, 75.

135. Homer C. Hockett to Phil L. Snyder, 6 January 1956, in Box 17.

Chapter Four

Alfred Thayer Mahan's
Style in History as a
Persuasive Paramessage:
A Subtle Impress

In September 1920, a U.S. Navy officer visited Kaiser Wilhelm's former residence in Potsdam, Germany. Commander Scott Umsted found its library in virtually the same condition as when the Kaiser hurriedly left for exile at the close of World War I. In the special nook where the Kaiser liked to read, the small bookcase within easiest reach of Wilhelm's favorite chair included *The Influence of Sea Power upon History,* published in 1890 by an American naval officer: Alfred Thayer Mahan. Not only had the Kaiser made extensive marginal notes, but he also had extensively underlined specific statements. Although U.S. Naval Intelligence later attempted to contact the Kaiser in exile and obtain the book, that underlined volume had been sold or stolen by then.[1] Actually, Mahan heard indirectly through his publisher of the impression his book had made on the Kaiser. In 1894, Wilhelm telegraphed the *New York Herald* foreign correspondent in England, Poultney Bigelow, giving him his reaction to Mahan's narration about the influence of sea power: "I am just now, not reading but devouring Captain Mahan's book and am trying to learn it by heart. It is a first class work and classical in all points. It is on board all my ships and constantly quoted by my captains and officers."[2] Although Mahan, on a European cruise in 1893 and 1894, refused to meet with him in Germany, Wilhelm nevertheless prevailed upon Queen Victoria to arrange dinner with the American naval historian in England, both at the Osborne House and on board the British royal yacht at Cowes, where Mahan learned directly that the Kaiser was "very much interested in my books."[3] As Germany approached the turn of the century with desires to become a world power, the Imperial German Navy subsequently requested that a translation of the book "be supplied to all the public libraries, schools and government institutions."[4] After World War I, *The Influence of Sea Power upon History* was required reading in Germany. "I had the chance to remember very much of Mahan's theories and ideas," wrote one such student; "I had to study him in the German Naval Academy as a Navy Officer, several years ago." After World War II, however, libraries were "not allowed to lend the works by Mahan in Germany," the officer continued, "because it is militaristic literature."[5]

Any history book that can make a world leader want "to learn it by heart" merits scholarly scrutiny for the sources of its rhetorical impact. An imperative for such scrutiny may be even greater when one suspects that such a book was conceived and written without acceptance by other historians as one of its central aims. While arguing that "Mahan's research methods would not pass muster in a modern Ph.D. seminar in historiography," Robert Seager offers an indelible image of Mahan as an author for whom an impelling motivation was "to write swiftly and write for money." From a perspective oriented to historiographical considerations, Mahan can be viewed as having the shortcomings that he himself suggested in his assessment of his books and other writings:

> I bring to them no special knowledge of details, only a few general principles, and I have laboriously to apply these, and under the pressure of time to solve difficulties, whose solution to a man who had studied before would be rapid. . . . Original research was not within my scope, nor was it necessary to the scheme thus outlined. . . . Of course, I cannot contemplate exhaustive research, or full treatment, of our now three century record. My hope is to strike a ruling thought, like Sea Power, and to string my account so upon that as to present a more vivid and coherent whole than more elaborate and comprehensive works do—or can do. . . . Facts won't lie if you work them right; but if you work them wrong, a little disproportion in the emphasis, a slight exaggeration of color, a little more or less limelight on this or that part of the grouping and the result is not truth, even though each individual fact be as unimpeachable as the multiplication table. . . . There is no use of a man writing what he has no reason to believe the many will read . . . large, plain, simple ideas . . . more suggestive to the man in the street.[6]

Despite scholarly criticism of Mahan's historiographical prowess, he nevertheless deserves attention for the manner in which *The Influence of*

Sea Power upon History was approached, read, and accepted as historical discourse by the people in public affairs he hoped to persuade. For in the final analysis, as Seager suggests, "with the possible exception of Harriet Beecher Stowe's *Uncle Tom's Cabin,* published in 1852, no book written in nineteenth-century America by an American had greater immediate impact on the course and direction of the nation."[7] Mahan's opinion leadership and guidance on naval matters is worthy of close analysis to discover the stylistic sources of its impact.

Evolving out of his lectures at the Naval War College in New-port, Rhode Island, Mahan's eminently influential book demonstrated authoritatively how the rise and fall of nations always has been linked inextricably with commercial and military command of the sea. In thereby explaining social, economic, and geographic factors governing the development and maintenance of sea power, that discourse became not only a basic essay on the strategy of war but also a major treatise on international geopolitics; its impact was profound and far-reaching. Not only had Kaiser Wilhelm used the book to justify German naval expansion prior to World War I, but Great Britain acclaimed its views as they substantiated the need for a larger navy and for colonial expansion, and Japan adapted his theories extensively in naval and military colleges.[8] In the United States, Mahan validated our emergence as a sea power and our goal of imperialism.[9] Indeed, this book likely affected the outcome of both the great world wars.[10] Even during the Cold War, Soviet naval expansion was analyzed in *Time* magazine as it "might almost have been inspired by the prophetic writings of the American naval strategist Alfred Thayer Mahan."[11]

The 1890s admittedly were receptive to messages like Mahan's. In the United States, his writing could be read as a hortatory, Jeremianic message that portrayed Americans favorably as a chosen people, destined to overcome adversity by returning to their former traits such as "healthy excitement of exploration and adventure," "wisdom," "up-rightness," "quick instinct," and firm dedication to "personal freedom and enterprise" (in contrast to the French, who had a tendency toward "hoarding," or the Spanish and Portuguese, who brought "a blot" on their national character because "the desire for gain rose in them to fierce avarice").[12] The author himself expressed his belief several times that his conception of Sea Power "came from within" only through God's help.[13] Accordingly, people who were opinion leaders in their own rights recommended values articulated by Mahan. For instance, Secretary of the Navy

Josephus Daniels wrote in 1914 to Mahan to say in his own Jeremianic mode that "it is most helpful to younger men to read your clear call to hold fast to the ancient landmarks our fathers set."[14] In the overt content of his discourse, the historian thus projected a traditional dimension of ethos or credibility known in the Aristotelian paradigm as good will or high moral character. For his readers in both America and Europe, that ethos manifest in its substance made Mahan's message all the more persuasive at a time when rapid industrial growth demanded raw materials as well as foreign markets, all of which depended upon the use and control of the seas. And while some national impulses to expand were disguised as missions of bringing democracy, civilization, and Christianity to backward peoples of the world, their avenues of approach also were the seas.

In this historical context, imperialism was a broad theme articulated by many; few found their discourse to be as persuasive as Mahan's, however. A pivotal factor was style. As Barbara Tuchman concluded, his "pronouncements were somehow couched in tones of such authority, as much a product of character as of style, as to make everything he wrote appear indisputable."[15] Like many people who acknowledge an impact of discourse read as history, Tuchman does not identify specific facets of syntax and lexicon achieving such effectiveness. She nevertheless suggests a possible functional relationship between nuances of style in discourse and a resultant image from its form *per se* which complemented the ethos or credibility characteristically derived more from manifest content of his discourse. To demonstrate this effect, one must first explain a rhetorical context in which stylistic form or manner of writing, in and of itself, may complement content and function as a paramessage to enhance the impact of the substantive matter of the discourse. And in Mahan's case, this effort entails discussion of his specific predilections for pithy or epigrammatic generalizations whose form or phraseology suggest his wisdom as well as sentences with extensive embedding of subordinate or qualifying clauses whose discrete but contrapuntal mode of syntax convey his caution or prudence.

I

To many critics, an intriguing notion about style is epitomized in George Louis Buffon's celebrated epigram of 1753, "style is the man himself."[16] Buffon's original statement—*le style est l'homme meme*—referred to mankind in general. To a zoologist primarily interested in biological rather than aesthetic ideas, the variety implicit in style distinguished man's language from the more limited if not monotonous communication patterns of other species. In its popular paraphrase as "style is the man"—in French, *le style c'est l'homme*—Buffon's concept advances a somewhat different but nevertheless provocative assumption: one's style in discourse reflects his or her essence as an individual. And if style in discourse does evince individuality, those language options at subtle levels of syntax and lexicon can be analyzed as a potential source of an image complementing the ethos or credibility typically derived more from the patent content of discourse.

In their more customary attempts to ascertain how persuaders project their credibility, rhetorical critics typically identify those aspects of discourse content which, as arguments or appeals, project competence and trustworthiness (or in the Aristotelian view, knowledge or sagacity, high moral character, and good will). Accepting a view that analyses of style may be concerned more with *how* people talk about something than with *what* they talk about, options in syntax and lexicon that primarily reflect a writer's unique individuality moreso than ideational content thereby are functions of what psycholinguists regard as "surface" structure, which does not affect meaning, rather than "deep" structure, which does.[17] Thus, any possible function of subtle stylistic traits to complement an author's ethos derived from patent substantive appeals are a phenomenon of that "paramessage" which stands in contradistinction to the "message" of a speaker or writer; for some stimuli, "although peripheral to the ideational content of the message, can materially affect the overall impact upon the receiver" by conveying subtle but nevertheless influential "information about the source" of that discourse:

Inferences about the source may also derive from the message, even though it contains no direct personal references. Because it is the product of human thought processes, a discourse can provide some degree of information about the personality that created it. The nature and originality of the subject matter, the quality and organization of the supporting materials, and the language in which the whole is expressed are forms of "real" evidence from which inferences about the competence, values, attitudes, *etc.*, of the source may be drawn. The topics a speaker chooses to discuss or avoid, the precision or lack thereof with which he orders his thoughts and marshals his

support, the character of his vocabulary and diction—his literacy—
are indicators of personality reflected in the discourse he produces,
quite apart from the representational meaning of the message itself.[18]

A methodology for explicating this dimension of stylistic functionalism
is to establish causal relationships between unique mannerisms of language and the persuasive image they create. For Alfred Thayer Mahan's
style, this means isolating characteristic usages giving direction and force
to his readers' positive reactions toward him as a credible source. Unlike many other studies of authors and their style, however, this critical
inquiry will not begin with operational definitions of typical but nebulous attributes such as "forcefulness" or "impressiveness," for instance.
Nor will the historian's book then be quoted extensively to identify those
conformations which ostensibly evince such presumed qualities of style
(although some will be provided for purposes of illustration). After all,
stylistic functionalism is not always explained best by a critic who—
operating basically outside a rhetorical transaction—nevertheless imposes preconceived notions of language qualities and their assumed
conformational determinants as the bases of a paramessage. As was
shown in the preceding chapter to be the case with Carl Becker, the effectiveness of style often is situational and thereby most accurately discernible in responses of people for whom the discourse was intended.

    The methodological focus here, therefore, is one of systemati-
cally cataloguing, analyzing, and synthesizing situationally bound
reactions to stylistic tendencies in *The Influence of Sea Power upon
History*. Those reactions have been found in the substantial Alfred
Thayer Mahan collection at the Library of Congress (MS-67-618),
primarily in the letters Mahan received after publication of his book
(but also in his file of newspaper and periodical reactions, foreign
and domestic, as well as in obituaries and letters to the family upon
Mahan's death, wherein his contemporaries epitomized their reactions to the man and his work). Additional reactions have been
gleaned from the Library of Congress Naval Historical Foundation
Collection, in the correspondence of Mahan's naval-officer peers as
they wrote to one another (examined specifically were letters of officers on active duty in the five years after publication of Mahan's
book, as well as those in subsequent positions of high command who
likely might have reacted to his work). Still other pertinent correspondence is now available among the extensive primary-source

materials recently collected by Robert Seager II and Doris Maguire in their *Letters and Papers of Alfred Thayer Mahan*. As complemented by the historian's personal observations about authoring *The Influence of Sea Power upon History*, responses of readers in this country and abroad are the significant data for investigation. And of specific interest are those comments by respondents within the situation who suggest the effects of his style upon them and the rather discrete, "exceptional" classes of language manipulation to which they themselves attributed that stylistic functionalism.

Excluded from consideration, however, are such imprecise remarks by Mahan's readers as their as references to "literary power," "grace," and "beauty" of style.[19] As a lecturer at the War College prior to publication of *The Influence of Sea Power upon History*, Mahan was known for "elegance" of style. Like "grace" and "beauty," however, "elegance" is not easily traced conclusively to replicable precepts of specific languages usages.[20] Also excluded are readers' remarks about being given "much pleasure" and being "entertained" by the "enchanting" book— remarks which seemingly appear in the correspondence as social amities.[21] Although they contributed to Carl Becker's overall stature among professional peers, such glowing responses to his style are too imprecise to identify in a meaningful way the subtle nuances of the stylistic means by which Mahan projected a persuasive image for a wider audience, particularly of people in public affairs. Moreover, because readers offered no meaningful clues to specific language variables that caused these responses, they are insufficiently discrete to be of value here. In the final analysis, a viable account of stylistic functionalism is founded upon replicable precepts of usage; and when the generality of a response about language precludes a notion of how to achieve that style, its usefulness as a rhetorical precept is nil. The paramessage projected by Mahan's style, however, did evolve from replicable precepts of language that he consciously applied in developing *The Influence of Sea Power upon History*. Moreover, that style was apt for the rhetorical situation to which he adapted, for the exigencies that call forth discourse typically constrain rhetorically sensitive speakers and writers to produce discourse which is a "fitting" response to the occasion.[22]

In 1884, while accepting a lectureship at the new U.S. Naval War College, Alfred Thayer Mahan agreed to use historical analogies to derive "certain general principles" and a system of "tactics applicable to modern naval warfare."[23] He was a likely choice for the position. Earlier, during 1880 duty at the New York Navy Yard, his Civil War block-ade service and a reputation for being particularly well-read in history came to the attention of Scribner's, who asked him to write *The Gulf and Inland Waters*—the last volume in their series on the navy in the Civil War. Completed expeditiously, the book was a clear, accurate account of those operations. Along with the 1878 Naval Institute Prize essay "Naval Education for Officers and Men," *The Gulf and Inland Waters* established its author as the strong candidate not only to lecture at the Naval War College but also to succeed Admiral S. B. Luce as its commanding officer.[24] Luce hoped the lectureship would develop a sorely needed "science" of naval warfare that included a "complete system of Naval Tactics under Steam."[25] Although navies of the world had converted to steam and developed relatively sophisticated ordnance for that time, no one knew "how any of the latest devices will turn out in actual service" or "the merits of this or that type of ship, weapon, or armor."[26] Luce, as well as other high-ranking officers in this country and abroad, desperately awaited what a reader in Japan called this "most important knowledge."[27] As reviewers of *The Influence of Sea Power upon History* consistently noted, however, the book that grew out of Mahan's lectures did not deal as expected with tactics but instead with an innovative, broad theory of strategy and international geopolitics.[28]

An experience during a summer cruise in 1885 changed the thrust of Mahan's thinking and preparation for the War College assignment. He read Mommsen's *History of Rome*. Reacting to the Hannibalic episode and Romans' use of sea power in the Second Punic War, his thoughts were less about tactics and more about broader strategic implications:

It suddenly struck me, whether by some chance phrase of the author I do not know, how different things might have been could Hannibal have invaded Italy by sea, as the Romans often had Africa, instead of by the long land route; or could he, after arrival, have been in free communication with Carthage by water. This clew, once laid hold of, I followed up in the particular instance. It and the general theory already conceived threw on each other reciprocal illustration; and between the two my plan was formed by the time I reached home, in September, 1885. I would investigate coincidently [*sic*] the general history and naval history of the past two centuries, with a view to demonstrating the influence of events of the one upon the other.[29]

He apparently often told people of this specific origin of his book.[30] And in 1886, Mahan himself acknowledged that his new role would be to derive "the great moral lessons" upon which sea power and thereby international strength were predicated.[31] Thus, heretofore unknown strategic issues came to characterize a concept that was ultimately given shape in *The Influence of Sea Power upon History*, particularly in its opening chapter of fifty-five pages, "Discussion of the Elements of Sea Power." In an analysis that reads much like an entry in an intelligence dossier, Admiral Raoul Castex stressed Mahan's innovation in dealing with these strategic questions: "He was the first to apprehend the true philosophy of naval war. He fully understood what no author before him had entirely grasped, namely the paramount importance of command of the sea and the part played by such command in the history of the world. . . . The true value of Mahan's theories lay in their innovating character. His works would doubtless have been less noticed in other periods. His wide success was really due to his having been the first to deal seriously with strategic questions."[32] In a somewhat similar self-appraisal, the historian himself admitted that "the point of view apparently possessed a novelty, which produced upon readers something of the effect of a surprise."[33]

Some readers were disappointed, however, because the book was neither focused on nor explicit about tactics for steam navies. A naval captain in 1892 admitted, "it seemed to me that there loomed up through the account of the various naval engagements a vague suggestion of a right way and a wrong way to do the thing and I wondered whether anyone is looking up the question of tactics."[34] Admiral Luce also agreed reluctantly that the book dealt only with the "general principles" of "Naval Strategy."[35] Individuals seeking advice on tactics under steam reported that they had do "careful" reading, even going back "two or three" times to find "anything that suggests itself" concerning that subject; that they had to exercise "a patience and comprehensiveness" coupled with "time and iteration" to find the "true meaning" for tactical implications.[36] Concern also was expressed that the book was not purely a chronicle of naval events, as the word "history" in its title might suggest; indeed, one authoritative reviewer commented that some readers had found the title "misleading or insufficient."[37]

Most reader reactions were extremely favorable, however. One British respondent said Mahan "ought to open the eyes of many on this side who are obstinately blind"; other Englishmen praised his "correctness" of insight, the "force" of arguments, and his overall ability "to reason our past events."[38] American readers praised the "logical" and "convincing" manner of the book, one remarking that its "conclusions were disclosed in a logic which could not be denied."[39] Such authoritativeness seems to evolve from Mahan's style functioning as paramessage. This interpretation is not merely a restatement of Tuchman's appraisal of how the book's "pronouncements were somehow couched in tones of such authority."[40] For Mahan's contemporaries also describe his treatment as "authoritative" and "masterly."[41] With the "supremacy" of having written the "conclusive discussion . . . on naval warfare," he was *the* expert—"the greatest authority living or dead," "head and shoulders" above others, the one whom "authorities" should consult on national courses of action.[42] Those favorable reactions can be linked to the two dominant but contrapuntal language tendencies isolated by readers themselves as sources of Mahan's style in discourse: pithy or epigrammatic generalizations and prolixity derived from the embedding of extensive subordinate clauses with qualifying materials.

II

Mahan's readership consistently lauded his particularly apt and pithy generalizations that achieved a penetrating synopsis of both a mass of detail and, more importantly, a relatively complex or abstract idea. One respondent praised "the great principles herein set forth by your forcible pen"; another affirmed that Mahan "possessed a peculiar power to grasp principles which others had seen only dimly and to set them forth with such clearness and force that all could understand them."[43] Also extolled were his "keen eye for discovering what is permanent," his "rare insight" that was "penetrating," and the "convincing truths" he brought "into array."[44] These reactions are clearly a product of style; for as one reviewer put it, "sentences frequently occur which show that the author is no ordinary inquirer."[45] In many instances, those sentences rely on antitheses which bestow an epigrammatic quality on statements, as in the following examples from "Discussion of the Elements of Sea Power," Mahan's pivotal opening chapter: "But if England was drawn to the sea, Holland was driven to it; without the sea England languished, but Holland died"; and "Men may be discontented at the lack of political privilege; they will be more uneasy if they come to the lack of bread"; or "While as an open enemy she struck at France upon the sea, so as an artful friend, many at least believed, she sapped the power of Holland afloat."[46] Or as the historian observed about the Confederacy in the American Civil War, "But as the Southern coast, from its extent and many inlets, might have been a source of strength, so, from those very characteristics, it became a fruitful source of injury."[47] These are among many examples of Mahan's "appealing eloquence," embodied in statements that "wrest the core of truth out of the period of which he wrote."[48] Whereas Carl Becker's epigrammatic antitheses achieved quotable eloquence in sentences which articulated well those sentiments in which readers already believed, those same syntactical conformations contributed to a somewhat different effect for Mahan.

Stylistic prowess exercised on behalf of generalizations seemed to endow Mahan with an image of wisdom founded upon extraordinary synthesizing powers to clarify a complex conceptualization. Moreover, readers' perceptions of his knowledge or sagacity evolved not only from the author's mass of detailed information as content but his manner of presentation through style. Consider these British reactions. Upon visiting England in 1893 and 1894 as commanding officer of the *U.S.S. Chicago,* Mahan was awarded honorary degrees from Oxford and Cambridge. And after announcing that Mahan would be in England while the *Chicago* was on European station, the United States Embassy in London was deluged with invitations for the ship's commander to attend meetings and dinner parties with "the leading and literary people" who were eagerly awaiting the opportunity to welcome him.[49] These included, of course, not only Queen Victoria but her guest Kaiser Wilhelm. On 20 June 1894, while awarding Mahan's D.C.L., Oxford's Public Orator praised him as a man "who in the skillful order of his writings, showed in a lucid manner how much the power of the sea is to be valued in the history of war."[50] Clarity was a dominant effect singled out by Englishmen, some of whom saw *The Influence of Sea Power upon History* as "clearly written" and capable of "getting people to understand what they had not understood before."[51] The book's clarity was lauded by Americans, too. In a letter to Mahan, Theodore Roosevelt called it "the clearest and most instructive general work of the kind with which I am acquainted"; and Roosevelt's praise for that clarity prevailed in two published reviews of the work.[52] Indeed, praise of Mahan's ability to explain a complex subject was the characteristic American reaction to the work—in correspondence to and about the historian and in published reviews.[53]

Mahan's word choice itself contributed greatly to the effectiveness of his generalizations. As one reviewer remarked, "the use of technical language has been avoided"; essential concepts are presented in such a way that, as another reviewer avowed, "the veriest landlubber should find no difficulty in apprehending them."[54] Mahan's avoidance of nautical jargon apparently made his book easily comprehensible "even . . . to the layman," and the level of writing therein was regarded by a reviewer as having brought "the work within the comprehension of the unprofessional reader."[55] While assistant secretary of the navy in 1914, for instance, Franklin Roosevelt lauded the Mahan's abilities to write in such a way that "fleet operations" could be understood by "the average 'man in the street.'"[56] Mahan's stylistic care in the phrasing of generalizations also seemed to create a rhetorically advantageous subordination which set the major tenets of a concept in relief, "foregrounded" against a mass of historical detail. Theodore Roosevelt praised *The Influence of Sea Power upon History* immediately in 1890 for its author's "faculty of grasping the meaning of events and their relations to one another and of taking in the whole situation," all of which helped contribute to "the clearest and most instructive general work of the kind with which I am acquainted."[57] In his published reviews of the book, Theodore Roosevelt said Mahan "subordinates detail to mass-effects, trying always to grasp and make evident the essential features of a situation"; also extolled by Roosevelt was "the skill with which he has subordinated the lesser to the main points of interest. While showing his thorough acquaintance with detail, he has never for a moment permitted that detail to absorb more than its proper amount of attention."[58] As a future president and exponent of American naval supremacy, Roosevelt proclaimed that Mahan "really helped me to formulate certain things which I had only vaguely in mind."[59] Again, the response suggests a reader's being impressed with a writer's ability to synthesize complex ideas.

In the rhetorical situation for which Mahan was constrained to produce a fitting response, the time was right for a writer with stylistic capabilities to exert subtle influence in the form of a paramessage projecting his or her extraordinary powers of synthesis. As America and the Western world approached the turn of the century and "apparent contradictions, irrationalities, dichotomies, and conflicts in the chronicle of mankind or in the life of a man," many writers "were busily at work in the 1880s and 1890s trying to design philosophies of history that would explain in scientific terms in what direction the world was moving, how it moved and why—if it was moving at all." Herbert Spencer, Brooks Adams, and Henry Adams, for instance, sought to achieve what Robert Seager has called a "philosophical synthesis of human affairs." That Mahan sensed the appropriateness of such inquiry and writing is suggested by his own appreciation of what he termed "really a remarkable pamphlet" by Sir Halford Mackinder in 1904: a journal essay explaining the concept of "The Geographical Pivot of History"—or, in other words, how those who controlled the Eurasian "heartland" (Russia) effectively would control the world.[60] Mackinder's heartland theory ultimately derived its persuasive force from his particularly apt generalization cast as a *klimax* or *scala*, "*Who rules East Europe commands the Heartland: Who rules the Heartland commands the World-Island: Who rules the World-Island commands the World.*"[61] The concept was to be studied during the Cold War of the 1950s by United States Air Force ROTC students.

The functional relationship between epigrammatic generalizations and the ability to clarify complex ideas was a long-developing stylistic trait on Mahan's part. Yet even in their initial form for lectures at the War College, his "general principles" or "great moral lessons" achieved a "clearness of statement" that Admiral S. B. Luce, for one, attributed to Mahan's "faculty for generalization."[62] Mahan's lectures often were acclaimed for the "exactness" and "precision" of their style.[63] For years, he worked diligently at creating these pithy expressions; and when it became apparent to him that the lectures would be published, Mahan admitted "the question of style gradually forced itself on my consideration." He scrutinized the sentence constructions of other writers in order to establish a standard for coping with what he called "the besetting anxiety" of his soul—the need to be "exact and lucid." According his own analysis of his typical stylistic efforts, Mahan laboriously exercised "ingenuity" and "lavished" time to achieve sentences by which "the whole should be at once apprehended by the reader."[64] Unquestionably, he was preoccupied with achieving clarity in discourse, particularly through the use of pithy statements which synthesize the major tenets of a concept.

Mahan also stated formally his personal concept of style in "The Writing of History," his 1902 inaugural address as president of the American Historical Association. The primary goal of historical writing, he contended, is to articulate "the principles which animate our own life." The historian should ascertain the "key of the situation" or the "leading

general tendency, which is the predominant characteristic of an epoch."
Then, while writing, the historian as stylist should avoid a "formless
mass of ill-arranged particulars" and strive instead for an essential
"artistic" unity whereby details "are subordinated to the one dominant
thought or purpose of the designer, whose skill it is to make each and all
enhance the dignity and harmony of the central idea." Only by this mode
of writing could "the mass of readers receive that correct impression of
the general character and trend of a period that far surpasses in instructive quality any volume of details, however accurate, the significance of
which is not apprehended." Moreover, although such subordination
is largely a function of broader organizational considerations and
the relationships between evidence, assertions, and their placements in
paragraphs or chapters, Mahan also predicated those compositional skills
upon "sentences" that are "no vague collocation of words, but the concrete pithy expression of a trained habit of mind that dominates writing
necessarily, even though unconsciously to the writer."[65] To Robert Seager,
a contemporary scholar appreciating the soundest of methodologies in
historiography, Mahan's tendencies as a writer of "history" yielded a
"subjective process that permitted a tiny portion of the available data to
be manipulated in such a way that it appeared to document preconceived conclusions."[66] What would have been historiographically more
sound to scholars like Seager, however, would not necessarily be
rhetorically effective for the general public.

Consider a problem in writing history. Assume a historian wanted
to write a sentence about the discovery of America. Moreover assume,
as Louis Gottschalk did, that this historian was aware of the following
factors: "other methods of dating than the Gregorian calendar; doubts
regarding whether Columbus was the first of his men to step on American soil; contentions that others had reached America before Columbus's
men; conflicts regarding the nationality of Columbus; arguments that a
man who reaches a remote island cannot lay claim to the discovery of a
continent; and uncertainty regarding the particular island on which he
did land." More interested in accuracy than emphasis, that historian
might cast a sentence like "On a day conveniently October 12, 1492, a
group of sailors captained by a man known in English as Christopher
Columbus landed on an island which was probably the one now called
Watling Island."[67] But many Americans learned the event another way:
Columbus discovered America on 12 October 1492. Therein lies a stylistic moral: some sentences are more forceful than others in articulating

and "foregrounding" what we remember as "facts."

Reactions to *The Influence of Sea Power upon History*—within the age for which it was composed—are an index to the way Mahan's ability to synthesize historical facts was regarded. Were his generalizations emphatic to his readers? We only can speculate now about exactly which generalizations Kaiser Wilhelm underlined in his copy of the book, but what many other readers underlined—on the pages or in their minds— might be identified in part by what they repeated from the volume and how they structured their own thinking in response. For example, before beginning its over 400 pages of historical narrative developed in strict chronological order, the book identifies six essential conditions contributing to sea power: (1) geographical position, (2) physical conformation, (3) extent of territory, (4) number of population, (5) character of the people, and (6) character of the government.[68] As generalizing principles, these six factors are stated and described directly *only* in that first chapter. Yet in the most extensive and authoritative review of the book shortly after it was published, while criticizing Mahan for falling "below his usual high level" in the presentation of "details," J. K. Laughton organized his thirty-three page commentary—not chronologically, in the manner of the narrative body of the book—but topically, according to those six principles articulated just that once.[69] Thus, those generalizing precepts were salient to the scholar whom Mahan himself regarded as the one who "knows more naval history than any English speaking man living" (Mahan attributed the unsigned review to Laughton as soon as it appeared and deemed himself "fortunate to come off so easy at his hands").[70]

Other apt generalizations in the book prompted similarly positive responses. The "Introductory" explains the decisive role of Rome's sea power in the Second Punic War (the very factor that originally inspired Mahan to undertake his inquiry into the sources of sea power).[71] One reviewer's *only* lengthy quotation from the book is Mahan's exact, synthesizing generalization: "The Roman control of the water forced Hannibal to that long perilous march through Gaul, in which more than half of his veteran troops wasted away; it enabled the elder Scipio, while sending his army from Rome on to Spain to intercept Hannibal's communications, to return in person and face the invader at Trebia. Throughout the war the legions passed by water, unmolested and unwearied between Spain, which was Hannibal's base, and Italy."[72] Theodore Roosevelt also prominently recounted what he called that "striking illustration," concluding that it "makes this point so clear that it is difficult to see how it can be controverted successfully"; and in another review Roosevelt paraphrased Mahan's conclusion about Roman sea power and proclaimed it "good proof of the way in which he grasps the salient features of any case."[73] Even J. K. Laughton repeated that same generalization to illustrate the "permanence of principle" with which the book deals.[74]

A faculty for generalization also is suggested by Mahan's coinage of the term "sea power." Before publication of his book, the historian's War College lectures were called "The Influence of Naval Power on the Growth of Nations"; but as he isolated causes for that growth in addition to those merely of warships, the term "sea power" began to appear in his correspondence.[75] By substituting "sea" for "naval," the term crystallizes a combination of complex factors, including but not restricted to warships. Many people acclaimed the aptness of the phrase. One English respondent said, "It is Captain Mahan who has *given us the word 'Sea Power.'* Excellent use has been made of it since; but no one thought of using it before he put it into our mouths." And a London newspaper praised Mahan's "pregnant conception of 'Sea Power' and his masterly exposition of its influence."[76] In the United States, a reader called him "the inventor of the term Sea Power" and hailed him as the person "having done for the Ocean what Adam Smith has done for the land," comparing "Sea Power with the Wealth of Nations."[77] Still others of Mahan's statements can be singled out for their aptness in synthesizing concepts. For instance, "contact," wrote Mahan, is the word "which perhaps better than any other indicates the dividing line between tactics and strategy." Two of his antitheses epitomized the value of naval operations intended to interfere with the maritime trade of a nation: "Commerce-destroying by independent cruisers depends upon wide dissemination of force. Commerce-destroying through control of a strategic centre by a great fleet depends upon concentration of force. Regarded as a primary, not as a secondary, operation, the former is condemned, the latter justified, by the experience of centuries."[78] This contention also was noticed and restated by reviewers.[79] Because they conveyed an impression of a writer with an extraordinary wisdom in synthesizing a complex situation, Mahan's epigrammatic generalizations functioned subtly as one vector of the stylistic sources of his credibility complementary to that ethos derived as well from his content.

III

As the dominant stylistic counterpoint to his prowess at phrasing pithy statements, Mahan endowed *The Influence of Sea Power upon History* with a predilection for what at first glance might be characterized as wordiness. This prolixity was criticized severely by readers removed from the situational exigencies. Analyzing the work in retrospect, Admiral Castex noted with disapprobation Mahan's "ponderous, rambling, ambiguous and cloudy" style: "He frequently repeated himself. His prose ran on and on, one tiresome affirmation incessantly succeeding another. He was a doctrinaire. He pontificated. Consequently, he is extremely difficult to read. Genuine courage is required to persevere to the end of any of his books."[80] Even Mahan's son subsequently deplored his father's "prolix" style and concluded that *The Influence of Sea Power upon History* "could have been considerably shortened to advantage."[81] To Livezey, well-removed chronologically from the situation and reacting with scholarly detachment, that style was "marked by laborious fullness of statement and burdened with qualifications" which could only make "difficult reading."[82] But Mahan's prolixity did *not* have such negative effects in the 1890s. On the contrary, the book maintained interest well for substantial numbers of his contemporaries. For instance, while lamenting the absence of color plates "to catch the eye and tempt the inclination to look in," a glowing response said, "once the book has fastened its hold on a reader, I consider that reader *belongs to the book!*"[83] Similarly, respondents wrote of reading *The Influence of Sea Power upon History* with "deepest" and "keenest" interest.[84] As suggested by responses of many of Mahan's contemporaries, prolixity of style in the book contributed to a persuasive paramessage that evolved from discrete and characteristic tendencies reflecting a rhetorically sensitive writer's appraisal of what the situation required as a fitting response.

First, consider the "fullness of statement" which Livezey disparaged from his twentieth-century perspective. That completeness and comprehensiveness were intentional. Although confident before publication that his overall conception was "entirely accurate," Mahan nevertheless "felt the necessity of supporting my case all through."[85] The resultant fullness of statement was adhered to, despite the author's early hesitancy to publish the lectures precisely because his characteristic prolixity could not be subject to "judicious curtailing" once in print (as it could be in his oral lectures).[86] In the 1890s, however, such wordiness had positive effects upon readers. While acclaiming "his grasp of the subject and all the facts bearing upon it, great and small," newspaper and periodical reactions praised the book for its "abundant" proof, "exhaustive" argument, and "fullness" of information, its subject covered "thoroughly," "completely," and "carefully."[87] Writing directly to Mahan, readers similarly praised the "scope" and "largeness" of his viewpoint as well as the likelihood that no other writer had ever displayed "fuller and more accurate knowledge of the subject."[88] In the 1890s, Mahan's prolixity seemed to suggest expertise to readers. Because of his ability to say so much so fully within individual sentences—quite apart from the mass of detail in the book overall—Mahan was perceived as a particularly knowledgeable man on his subject.

Although it may be a function of style or form, prolixity also can be the result of a writer's substance or content. Praise of "abundant" proof, "exhaustive" argument, and "fullness" of statement indicates the extent to which Mahan brought subject matter to bear in support of assertions in his narrative. The syntactical manner in which that material is cast into sentences is more clearly in the realm of style in discourse, however. In their customary and familiar constructions of sentences in English, native speakers of the language tend to rely on syntactical conformations that are relatively easy to construct. These statements typically are "progressive" or "right-branching" because qualifying or subordinate material appears after—or to the right of—the kernel subject and predicate which begin the sentence.[89] When qualifying or subordinate segments appear before—or to the left of—the kernel subject and predicate, the sentence is "recursive" or "regressive." Such "left-branching" or periodic sentences are not in the common idiom of English because "as *regressive* structures grow longer they require more and more memory; but *progressive* structures do not. They can continue indefinitely with a minimum of memory."[90] When the kernel subject and predicate of a sentence are "postponed" to appear after imbedded qualifying phrases, the writer in effect is making "a promise that must be remembered until the time comes to develop it; as the number of promises grows, the load on the memory also grows."[91] Because an increased strain on the memory makes the writing process require a greater effort, people customarily favor conformations which are more economical in expenditures of mental energy.[92] Mahan, though, was willing to do the additional work.

When Mahan's prolixity evolved from numerous and extensive

qualifying clauses embedded within sentences or at their beginnings—the "burdened with qualifications" censured by Livezey in retrospect—the historian achieved a second characteristic usage which evinces his sense of style. He wrote cautiously. In addition to clarity, Mahan admitted to the demand for exactness and accuracy as the other "besetting anxiety of my soul." And his stylistic means for achieving this end was often the very long sentence characterized by the careful and lengthy qualification of ideas, as this passage on the very subject illustrates: "My cautious mind strove to introduce between the same two periods every qualification, whether in abatement or enforcement of the leading idea or statement. This in many cases meant an accumulation of clauses. . . . It was not enough for me that qualifications should appear a page or two before, or after, and in this I think myself right; but in wanting them all in the same period, as I instinctively did,—and do, for nature is obstinate,—I have imposed on myself needless labor, and have often taxed attention as an author has no right to do."[93] To phrase appropriately the first sentence of his "Introductory" for *The Influence of Sea Power upon History*, Mahan saw fit to embed a cautious, qualifying phrase to precede the opening assertion about what his narrative might achieve: "The history of Sea Power is largely, *though by no means solely* [italics mine], a narrative of contests between nations, of mutual rivalries, of violence frequently culminating in war." Even in his opening chapter, "Discussion of the Elements of Sea Power"—surely the most polemical in the book—Mahan's peroration is characterized by the same caution of structuring sentences with qualifying phrases imbedded in them:

> In the matter of particular battles, while freely admitting that the change of details has made obsolete much of their teaching, the attempt will be made to point out where the application or neglect of true general principles has produced decisive effects; and, other things being equal, those actions will be preferred which, from their association with the names of the most distinguished officers, may be presumed to show how far just tactical ideas obtained in a particular age or a particular service. It will also be desirable, where analogies between ancient and modern weapons appear on the surface, to derive such probable lessons as they offer, without laying undue stress upon the points of resemblance. Finally, it must be remembered that, among all changes, the nature of man remains much the same; the personal equation, though uncertain in quantity and quality in the particular instance, is sure always to be found.[94]

While Mahan was pessimistic about the influence of his style on readers, that negative effect seems to have operated primarily upon people
reacting to the book outside the situation for which it was written. To
Mahan's immediate contemporaries, his tendency to qualify his ideas
evinced an image of prudence and caution. He seemed to acquire an air
of impartiality which complemented his ethos or credibility derived
from manifest content, for any persuaders perceived as obviously biased in their points of view are less likely to be trusted than those creators of discourse perceived to fair and objective in their treatment of
the topic at hand. Situational ramifications of this aspect of style as
paramessage were substantial, and constraints upon this rhetor to produce a "fitting" response in discourse were heeded by him.[95]

While preparing his lectures for publication as *The Influence of Sea
Power upon History*, Mahan was cognizant of an "indifference to service
matters among our people." And because they still were "interested in
other matters," (i.e., westward expansion rather than imperialism), his
was "not necessarily, nor on the face, an attractive subject to the public."[96] To a career naval officer, that political climate was significant.
With some bravado, the historian staunchly said there was "no reason why an officer, being also a citizen, should not express opinions
on matters which are not merely politics, but affect the national interest."[97] To more intimate friends, however, he confided it would
be "imprudent" to say things "too explicitly" because of "the way
our government looks on the expression of political opinions, however general, by officers—particularly if diametrically opposed to the
traditions of the party in office."[98] Or as a British officer explained the
problem of promoting sea power, "the naval officer if he does consider
the intensity of its importance . . . is hardly in a position to parade his
views."[99] So adapting to "the exigencies of politics," Mahan admitted to
the prudent necessity of writing "passively" so that his arguments would
not "rise too obtrusively to the surface."[100] After all, an audience need-
ing to be persuaded about the importance of sea power might expect a
naval officer to be biased on the subject, perhaps polemical moreso than
objective, and thereby not likely a source to be trusted to any appreciable extent. Mahan had to win his readers' trust in him as an unbiased,
objective writer with nothing personally to gain from any increased national interest or expenditures on behalf of the U.S. Navy; and that impulse influenced his style in many of his sentences. Congruent with
Mahan's avowed intention of writing in such a way that everything be

carefully qualified to avoid polemical overstatement, that stylistic caution also created a favorable image of him in the eyes of many readers.

In Great Britain, Mahan was perceived as the "impartial authority,"
the "expert who approaches the question without national bias."[101]
Admittedly, that British response was due in part to the fact that "as an
American citizen and sailor," Mahan often praised "men and deeds of
the British Navy"; and this was interpreted as evidence of the author's
"magnanimity."[102] Naturally, British readers would appreciate an American who praised their Royal Navy. Still, their positive feelings could
have been amplified by the caution with which Mahan wrote, for in
America, he was praised for being "singularly fair in his judgments"
with a "deep sense of truth and perfect sincerity."[103] According to
Theodore Roosevelt, *The Influence of Sea Power upon History* is characterized by a "dispassionate spirit" and the absence of "forced analogies."[104]
In the United States, the book was accepted as a work of "admirable
impartiality" with sober, restrained conclusions "throughout" and no
"undue magnification of the influence of sea power" as might be
expected from a professional naval officer. And if some of its conclusions gave rise to professional controversy, "no statement is hazarded
. . . without deliberation."[105] Although another reviewer concluded that
"in his constant tendency to point a moral for our fresh-water Congress-
men, and to preach the gospel of American commerce and a new navy,
he mars to a considerable degree the force of his thesis," Mahan more
often was perceived as unbiased: "with politics he has little to do; with
ethics, national or international, nothing."[106] For readers, an air of
impartiality created stylistically with careful qualifying of ideas was an
asset along with the expertise suggested by completeness and comprehensiveness of statement. That style functioned subtly, however. For
although Mahan has "nowhere specifically" stated his motive, said one
reviewer, it "is still evident. It is to turn the minds of his countrymen to
sea affairs."[107] In combination, perceived effects of Mahan's characteristic prolixity strongly resemble and complement traditional dimensions
of ethos known as knowledge and good will. As these attributes were
evinced stylistically to his readers by the form of his sentences moreso
than by their manifest content, they portrayed a man whose "statement was not superficial" but rather whose "words convey unconsciously, the impression of responsibility and of duty" whereby
people are drawn "inevitably to his opinions and conclusions."[108] To
paraphrase Buffon, the style *was* the man as perceived persuasively

by readers in positions of political power.

When its stylistic form so complements ideational content, historical writing becomes increasingly persuasive for its readers. For *The Influence of Sea Power upon History,* that overall rhetorical impress may be illustrated most aptly by our considering further how Theodore Roosevelt came to his admission to Mahan that this book "really helped me to formulate certain things which I had only vaguely in mind." Roosevelt had read Mahan's book over the weekend of 10 and 11 May 1890 and, in the words of Edmund Morris, "flipped the book shut a changed man." After publication of his own *Naval War of 1812* in 1881—as Morris goes on to explain—Roosevelt considered himself an expert on this very subject of warships, yet he never questioned traditional naval strategy "based on a combination of coastal defense and commercial raiding." But after "one of the most important weekends of his life," Roosevelt was persuaded "that real national security—and international greatness—could only be attained by building more and bigger ships and deploying them farther abroad." A warm relationship soon developed between Mahan and Roosevelt, one whereby the naval officer often was a guest at Roosevelt's Sagamore Hill home for dinner and long conversations. Roosevelt came to feel he "could call upon Mahan in confidence," whether about naval matters or his political aspirations.[109]

During 1897 while revising his *Naval War of 1812* for a new edition, Roosevelt admitted to his family that he would include therein, as Morris puts it, "a pretty strong plea for a powerful navy," and he thereby admitted his own inclination to utilize historical writing as a mode of rhetoric to shape attitudes and actions of readers.[110] Among Roosevelt's more direct and forceful arguments on behalf of sea power, however, were his remarks in an address to the Naval War College as assistant secretary of the Navy on 2 June 1897. Although he reiterated George Washington's maxim that "to be prepared for war is the most effectual means to promote peace," Roosevelt's appeal for "an immediate, rapid build-up of the American Navy" was blatantly bellicose on behalf of war as a healthy endeavor. "All the great masterful races have been fighting races, and the minute that a race loses the hard fighting virtues, then . . . it has lost its proud right to stand as the equal of the best"; "cowardice in a race, as in an individual," he declared, "is the unpardonable sin." As if to outdo Mahan's hortatory characterization of Americans' dedication to "personal freedom" and "healthy excitement of exploration and adventure," Roosevelt—in the advent of the Spanish-American War—argued that "better a thousand times err on the side of over-readiness to fight, than to err on the side of tame submission to injury, or cold-blooded indifference to the misery of the oppressed." Thus, American sea power had its purpose: "No triumph of peace is quite so great as the supreme triumphs of war. . . . It may be that at some time in the dim future of the race the need for war will finish; but that time is yet ages distant. As yet no nation can hold its place in the world, or can do any work really worth doing, unless it stands ready to guard its rights with an armed hand."[111] In 1897, Mahan published *The Interest of America in Seapower, Past and Future*, and Roosevelt's review of the volume praised the "noble passage" in which the naval historian deplored as "ominous for the future of the race" the "tendency, vociferous at present, which refuses to recognize in the profession of arms, in war, that something which inspired" poets and heroes, "that something which has made the soldier to all ages the type of heroism and self-denial."[112] So Theodore Roosevelt had a vision of "Anglo-Saxon world conquest" as heady as anything Mahan ever wrote.[113]

Theodore Roosevelt became enamored of battleships as a key element in achieving conquest through what Mahan called sea power. Again proclaiming that "we must prepare for war in order to preserve peace," Roosevelt told the New York yacht club in 1897 that he hoped America would "build ten new battleships." For although "there may be a time in eight or ten thousand years, when there will be no need to prepare for war; but until then, we need try to secure peace with a sword girt at our side."[114] In September 1897, after observing U.S. Navy fleet maneuvers, Roosevelt wrote rapturously to the Chairman of the House Naval Affairs Committee, Charles Boutelle: "Oh, Lord! if only the people who are ignorant of our Navy could see those great warships in all their majesty and beauty, and could realize how . . . well fitted" they are "to uphold the honor of America."[115] When Roosevelt acknowledged to Mahan the fact that America must meet successfully "the vital need for more battleships," the reader of the history acknowledged its author's ability to be an opinion leader providing guidance and reinforcement.[116]

And Mahan dutifully responded with lengthy, specific advice about what those battleships should be like in speed, armaments, and construction. For example, in a long letter in which Mahan reiterated for Roosevelt the conclusions in "my *Lessons of the War with Spain*, pp. 36-42," Mahan quoted himself: "War depends largely upon combination, and facility of combination increases with numbers. Numbers therefore, mean

increase of offensive power, other things remaining equal" (again, a qualifying phrase: "other things remaining equal"). The naval historian
explained for Roosevelt how a battleship built with its weight increased
"from the 10,000 to the 15,000 ton ship" nevertheless acquired "little
more broadside gain than one six-inch rapid fire gun" and thus why "it
can in no wise justify an increase of nearly fifty per cent in tonnage with
less than ten per cent of offensive power." Mahan then explained relationships among the weight of a battleship, its speed, and the amount of
coal thereby required for "the fighting efficiency of the ship."[117]

Theodore Roosevelt's resultant American armada ultimately was
flaunted to the world in the cruise of the "Great White Fleet." Mahan
claimed that display of force was intended primarily as "a matter of
practice, to encounter now the difficulties, run our heads against them,
so as to know how to manage all questions of supply, should War some-
day come." For he, like Roosevelt, was concerned about "the question
of Japs settling in California" and "yellow immigration" which "would
soon fill our country west of the Rockies with another race, involving
interminable trouble." For if Japan were "to insist on the right of immigration for its coolies," the result "would fetch us mighty close to war."
Yet Mahan worried that "Japan should resent our sending our own fleet
where we wished." Admitting "I feared and still fear popular commo-
tion . . . the Jap people in the ferment of their radical changes are more
out of hand than even our Pacific hoodlums," Mahan said he would
therefore "be more at ease when the fleet gets safely away from Japan."[118]
He also wrote to the *New York Times* forcefully defending Roosevelt
against charges of "desiring hostilities with Japan"; the newspaper's
political commentary against Roosevelt in 1910 was, in Mahan's view,
"neither rational nor moral. Not rational, because it was not needed to
account for the act, which had other abundant justification; immoral,
because it was a wanton attribution of wrong purpose."[119] Theodore
Roosevelt and Alfred Thayer Mahan were kindred spirits.

In the content of his historical writing, Mahan found in Roosevelt a
sympathetic eye to his views about battleships and sea power. Yet as
Barbara Tuchman has observed, the naval historian's impress on readers also had origins in the fact that his "pronouncements were somehow couched in tones of such authority, as much a product of character
as of style, as to make everything he wrote appear indisputable." In his
published reviews of Mahan's writing and in his personal letters to the
historian, Roosevelt was among the readers who attested to the stylistic

sources of persuasiveness that complemented the ideational content thereby articulated. Unlike the overt impact of Carl Becker's epigrammatic style, though, Mahan's rhetoric of style was subtle, serving but to help evince a paramessage of competence, impartiality, and prudence which complemented the ethos generated by the manifest content of *The Influence of Sea Power upon History*. Despite the subtlety of its effects, stylistic prowess contributed to Mahan's emergence as a "super representative" who exerted opinion leadership through historical writing.

Mahan's predilection to be a writer of history was one of a lifelong aspiration. As a seventeen-year-old midshipman on a training cruise in 1858, Mahan had listened to his peers talk about becoming heroes like Perry or Decatur, but he decided on a different course, telling his friend Samuel Ashe: "The time for opportunity to win distinction for *bravery* was passed. I hope to win distinction in another field—*intellectual* performance."[120] Admittedly, some of Mahan's contemporary naval officers deplored the historian's activities as a writer. As one of them observed, "Capt. Mahan always appears to advantage in all that does not appertain to ship life or matters, but in this particular he is lacking in interest, as he has frankly admitted to me. His interests are entirely outside the service, for which, I am satisfied, he cares but little, and is therefore not a good naval officer. . . . In fact, Capt. Mahan's interests lie wholly in the direction of literary work and in no other way connected with the service."[121] As revealed in the responses of certain readers— particularly those in positions of political power—*The Influence of Sea Power upon History* had a different impact, acquiring for its author a position and reputation not enjoyed by any other naval officer in the world. Perhaps Theodore Roosevelt articulated the ultimate compliment to Mahan: "He was one of those few men who leave a permanent mark on history and literature, aside from their profound and far reaching influence on contemporary thought."[122]

Alfred Thayer Mahan as a writer of discourse read as history qualifies as a persuader of substantial influence upon the course of events, and style well may have been a subtle but nevertheless causal factor in his achieving that persuasiveness. For as they functioned rhetorically as paramessage, his discrete but contrapuntal stylistic tendencies contributed to a persuasive image of Mahan the man. His epigrammatic generalizations evinced sagacity founded upon what was perceived as an exceptional ability to synthesize a complex concept. Furthermore, and despite what twentieth-century commentary might say to the contrary, his prolix style also was advantageous in that rhetorical context when its completeness suggested expertise to readers. More importantly, because that comprehensiveness of statement was founded to an appreciable extent on cautious attempts to qualify fully and carefully what was said, the resultant suggestion of prudence evinced a desirable image of the impartiality of the author. In their combined, contrapuntal roles in helping achieve the persuasiveness of Mahan's book, these language tendencies illustrate the subtle influence of style as paramessage complementing the ethos or credibility typically achieved by manifest content of discourse. Such stylistic efficacy can function rhetorically, however, only when nuances of syntax and lexicon are read in their original language. When historians' discourse is translated into other languages, other factors more likely are persuasive—as is indicated in the next chapter about the impress of Mahan's historical narratives, particularly *The Influence of Sea Power upon History* and *Lessons of the War With Spain*, upon Japanese naval officers who planned and executed the attack on Pearl Harbor.

Notes

1. Commander Scott Umsted to W. D. Puleston, Director of U.S. Naval Intelligence, 18 March 1936; and Benjamin Dutton, American Embassy, Berlin, to Puleston, 6 November 1936, in Box 15, Alfred Thayer Mahan Papers, Library of Congress, Washington, D.C. Unless stipulated otherwise, all correspondence and primary source materials used in chapter 4 are from this collection.

2. Bigelow in turn sent a handwritten copy to Mahan, 26 May 1894, in Box 3.

3. See Robert Seager II, *Alfred Thayer Mahan: The Man and His Letters* (Annapolis: Naval Institute Press, 1977), 215, 279, 298.

4. *Alfred Thayer Mahan*, 215.

5. Karl-Heinz Menzel to Merle Curti, 30 December 1948, in Box 24, File 5, Merle Curti Papers, State Historical Society of Wisconsin, Madison, Wis.

6. Seager, *Alfred Thayer Mahan*, xii; Alfred Thayer Mahan, cited in *Alfred Thayer Mahan*, 432–34.

7. *Alfred Thayer Mahan*, 218.

8. For discussions of Mahan's reception abroad, see W. D. Puleston, *Mahan* (New Haven: Yale University Press, 1939) and William E. Livezey, *Mahan on Sea Power* (Norman: University of Oklahoma Press, 1947).

9. See Barbara Tuchman, *The Proud Tower: A Portrait of the World before the War 1890–1914* (New York: Macmillan, 1962), 130–37, 148–49, 248–53. See also Howard K. Beale, *Theodore Roosevelt and the Rise of America to World Power* (Baltimore: Johns Hopkins University Press, 1956).

10. See, in particular, Louis Hacker, introduction to Alfred Thayer Mahan, *The Influence of Sea Power upon History 1660–1783* (New York: Hill and Wang, 1957), vi.

11. "Reaching for Supremacy at Sea," *Time*, 31 January 1972, 28–33. See especially p. 29.

12. Mahan, *The Influence of Sea Power*, 25, 43–50. See also my "The Historical Jeremiad as Rhetorical Genre," in *Form and Genre: Shaping Rhetorical Action*, ed. Karlyn Campbell and Kathleen Jamieson (Falls Church, Va.: Speech Communication Association, 1977), 103–17.

13. Cited in Seager, *Alfred Thayer Mahan*, 430–31.

14. Josephus Daniels to Mahan, 1 May 1914, in Box 3.

15. Tuchman, *The Proud Tower*, 131.

16. Georges-Louis Buffon, "Discours sur le Style," in *The Art of the Writer*, ed. Lane Cooper (Ithaca: Cornell University Press, 1952), 146–55. See in particular p. 154.

17. See Rulon Wells, "Nominal and Verbal Style," in *Style in Language*, ed. Thomas A. Sebeok (Cambridge: M.I.T. Press, 1960), 215; and Charles E. Osgood, "Some Effects of Motivation on Style of Encoding," in *Style in Language*, 293. For discussion of the distinction between "surface" and "deep" structure, see Noam Chomsky, *Aspects of the Theory of Syntax* (Cambridge: M.I.T. Press, 1965), 16–17; and Paul M. Postal, "Underlying and Superficial Linguistic Structure," *Harvard Educational Review* 34 (1964): 246–66.

18. Paul I. Rosenthal, "The Concept of the Paramessage in Persuasive Communication," *Quarterly Journal of Speech* 58 (February 1972): 15–17. Italics are mine.

19. J. K. Laughton, "Captain Mahan on Maritime Power," *Edinburgh Review*, 172 (October 1890): 453; and letters to Mahan from Admiral L. A. Columb, 26 April 1891, and T. F. Clark, 2 May 1891, in Box 3. See also reviews in *Literary World*, 5 July 1890: 217–18; and the *New York Daily Tribune*, 22 January 1893.

20. See Admiral S. B. Luce to John Barnes, 5 August 1889; and P. F. Harrington to Captain Harry Metcalfe, 10 October 1917, in Box 2.

21. See, for example, Captain A. S. Barker to Mahan, 30 September 1890; Captain W. S. Schley to Mahan, 17 September 1891; Captain C. F. Goodrich to Mahan, 14 May 1892; and Admiral Sir August Millimore to Mahan, 22 June 1892, in Box 3. See also R. B. Marston to Mahan, 6 January 1893, in Box 4; and Captain T. F. Meigs to Admiral S. B. Luce, 11 June 1890, in Box 9, S. B. Luce Papers, Naval Historical Foundation Collection; Library of Congress, Washington, D.C., hereafter cited as NHFC.

22. See Lloyd F. Bitzer, "The Rhetorical Situation," *Philosophy and Rhetoric* 1 (1968): 1–14.

23. Mahan to Admiral S. B. Luce, 4 September 1884, in Box "Miscellany T–Z," S. B. Luce Papers, NHFC.

24. See Puleston, *Mahan*, 56–68.

25. Admiral Luce to Lt. J. F. Meigs, 29 October 1888, in Box "Miscellany T–

Z," S. B. Luce Papers; Luce to B. F. Tracy, Secretary of the Navy, 14 March 1889, in Box 2.

26. *New York Daily Tribune*, 18 May 1890; *Literary World*, 5 July 1890.

27. Admiral Luce to Secretary Tracy, 14 March 1889, in Box 2, ATM. See also Admiral William S. Sims to C. Carlisle Taylor, 2 May, 1918, in Box 71, William S. Sims Collection, NHFC; Sir Gerard H. V. Noel to Mahan, 23 December 1890, in Box 3; Secretary of the Oriental Association Tokyo to Mahan, 1 April 1897, in Box 3.

28. See, for example, the reviews of *The Influence of Sea Power upon History* in *Boston Evening Transcript*, 14 May 1890; *New York Daily Tribune*, 18 May 1890; *Louisville Courier Journal*, 24 May 1890; *San Francisco Chronicle*, 1 June,1890; *Chicago Daily Inter-Ocean*, 7 June 1890; *Literary World*, 5 July 1890; *Royal United Service Institution Journal* 34 (1890–1891): 1067; *London Times*, 23 October 1893; and *Le Journal* (Paris), 3 December 1914.

29. Alfred Thayer Mahan, *From Sail to Steam* (New York: Harper and Brothers, 1907), 277.

30. See Mahan to Roy B. Marston, 19 February 1897. The letter is published in R. B. Marston, "Captain Mahan and Our Navy," *The Sphere* 17 (11 June 1904), 250.

31. Mahan to Luce, 22 January 1886, in Box 3.

32. Raoul V. P. Castex, *Théories Stratégiques* (Paris: Société d'Editions Géographiques, Maritimes et Coloniales, 1929), 1:39–43. The translation is included in Box 16.

33. Mahan, *From Sail to Steam*, 302.

34. Captain C. F. Goodrich to Mahan, 14 May 1892, in Box 3.

35. Luce to Mahan, 15 July 1907, in Box "Miscellany T–Z," Luce Papers.

36. C. F. Goodrich to Mahan, 14 May 1892; and Thomas G. Bowles to Mahan, 14 January 1893, in Box 3. See also an unidentified newspaper article, 2 December 1914, in Box 1 (although the date is evident, the name of the newspaper has been cut off).

37. Laughton, *Edinburgh Review*, 420.

38. J. K. Laughton to Mahan, 11 March 1893; Thomas C. Bowles to Mahan, 14 January 1893; Admiral L. A. Columb to Mahan, 26 April 1891; and Admiral Sir Phipps Hornby to Mahan, 18 June 1890, in Box 3.

39. Captain W. S. Schley to Mahan, 17 April 1891, in Box 3, ATM; P. F. Harrington to Captain Henry Metcalfe, 10 October 1917, in Box 2. A review of *The Influence of Sea Power upon History* in *New York Tribune*, 18 May 1890, declared that Mahan's work was "exact and logical in its conclusions."

40. Tuchman, *The Proud Tower*, 131.

41. Admiral Sir Phipps Hornby to Mahan, 18 June 1890, in Box 3; *London Times*, 23 October 1893; *Melbourne Argus*, 22 January 1893.

42. William McAdoo to Mahan, 6 May 1893; Henry Cabot Lodge to Mahan, 19 October 1898; and Theodore Roosevelt to Mahan, 21 March 1898 and 8 June 1911, in Box 3.

43. M. Minakami, Naval Commanding Staff Imperial Japanese Navy Dept., to Mahan, 15 July 1899, in Box 3; John Moore to Mahan's wife, 1 December 1914, in Box 2.

44. *Literary World*, 5 July 1890; *Göteborgs Handels Tidning*, 4 December 1914; *New York Daily Tribune*, 18 May 1890; and Captain W. S. Schley to Mahan, 17 September 1891, in Box 3.

45. *Living Age* 187 (1890): 402.

46. Mahan, *The Influence of Sea Power*, 32–33, 53.

47. Mahan, *The Influence of Sea Power*, 38.

48. Unidentified newspaper article, 2 December 1914, in Box 1. One of the obituaries published after Mahan's death, this piece from which I quote includes a comprehensive evaluation of his style.

49. Henry White to Mahan, 15 July 1893; Lord Bryce to Mahan, 21 July 1893; and John Hay to Mahan, 2 August 1893, in Box 3. For an overview of British acclaim of Mahan, see Puleston, *Mahan*, 154–62. Mahan described his personal reaction to the warm British reception to Admiral Luce in a letter dated 22 May 1893 (in Box 9, Luce Papers). Mahan's positive reception in England and his honorary degrees were covered favorably in the *New York Daily Tribune*, 11, 23, and 25 May; 19 and 21 June, 1894.

50. The Latin text of the speech and its translation are in Box 6.

51. Admiral Sir Gerard Noel to Mahan, 23 December 1890; Admiral L. A. Columb to Mahan, 26 April 1891; both in Box 3. For another indication of how Mahan "made clear" the role of sea power, see the review of *The Influence of Sea Power upon History* in the *Royal United Service Institution Journal* 34 (1890–1891): 1067.

52. Theodore Roosevelt to Mahan, 12 May 1890, in Box 3; [Theodore Roosevelt], review of *The Influence of Sea Power*, by Alfred Thayer Mahan, *Atlantic Monthly* 66 (1890): 563–67; Theodore Roosevelt, review of *The Influence of Sea Power*, by Alfred Thayer Mahan, *Political Science Quarterly* 9 (1894): 171–73. Roosevelt's *Atlantic Monthly* review was unsigned; but in his research for a biography of Mahan, W. D. Puleston ascertained Roosevelt's authorship of that piece. See letter from "The Editors" of *Atlantic Monthly* to W. D. Puleston, 24 November 1936, in the box labeled "Puleston's Correspondence," Mahan Papers.

53. See, for instance, *New York Daily Tribune*, 18 May 1890; *San Francisco Chronicle*, 1 June 1890; *Living Age* 187 (1890): 402; Captain W. S. Schley to Mahan, 17 September 1891, in Box 3; Admiral William S. Sims to British Counsel General C. Carlisle Taylor, 2 May 1918, in Box 71, Sims Collection, NHFC.

54. *Louisville Courier Journal*, 24 May 1890; *New York Daily Tribune*, 18 May 1890.

55. See the obituary of Mahan, *Göteborgs Handels Tidning*, 4 December 1914 and the "Just Reading" column of the *Boston Evening Transcript*, 10 May 1890.

56. Franklin D. Roosevelt to Mahan, 28 May 1914; cited in Richard W. Turk, *The Ambiguous Relationship: Theodore Roosevelt and Alfred Thayer Mahan* (New York: Greenwood Press, 1987), 166–67.

57. Theodore Roosevelt to Mahan, 12 May 1890, in Box 3.

58. Roosevelt, *Atlantic Monthly*, 563, and *Political Science Quarterly*, 171.

59. Theodore Roosevelt to Mahan, 21 March 1898, in Box 3.

60. Cited in Seager, *Alfred Thayer Mahan*, 438–39. See Sir Halford Mackinder, "The Geographical Pivot of History," *Geographical Journal* 23 (April 1904): 421–44.

61. Sir Halford Mackinder, *Democratic Ideals and Reality* (New York: Henry Hold and Company, reprinted 1942), 150. See my discussion of Mackinder as a persuader in "The Historical Jeremiad as Rhetorical Genre," 112–13, 117.

62. Admiral S. B. Luce to John Barnes, 5 August 1889, in Box 2. Although this is an unsigned typewritten copy of an original letter, the sender's address is that of Admiral Luce. Moreover, the letter refers to Mahan as the Jomini of Naval Science, Luce's rather consistent sobriquet for Mahan.

63. P. F. Harrington to Captain Henry Metcalfe, 10 October 1917, in Box 2, ATM. Harrington was Commandant of Midshipmen at the Naval Academy.

64. Mahan, *From Sail to Steam*, 285, 286–88.

65. Alfred Thayer Mahan, "The Writing of History," *Atlantic Monthly* 91 (1903): 289–90, 292, 295, 297.

66. Seager, *Alfred Thayer Mahan*, 433.

67. Louis Gottschalk, "The Evaluation of Historical Writings," in *The Practice of Book Selection*, ed. Louis R. Wilson (Chicago: University of Chicago Press, 1940), 101–15.

68. Mahan, *The Influence of Sea Power*, 25–77.

69. Laughton, *Edinburgh Review*, 446, 450.

70. Mahan to Luce, 20 December 1890, in Box 9, Luce Papers, NHFC. Laughton acknowledged his authorship of that piece in a letter to Mahan dated 11 March 1893, in Box 3.

71. Mahan, *The Influence of Sea Power*, 13–18.

72. *Boston Evening Transcript*, 14 May 1890.

73. Roosevelt, *Atlantic Monthly*, 564, and *Political Science Quarterly*, 171–72.

74. J. K. Laughton, *Edinburgh Review*, 422.

75. Admiral Luce to Lt. T. F. Meigs, 29 October 1888, in Box "Miscellany T–Z," Luce Papers, NHFC; Mahan to Luce, 22 January 1886, in Box 3.

76. Louisa Tyndall to Mahan, 4 May 1894, in Box 3; *London Times*, 23 October 1893.

77. To Mahan, 21 April 1893, in Box 3. The letter is from someone at the Treasury Department's Light-House Board, but the signature is an illegible scrawl. Mahan's brother Dennis worked there in 1893; however, the resemblance of the scrawl to a "B" suggests that the writer was Captain A. S. Barker, a longtime correspondent with Mahan who had duty that year as a lighthouse inspector.

78. Mahan, *The Influence of Sea Power*, 7 and 481, n. 15.

79. See Laughton, *Edinburgh Review*, 441; and Roosevelt, *Political Science Quarterly*, 172–73.

80. Castex, *Theories Strategiques*, 39–43.

81. Lyle E. Mahan to W. D. Puleston, 2 March 1936, in Box 15.

82. Livezey, *Mahan on Sea Power*, 32.

83. William M. Little to Mahan, 22 May 1890, in Box 3.

84. For example: Admiral Sir Gerard Noel to Mahan, 23 December 1890; Lord Charles Beresford to Mahan, 12 January 1891; Captain C. F. Goodrich to Mahan, 14 May 1892; R. B. Marston to Mahan, 6 January 1893; and L. Bowenhagen, Directions Officier der Marine Academie and Schule Keil, to Mahan, 11 November 1893, in Boxes 3 and 4. Direct references to the "interest" value of the book also appear in the *New York Daily Tribune*, 22 January 1893, as well as in Roosevelt's review in the *Atlantic Monthly*, 563, 567.

85. Mahan to Admiral Luce, 16 October 1889, in Box 2; Mahan to Sir George S. Clarke, 5 November 1892, in Box 3.

86. Mahan to the secretary of the Naval Institute, 27 November 1888, in Box 2.

87. *San Francisco Chronicle*, 1 June 1890; *Journal Des Debates* (Paris), 4 December 1914; *New York Daily Tribune*, 18 May 1890; *Boston Evening Transcript*, 14 May 1890; *Chicago Daily Inter-Ocean*, 7 June 1890; *Louisville Courier Journal*, 24 May 1890; *Edinburgh Review* 172 (1890): 453; and *Political Science Quarterly* 9 (1894): 171.

88. Theodore Roosevelt to Mahan, 18 May 1893; Thomas G. Bowles to Mahan, 14 January 1893; and Admiral Sir Gerard H. V. Noel to Mahan, 23 December 1890, in Box 3.

89. See Noam Chomsky, "On the Notion 'Rule of Grammar,'" in *Structure of Language and Its Mathematical Aspects*, ed. Roman Jakobson, vol. 12 of *Proceedings of Symposia in Applied Mathematics* (Providence, R.I.: American Mathematical Society, 1961), 10; George A. Miller and Noam Chomsky, "Finitary Models of Language Users," in *Handbook of Mathematical Psychology*, ed. Robert D. Luce, Robert R. Bush, and Eugene Galanter (New York: John Wiley and Sons, 1963), 2:472; or the shorter discussion in my "The Essential Schemes of Syntax: An Analysis of Rhetorical Theory's Recommendations for Uncommon Syntax," *Quarterly Journal of Speech* 55 (April 1969): 161–68.

90. Victor H. Yngve, "The Depth Hypothesis," in *Structure of Language*, 134.

91. Miller and Chomsky, "Finitary Models of Language Users," in *Handbook of Mathematical Psychology*, 474.

92. See George Kingsley Zipf, *The Psycho-Biology of Language* (Cambridge: M.I.T. Press, 1965); see also his *Human Behavior and the Principle of Least Effort* (Cambridge: Addison Wesley Press, 1949), 20.

93. Mahan, *From Sail to Steam*, 288.

94. Mahan, *The Influence of Sea Power*, 77.

95. See Bitzer, "The Rhetorical Situation," *Philosophy and Rhetoric* 1 (Winter 1968): 1–14.

96. Mahan to Luce, 22 May 1893, in Box 9, Luce Papers, NHFC; Mahan to Admiral Sir B. G. Clark, 22 May 1891, in Box 3; Mahan to Luce, 7 May 1890, in Box 2.

97. Mahan to Admiral Luce, 17 September 1890, in Box 9, Luce Papers, NHFC.

By this time, Mahan also was laying groundwork for a series of polemic magazine articles.

98. Mahan to Sir George Clarke, 29 July 1894, in Box 3.

99. Admiral Sir Gerard H. V. Noel to Mahan, 23 December 1890, in Box 3.

100. Mahan to Clarke, 5 November 1892, in Box 3.

101. *London Times,* 23 October 1893; Laughton, *Edinburgh Review,* 420.

102. T. F. Maynard to Mahan, 22 June 1894, in Box 3.

103. John Moore to Mahan's wife, 1 December 1914, in Box 2.

104. Roosevelt, *Atlantic Monthly,* 563–64. Part of Roosevelt's reaction also reflects his appreciation for Mahan's use of French sources which made "it possible to arrive at the true facts" of the naval struggles between France and England.

105. *New York Daily Tribune,* 18 May 1890.

106. *Literary World,* 5 July 1890.

107. *Living Age* 187 (1890): 401.

108. P. F. Harrington to Captain Henry Metcalfe, 10 October 1917, in Box 2.

109. Edmund Morris, *The Rise of Theodore Roosevelt* (New York: Coward, McCann and Geohegan, 1979), 424–25, 540, 558, 575.

110. Cited in *The Rise of Theodore Roosevelt,* 558.

111. Cited in *The Rise of Theodore Roosevelt,* 569. See also the discussion of this address in Beale, *Theodore Roosevelt,* 40.

112. Theodore Roosevelt, review of *The Interest of America in Sea Power, Past and Future,* by Alfred Thayer Mahan, *New York Sun,* 26 December 1897; cited in Beale, *Theodore Roosevelt,* 37.

113. Morris, *The Rise of Theodore Roosevelt,* 575.

114. Theodore Roosevelt's remarks were reprinted in the *New York Sun,* 10 February and 23 February 1897; *New York Press,* 23 February 1897; and *New York World,* 23 February 1897 (cited in Beale, *Theodore Roosevelt,* 57).

115. Roosevelt to Charles A. Boutelle, 16 September 1897; cited in Beale, *Theodore Roosevelt,* 56.

116. Cited in Morris, *The Rise of Theodore Roosevelt,* 574.

117. Mahan to Theodore Roosevelt, 16 October 1902, in *Letters and Papers of Alfred Thayer Mahan,* 3 vols. ed. Robert Seager II and Doris D. Maguire (Annapolis: Naval Institute Press, 1975), 3 :38–39.

118. Mahan to Bouverie F. Clark, 6 September 1907, in *Letters and Papers* 3: 225–26; Mahan to Clark, 11 September 1908, in *Letters and Papers* 3: 263.

119. Mahan, cited in *New York Times,* 26 October 1910 (reprinted in *Letters and Papers* 3: 363–64).

120. Samuel A. Ashe quoted that statement to Mahan's daughter Helen, 8 January 1931; in Box 2.

121. Henry Erben to Francis M. Ramsay, Bureau of Navigation, 31 December 1893, in cited in Seager, *Alfred Thayer Mahan,* 278.

122. Theodore Roosevelt to Mahan's wife, 5 December 1914, Box 2.

Part II

The Rhetoric of Narrative in History

Rationality is determined by the nature of persons as narrative beings—their inherent awareness of *narrative probability*, what constitutes a coherent story, and their constant habit of testing *narrative fidelity*, whether the stories they experience ring true with the stories they know to be true in their lives.

Walter R. Fisher,
"Narration as a Human Communication Paradigm,"
Communication Monographs

Chapter Five

Alfred Thayer Mahan
as Opinion Leader for the
Japanese Attack on Pearl Harbor:
Narrative Fidelity with Fact

After aircraft of his attacking squadrons completed their surprise raid on Pearl Harbor, Commander Mitsuo Fuchida remained to fly alone over the scene for a final appraisal before returning as the last plane back to his aircraft carrier.[1] Upon landing on the *Akagi*, Fuchida rushed up to the bridge to make his personal report to the task-force commander, Admiral Chuichi Nagumo. As he exclaimed with glowing pride and excitement, "four battleships sunk" and "four battleships damaged," Nagumo interrupted with the question uppermost in his mind as task-force commander: "Do you think that the U.S. Fleet could come out from Pearl Harbor within six months?" Fuchida replied, "The main force of the U.S. Fleet will not be able to come out within six months." Then, although Fuchida pressed for a second strike against "dockyards, the fuel tanks, and an occasional ship," Nagumo dismissed him with a "few words of praise."[2] Thus, in the heat of battle, for a tactical decision which greatly affected the course of World War II, "six months" was a criterion for judgment. The task-force commander did not think generally in terms such as the U.S. Fleet's being able to come out "soon" or in "several months," nor was his decision contingent upon other criteria as specific as four months, eight months, or a year, for instance. *The* criterion was *six* months. And that exact time reference was a product of what leading Japanese naval officers knew to be "history"—not only from what they understood to be the facts of the earlier experiences of their nation at sea but also from what they had assiduously read and learned about "sea power" in writings of Alfred Thayer Mahan.

By 1897, *The Influence of Sea Power upon History* had been translated into the Japanese language, and copies were not only in the hands of the

Emperor and Crown Prince but widely distributed among government leaders and the officer corps of the services.[3] As indicated directly to the book's author by a member of the Imperial Japanese Navy Department in 1899, that nation appreciated "the great principles herein set forth by your forcible pen"; and because the Japanese Naval and Military Colleges adopted it as their textbook, *The Influence of Sea Power upon History* also was in "every middle, higher middle and normal school in Japan."[4] Mahan himself at first seemed skeptical about his popularity in Japan. After learning from the Oriental Association of Tokyo that the Japanese Club of Naval Officers had had the book translated and that "several thousand volumes were sold in a day or two," he deemed such instant popularity "a little fishy" and asked his publisher to find "some correspondent in Japan who could investigate the matter."[5] Mahan's popularity and credibility there indeed were substantial, however. During a six-year tour of duty in Japan, a British naval officer observed as early as 1894 that "Japanese naval officers are much impressed with the advantage in a land war of superiority at sea. They have been, I know, faithful students of the American naval historian, Captain Mahan."[6] This American author, "with his theories of the influence of sea power upon history, was one of the gurus of Japanese naval officers."[7] In succeeding years, when he had to defend his extensive writing at the expense of time devoted to more orthodox naval duties, the historian lauded himself as "an authority . . . not in the United States only, but throughout the world, my . . . works having been translated into the principal European languages, as well as into Japanese."[8] As Ronald Spector concludes, sources of Japanese decisions about Pearl Harbor include impressions ranging from "the British Royal Navy to the histories of Alfred Thayer Mahan," and other historiographical research with diaries and correspondence indicates that Admiral Yamamoto, his planning staff, and attack commanders were "true disciples of Mahan."[9] Those rich primary sources facilitate analysis of a rhetorical process by which the course of Japanese strategy and tactics at Pearl Harbor was vectored in part by an American's historical writing.

For Japanese readers of Mahan's translated work, the persuasive role of his stylistic predilections likely was lost: English syntax had been transformed into ideographs of the Japanese language. Even members of the Japanese Imperial Navy who read Mahan in English likely were not affected in significant ways by any possible paramessage evolving from subtle nuances of syntax such as periodic suspensions or the embedding of numerous qualifying clauses, for the functional effects of such facets of style are generally constrained by cultural differences in how people use and respond to language. The rhetorical impact of Mahan's historical writing in Japan therefore must be explicated in terms of a broader variable not altered greatly by translation into another language, particularly an ideographic one. In this case, that factor is simply the story being told—and the way that narrative could interact rhetorically with other "stories" the Japanese accepted as embodying truth.

Characterizing historians as "rhetorical agents" who "are always in search of those proofs that are able to explain the past to the present in the most persuasive terms," E. Culpepper Clark asks: "What makes certain explanations more satisfactory than others?" For him, historical writing is an analog of an oration's *narratio* or "statement of facts" wherein "stylistic devices are to emplot the story . . . transform the warrant from its status as a general inferential rule to a connector between thought and action that is grounded in experience and appeals to common sense."[10] In this view, sources of historians' persuasiveness reside largely in their texts. A different purview here holds that for Japanese naval personnel who planned and executed the Pearl Harbor raid, Mahan's writing became increasingly influential as doctrine espoused therein was corroborated by several historical events, each of which in turn helped endow his discourse with "narrative fidelity." For as Walter Fisher observes about the narrative paradigm operative in human communication, the critic who would account for persuasiveness of discourse must view such endeavors as stories "competing with other stories . . . and as rational when they satisfy the demands of narrative probability and fidelity."[11] Mahan's story came to "ring true" for the Japanese prior to the attack on Pearl Harbor because of (1) elements internal to his text which initially enticed Japanese readers to favorable reception of his work, and then, more significantly, (2) a series of discrete events which, as facts known in a communication "mosaic," corroborated the American's historical writings, and finally (3) a singularly important "bolstering" event which likely influenced final deliberations about whether or not to attack Pearl Harbor.

I

Although rhetorical interaction between discourse and corroborating events is integral to attaining narrative fidelity, Mahan's prior ethos or credibility complemented the process of persuasion. His reputation among Westerners caused the Japanese to read him initially as they entered the twentieth century with a "catch up" mentality about naval warfare. The means of achieving naval supremacy admittedly were very much on the minds of other world leaders and their military and naval commanders. In both Great Britain and Imperial Germany, for instance, varied voices forcefully articulated the advantages of larger navies as they contributed to world power. In Japan, however, a voice which was particularly enticing was that of Mahan, for he was a distinguished historian who seemed to write directly about that nation and to advocate models for its behavior. Readers so persuaded are drawn to such models initially because they perceive similarities—real or imagined—between themselves and the people whose behavior should be emulated.[12] To Kenneth Burke, such identification is an *"acting together."*[13] But as Fisher also observes, "any story, any form of rhetorical communication, not only says something about the world, it also implies an audience, persons who conceive of themselves in very specific ways. If a story denies a person's self-conception, it does not matter what it says about the world. . . . The only way to bridge this gap, if it can be bridged through discourse, is by telling stories that do not negate the self-conceptions people hold of themselves."[14] Mahan's "story"—quite exclusive of the style in which it was cast—appealed forcefully to Japanese self-conceptions and functioned as a potential source of initial rhetorical identification between author and readers.

From the rhetorical perspective of opinion leadership and the issue of how historical writing of an American could appeal to Japanese readers—or those of other nationalities who might identify with viewpoints expressed therein—the most significant section of *The Influence of Sea Power upon History* was its opening chapter, "Discussion of the Elements of Sea Power." Indeed, as Robert Seager has remarked, "many American newspaper reviewers and some foreign ones as well, seem not to have read past the controversial 'Elements of Sea Power' or to have done much more than scan the chapter headings of the remainder of the volume."[15] Preceding 421 pages of a highly detailed, historical narrative about naval engagements between 1660 and 1783—typically won by British naval prowess—these 55 pages identify and explain six discrete sources from which a nation achieves greatness at sea and thereby in the world: (1) geographical position whereby the significant boundaries of a nation are not those of land, which require local military strength for defense, but rather those of the sea, which also offer easy access to projection of naval power; (2) physical conformation characterized by numerous deep harbors, particularly if they are the outlets of navigable streams; (3) extent of territory *not* as the total number of square miles but rather as the length of the coastline and the character of its harbors; (4) population not simply as the number of people or the grand total residing in the nation but rather the number of those who specifically follow the sea for their livelihood or are at least readily available for shipboard duties and the creation of naval stores and matériel; (5) national character whereby the population embodies such qualities as boldness, industriousness, patience in times of suffering, and industriousness, and are gifted with intense national feeling; and (6) a character of government whereby those in positions of leadership are in full accord with the natural bias of its people and promote growth in every respect.[16] Although Mahan's model for that chapter was the British Isles (rather than continental France or Holland), he easily could have been writing about Japan. That island nation *obviously* shared several sources of potential sea power with Great Britain.[17] Immediately perceiving bases of similarity with Great Britain, Japanese naval personnel *then* read Mahan's extensive if not exhaustive, patent praise for "men and deeds of the British Navy."[18] For as the reviewer for the *Chicago Tribune* put it, "the grand theme of naval strategy . . . is engrossing," but a reader likely "follows Captain Mahan's battle narratives . . . of sea fights with amused and amusing patience."[19] Still, the moral from the body of the book was always the same: the Royal Navy did it the right way and thereby contributed greatly to the power of Great Britain in the world.

Naval prowess of Great Britain was emulated by Japan. During the Russo-Japanese War of 1904–05, Captain William C. Pakenham of the Royal Navy was with Admiral Togo as an observer and a firm friend. He was aboard ship for fourteen months, during which Togo consulted Pakenham and another British naval attache, Captain Thomas Jackson. Moreover, Japanese naval "training methods and organization were on British models."[20] As commander-in-chief of the Combined Fleet of the Imperial Japanese Navy, and a prime mover behind the attack on Pearl Harbor, Admiral Isoroku Yamamoto also was a product of Royal Navy training methods and traditions. Such emulation was warranted in Japan not only because the Royal Navy was "the world's premier fleet and was obviously the best one to copy" but also because its "traditions seemed to slot in naturally with indigenous Japanese traditions" of "loyalty, hard work, conformity and discipline."[21] Japanese emulation of British naval practices included using a "traditional" flag signal "Z," which conveyed the message "The rise or fall of the Empire depends upon this battle; everyone will do his duty with utmost efforts" (a paraphrase of the Nelsonian signal at Trafalgar, "England expects every man to do his duty").[22] In the Imperial Japanese Navy, the "Z" flag had special significance. It had been hoisted on Admiral Togo's flagship during the Russo-Japanese War battle of Tsushima in 1905; the exact same flag was raised on the *Akagi* on 7 December 1941 as she turned into the wind to launch aircraft for the raid on Pearl Harbor; and a sentence that was virtually the flag's message was included in the Emperor's "Imperial Rescript" read aloud to *Akagi* crewmen that morning.[23] Officers on other ships in the Pearl Harbor task force recalled the inspirational impact of the "Z" signal. When he saw this flag "gallantly hoisted," a destroyer officer was "excited over the honor," for "I have heard many times of that order given by the 'Z' flag from Admiral Togo. . . . Now I have actually received the same order myself." And a battleship officer wrote in his diary, "nothing more contents us, as fighting men, then to look at the same signal hoisted when we are about to meet the enemy's Pacific Fleet. . . . There is none who does not make up his mind to accomplish a great deed comparable to that accomplished by his ancestors."[24] Historical precedent was important to Japanese naval officers.

Other evidence of how Japanese naval officers emulated British sea power is an exultant newspaper release after Pearl Harbor, on Navy Day in Japan (27 May 1942), which was celebrated with parades, ceremonies, and this proud proclamation of achievement published in English:

> This year, Navy Day is not a day of mere remembrance, not a mere reminder; it is a day of fulfillment. The Japanese Navy has not only duplicated the exploits of 37 years ago, but it has repeated it [*sic*] time and time again and on an unbelievably greater scale. . . . This is the moment of culmination, the moment of fulfillment.
>
> Today, Britain's control over the seas has vanished, thanks to the work of the German and Italian submarines and more to the work of the Japanese Navy. Britain's auxiliary, the United States, has likewise had her navy practically destroyed by the Japanese Navy. As a result, Japan stands today as the premier naval power of the world. It may well presage the rise of Japan in the future history of the world to a position comparable to that which Britain has occupied in the past.[25]

That "work of the Japanese Navy" included on 10 December 1941 the sinking in short order (approximately 90 minutes of aerial attack) of the 32,000-ton battle cruiser HMS *Repulse* and the 35,000-ton battleship HMS *Prince of Wales*, both sent by the Royal Navy to help repel an invasion of Malaya and "impregnable" Singapore (which also fell in short order).[26] Japanese success in emulating—and defeating—the British Royal Navy lauded in *The Influence of Sea Power upon History* was made possible in part by learning lessons reinforced by story after story within that broader historical narrative. That success also was made possible by interaction between Mahan's discourse and a notable event in 1905 which helped endow his stories with "narrative fidelity" for the Japanese: the battle of Tsushima during the Russo-Japanese War.

In his "Introductory," Mahan argues that "at a very conspicuous and momentous period of the world's history, Sea Power had a strategic bearing and weight." He immediately provides the supporting "story" of Rome's victory over Hannibal in the Second Punic War.[27] His autobiography also summarizes that conceptualization (which he formulated in 1885 while reading Mommsen's *History of Rome*) and explains how it led him to "investigate coincidentally the general history and naval history of the past two centuries, with a view to demonstrating the influence of events of the one upon the other"; "It suddenly struck me, whether by some chance phrase of the author I do not know, how different things might have been could Hannibal have invaded Italy by sea, as the Romans often had Africa, instead of by the long land route; or could he, after arrival, have been in free communication with Carthage by water."[28] Thus, *The Influence of Sea Power upon History* begins by calling attention to what Japanese readers would perceive immediately as the direct, historical analog of Japan and Russia at Tsushima in 1905. After the Japanese surprise attack on the Russian fleet at Port Arthur ("the first Pearl Harbor"), their mainland war was one of sieges, frontal assaults, and massive bodies of troops (at Mukden no larger forces ever had met in the history of war). Hampered by a long, overland supply route for which the TransSiberia Railroad was inadequate, Russia sent an armada from Europe to interdict Japanese supplies and reinforcements for mainland operations. In the Straits of Tsushima between Korea and Japan, that fleet was destroyed decisively by Admiral Togo (with Captain Pakenham on the flagship *Mikasa* and with battle preparations made "according to the best British traditions," including the "Z" flag). According to Togo himself, "the fate of our empire was really settled within the first half hour" on 27 May 1905 (hence the date of Navy Day).[29] Tsushima brought Russia earnestly to the conference table.[30] Japanese naval planning thereafter favored a "statutory Great All-Out Battle" because "decisive victory" allowed the winner "to 'control the seas,' to cut off the enemy's seaborne supplies and reinforcements, and to ensure the arrival of one's own."[31] Indeed, as a Japanese naval officer wrote in retrospect after World War II, "the idea of the Battle of Tsushima has prepossessed us, this fatal 'One Decisive Battle Idea.'"[32] Clearly, historical precedent was significant in Japanese naval planning. Rome against Hannibal directly paralleled Japan against Russia, and Mahan's detailed chronicles of other "decisive" sea battles won by "men and deeds of the British Navy" corroborated extensively and authoritatively what Japanese readers in the twentieth century believed already.

Another source of potential identification between Mahan and his Japanese naval readers stemmed not only from geographical and political similarities with Great Britain but also from cultural predilections that complemented admiration of the Royal Navy and its deeds. In one analysis of Yamamoto's "unswerving target, the destruction in one decisive battle of the enemy fleet," Stephen Howarth explains in detail how "the concept of the decisive battle was deeply ingrained" by sports played by cadets in the Imperial Japanese Naval Academy at Etajima.[33] Although that program included some Western imports such as soccer, prospective naval officers at Etajima concentrated on "four essentially Japanese" competitions. These included judo, a mode of martial arts in which the opponent's physical strength is used against him; sumo wrestling, wherein the objective is not to win points but to have the opponent lose points; and kendo, a relic of Samurai sword-fighting that uses four-foot staves instead of swords. Unlike European fencing, in which the opponent's strength is whittled away by repeated small strikes, kendo has as its most artful end but a single blow at one of five specific places on the body where a Samurai sword wound is fatal. And a Samurai "sword" metaphor prevailed when Admiral Kusaka (Nagumo's chief of staff on the *Akagi*) reminisced about the Pearl Harbor raid: "The operational objective of this attack was . . . to destroy the U.S. Pacific Fleet . . . to cut it down with one stroke of a big sword to be swung from overhead." Moreover, indecision about canceling the raid because American aircraft carriers were not in Pearl Harbor on 7 December 1941 "would only result in blunting the cutting effect of a sword swung down from overhead."[34]

Another sport popular at Etajima was *botaoshi*, "played in the academy and nowhere else." In this competition, typically over in "three or four minutes," two opposing teams charged from opposite ends of the field. The sole objective was pull down the opponent's pole with flags on it, and the entire event, often leaving unconscious players on the field, was "extremely vicious," Howarth affirms, "incredibly exciting and swiftly finished—one quick decisive battle." Through sports, cadets acquired "consciously or unconsciously, their principles of war. . . . The seeds of thought in every officer's mind were there: the beliefs that they could tackle an enemy, however strong, by using his strength against him; that a single, well-calculated blow was always worth more than a dozen smaller ones; that they could always win, not by overwhelming force, but by inflicting greater loses than they sustained; and finally, that it would all be over in one fast decisive battle. This was more than a rational strategic ideal; it was an eternal conviction, deeply rooted in the psyche of every Japanese naval officer." Unfortunately, the experience also conduced to "a severe narrow-mindedness, an inability to improvise against the unexpected, a phobia of doing the wrong thing and a reluctance to operate without exact orders for every eventuality."[35]

Against that backdrop of cultural predispositions, Mahan's eminence in Japan also is explained therefore as "opinion leadership." Perceived as "characteristically more competent, within his specialty, than are his fellows," with "access to wider information," and "like everyone else only moreso," this "super-representative" could reinforce extant group norms. Mahan's credibility in Western eyes demonstrated competence to the Japanese; scope of detail in his book evinced "access to wider information"; and the historian's praise of "elements of sea power"— which Japan *shared* with Britain, geographically, politically, and culturally—displayed a similarity in values with Japanese naval personnel. Thus, by "predicting" in 1890 the impact of Togo's naval victory at Tsushima in 1905, Mahan's treatise about the past offered guidance for those who planned and executed the future attack on Pearl Harbor. The experience of the Japanese in their war with Russia confirmed the veracity of his narrative and fulfilled the early expectation of officers in the Japanese Navy Department that his work could "awaken our nation and as in Moses time may be the pillar of fire leading our nation in the century to come."[36]

II

Still another persuasive aspect of Mahan's story was his terminology made salient by the course of events. For Western readers, "Sea Power" was such a term.[37] Even when translated by another Japanese officer back into English, the diary of a World War II Imperial Navy admiral noted that the "chance of our absolute success" was equated with the ability to "destroy more of the enemy's sea power."[38] Nevertheless, not easily conforming to a Japanese ideograph, "sea power" may have had less influence upon naval thinking in Japan than the expression "fleet in being," a more precise term referring to a concentration of warships sufficient for offensive success. Narrative fidelity of the concept was confirmed for careful Japanese readers of Mahan by events during the Spanish-American War, which lasted 113 days. First, the battle of Manila Bay impressed the Japanese. Two months before formal outbreak of hostilities on 22 April 1898, Assistant Secretary of the Navy Theodore Roosevelt cabled Commodore Dewey, commanding the U.S. Navy Asiatic Squadron, to be ready at Hong Kong for "offensive operations in Philippine Islands" upon the declaration of war against Spain. So in Manila Bay at 5:40 A.M. on 1 May, Dewey said to the commander of the *Olympia*, "You may fire when you are ready, Gridley"; at 7:35 A.M., after five passes at the Spanish ships, the squadron withdrew to redistribute ammunition and have breakfast; at 11:16 A.M., Dewey resumed the attack; at 12:30 P.M., the Spanish surrendered. American casualties were "none killed and but six slightly wounded."[39] In a few hours—including a break for breakfast—America acquired a forward Philippine naval base from which the United States Fleet could "dominate the Far East."[40] Second, the American naval triumph at Santiago de Cuba was significant. The Spanish fleet under Admiral Cervera left harbor shortly before 10:00 A.M. on 3 July 1898 to battle the blockading U.S. Navy; by 1:15 P.M., its last vessel was destroyed; one American was killed. With morale shattered, Spanish troops there surrendered, and peace was proclaimed on 12 August. As a World War II Japanese admiral reminiscenced, these two American naval triumphs had made an "especially deep impression" and caused "the blood of our young officers to boil with emulation."[41] Moreover, triumph at Santiago was witnessed firsthand by Lieutenant Akiyama Saneyuki, of the Imperial Japanese Navy, as an observer aboard Admiral Sampson's flagship.[42]

Saneyuki became a pivotal figure who between 1900 and 1912 exerted a "dramatic and comprehensive impact on Japanese naval thinking."[43] During duty in America (1897–1899), he conferred with Mahan, who recommended readings for his professional education. Saneyuki was among Imperial Japanese Navy officers who "counted themselves" among the American's "disciples."[44] Although Saneyuki had been denied admission to the United States Naval Academy and to the Naval War College, his assignment on Admiral Sampson's flagship allowed him the distinction of being the first Japanese naval officer to be a direct witness of Western sea power in action. His observations about Sampson's "bold initiatives" using modern battleships became Secret Intelligence Report 108, the "classic source of information on the U.S. Navy for Japanese planners," and his analysis of the American blockade at Santiago guided the successful blockade by the Japanese of Port Arthur six years later—which Mahan in turn characterized in *Naval Strategy* (1911) as a model of a "fleet in being" engaged in offensive operations.[45] Assigned to the Japanese Naval Staff College in 1900, Saneyuki "brought a sense of authority to his lectures" founded upon wide readings and, more significantly, his status as an eyewitness to what American battleships could do. Previous to Saneyuki's direct observations, a few Japanese officers had visited sites of naval battles. In the Sino-French War of 1884 and the Greco-Turkish War of 1897, for example, they had interviewed participants after the encounters.[46] But Saneyuki saw firsthand what U.S. Navy battleships as a "fleet in being" did in a decisive "big battle" as advocated by Mahan.[47] Then, after reflecting upon medieval Japanese treatises, such as *The Ancient Corsair Tactics of the Yashima School* written in the fourteenth century, Saneyuki advocated as part of his emergent doctrine (like Mahan's) a "concentration of forces" but added the destruction of the enemy's "will" as equally important, if not moreso, than great numbers of ships. By overlaying Mahan's ideas with his personal perspective, Saneyuki likely enhanced his own ethos or credibility. Merely to translate a book bestows no aura of special expertise upon someone aspiring to be a naval strategist, but by demonstrating how its doctrine could be adapted to conform to unique Japanese naval inclinations, Saneyuki showed himself to be especially knowledgeable about how Japan might exert influence upon the seas.[48] By 1904, as the "unrivaled tactical genius" in the Imperial Japanese Navy, Saneyuki was aboard Togo's flagship drafting the battle plan for Tsushima and subsequently writing the report of the engagement, thus being both architect and scribe of victory. And so it was that impressions made upon a Japanese officer during the Spanish-American War helped to shape not only the tactics for Japanese naval triumphs against Russia and but also the resultant Japanese naval doctrine favoring "concentrated fleets of battleships" to win "command of the sea" in decisive battles.[49]

Still another of Mahan's ideas—and the exact wording of a phrase—helped shape Japanese naval planning. Two and one-half weeks before the Spanish-American War began formally, Admiral Cervera's fleet sailed from Cádiz for the Western Hemisphere (the *Maine* disaster in Havana preordained the conflict). While its location was unknown, that Spanish "fleet in being" caused panic along the eastern seacoast of America. A Georgia congressman asked the Navy Department for a ship to defend Jekyll Island "because it contained the winter homes of certain millionaires," and an influential women insisted that "a ship should be anchored off a huge sea-side hotel because she had a house in the neighborhood." The Atlantic Fleet remained concentrated, though, for *offensive* operations to blockade Cuba and then "force Spain to surrender by threatening a naval attack on her coasts."[50] The moral about a concentrated fleet of battleships had not gone unnoticed by Theodore Roosevelt, for example, who wrote to Mahan: "I shall urge, and have urged, the President and the Secretary to pay absolutely no heed to the outcries for protection from Spanish raids. Take the worst—a bombardment of New York. It would amount to absolutely nothing, as affecting the course of a war, or damaging permanently the prosperity of the country. I should not myself divert a ship from the Cuban waters for any threat against our coast, bar always that I should protect the battleships building at Newport News."[51]In *Lessons of the War with Spain,* undoubtedly read in Japan by his ardent disciples and admirers of Admirals Sampson and Dewey and their exploits at Santiago and Manila Bay, Mahan explained further why American battleships must not be detached as single units to be overwhelmed by larger forces: "The Navy Department had . . . to keep in mind . . . that we had not a battleship in the home ports that could in *six months* be made ready to replace one lost or seriously disabled. . . . *If we lost ten thousand men, the country could replace them; if we lost a battleship, it could not be replaced.* The issue of the war, as a whole and in every locality to which it extended, depended upon naval force. . . . A million of the best soldiers would have been powerless in the face of hostile control of the sea."[52] *The Influence of Sea Power upon History* similarly had quoted "a most accomplished French officer of the day" about another war: "Behind the squadron of twenty-one ships-of-the line . . . there was no reserve; not another ship could have been commissioned within *six months.*"[53] For careful Japanese readers, "six months" became a potent frame of reference; it later constrained decisions about an American "fleet in being" of battleships which, by U.S. Naval doctrine, were to be kept together as a group. In the spring of 1941, Britain asked the United States to divide its Pacific Fleet and detach some of those ships to help defend Singapore, but the request was denied because "it was fundamental that the Pacific Fleet be held intact."[54] Without American battleships, the British Far Eastern Empire would be easy prey to the Japanese; and Singapore, specifically, would be "a base without a fleet and without prospect of one."[55] Again, facts of actual events made Mahan persuasive to all parties.

The Washington Naval Conference Treaty of 1922 did not favor Japan. Great Britain, the United States, and Japan could build battleships in a 5-5-3 ratio, respectively, for a 40 percent American superiority over the Japanese (and the London Naval Treaty of 1930 specified 10-10-7, respectively, for cruisers). Japan experienced a "ratio neurosis" about being outgunned by the greater number of British and American battleships in the Pacific.[56] Two "super battleships," *Yamato* and *Musashi,* were built secretly to offset the imbalance. With eighteen-inch guns (instead of the sixteen-inch guns on American battleships) and displacing 70,000 tons, these behemoths substituted "striking power per ship for number of vessels"; and faith in such "huge battleships and big guns" constituted "mainstream" and "conservative" thought in Japan's navy.[57] Even after their successful aircraft-carrier strike against Pearl Harbor, the Japanese Naval General Staff still believed widely that "the battleship constitutes the nucleus of naval power."[58] For example, on 9 August 1942, when the outcome of the American amphibious landing at Guadalcanal was in doubt, the U.S. Marines' ability to hold their tenuous position during the first three days depended upon their receiving supplies and reinforcements from a fleet of U.S. Navy transport and cargo ships off the island. Aircraft of the Japanese Navy en route to raid the landing area were diverted, however, when a scout plane patrolling elsewhere mistook and reported the damaged American destroyer *Jarvis* to be a "battleship." Accordingly, those Japanese naval aircraft abandoned their attack on plebeian transport shipping—an assault which likely "would have ended the campaign shortly in ignominious defeat for the Allies"— to achieve instead the "flawed victory" of sinking the *Jarvis*. Admiral Mikawa's decision reflected traditional Japanese Navy thinking, "one of its sacred tenets . . . the destruction of the enemy's surface fleet."[59] In their overall assessment, subsequent strategists conclude that "Japan, in keeping with her program of Westernization, emulated Great Britain and the United States in embracing the fleet concept with the battleship as the ultimate arbiter."[60] That battleship mentality was maintained by Rear Admiral Matome Ukagi, for instance, who as Combined Fleet chief of staff "had almost reverent faith in the lessons taught in the Naval General Staff College and in the concept of the Great All-Out Battle." And Admiral Yamamoto, despite his pioneering efforts to foster development of aircraft carriers and naval aviation, was said to be "under the influence of Alfred Thayer Mahan" and to have "visualized the battleship as the queen of the fleet."[61] For as Theodore Roosevelt had concluded in his review of *The Influence of Sea Power upon History*, an underlying but clear moral of the book was its proof of the importance of "a large navy, composed not merely of cruisers, but containing also a full proportion of powerful battleships able to meet those of any other nation."[62] Orthodoxy about "powerful battleships" became more significant, however, as Japan moved inexorably closer to attacking Pearl Harbor.

Bogged down since 1937 in war with China, Japan sought expansion in Southeast Asia for raw materials, especially oil. Holland and France were defeated by Nazi Germany in 1940. Great Britain seemingly awaited only Hitler's final blow; its Asian empire was vulnerable. In July 1941, Japanese troops entered French Indochina and secured the flank for a drive to obtain oil in the Dutch East Indies. Although many Americans were isolationists, despite Franklin Roosevelt's appeal in 1937 to "quarantine" aggressors, sentiment was turning against Japan due to pro-Chinese propaganda, including the widely published photograph of a Chinese baby crying amid rubble after a Japanese air raid.[63] The French Indochina incursion prompted a stern warning from Roosevelt and an embargo on American shipments of strategic materials to Japan, including high-octane gasoline and crude oil. Time was running out. The Japanese Navy wanted 500,000 tons of oil on reserve "for the Great All-Out Battle," but peacetime consumption was 300,000 tons every month. Japan could not meet extensive oil needs with synthetics or purchases abroad; its navy "would be disabled in two years, and important industries paralyzed in less than half that time" (in another estimate, the navy "had enough oil for only eighteen months of operations under war conditions"). But military seizure of oil and raw materials in Southeast Asia "would almost certainly precipitate war with the United

States."[64] Largely because of such factors—"the most important was fuel"—Japanese naval officers in 1941 agreed with a "Jingo" at that time that their nation was "headed for sure ruin" and, therefore, that "this is the one supreme moment. Now or never! Japan is at the crossroads."[65]

One American force—the U.S. Navy Pacific Fleet—was, in Yamamoto's words, a "dagger being pointed at our throat."[66] Formerly based on the west coast, those ships were sent to Hawaii in May 1940 as a "putative deterrent to Japanese aggression against British or Dutch possessions in Southeast Asia."[67] In ordering that fleet in being to Hawaii, President Franklin Roosevelt reflected his own Mahanism, for, in the words of John Toland, "ever since his school days at Groton, Roosevelt had been convinced of Japan's long-range plans of conquest. He pored over Admiral Mahan's *Influence of Sea Power upon History* until, according to his mother, he had 'practically memorized the book.' Later he corresponded with Mahan and learned that the admiral shared with him a strong concern over Japan as a major threat in the Pacific."[68] As assistant secretary of the navy in 1913, for example, Franklin Roosevelt was corresponding with his cousin Theodore Roosevelt about naval matters. Although Theodore did not believe it likely that war with Japan actually would come as a result of disagreements over immigration, "it may come, and if it does it will come suddenly"; and thus the former president warned his younger cousin about why the American fleet must not be separated: "Russia's fate ought to be a warning for all time as the criminal folly of dividing the fleet if there is even the remotest chance of war."[69] Sensing the uneasiness of Americans on the West Coast about a war with Japan, FDR took it upon himself in 1914 to urge Mahan—whose statement would "carry more conviction than that of anybody else"—to write an article for the *North American Review* which demonstrated, for the "average 'man in the street,'" the importance of keeping American battleships together in one concentrated force rather than in diverse places as detached units.[70] In a personal letter to FDR some weeks later, with prescient overtones about later naval decisions with respect to Japan, Mahan re-echoed his own and FDR's belief in the importance of concentrating the main fleet because "I feel that our danger in the Pacific much exceeds that in the Atlantic."[71] Indeed, years later, when he was president himself, "F.D.R.'s Mahanism" caused consternation to an historian such as Charles A. Beard, who took issue with such an outlook toward world affairs.[72] Relocation of that concentrated fleet of warships to Pearl Harbor and their subsequent maneuvers were regarded in Tokyo as a "brandishing of the big sword" (the "sword" metaphor from the Japanese naval academy at Etajima) calling forth "vigorous protests," for those ninety-six vessels—including eight battle-ships—constituted a "fleet in being" which "created a *strategical* situation incomparably more tense and threatening to the Japanese than had existed when it was based on the Pacific coast."[73] And as Japanese naval personnel sensed the importance to Americans of a concentrated fleet of battleships, their imperative to destroy or cripple that source of naval power became all the more logical to senior officers in the Imperial Navy. An attack on Pearl Harbor, once only a possibility in Japanese planning, became a probability.

Japanese naval officers long had thought about war with the United States. As early as 1907, such planning was underway because of tensions over American discrimination against Japanese immigrants. The world cruise of Theodore Roosevelt's "great white fleet" had impressed the Japanese again with American battleships (see chapter 4 above). So the early plan of the Japanese Imperial Navy was to seize Guam and the Philippines; battleships sent to recover United States possessions then would be intercepted near Japan and destroyed in decisive battle. For thirty years, the Japanese "long-cherished" naval posture was a "conservative," *defensive* one of "calmly remaining in waiting" in "seas adjacent to Japan" for "its sole imaginary enemy," the United States Navy.[74] In 1936, however, a Japanese Naval War College officer, Captain Kameto Kuroshima, produced an *offensive* view of "Strategy and Tactics in Operations Against the United States," the surprise attack on Pearl Harbor.[75] At the Japanese Naval Academy, cadets soon learned about "sudden attack" against "the United States fleet, the strongest in the world."[76]

By 7 January 1941, events—and the factor of time as related to dwindling oil reserves—led Admiral Yamamoto as Combined Fleet Commander to write to Navy Minister Admiral Koshiro Oikawa that "a conflict with the U.S. and Great Britain is inevitable." The Japanese Navy, he said, should therefore "fiercely attack and destroy the U.S. main fleet at the outset of the war, so that the morale of the U.S. Navy and her people goes down to such an extent that it could not be recovered." Furthermore, Yamamoto believed that "we should do our very best at the outset" to determine "the fate of the war on the very first day" with aircraft carriers launching a "surprise attack . . . on a moonlight night or at dawn" against Pearl Harbor.[77] In late January of that year, Yamamoto told Rear Admiral Takijiro Onishi that he was intent upon "smashing the morale of the American people by sinking as many battleships as possible," for "most Americans—like most Japanese—still believed battleships to be the mightiest weapons of war. The sinking of one or, better yet, a number of these giant vessels would be considered a most appalling thing, akin to a disaster of nature."[78] In October 1941, Yamamoto thus wrote to the new Navy Minister, Vice Admiral Shigetaro Shimada: "after much study, therefore, I have come to the opinion that the only way is to have a powerful air force strike deep at the enemy's heart at the very beginning of the war and thus deal a blow, material and moral, from which it will not be able to recover for some time."[79] That likely negative effect on American morale was shared by Admiral Kusaka who agreed that "to give a fatal blow to the enemy's main strength at the outset of the war could raise the morale of the whole friendly forces, while on the other hand [be] extremely discouraging to the morale of the enemy."[80]

The Japanese Navy was astute in its assessment of how the morale of Western nations might suffer if their battleships were sunk. Consider the British view both before and after the raid on Pearl Harbor, which demonstrated the vulnerability of battleships to attack from the air— whether from aircraft carriers off Oahu or from land-based planes such as those which readily sank the *Repulse* and the *Prince of Wales* off the coast of Malaya on 10 December 1941. Winston Churchill had ordered those ships to the Far East in August 1941, based on his assessment of how the only remaining German battleship, the *Tirpitz*, caused the Royal Navy to be so endlessly preoccupied with its potential threat as to have fifteen battleships and cruisers available just to counter that powerful capital ship. Churchill had believed the *Repulse* and the *Prince of Wales* similarly would constitute "a small but very powerful and fast force in Eastern waters" exerting the same restraining effect on Japan as did the *Tirpitz*, a vessel that "exercises a vague, general fear and menaces all points at once. It appears, and disappears, causing immediate reactions and perturbations on the other side." Perceiving that a battleship "might indeed be a decisive deterrent," Churchill boasted to President Franklin Roosevelt that "there is nothing like having something that can catch and kill anything." After those two ships had been sunk so easily, Churchill admitted that "in all the war I never received a more direct shock."[81] In turn, that effect upon morale influenced a subsequent naval decision in the summer of 1942 during planning for the British amphibious landing on the coast of France for the raid at Dieppe. Reflecting the prevailing view in the government that "the greatest danger faced by Britain was not the loss of any particular area but rather that 'the number of . . . capital ships may gradually be whittled away until their present margin of superiority disappears,'" the conclusion was that "in the narrow waters of the Mediterranean, as in those of the Channel . . . the operations of capital ships are proving dangerous and costly both in casualties and damages." Therefore, no battleships were used to support what turned out to be the disaster at Dieppe. As Admiral Sir Dudley Pound then explained that decision, "a capital ship in the Channel, you must be joking," for the loss of a battleship would have a grave effect on "morale."[82] So in Japan, Mahanism—favoring bold, offensive applications of sea power against battleships—complemented traditional doctrine from Saneyuki, which advocated striking a decisive blow at the enemy's morale. And together, the two viewpoints began to modify a conservative, defensive naval posture toward the United States.

Japanese naval planners chose Pearl Harbor as the location of such an attack not only because of the concentration of American battleships there but also because of the likelihood that the raid would be a surprise. Being close readers and students of Mahan, the Japanese might know that the American naval historian himself deemed an attack there as unlikely. He had been asked to react to the U.S. Naval War College Strategic War Plan of 1911, which assumed a naval war in the Pacific between Japan (Orange) and the United States (Blue) as "a theoretical problem that would dominate the U.S. Navy's strategic thinking and planning in the Pacific until the Imperial Japanese Navy attacked Pearl Harbor and the Philippines in December 1941." Mahan's evaluation, made when he was lecturing at that War College, was that the island of Guam "was the key to the Pacific interests of the United States." And he even ventured a statement to the editor of *Century Magazine* about the likelihood of a Japanese strike on Pearl Harbor: "If the Navy be there in force, the attack will not be made."[83] Even after 7 December 1941, the American commander then at Hawaii, Admiral Kimmel, proclaimed before a U.S. Naval Court of Inquiry his belief that "it was much more probable that the Japs would attempt a raid on Pearl Harbor if the Fleet were away than if it were there."[84] Just as Saneyuki could enhance his credibility by adding a personal interpretation to Mahan's writings, so too could subsequent Japanese planners perhaps take pride in being able to use Mahan's predictions about Pearl Harbor as an unlikely target to their advantage in helping achieve surprise.

III

In February 1941, an air officer on the carrier *Kaga* was ordered to develop an operational concept for an attack on Pearl Harbor. As "one of the most brilliant 'Young Turks' of naval aviation in Japan," Commander Minoru Genda completed his assignment quickly; and while differing from Yamamoto in that the main objective was the two aircraft carriers at Hawaii rather than battleships, Genda saw the raid as "difficult but not impossible."[85] From the outset, Genda understood he was to devise an operational plan that would deal a "crushing blow to the main force of the American Fleet in Hawaiian waters." And although he believed firmly that American aircraft carriers should be "selected as primary targets," Genda's operational plan was predicated upon orders for "use of sufficient force to put the main force of the American Fleet out of action for at least six months at one blow."[86] Understanding that the Imperial Japanese Navy "adhered to having the main target as battleships," Genda argued forcefully but unsuccessfully to have "the aircraft carriers as the main target"; he concluded in retrospect that "at this time the leaders of both Japan and America, the greater part of the navy personnel and the people as a whole had overestimated the power of the battleships because most of their thinking was just wishful thinking."[87] Nevertheless, "if Yamamoto was the father of the Pearl Harbor plan," Genda was a "spiritual and intellectual mother, coaxing it to life, nourishing it from the well springs of his own heart and mind, defending it against all comers."[88] As of April, however, some members of the Naval General Staff felt that "Hawaii Operation" planning should be abandoned, but Yamamoto's staff of "very loyal" and "powerful supporters" now included Captain Kameto Kuroshima, who authored that pivotal 1936 Naval War College paper.[89]

Yamamoto's forceful personality and his planners' loyalty resembled "groupthink," wherein "members use their collective resources to develop rationalizations supporting shared illusions about the invulnerability of their organization or nation." Along with their willingness to take extreme risks and collective discounting of warnings to reconsider assumptions, such groups often achieve conformity by stifling counterarguments and adverse information that might undermine faith in their decision.[90] When the Imperial General Headquarters did not give serious consideration at first to the idea of a Pearl Harbor raid, Yamamoto—whose "position and influence in the Japanese Navy were unique"—threatened "to resign from his post if his plan was not accepted."[91] Illusions about invulnerability were evident in the planners' table-top war games (as practiced at the U.S. Naval War College and introduced to Japan by Saneyuki).[92] During September 1941, Yamamoto stood "over the table" and "dominated" exercises in which one team executed his plan "as faithfully as possible" and another team simulated various American responses. When attackers suffered heavy losses, games were replayed with new dice, or umpires decreed the Japanese fleet "was divinely aided by a squall just in time to permit it to leave the Pearl Harbor area without serious damage." In post-war interviews, participants characterized their procedures as "unrealistic" and "self-indulgent thinking" wherein umpires would "slant their decisions" to favor the attackers.[93]

Despite the planners' conformity and illusions of invulnerability, however, Japan wavered. By October 1941, torpedoes still were not perfected for shallow waters of Pearl Harbor (when dropped from aircraft, they nosed down too sharply and hit bottom); practice bombing results still left doubts in planners' minds; and Admiral Nagumo, who would command at sea, remained unconvinced about the attack.[94] Even at sea on the way to Pearl Harbor, Nagumo admitted to his chief of staff, Admiral Kusaka, "I now think that I have accepted too big a task. It seems to me that I had better have refused it, having taken a stronger attitude."[95] Serious reservations about feasibility of the attack also were held initially by Commander Mitsuo Fuchida, who would lead aircraft over Pearl Harbor.[96] Air crews stepped up training and increased their proficiency, however; and after the Yokosuka Air Group experimented with torpedoes to which a special stabilizing fin had been added, the Mitsubishi firm quickly adapted its Mark 11 torpedoes and delivered a sufficient quantity to the striking force in time for their departure.[97] As of 18 October, though, some Navy General Staff members remained reluctant to launch the raid. Admiral Shigeru Fukudome recalled in 1950, "we in Tokyo were against the Pearl Harbor plan." Nevertheless, because of Yamamoto's threatened resignation if his plan was not accepted, the Navy General Staff acquiesced on 21 October, with Chief of Staff Admiral Nagano saying, "If he has that much confidence, it's better to let Yamamoto go ahead."[98] But the Naval General Staff still was not ready to endorse the plan forward for Imperial sanction!

Japan could not attack Pearl Harbor because Yamamoto threatened resignation. In the psychology of groups, even those characterized by "groupthink," decisions often require "bolstering" before final implementation. "*Bolstering* is an umbrella term that includes a number of different psychological tactics that contribute to creating and maintaining the decision maker's image of a successful outcome with high gains and tolerable losses"; and when decisions must be made under "strong deadline pressures along with little or no opportunity to shift responsibility," the "classic pattern of *selective exposure* becomes dominant, marked by active search and preference for supportive information and avoidance of discrepant information."[99] That "supportive information" was obtained promptly on 23 October 1941 when Lieutenant Commander Takeshi Naito lectured to Yamamoto's planning staff, which now included Fuchida. In 1940, Naito was assistant naval attaché in Berlin when British carrier aircraft launched a torpedo raid against the Italian fleet in Taranto Harbor. The Germans flew him to Taranto to appraise the damage. Back in Japan, Naito reported his direct observations to the planners, and Fuchida as a good friend "interrogated him extensively all the next day."[100] To bolster a decision in the face of "strong deadline pressures," Naito's news was superb.

On the evening of 11 November 1940, the British aircraft carrier HMS *Illustrious* was 170 miles from Taranto where the Italian Navy had moored six battleships and three of its cruisers. The Royal Navy Fleet Air Arm launched twenty-one aircraft, eleven of which carried torpedoes (the others carried bombs and flares to light targets and help pilots avoid barrage balloons and their steel cables). The first planes attacked at 10:56 P.M.; within sixty-five minutes, the last planes turned back to their aircraft carrier. Two battleships were so heavily damaged they were beached; another battleship and two cruisers were severely damaged; two destroyers were damaged and two auxiliary vessels sunk. Losing only two aircraft, the *Illustrious* escaped unscathed. Italy withdrew remaining major warships to safer harbors from which they never again conducted offensive operations. Just as Japanese supplies could flow unmolested to the Asian mainland after Tsushima, British convoys to Malta, Egypt, the Suez Canal, and India and beyond were no longer interdicted by an Italian "fleet in being." British naval prowess lavishly praised by Mahan again attained decisive victory, this time with aircraft carrier operations which Japan began imitating shortly after World War I.[101] But the Fleet Air Arm used twenty-one Fairey Swordfish aircraft—fabric-covered, open-cockpit biplanes, affectionately known as "Stringbags," with a top speed of 138 miles per hour.[102] If the Royal Navy accomplished so much at Taranto with an insignificant number of paltry, obsolescent biplanes, Japan should attain more by surprise on a Sunday morning, against Pearl Harbor at peace, with six aircraft carriers and three hundred and fifty-three clearly superior aircraft.

From March 1939 to September 1940, Genda had been assistant naval attaché in London, so he derived his only knowledge of Taranto later from reading British censor-cleared releases, but the profound "lessons I learned" about successful applications of air power in the "European War" undoubtedly influenced his thinking.[103] In late October 1941, Naito's eyewitness report about the British naval success was more pertinent as the Japanese Naval General Staff moved closer to its final decision, which was not reached until 5 November 1941. Indeed, the actual decision for war which approved the raid was not made by an Imperial Conference with the emperor until the afternoon of 1 December, when the task force already was on its way to Hawaiian waters (the armada could have been recalled, however, in the unlikely event that diplomatic overtures to the United States were successful).[104] Saneyuki's earlier eyewitness analyses stood the test of time and contributed to a "self-conception" of Japanese naval prowess. For Japanese planners making the final decision about Pearl Harbor, though, Naito's eyewitness report about a corroborative event was an important addition to interact with other input, including orthodox attitudes about Mahan's "fleet in being"—particularly when Yamamoto's plan was so pragmatic and limited in its ultimate goals.

Despite bravado about deciding "the fate of the war on the very first day," Yamamoto really hoped the Pearl Harbor strike would gain for Japan six months. As a man who would avoid war with America if possible, he did not anticipate landing troops in California, fighting across a continent, and capturing Washington, D.C. Having served tours of naval duty in the United States during the 1920s, Yamamoto "had seen for himself how far American resources outstripped those of Japan, and understood clearly that if a war should ever come—and if it should be prolonged—Japan would have no prospect of ultimate victory." Moreover, "if war could not be avoided then, as he saw it, his next best duty was to do his best to ensure that Japan entered the conflict on the best possible terms. That meant the prompt destruction of America's Pacific Fleet; and the example of how such an object could be achieved was offered on 11 November 1940 by the successful British attack, using aerial torpedoes, against the Italian fleet as it lay at anchor in Taranto harbour."[105] After all, Yamamoto's primary goals were (1) protecting the drive south for desperately needed oil and other raw materials and (2) securing sea lanes by which these resources came home. By destroying or crippling the U.S. Navy "fleet in being" which was threatening those operations with offensive attacks, and taking away its forward base in Manila Bay (won by Dewey's "fleet in being" in six and one-half hours, including a break for breakfast), Japan would obtain time to seize and strengthen forward island bases behind which its new empire would be secure until a rebuilt fleet advanced to the "Great All-Out" naval engagement far in the western Pacific. Thus in January 1941, as he wrote letters to several naval officer peers as well as government officials, Yamamoto saw the Pearl Harbor attack specifically as gaining "approximately six months" and thereby assuring success for the Japanese primary objectives, those "southern operations" to secure oil and thereby "determine the nations's rise or fall."[106] Accordingly, Genda prepared his operational plan to achieve "six months." And thus to Premier Konoye, Yamamoto boasted that "in the first six months to a year of war against the U.S. and England I will run wild, and I will show you an uninterrupted succession of victories."[107] For as Mahan the opinion leader authoritatively proclaimed in *Lessons of the War with Spain*, America "had not a battleship in the home ports that could in six months be made ready to replace one lost or seriously disabled."

A "fleet in being" was the primary target at Pearl Harbor. Air crews training for their mission familiarized themselves with models of ships they would attack, and a full size replica of a U.S. battleship was built and bombed as part of that training.[108] As Gordon W. Prange attests, "the Japanese were after the U.S. Pacific Fleet and Oahu's air power— not the military installations, the tank farms, the dry docks, the machine shops, or the submarine base" (and the attack to suppress American air power in Hawaii was only to insure success of the raid upon warships). On 23 November, Admiral Nagumo convened task-force ship commanders and finally announced "our mission is to attack Pearl Harbor." Having solved the problem with their torpedoes, the raiders departed on 26 November. On the way, Fuchida's airmen "drilled incessantly" on recognizing the ships that were their only designated targets as individual units in the air over Pearl Harbor, for Yamamoto's direct order was to "operate in such a manner as to destroy the U.S. Fleet at the outset of the war."[109] Indeed, the direct "Carrier Striking Force Operations Order" issued on 23 November 1941 specified that "the order of targets will be battleships and then aircraft carriers."[110] So in their focus on bombing battleships first, a strategic goal dominated Japanese naval planning. But tactics deserve consideration, too. For "a word which perhaps better than any other indicates the dividing line between tactics and strategy," Mahan recommended "con*tact*."[111] Once the attackers made contact in the air over Pearl Harbor, decision-making shifted from Yamamoto in Tokyo to Nagumo on his flagship *Akagi* about 200 miles north of Oahu.

In under two hours, "Battleship Row" in Pearl Harbor became a disaster scene for America. The *Arizona* and the *Oklahoma* were totally lost (as well as the target ship *Utah* and two destroyers); the *West Virginia*, the *California*, and the *Nevada* were sunk or beached (but salvageable); the *Tennessee*, the *Maryland*, and the *Pennsylvania* were damaged (as well as three cruisers and a destroyer). American air power in Hawaii was shattered: 188 army and navy planes were destroyed, and 159 were damaged. Japan lost 29 planes and their 64 crewmen (74 other planes suffered some damage).[112] In Tokyo, as reports of results came in, the Naval General Staff became "wild with joy" as the attack "greatly exceeded its most optimistic expectations."[113] In a message thereupon to the task force, the emperor announced that the raid "rejoiced me very much" (although the success of the attack also was attributed in part to "providential help").[114] After his pilots returned to aircraft carriers, also "wild with joy," Fuchida landed and hurried to the bridge to make that report to Admiral Nagumo, "four battleships sunk" and "four battleships damaged." And as recounted earlier, the task-force commander interrupted with the question uppermost in his mind: "Do you think that the U.S. Fleet could come out from Pearl Harbor within six months?" After replying that "The main force of the U.S. Pacific Fleet will not be able to come out within six months," Fuchida made an immediate, urgent plea for a second strike against "dockyards, the fuel tanks, and an occasional ship." But his effort was futile. Nagumo's mind was made up: "We may then conclude that anticipated results have been achieved."[115] The lessons of history were forceful.

A second strike was well within Nagumo's capability, however. Despite higher seas, his returning aircraft landed without incident, and over 200 of those planes could have been refueled, rearmed, and launched again for a second strike. Fuchida's plea for the return raid also was endorsed by Lieutenant Jinichi Goto (commanding the *Akagi*'s torpedo planes), Lieutenant Saburo Shindo (commanding fighter aircraft), and

Genda (who wanted to find and destroy the American aircraft carriers *Lexington* and *Enterprise,* which had not been in the harbor that morning). For these Japanese pilots, Pearl Harbor was "the chance of a lifetime." After weighing alternatives, including possibilities that Japanese submarines also sent to Hawaii would sink the American carriers, Nagumo—in total command once "con*tact*" was made—ordered "Preparations for attack canceled." Upon seeing the *Akagi* signal flags sending the armada homeward, Fuchida rushed once more to the bridge and protested, "why are we not attacking again?" Before Nagumo could speak, his chief of staff, Rear Admiral Ryunosuke Kusaka, replied, "The objective of the Pearl Harbor operation has been achieved." Fuchida saluted, turned on his heel, and stalked out "a bitter and angry man."[116]

Nagumo's decision partly reflected Kusaka's stated concerns then that the Japanese strike force might suffer "heavier losses if a secondary attack was carried out." After all, reluctance to launch a second attack might be attributed in part to Nagumo's uncertainty about whether or not American land-based air power on Hawaii was shattered (it was) and his fear of counterattack (unlikely, or without appreciable effect if attempted).[117] He also held some apprehensions about American aircraft carriers not in Pearl Harbor that morning but whose location was unknown, yet Nagumo need not have worried about counterattack from them either. Japanese Zeros were superior to Grumman F4F Wildcat fighters and to any American naval aircraft then, the latter's slower speeds not yet counterbalanced by perfected flyer tactics. The U.S. Navy torpedo bomber, the Douglas TBD-1 Devastator, was inadequate as a frontline aircraft (at Midway, *all* of Torpedo Squadron 8 was destroyed by Zeros or antiaircraft fire before achieving a single hit). Japanese pilots then were "among the best in the world," many with years of combat experience in China.[118] Moreover, aviators from *Lexington* and *Enterprise* likely could not have found Japanese ships because they believed the raid was launched from *south* of Oahu rather than the north from which the raiders came.[119] But Nagumo could not capitalize upon the position of tactical strength from which he operated to alter a strategic goal.

As a commander who from the outset "had not had much confidence in the success of the Pearl Harbor plan," Nagumo "led the attack timidly" and his more prudent decision well might be a course of "retreating as quickly as possible to an area outside the range of US aircraft." And as Fuchida himself dispassionately described his superior's personality in retrospect, "Nagumo's leadership as a commander was extremely conservative and he would never take the initiative. In the end he would always agree with the Staff Officer's opinion and just give a short 'I see . . . very well' when taking decisions. The credentials of a commander are the ability to foresee the development of a battle and calculate accordingly. These qualities were lacking in Commander-in-Chief Nagumo." As superiors in the Tokyo naval headquarters soon recognized the "incompleteness of the attack," Nagumo received a more scathing characterization from Admiral Matome Ugaki, Chief Staff Officer of the Combined Fleet: "He was like a robber fleeing the scene, happy with small booty."[120] But the significant factor affecting Nagumo's *tactical* decision also was his commitment to a *strategic* goal. As a doctrinaire, Nagumo from the outset had been insistent: "One attack only! One attack only!"[121] Even on 27 November, as the strike force was at sea on the way to Pearl Harbor, Nagumo on the bridge of the *Akagi* whispered his reservations about the attack to Kusaka: "Chief Staff Officer . . . What do you think? Do you think I should have been a little more forceful [in opposing the raid]? . . . Well, we're on our way now but do you think we will be able to pull it off?" Kusaka was "shocked" to hear such remaining indecision from his commander.[122] But Kusaka himself originally deemed the Pearl Harbor raid "too risky an operation," and the mission seemed to him to be a last resort measure whereby "a long-trained sword was swung down under minute planning after making up our mind to swing it once and for all" (again, the Samurai sword metaphor from the Japanese naval academy at Etajima).[123] Nagumo also considered aborting the raid as late as 6 December when intelligence from the Japanese consul in Hawaii (relayed though Tokyo) reported the American aircraft carriers absent from Pearl Harbor. But Admiral Kusaka argued, "We can't do anything about carriers that are not there. I think we should attack Pearl Harbor tomorrow."[124] As Admiral William Furlong concluded in 1962, "Nagumo followed classic naval doctrine in staying within the established boundaries of his task and refusing to be tempted into alluring side paths," and although "that mission may have been wrong," the tactical commander "stuck with it."[125] He gained "six months" by destroying battleships, the core of a "fleet in being." Mahanism could not have been served better, particularly when Nagumo's "fleet in being" remained intact for subsequent "decisive" engagements and that statutory "Great All-Out Battle."

Admiral Nagumo would have had no substantive reason to entertain second thoughts about his decision to disregard combined pleas of

Fuchida, Goto, Shindo, and Genda. Their interchange on the bridge of the *Akagi* conforms closely to an observation of General Douglas MacArthur about such deliberations and their subsequent decisions for battle. During darker days of the Korean War, MacArthur's proposal for an audacious amphibious landing by Marines at Inchon was received with grave doubts and consternation by the Joint Chiefs of Staff in Washington, and General Lawton Collins and Admiral Forrest Sherman flew out to Tokyo in late August 1950 to confront MacArthur in a briefing session and persuade him to another course of action. After hearing all the reasons why Inchon was unsuitable for a landing, and before articulating his own views eloquently, MacArthur to himself heard "my father's voice telling me as he had so many years ago, 'Doug, councils of war breed timidity and defeatism.'"[126] With an oratorical tour de force then in 1950, MacArthur overcame the doubts of the Joint Chiefs of Staff, and the Inchon landing took place with substantial implications for the remaining course of the war.[127] In December 1941, however, no appeals could alter Nagumo's timidity and conservatism, for his natural inclinations were bolstered by the weight of history as he knew it: the Japanese naval victory at Tsushima (a classic engagement between battleships) had favorably determined the course of the Russo-Japanese war; the more recent successful British aircraft carrier strike against capital ships anchored at Taranto had knocked Italy out of the naval war in the Mediterranean Sea. And in his *Lessons of the War with Spain,* the foremost naval historian in the world, Alfred Thayer Mahan, proved the importance of battleships to the triumph of America at sea in 1898 (also witnessed firsthand by Saneyuki) and potentially the world thereafter. All these factors conjoined to instill in Japanese planners unshakable faith in history, one whereby the past was but prologue to naval aspirations of Japan in the Second World War.

The second strike proposed by Fuchida and the other air commanders would have altered the course of the war, however. In retrospect, Admiral Chester Nimitz "knew what a close thing Pearl Harbor had been" because the Japanese did not "complete the job" and destroy "the oil supply," thereby creating a shortage which "would have prolonged the war another two years." Admiral Raymond Spruance agreed that "the Japanese could have done much more damage. . . . So long as anything was left, they had not completed the job."[128] Amid the immediate disaster scene, even Admiral Kimmel saw "some positive aspects to his situation. His precious oil tanks had escaped destruction; so had his machine shops, his 'Navy behind the Navy.'" Indeed, he fully expected another strike against shipyards and docks still "relatively undamaged, and above all, the tank farms," for "if they had destroyed the oil which was all above ground at that time . . . it would have forced the withdrawal of the fleet to the coast because there wasn't any oil anywhere else out there to keep the fleet operating."[129] As Japanese naval historians themselves later concluded, Nagumo's

> error was that the attack concentrated almost exclusively on ships, especially battleships, and left facilities such as oil dumps and factories unscathed. This mistake was not made by him alone. The strategic concept of the entire Japanese navy up to the opening of the Pacific War was based on the idea that naval conflicts were won by fleets, and that big ships and big guns were the key to victory. However, as a result of leaving the manufacturing facilities, which could provide the capability to rebuild strength, unscathed, almost all of the ships left on the bottom of Pearl Harbor after the attack were later refloated and were able to take part in the fighting from the middle stages of the war.[130]

As a planner less beholden to the lessons of history, Genda had foreseen this exact outcome: "because the depth of the harbor was such that even if a bomb would make a leakage and sink the ship, the Americans could repair that hole completely and have the ship read for action with their large repairing equipment. . . . For this reason, we could not expect too great a success in the attack."[131] Still another, younger Japanese officer perceived that at Pearl Harbor, "serious damages could not be inflicted by bombing" of American battleships because "even though they were damaged, they would be repaired by use of the Navy Yard."[132] Because of inflexible adherence of the elder Japanese officers to their perception of Mahanism, however, the American naval war in the Pacific would not be fought from the West Coast.[133]

But Mahan did identify shore installations as contributing to sea power. While discussing "the making and repairing of naval material," *The Influence of Sea Power upon History* had lauded that "staying power, or reserve force, which is even greater than appears on the surface"— the rear echelon (if you will) capability to service, supply, and repair warships. The topic was treated, though, under "Number of Population," and the importance of destroying an enemy's dockyards was buried in commentary about "Character of Government."[134] Thus, clues to the importance of tactical targets were subordinated to strategic concepts. As a reader had suggested to Mahan in 1892, "it seemed to me that there loomed up through the account of various naval engagements a vague suggestion of a right way and a wrong way to do the thing and I wondered whether anyone is looking up the question of tactics," and for that specific advice from the world's authority on sea power, people needed "careful" reading, even "two or three" times to find "anything that suggests itself," exercising "patience and comprehensiveness" coupled with "time and iteration" to find "true meaning" for tactical consideration.[135] Recalling how "the histories of the American and European wars formed one of the curricula of the Naval College," a Japanese analyst made this characterization of senior officers in the Imperial Navy: "In the study of the two navies of both Britain and America alike, they have limited their attention to naval tactics in the narrow, limited sense."[136] Ignoring finer points of Mahan's writing about shore installations had ironic implications for the Japanese in World War II.

To many naval historians, the turning point of the war in the Pacific against Japan was the battle of Midway on 4 June 1942. Here the tide was turned, and Japan thereafter was on the defensive. Having broken the Japanese operational naval code, JN-25, a U.S. Naval Intelligence unit at Pearl Harbor, under Lieutenant Commander Joseph Rochefort, ascertained beforehand that Japan was attacking Midway Island with an armada of 8 aircraft carriers, 11 battleships, 20 cruisers, 60 destroyers, and nearly 50 auxiliary ships and transports carrying 5,000 troops. Knowing where those Japanese forces would be concentrated for an assault, American naval forces were waiting. And superior naval intelligence more than compensated for the small size of the U.S. Navy's force: 3 aircraft carriers, 8 cruisers, 14 destroyers, and no battleships. As that epic sea battle evolved (in which opposing ships themselves never were in sight of one another), a pivotal factor was the presence of the third American aircraft carrier. During the first week of May 1942, a Japanese naval force had attempted to occupy Port Moresby on the southeastern tip of New Guinea, thereby threatening to cut off Australia. A U.S. Navy task force with the aircraft carriers *Lexington* and *Yorktown* (with the *Hornet* and the *Enterprise* in reserve) attacked the Japanese armada in the Coral Sea on 4 May (the first major sea battle in which opposing ships never saw one another). American pilots from aircraft carriers sank the Japanese carrier *Shoho* and damaged the carriers *Shokaku* and *Zaikaku* so badly that they were out of action for refitting during the battle of Midway. The Japanese were thwarted in their attempt to take Port Moresby. The *Lexington* was sunk by Japanese pilots, and the *Yorktown* was so badly damaged that it returned to Pearl Harbor on 27 May trailing a ten-mile oil slick. The *Yorktown* commanding officer estimated that repairs to restore the ship to fighting capabilities would take ninety days. Forewarned of the attack on Midway, the American trap for the Japanese required that the *Yorktown* be ready to join the *Hornet* and the *Enterprise* quickly, nearly a thousand miles away at Midway. Admiral Nimitz ordered the *Yorktown* repaired and out to sea in seventy-two hours! After round-the-clock work—at ship repair facilities undamaged during the attack on Pearl Harbor—the *Yorktown* left harbor on 30 May to join the rest of the American task force at Midway and add immeasurably to a decisive battle in which the Japanese lost 4 aircraft carriers (including the *Akagi*), a cruiser, 322 planes, and 100 irreplaceable first-line pilots.[137] The Japanese Navy thereafter was never a genuine offensive force in the Pacific—in part because the *Yorktown* was repaired so quickly at Pearl Harbor after the battle of the Coral Sea. If ship repair facilities at Pearl Harbor had been destroyed in a second strike by Fuchida's planes, war in the Pacific would have been substantially different. But coinciding with Yamamoto's objectives for the attack, Admiral Nagumo's major goals were the battleships and Mahan's "six months."

Pearl Harbor served Japanese strategy. In addition to providing the time deemed essential for success of the "southern operations," the attack rendered irrelevant the naval treaties which had caused Japan to suffer a "neurosis." By destroying an American "fleet in being," the Japanese navy was no longer "outgunned" by battleships in the Pacific, and Yamamoto believed the "balance of power" was tipped "in our favor."[138] That orthodox view was shaped in part by Mahan's historical narrative. For final decisions about and at Pearl Harbor, however, that discourse was influential because it told "stories that do not negate the self-conceptions people hold of themselves." In the final analysis, much of discourse read as history often is measured against what readers "know" already from other "stories," whether as narrative discourse or historical events remembered as "facts." When discourse accepted as "history" is consonant with those other stories, its narrative fidelity is persuasive. Mahan corroborated the Japanese venerated victory over Russia at Tsushima and in turn was corroborated by the pivotal "bolstering" event of the British Fleet Air Arm triumph at Taranto. Within a narrative paradigm, that interaction between events and discourse could be rhetorically potent, particularly to people oriented toward lessons of history as guidelines for future actions. In the predawn of 7 December 1941, as the *Akagi* turned into the wind to launch aircraft, an unique flag flew from its mast: Admiral Togo's "Z" banner from Tsushima.[139] In attacking Pearl Harbor, the Imperial Japanese Navy demonstrated irrevocable faith in the lessons of history. What Japanese naval planners knew as history, however, evolved from interaction between their experiences as a nation and an American admiral's discourse. Because Mahan's narrative of sea power achieved credibility from actual events, his rhetoric about the past guided the future of Japan, briefly but momentously. And the magic of Mahan's "six months" remained evident to Japan as its own formidable "fleet in being" roamed with impunity from Pearl Harbor on 7 December 1941 until the decisive naval victory of America at Midway on 4 June 1942, as history repeated itself for Japan—for a while.

Notes

1. Ryunosuke Kusaka, *"Rengo Kantai* (Combined Fleet), Extracts," in *The Pearl Harbor Papers: Inside the Japanese Plans,* ed. Donald M. Goldstein and Katherine V. Dillon (Washington, D.C.: Brassey's, 1993), 161.

2. Quotations from the Fuchida-Nagumo interchange are from Fuchida's recollections during an interview in 1963, published in Gordon W. Prange, *At Dawn We Slept: The Untold Story of Pearl Harbor* (New York: McGraw-Hill, 1981), 541–43. In Fuchida's published account of the attack for the U.S. Naval Institute, "Six Months," is not included as part of the dialogue with Admiral Nagumo; however, Nagumo is quoted as having said after hearing the report of the number of battleships sunk, "We may then conclude that anticipated results have been achieved." See Mitsuo Fuchida, "The Attack on Pearl Harbor," in *The Japanese Navy in World War Two: An Anthology of Articles by Former Officers of the Imperial Japanese Navy and Air Defense Force* (Annapolis: United States Naval Institute, 1971), 27.

3. Robert Seager II, *Alfred Thayer Mahan: The Man and His Letters* (Annapolis: Naval Institute Press, 1977), 215.

4. M. Minikami, Naval Commanding Staff Imperial Japanese Navy Dept., to Mahan, 15 July 1899; and the Secretary of the Oriental Association, Tokyo, to Mahan, 1 April 1897, in Box 3, ATM. See also W. D. Puleston, *Mahan* (New Haven: Yale University Press, 1939), 106–9; and William Livezey, *Mahan on Sea Power* (Norman: University of Oklahoma Press, 1947), 70.

5. Mahan to John M. Brown, 31 May 1897, in *Letters and Papers of Alfred*

Thayer Mahan, 3 vols., ed. Robert Seager II and Doris D. Maguire (Annapolis: Naval Institute Press, 1975), 2:511.

6. *The Standard* (London), 18 August 1894; cited in Seager, *Alfred Thayer Mahan*, 659, n. 30.

7. Goldstein and Dillon, eds., *The Pearl Harbor Papers*, 1.

8. Mahan to R. J. Tracewell, 9 March 1910, in *Letters and Papers* 3:331.

9. Ronald H. Spector, *Eagle against the Sun: The American War with Japan* (New York: Free Press, 1985), 33, 293. See also Prange, *At Dawn We Slept*, as well as his *Miracle at Midway* (New York: McGraw-Hill, 1982).

10. For another view of historians as "rhetorical agents," see E. Culpepper Clark, "Argument and Historical Analysis," in *Advances in Argumentation Theory and Research*, ed. J. Robert Cox and Charles A. Willard (Carbondale: University of Southern Illinois Press, 1982), 298–317.

11. Walter R. Fisher, "Narration as a Human Communication Paradigm: The Case of Public Moral Argument," *Communication Monographs* 51 (1984): 2, 6–8, 10, 15. For another view of rhetorical narration, see Thomas S. Frentz, *Mass Media as Rhetorical Narration*, Van Zelst Lecture in Communication, Northwestern University (Evanston: Northwestern University, 1985), 6–7.

12. See Jerome Kagan, "The Concept of Identification," *Psychological Review* 65 (1958): 304; and Walter Weiss, "Effects of the Mass Media of Communication," in *Handbook of Social Psychology*, 2d ed., ed. Gardner Lindzey and Elliot Aronson (Reading, Mass.: Addison-Wesley, 1969), 5:98–100.

13. See Kenneth Burke, *A Rhetoric of Motives* (New York: George Braziller, 1955), 19–23, 55–59.

14. Fisher, "Narration as a Human Communication Paradigm," 14.

15. Seager, *Alfred Thayer Mahan*, 211.

16. For other indices of the potency of Mahan's generalizations, see chapter 4 above.

17. See Theodore H. White, "The Danger from Japan," *New York Times Magazine*, 28 July 1985, 19ff.

18. For further discussion of Mahan's praise of British naval prowess, and of Lord Nelson specifically, see Julius W. Pratt, "Alfred Thayer Mahan," in *The Marcus W. Jernigan Essays in American Historiography*, ed. William T. Hutchinson (Chicago: University of Chicago Press, 1937), 221–22. See also chapter 4 above.

19. *Chicago Tribune*, 6 June 1891.

20. Samuel Eliot Morison, *The Rising Sun in the Pacific 1931–April 1942*, vol. 3 of *History of United States Naval Operations in World War II* (Boston: Little, Brown, 1948), 21. See also Denis Warner and Peggy Warner, *The Tide at Sunrise: A History of the Russo-Japanese War 1904–1905* (New York: Charterhouse, 1974), 184.

21. Stephen Howarth, "Admiral of the Fleet Isoroku Yamamoto," in *Men of War: Great Naval Leaders of World War II*, ed. Howarth (New York: St. Martin's Press, 1992), 111.

22. Minoru Genda, "Analysis No. 2 of the Pearl Harbor Attack," in *The Pearl*

Harbor Papers: Inside the Japanese Plans, ed. Donald M. Goldstein and Katherine V. Dillon (Washington, D.C.: Brassey's, 1993), 39.

23. Kusaka, *"Rengo Kantai* (Combined Fleet), Extracts," in *The Pearl Harbor Papers,* 155.

24. Sadao Chigusa, Rear Admiral (Ret.), Japanese Maritime Self-Defense Force, "Conquer the Pacific Ocean aboard Destroyer *Akigumo*: War Diary of the Hawaiian Battle"; and Gunichi Mikawa, "War Diary of the 3rd Battleship Division, 4–25 December 1941," in *The Pearl Harbor Papers: Inside the Japanese Plans,* ed. Donald M. Goldstein and Katherine V. Dillon (Washington, D.C.: Brassey's, 1993), 191, 254.

25. *Japan Times and Advertiser,* 27 May 1942; cited in Prange, *Miracle at Midway,* 88. Italics are mine.

26. See the detailed account of the sinkings in John Toland, *The Rising Sun: The Decline and Fall of the Japanese Empire 1936–1945* (New York: Random House, 1970), 238–43.

27. Alfred Thayer Mahan, *The Influence of Sea Power upon History 1660–1783* (New York: Hill and Wang, 1957), 11–18.

28. Alfred Thayer Mahan, *From Sail to Steam* (New York: Harper and Brothers, 1907), 277.

29. This discussion is draws from Warner and Warner, *The Tide at Sunrise*: on Tsushima, see 494–520; on "the first Pearl Harbor," see 3–20; on Togo and Mahan, see 513. The quotation from Togo, drawn from official documents, is on p. 520.

30. For discussion of the impact of the Japanese victory at Tsushima, see Eugene P. Trani, *The Treaty of Portsmouth: An Adventure in American Diplomacy* (Lexington: University of Kentucky Press, 1969), 46, 56, 110. Trani also found evidence that the Japanese sought advice from Admiral Mahan for the final terms of settlement in the Treaty of Portsmouth (see 92).

31. Prange, *Miracle at Midway,* 116; Spector, *Eagle against the Sun,* 511.

32. Masataka Chihaya, "An Intimate Look at the Japanese Navy," in *The Pearl Harbor Papers: Inside the Japanese Plans,* ed. Donald M. Goldstein and Katherine V. Dillon (Washington, D.C.: Brassey's, 1993), 372.

33. Howarth, "Admiral of the Fleet Isoroku Yamamoto," in *Men of War,* 120ff.

34. Kusaka *"Rengo Kantai* (Combined Fleet), Extracts," in *The Pearl Harbor Papers,* 156–57.

35. Howarth, "Admiral of the Fleet Isoroku Yamamoto," in *Men of War,* 121–22.

36. M. Minikami, Naval Commanding Staff, Imperial Japanese Navy Dept., to Mahan, 15 July 1899, in Box 3, ATM.

37. See reactions in the *Boston Evening Transcript,* 14 May 1890; *New York Daily Tribune,* 18 May 1890; *Louisville Courier Journal,* 24 May 1890; *San Francisco Chronicle,* 1 June 1890; *Chicago Daily Inter-Ocean,* 7 June 1890; *Literary World,* 5 July 1890; *Royal United Service Institution Journal* 34 (1890–1891): 1067; *London Times,* 23 October 1893; and *Le Journal* (Paris), 3 December 1914.

38. "Diary of Rear Adm. Giichi Nakahara, Extracts, 11 August 1941–1 January 1942," in *The Pearl Harbor Papers: Inside the Japanese Plans*, ed. Donald M. Goldstein and Katherine V. Dillon (Washington, D.C.: Brassey's, 1993), 75.

39. G. J. A. O'Toole, *The Spanish War: An American Epic—1898* (New York: W. W. Norton, 1984), 102–3, 136–37, 174–93. Dewey then held Manila under siege, not attacking the city itself and forcing its surrender until 13 August, the day after the peace protocol was signed by both countries.

40. See discussion of these concerns in Asada Sadao, "The Japanese Navy and the United States," in *Pearl Harbor as History: Japanese-American Relations 1931–1941*, ed. Dorothy Borg and Shumpei Okamoto (New York: Columbia University Press, 1973), 243–44; see 650–63 for an indication of the extensive primary sources used in this analysis. Naval presence in the Philippines still was deemed important to the United States as late as the 1990s, when the Philippines finally sought to abrogate treaty obligations for U.S. Naval bases there. See the *New York Times*, 23 February 1986, E1 and E3.

41. Chihaya, "An Intimate Look at the Japanese Navy," in *The Pearl Harbor Papers*, 329.

42. For an account of the battle of Santiago, see O'Toole, *The Spanish War*, 328–39. Saneyuki's role as observer also is noted in Spector, *Eagle against the Sun*, 43.

43. Mark R. Peattie, "Akiyama Saneyuki and the Emergence of Modern Japanese Naval Doctrine," *U.S. Naval Institute Proceedings* 103 (January 1977): 62–65.

44. Seager, *Alfred Thayer Mahan*, 472.

45. Mahan's chapter "Fleet in Being and Fortress Fleet: The Port Arthur Squadron in the Russo-Japanese War" is reprinted in *Mahan on Naval Warfare: Selections from the Writings of Rear Admiral Alfred T. Mahan*, ed. Allan Westcott (Boston: Little, Brown, 1920), 256–75.

46. See Peattie, "Akiyama Saneyuki and the Emergence of Modern Japanese Naval Doctrine," 69. Other mention of Saneyuki as a student of Mahan is made in Warner and Warner, *The Tide at Sunrise*, 500.

47. Seager, *Alfred Thayer Mahan*, xiii.

48. For this insight I am indebted to Michael Osborn, who suggests that by adding that personal perspective, Saneyuki made himself all the more influential in the Imperial Japanese Navy. See also my "Admiral Mahan, 'Narrative Fidelity,' and the Japanese Attack on Pearl Harbor," *Quarterly Journal of Speech* 72 (August 1986): 290–305.

49. Spector, *Eagle against the Sun*, 18–9.

50. O'Toole, *The Spanish War*, 194–95, 209, 223, 325.

51. Theodore Roosevelt to Mahan, 14 March 1898; cited in Richard W. Turk, *The Ambiguous Relationship: Theodore Roosevelt and Alfred Thayer Mahan* (New York: Greenwood Press, 1987), 122–23.

52. Alfred Thayer Mahan, *Lessons of the War with Spain* (New York: Little, Brown, 1899), 185. Italics are mine.

53. Mahan, *The Influence of Sea Power,* 39. Italics are mine.

54. Morison, *The Rising Sun in the Pacific,* 50.

55. For discussion of British efforts before Pearl Harbor to persuade Roosevelt to send American capital ships to help defend Singapore and other Far East possessions, see Correlli Barnett, *Engage the Enemy More Closely: The Royal Navy in the Second World War* (New York: W. W. Norton, 1991), 385–88.

56. See the discussion, based on Japanese naval documents, in Sadao, "The Japanese Navy and the United States," in *Pearl Harbor as History,* 240–43. See also Spector, *Eagle against the Sun,* 20–21, 39–40.

57. Sadao, "The Japanese Navy and the United States," in *Pearl Harbor as History,* 238–42; Spector, *Eagle against the Sun,* 47; and Prange, *Miracle at Midway,* 15.

58. Captain Hideo Hiraide, cited in *Japan Times and Advertiser,* 27 May 1942; in Prange, *Miracle at Midway,* 89.

59. See Richard B. Frank, *Guadalcanal: The Definitive Account of the Landmark Battle* (New York: Random House, 1990), 120–21.

60. See Raymond O'Conner, "Commentary," in *The Japanese Navy in World War Two: An Anthology of Articles by Former Officers of the Imperial Japanese Navy and Air Defense Force* (Annapolis: United States Naval Institute, 1971), 136.

61. Prange, *Miracle at Midway,* 34, 305. For discussion of Yamamoto's efforts on behalf of naval aviation and aircraft carriers, see Sadao, "The Japanese Navy and the United States," in *Pearl Harbor as History,* 238.

62. [Theodore Roosevelt], *Atlantic Monthly* 66 (October 1890): 563.

63. For public-opinion-poll data at this time, see Morison, *The Rising Sun in the Pacific,* 39 and 58–61.

64. Prange, *At Dawn We Slept,* 169, 191; Shigeru Fukudome (Rear Admiral and Chief of Staff under Yamamoto at the time of Pearl Harbor), "Hawaii Operation," in *The Japanese Navy in World War Two: An Anthology of Articles by Former Officers of the Imperial Japanese Navy and Air Defense Force* (Annapolis: United States Naval Institute, 1971), 8–9. For similar conclusions based on the United States Strategic Bombing Survey, see Morison, *The Rising Sun in the Pacific,* 36, 62–63, 70, 78. See also Spector, *Eagle against the Sun,* 75–76.

65. A Japanese "Jingo," cited in Chihaya, "An Intimate Look at the Japanese Navy," in *The Pearl Harbor Papers,* 321, 331.

66. Isoroku Yamamoto, cited in Fukudome, "Hawaii Operation," in *The Japanese Navy in World War Two,* 5, 8.

67. Spector, *Eagle against the Sun,* 1.

68. Toland, *The Rising Sun,* 47. Toland also notes that "at Harvard, in 1920 [*sic*], a Japanese student told Roosevelt in confidence about his nation's hundred-year plan for conquest, drafted in 1889" which included Manchuria, China, and British and American possessions in the Pacific including Hawaii. In 1934, Roosevelt informed Henry L. Stimson of this "plot" and pointed out how "many of its particulars had already been verified."

69. Theodore Roosevelt to Franklin D. Roosevelt, 10 May 1913; cited in Turk, *The Ambiguous Relationship*, 97.

70. Franklin D. Roosevelt to Mahan, 28 May 1914; cited in *The Ambiguous Relationship*, 98. The entire letter is reprinted on 166–67.

71. Mahan to FDR, 26 June 1914; cited in *The Ambiguous Relationship*, 98. The entire letter is reprinted on 168–69.

72. Charles A. Beard to Merle Curti, 5 January 1948, in Box 4, File 13, Curti Papers, State Historical Society of Wisconsin, Madison, Wis.

73. Fukudome, "Hawaii Operation," in *The Japanese Navy in World War Two*, 5. Italics are mine. See also Morison, *The Rising Sun in the Pacific*, 42–43; and O'Conner, "Commentary," in *The Japanese Navy in World War Two*, vi.

74. "Hawaii Operation," in *The Japanese Navy in World War Two*, 4–5. See also the post-war testimony of Admiral Osami Nagano, Chief of the Naval General Staff, in *What Happened at Pearl Harbor: Documents Pertaining to the Japanese Attack of December 7, 1941, and Its Background*, ed. Hans Louis Trefousse (New York: Twayne, 1958), 254ff.

75. See Spector, *Eagle against the Sun*, 44 and 79. The Americans also devised their corresponding "Orange Plan" for war in the Pacific.

76. Kazuo Sakamaki, *I Attacked Pearl Harbor* (New York: Association Press, 1949), 28. He had entered the Academy in 1937 and graduated in 1940.

77. Isoroku Yamamoto to Admiral Koshiro Oikawa, 7 January 1941, in *The Pearl Harbor Papers: Inside the Japanese Plans*, ed. Donald M. Goldstein and Katherine V. Dillon (Washington, D.C.: Brassey's, 1993), 115–18.

78. Onishi, in turn, repeated Yamamoto's goal to Commander Minoru Genda who was responsible for planning the role of naval aircraft in the attack. Genda was interviewed by Prange in 1947. According to Prange, the first time Yamamoto spoke about attacking Pearl Harbor was to Fukudome in March or April 1940. For discussion of Onishi's role in planning the attack, see Fukudome, "Hawaii Operation," in *The Japanese Navy in World War Two*, 6.

79. Yamamoto to Vice Admiral Shigetaro Shimada, 24 October 1941; translated in its entirety in *The Pearl Harbor Papers*, 118–20.

80. Kusaka, "*Rengo Kantai* (Combined Fleet), Extracts," in *The Pearl Harbor Papers*, 140.

81. Winston Churchill, private correspondence; cited in Brian Loring Villa, *Unauthorized Action: Mountbatten and the Dieppe Raid* (Toronto: Oxford University Press, 1989), 105, 283n.21.

82. Admiral Sir Dudley Pound, cited in *Unauthorized Action*, 125 and 285n.60.

83. Mahan, cited in Seager, *Alfred Thayer Mahan*, 482–89. See also Mahan to Philip Andrews, 24 September 1910; Mahan to Raymond P. Rodgers, 22 February 1911 (also in response to the Naval War College Strategic War Plan of 1911); and Mahan to Robert U. Johnson, 31 March 1911, in *Letters and Papers* 3:356, 380ff., 396.

84. Admiral Husband E. Kimmel, cited in Prange, *At Dawn We Slept*, 627.

85. See Spector, *Eagle against the Sun*, 79–80, as well as the several primary sources cited in Prange, *At Dawn We Slept*, 20–27.

86. Minoru Genda, "Affidavit of Minoru Genda," 15 March 1948, in *The Pearl Harbor Papers: Inside the Japanese Plans*, ed. Donald M. Goldstein and Katherine V. Dillon (Washington, D.C.: Brassey's, 1993), 13.

87. Minoru Genda, "Analysis No. 1 of the Pearl Harbor Attack, Operation AI," trans. in *The Pearl Harbor Papers: Inside the Japanese Plans*, ed. Donald M. Goldstein and Katherine V. Dillon (Washington, D.C.: Brassey's, 1993), 18–20.

88. Prange, *Miracle at Midway*, 136.

89. Fukudome, "Hawaii Operation," in *The Japanese Navy in World War Two*, 6. See also Prange, *At Dawn We Slept*, 98, 226 (on Admiral Matome Ukagi's "shatterproof convictions of the loyalty a chief of staff owed to his commander in chief," Yamamoto, see 235); and Prange, *Miracle at Midway*, 69.

90. Irving L. Janis and Leon Mann, *Decision Making: A Psychological Analysis of Conflict, Choice, and Commitment* (New York: Free Press, 1977), 129–31. For analysis of American unpreparedness at Pearl Harbor, see Irving L. Janis, *Groupthink: Psychological Studies of Policy Decisions and Fiascos*, 2d ed., (Boston: Houghton Mifflin, 1983).

91. See Prange, *At Dawn We Slept*, 297–303; and Spector, *Eagle against the Sun*, 81–82. On Yamamoto's "threatening to resign if he did not get his way, and the Naval General Staff yielding to his polite blackmail," see Prange, *Miracle at Midway*, 23. See also Kusaka, "*Rengo Kantai* (Combined Fleet), Extracts," in *The Pearl Harbor Papers*, 140.

92. Peattie, "Akiyama Saneyuki and the Emergence of Modern Japanese Naval Doctrine," 63–64. See also Spector, *Eagle against the Sun*, 43–44.

93. See Prange, *At Dawn We Slept*, 223–31, 234; see also Spector, *Eagle against the Sun*, 81–82.

94. Spector, *Eagle against the Sun*, 81–82; Prange, *At Dawn We Slept*, 225, 236, 258–60.

95. Kusaka, recounts those exact words in his "*Rengo Kantai* (Combined Fleet), Extracts," in *The Pearl Harbor Papers*, 151.

96. Fuchida, "The Attack on Pearl Harbor," in *The Japanese Navy in World War II*, 18.

97. Prange, *At Dawn We Slept*, 321–23.

98. Fukudome, "Hawaii Operation," in *The Japanese Navy in World War Two*, 8–9. For further discussion of Nagano's reaction to Yamamoto's threatened resignation, see Prange, *At Dawn We Slept*, 298–301.

99. Janis and Mann, *Decision Making*, 91, 205–6.

100. Prange, *At Dawn We Slept*, 320.

101. O'Conner, "Commentary," in *The Japanese Navy in World War Two*, vii. The success of the British air strike against Taranto had not gone unnoticed by U.S. Navy personnel, including Admiral Stark at Pearl Harbor (see Prange, *At Dawn We Slept*, 40, 45, 47, and 159). But inertia worked to the Americans'

disadvantage. As Spector concludes, "naval aircraft were improving rapidly during the late 1930s; they had performed impressively on maneuvers, but they had also proven to be highly dependent on good weather and visibility. Their carriers, meanwhile, had proven highly vulnerable to both surface and air attack. Tactics that were to prove decisive in the air-sea battles of the 1940s appeared impossible with the aircraft available in the 1930s. 'There was just not enough evidence [before 1941] that aircraft carriers had become the dominant ship type' to convince most of the navy's senior command to abandon the battleship as the basis of the combat fleet" (*Eagle against the Sun*, 23).

102. Ian G. Stott, *The Fairey Swordfish Mks. I–IV*, Profile # 212 (Windsor, England: Profile Publications, n.d.), 34–37, 43. See also A. B. C. Whipple, *The Mediterranean* (Chicago: Time-Life Books, 1981), 63–71.

103. Minoru Genda, "How the Japanese Task Force Idea Materialized," in *The Pearl Harbor Papers: Inside the Japanese Plans*, ed. Donald M. Goldstein and Katherine V. Dillon (Washington, D.C.: Brassey's, 1993), 8. See also John Deane Potter, *Yamamoto: The Man Who Menaced America* (New York: Viking, 1965), 55.

104. "Extracts from Diary and Duty Book of Capt. Shigeshi Uchida," in *The Pearl Harbor Papers: Inside the Japanese Plans*, ed. Donald M. Goldstein and Katherine V. Dillon (Washington, D.C.: Brassey's, 1993), 79, 83.

105. Howarth, "Admiral of the Fleet Isoroku Yamamoto," in *Men of War*, 112–13.

106. Yamamoto's statements are quoted and cited in Prange, *At Dawn We Slept*, 9–12, 18.

107. From Konoye's memoirs, cited in Morison, *The Rising Sun in the Pacific*, 46. Yamamoto's boast also is quoted in Prange, *At Dawn We Slept*, 10; and Roberta Wohlstetter, *Pearl Harbor: Warning and Decision* (Stanford: Stanford University Press, 1962), 350.

108. See Kusaka, "*Rengo Kantai* (Combined Fleet), Extracts," in *The Pearl Harbor Papers*, 158; and Yokosuka Naval Air Corps Air Branch Committee, Battle-lessons Investigating Committee, "Lessons [air operations] of the Sea Battle off Hawaii, Vol. I," in *The Pearl Harbor Papers*, 284.

109. Prange, *At Dawn We Slept*, 27, 373–79, 415; Fukudome, "Hawaii Operation," in *The Japanese Navy in World War Two*, 11.

110. "Pearl Harbor Operations: General Outline of Orders and Plans," in *The Pearl Harbor Papers: Inside the Japanese Plans*, ed. Donald M. Goldstein and Katherine V. Dillon (Washington, D.C.: Brassey's, 1993), 101.

111. Mahan, *The Influence of Sea Power*, 7.

112. Arthur Zich, *The Rising Sun* (Chicago: Time-Life Books, 1977), 72. See also Prange, *At Dawn We Slept*, 544–45.

113. "Extracts from Diary and Duty Book of Capt. Shigeshi Uchida" and "Extracts from Diary and Papers of Comdr. Sadamu Sanagi," in *The Pearl Harbor Papers: Inside the Japanese Plans*, ed. Donald M. Goldstein and Katherine V. Dillon (Washington, D.C.: Brassey's, 1993), 79 and 89. See also Prange, *At Dawn We Slept*, 548–49.

114. See "War Diary of the 3rd Battleship Division, 4–25 December 1941" and "Lessons [air operation] of the Sea Battle off Hawaii," in *The Pearl Harbor Papers: Inside the Japanese Plans*, ed. Donald M. Goldstein and Katherine V. Dillon (Washington, D.C.: Brassey's, 1993), 255–57 and 280.

115. Fuchida, "The Attack on Pearl Harbor," in *The Japanese Navy in World War II*, 27.

116. The interchange on the bridge of the *Akogi* is recounted in detail in Prange, *At Dawn We Slept*, 542–46. See also Fukudome, "Hawaii Operation," in *The Japanese Navy in World War Two*, 12–14.

117. Prange, *At Dawn We Slept*, 546.

118. Spector, *Eagle against the Sun*, 46–47.

119. Morison, *The Rising Sun in the Pacific*, 214–15, 218. Even when the Americans expected the Japanese at Midway, U.S. naval aviators almost missed finding the enemy fleet (this was a time before airborne radar and its search capabilities).

120. The characterization of Nagumo by Fuchida and Ukagi appears in Kyoshi Ikeda, "Vice Admiral Chuichi Nagumo," trans. Richard Harrison, in *Men of War: Great Naval Leaders of World War II*, ed. Stephen Howarth (New York: St. Martin's Press, 1992), 264–66.

121. Chuichi Nagumo, cited in Prange, *At Dawn We Slept*, 426.

122. This interchange is recounted in Ikeda, "Vice Admiral Chuichi Nagumo," in *Men of War*, 264.

123. Kusaka, "*Rengo Kantai* (Combined Fleet), Extracts," in *The Pearl Harbor Papers*, 139, 162.

124. Recounted by Fuchida in "The Attack on Pearl Harbor," in *The Japanese Navy in World War II*, 21.

125. William Furlong, cited in Prange, *At Dawn We Slept*, 549–50. For a subsequent defense of Nagumo's decision, see Fukudome, "Hawaii Operation," in *The Japanese Navy in World War Two*, 15.

126. Douglas MacArthur, *Reminiscences* (New York: McGraw-Hill, 1964), 349.

127. See my "General Douglas MacArthur's Oratory on Behalf of Inchon: Discourse that Altered the Course of History," *Southern Communication Journal* 58 (Fall 1992): 1–12.

128. Chester Nimitz, interview by Prange, 4 September 1964; cited in Prange, *Miracle at Midway*, 9; Raymond Spruance, interview by Prange, 5 September 1964; cited in Prange, *At Dawn We Slept*, 550.

129. Prange, *At Dawn We Slept*, 549–50, 565, 575, 587.

130. See Ikeda, "Vice Admiral Chuichi Nagumo," in *Men of War*, 266.

131. Minoru Genda, "Analysis No. 2 of the Pearl Harbor Attack," in *The Pearl Harbor Papers*, 36–37.

132. "Extracts from Diary and Papers of Comdr. Sadamu Sanagi," in *The Pearl Harbor Papers*, 87.

133. See Spector, *Eagle against the Sun*, 83–84; and Morison, *The Rising Sun in the Pacific*, 125–26.

134. Mahan, *The Influence of Sea Power,* 40, 55, 62–63.

135. C. F. Goodrich to Mahan, 14 May 1892; and Thomas G. Bowles to Mahan, 14 January 1893 (although the date is evident, the name of the newspaper has been cut off), in Box 3, Alfred Thayer Mahan Papers, Library of Congress, Washington, D.C. See also an unidentified newspaper analysis of 2 December 1914, in Box 1.

136. Chihaya, "An Intimate Look at the Japanese Navy," in *The Pearl Harbor Papers,* 328–29.

137. See Zich, *The Rising Sun,* 176–83; for a complete account of this epic battle, see Prange, *Miracle at Midway.*

138. Yamamoto's statement about the Pearl Harbor raid "tipping the balance of power in our favor" appears in Prange, *At Dawn We Slept,* 202.

139. That beau geste is noted in several sources in addition to the primary-source recollections of Japanese participants in the Pearl Harbor attack: see Prange, *At Dawn We Slept,* 472; Morison, *The Rising Sun in the Pacific,* 93; and Warner and Warner, *The Tide at Sunrise,* 20.

Chapter Six

Frank L. Owsley Competes Rhetorically but Unsuccessfully for the Hearts and Minds of the South:
Narrative Fidelity and Myth

Frank Owsley had high hopes for "The Irrepressible Conflict." The historian's chapter in 1930 for *I'll Take My Stand* would persuade. During an Agrarians' reunion at Vanderbilt University in 1956, he recalled "working in history . . . and more and more aware . . . that the people of America were losing the basic values of civilization, that we were going as a nation into materialism, that money value had become the real basic value. . . . We advocated . . . an agrarian way of life . . . and also a belief that the high-powered modern industrialization and materialism would not either develop or maintain civilization very long."[1] As he confided to fellow Agrarian Allen Tate shortly after publication of that essay, "the purpose of my life" is not reaching readers at large as much as other "historians who teach history classes and write text books and they will gradually and without their own knowledge be forced into our position."[2] Owsley hoped to use his rhetorical power to help inculcate and perpetuate a myth.

"The Irrepressible Conflict" did not exert that rhetorical influence, whether among general readers or fellow historians who as opinion leaders themselves might restate Owsley's views. Instead, he was "regarded with suspicion" for being "too militant [in] tone," and "The Irrepressible Conflict" as well as other essays in *I'll Take My Stand* evoked "ridicule or alarm," "bitter resentment," and perceptions that Owsley, specifically, was a "fire eater" deserving of being "attacked" by other historians.[3] The author's admission of being "deliberately provocative" is insufficient to account for his ineffectiveness.[4] Better evidence about "The Irrepressible Conflict" is in letters of Agrarian peers, and those primary sources suggest that Owsley (1) was a poor writer on behalf of Agrarianism who

nevertheless (2) hoped to compete rhetorically against the stylistic prowess and credibility of Woodrow Wilson's eminently well received *Division and Reunion 1829–1889* and (3) sought ultimately to undermine if
not supplant an American myth nurtured by other historians as opinion
leaders on behalf of industrialism and imperatives to succeed economically. An account of Owsley as a rhetorical failure is just as pertinent as
analyses of other historians who have been successful persuaders, for
the rhetoric of historical writing is explicated as much by what fails as
by what works.

I

As the Agrarians began identifying potential authors for *I'll Take My
Stand*, Allen Tate expressed concern to Donald Davidson about Owsley's
possible contribution: "We should probably have to rewrite it to make it
readable."[5] In 1932, after publication of that volume, Tate still deemed
the historian's writing of a subsequent book review as "so bad" and
requiring "so many changes in diction and construction" that "I quit
before the end." Tate added: "it amazes me that a man who has written
two books and innumerable articles can't write at least correctly. Some
of the sentences were so bad that they were ludicrous. What Frank has
to say is extremely valuable, and needs like hell to be said, but God
knows if he will ever learn how to write. . . . I believe he thinks it's
contemptible to write well—literary, artistic, *etc.* Well, if a historian is
not a writer, like any other writer, I'd like to know what he is."[6] By 1936,
that writing still caused misgivings among Agrarian peers. While pro-
posing membership for an American Academy of Letters, John Crowe
Ransom identified twenty-five writers "who seem most eligible" by virtue of their "*Style*" and "*Dignity* as exhibited in literary tone"; Owsley
was on "a list of *nearly* qualified."[7] Why was he was invited to write
with Donald Davidson, Andrew Lytle, John Crowe Ransom, Allen Tate,
John Donald Wade, or Robert Penn Warren? Their correspondence suggests selection by default.

The prime movers for *I'll Take My Stand* were men of letters, congre-
gated at Nashville and Vanderbilt University, who hoped that "profits
of the volume" might finance purchase of a "newspaper, weekly, quarterly, *etc.*" through which their "literary power" might gain what
Davidson called "access to the public mind."[8] From the outset, though,
they appreciated a broad-based appeal. Thinking about proposed "con-

tributors and subjects" for *I'll Take My Stand*, Tate wanted someone to write on "Economic Issues," but in arguing that "*we need a most efficient economist on our side*," he admitted that "the contributor here stumps me too" because of his erroneous assumption that Owsley would be "limited to facts" and thereby "dissipate us."[9] In addition to arguing for an authoritative essay on "education," Davidson insisted, "What we *must* find is an Economist and a Political thinker." But while considering "the right men for the various subjects," he too omitted Owsley and expressed a concern uppermost in his mind: "We run up against, here, the lack of knowledge of our own people that is a handicap to promoting anything in the South."[10] Thus, for a book that was to appear in 1930, Owsley had not been chosen—as of 26 October 1929— to write an essay. Although "stumped to find any contributors" on the subjects that needed to be covered, Tate nevertheless posed the question "Why won't Owsley write an essay in politics and economy?" (while still expressing the caveat that "We should probably have to rewrite it to make it readable").[11] Tate's assumption that he "evidently knows a lot about" politics and economics likely was based on the historian's *States Rights in the Confederacy* (1925) and *King Cotton Diplomacy* (to be published in 1931), whose very titles alone suggested expertise in "politics and economy." So an invitation came to Owsley for a chapter in a book which fellow contributor Lyle H. Lanier characterized as "contrived in a hurry."[12]

As of 11 December 1929, though, Tate bemoaned "people like Owsley, who may not enter the immediate arena" and submit the promised essay.[13] For negotiations were underway with possible publishers, and Tate contracted with Harper on 8 February 1930 for *I'll Take My Stand* to be in print that year.[14] As of 15 March 1930, however, Owsley was "too engaged for the present" to write his essay, and Ransom lamented that they might have "to aim at publication in 1931 and abandon the project for the moment." Moreover, "dumfounded" because the project had been "under discussion now for some two years," Ransom suggested going ahead for fall publication "even if we have to leave out some of our best men." Intended for those "who *might* make the sacrifice of their prior projects and write for us," that threat was predicated on an assumption that Owsley, specifically, could produce his essay "within two or three months anyway, by a great effort."[15] By 21 July 1930, galley proofs were available, so it is clear that Owlsey produced "The Irrepressible Conflict" within the short time anticipated by Ransom.[16] The essay thereby suffered.

Owsley ostensibly was "the child of a Rankean tradition of historical objectivity" about "real facts in the world," and "words, though agreeable if neatly turned, were an uncomplicated vehicle to allow the historian to transcribe the hard truths of an external reality."[17] As an undergraduate and M.A. student at Alabama Polytechnic Institute (now Auburn University), the future historian worked under George Petrie, whose "laboratory" approach centered in "manuscripts and maps, charts and diagrams, and . . . tables, cases, shelves, and walls utilized to display . . . new documents, papers and letters illustrative of Southern, and especially of Alabama history."[18] "The Irrepressible Conflict" hardly evinces "objectivity" of any "laboratory" approach, however. Its vitriolic tone and invective are illustrated in its peroration decrying efforts by an industrial North to subjugate an agrarian South: "It was the doctrine of intolerance, crusading, standardizing alike in industry and in life. The South had to be crushed out; it was in the way; it impeded the progress of the machine. So Juggernaut drove his car across the South."[19] Historian peers hardly would be impressed favorably by page after page blaming the North, complemented only by brief praise for a South in an "idyll of the soil" which did *not* agree with "hard truths of an external reality"—or as H. L. Mencken observed, if the contributors to *I'll Take My Stand* "really want to help their people they will stop blowing pretty soap-bubbles and devote themselves honestly and courageously to concrete and workable remedies."[20]

The Agrarians anticipated this problem while planning their book. In a perceptive audience analysis, Davidson wrote to Tate urging they "accumulate data" and endow their essays with concreteness making agrarian values and ways of life attractive: "One weakness in your program I should like to point out. The Southern people are not actually united on anything these days—except the Negro question, and they do not know each other as well as they used to. How are they going to be attracted to a Cause unless it is linked up to something very concrete and of an importance that overwhelms all else—it can't be a mere intellectual issue or pure sentiment. It must be as important as Food, Money, Sex, before real work can be done."[21] Here was a paradigm for persuasion which Owsley ignored; for although sensitive to Southerners on "the Negro question," he was diverted from his task to engage instead in what Fred Hobson calls "the Southern rage to explain":

> The radical need of the Southerner to explain and interpret the South is an old and prevalent condition, characteristic of Southern writers since the 1840s and 1850s when the region became acutely

self-conscious. The rage to explain is understandable, even inevitable, given the South's traditional place in the nation—the poor, defeated, guilt-ridden member . . . of a prosperous, victorious, and successful family. The Southerner, more than other Americans, has felt he had something to explain, to justify, or to affirm. If apologist for the Southern way, he has felt driven to answer the accusations and misstatements of outsiders and to combat the image of a benighted and savage South. If native critic, he has often been preoccupied with Southern racial sin and guilt, with the burden of the Southern past.

Moreover, although many "historians and scholars" have "told about the South . . . not in passion but, insofar as possible, with something approaching calm and deliberate reflection," Owsley is more that writer with "outrage but rarely with humor and sometimes not even with perspective."[22] The historian also was an unsuccessful rhetor.

For all he should have done to praise agrarian life, Owsley was diverted to blame Northern abolitionists: "slavery as a moral issue has too long been the red herring dragged across the trail. . . . to say that the irrepressible conflict was between slavery and freedom is either to fail to grasp the nature and magnitude of the conflict, or else to make use of deliberate deception by employing a shibboleth to win the uninformed and unthinking to the support of a sinister undertaking." Slavery therefore was depicted as a benign institution of Southerners who had "considered emancipation honestly and fairly," reluctantly rejected that alternative, and "deplored the necessity of continuing the negroes in bondage as the only alternative to chaos and destruction" because they were "cannibals and barbarians, and therefore dangerous." Furthermore, Southerners after the Civil War still could fear "three millions of former slaves, some of whom could still remember the taste of human flesh and the bulk of them hardly three generations removed from cannibalism." Any negative view of slavery simply reflected abolitionist William Lloyd Garrison's "typical 'radical' mind . . . which tries to force nature, which wants to tear up by the roots. Although he was completely ignorant of the South and of negro slavery, he dogmatically assumed an omniscient power of judgment over the section and the institution. . . . He set no bounds of accusation or denunciation." To illustrate Garrison's having "no balance or sense of consequence," Owsley devoted considerable space in "The Irrepressible Conflict" to restating the impassioned abolitionist's view of slavery as the greatest of evils:

The slave master . . . debauched his women slaves, had children by them, and in turn defiled his own children and sold them into the slave market; the slave plantation was primarily a gigantic harem for the master and his sons. The handsome octoroon coachman shared the bed of the mistress when the master was away from home, and the daughters were frequently away in some secluded nook to rid themselves of undesirable negro offspring. . . . The Southern slave owners were not merely moral lepers; they were cruel and brooding tyrants, who drove their slaves till they dropped and died, who starved them to save food, let them go cold and almost naked to save clothing, let them dwell in filthy pole pens rather than build them comfortable cottages, beat them unmercifully with leather thongs filled with spikes, dragged cats over their bodies and faces, trailed them with bloodhounds which rent and chewed them,—then sprinkled their wounds with salt and red pepper. Infants were torn from their mothers' breasts and sold to Simon Legrees; families were separated and scattered to the four winds.[23]

Additional evidence of his persistent, militant rage to explain occurs in Owsley's 1940 presidential address to the Southern Historical Association, with its assertion that Lincoln's Gettysburg Address "has little if any value as a statement of the basic principles underlying the war. The Civil War was not a struggle on the part of the South to destroy free government and personal liberty nor on the part of the North to preserve them."[24] In the 1930s, though, many white Southerners could agree that Garrisonian rhetoric was without "balance or sense of consequence" whereas Owsley's was more acceptable. Some readers also might conclude as a Vanderbilt graduate student did in 1929 that his presumed "Agrarian" professors likely were engaged in a conspiratorial effort to create a volume which was an apologia for the South. Indeed, the budding intellectual proclaimed, *the book waked me!*" But the focal point of his reaction was not so much the future of agrarianism but the Civil War of the past: "Perhaps we began for the first time to think seriously about our Civil War ancestors, about the ultimate decision that drove them to poverty or death. Were they, after all, villains, or madmen? We know well enough now that they were neither."[25] The guidance of opinion leaders, though, is about the future.

Both Owsley and Davidson actually lamented Robert Penn Warren's contribution, "The Briar Patch"—which was more enlightened about "the negro's fate" in the South, where he was deprived of the "democratic ideal of equal opportunity" and faced instead "the lack of opportunity which is there offered and the discriminations which exist against him."[26] Both men thought Warren's "progressive" assertions about "the negro problem" would "irritate and dismay the very Southern people to whom we are appealing":

> I was rather shocked with Red's essay. It hardly seems worthy of Red, or worthy of the subject. And it certainly is not very closely related to the main theme of our book. It goes off at a tangent to discuss the negro problem in general (which, I take it, is not our main concern in the book), and it makes only two or three points that bear on our principles at all. Furthermore, the ideas advanced about the negro don't seem to chime with our ideas as I understand them. Behind the essay, too, are implications which I am sure we don't accept—they are "progressive" implications, with a pretty strong smack of latter-day sociology. Furthermore, I think there are some things that would irritate and dismay the very Southern people to whom we are appealing. . . . I simply can't understand what Red is after here. It doesn't sound like Red at all—at least not the Red Warren I know. The very language, the catchwords, somehow don't fit. I am almost inclined to doubt whether RED ACTUALLY WROTE THIS ESSAY! . . . Owsley has read the essay, and thinks about as I do.[27]

To many Southerners in the 1930s, Owsley's arguments about race likely evinced "narrative probability and fidelity" by complementing "self-conceptions that people hold of themselves"—whether or not an accurate image of their factual selves.[28] Although the historian was "right" on race, he was wrong in his rhetoric on behalf of economic life of most whites farming in an agrarian South.

In 1929, historian Ulrich B. Phillips published *Life and Labor in the Old South*, a "genial portrayal of the antebellum South" generally and a work of "romanticism" about plantation life in particular. And although the book gained favorable attention from several Agrarians, Phillips declined to write an essay for *I'll Take My Stand*.[29] Davidson was not sorry, however, because Phillips's conception of the Old South "favors plantation and gentry too much."[30] Wanting someone who convincingly could laud yeoman farmers in an agrarian South, Davidson bowed to Tate's erroneous assumption that Owsley as historian would be "limited to facts" (even if they would "dissipate us").[31] Having squandered space on an invective against the North and a defense of slavery, however, "The Irrepressible Conflict" could offer only a few paragraphs of paean to white, small landowners who ostensibly were a mainstay of everything good about Southern agrarian life. The historian thus ignored portraying in a more persuasive way a "model of what the rhetor would have his audience become"—that rhetorical "second persona" or "beckoning archetype."[32]

"The Irrepressible Conflict" waxed grandiloquently—but briefly—about a Southern yeoman whose "close to the soil" life was "leisurely and unhurried":

> It was a way of life, not a routine of planting and reaping merely for gain. . . . close to the soil. . . . It might center around a small farm, ranging from a fifty-acre to a five-hundred-acre tract, tilled by the owner, undriven by competition, supplied with corn by his own toil and with meat from his own pen or from the fields and forest. The amusements might be . . . the three-day break-down dances which David Crockett loved, or horse races, foot races, cock and dog fights, boxing, wrestling, shooting, fighting, log-rolling, house raising, or corn-shucking. It might be crude or genteel, but it everywhere was fundamentally alike and natural. The houses were homes, where families lived sufficient and complete within themselves.[33]

That idyllic life of yeomen—but not their women—existed largely in Owsley's imagination. In his "rage to explain," he succumbed to predilections for overstatement characterizing earlier publications that elicited negative reactions. Reviewing *States Rights in the Confederacy*, for instance, Charles Ramsdell thought the historian had abandoned "his critical powers," "accepted isolated and casual statements as bases for sweeping assertions," "read into some of his sources statements that are not there even by implication," and "ignored evidence that tends to disprove or to qualify materially portions of his general thesis." In his cover letter when submitting the review, Ramsdell continued to stress the historian's failures as a writer: "to have called attention to all the errors would have required a book as long as Owsley's."[34] For many Southerners reading *I'll Take My Stand* in 1930 or later, "The Irrepressible Conflict" did not reflect "external reality." But such skepticism was partly the result of what Southerners had read as other historical discourse, including a book by Woodrow Wilson that had been required reading for Owsley as a student of history.

II

After undergraduate work from 1909 to 1911 at Alabama Polytechnic Institute, Owsley stayed on at the "Auburn Oasis" to complete a master of science in history. As both an undergraduate and a graduate student, he "came under the influence of the great teacher, George Petrie." And in characterizing further this "inspirational urge" which students received from Petrie, Wendell Stephenson describes a "laboratory" approach to the study of history in which graduate students had a required text: Woodrow Wilson's *Division and Reunion 1829–1889.*[35] That textbook figured in the later development of Owsley's contribution to *I'll Take My Stand*, which argued that the Civil War was "not between slavery and freedom, but between the industrial and commercial civilization of the North and the agrarian civilization of the South," for *Division and Reunion* drew a sharp dichotomy between the North, which progressed industrially as well as economically and thus won the Civil War, and the South, which had not been willing to change accordingly and thus lost the conflict.[36] Appreciating more than that dichotomy, though, Owsley also sensed the significance of how Wilson's volume was different from other American history textbooks for Southerners since the end of the Civil War:

> For thirty years after the Civil War the intellectual life of the South was as sterile as its own rocky uplands and sandy barrens. The rising generations read Northern literature, shot through with the New England tradition. Northern histories, despite the frantic protests of local patriotic organizations, were almost universally taught in Southern High Schools and colleges,—books that were built around the Northern legend and either completely ignored the South or insisted upon the unrighteousness of most of its history and its philosophy of life. . . . In short, the South either had no history, or its history was tainted with slavery and rebellion and must be abjured. There was for the Southern child and youth *until the end of the nineteenth century* very little choice. They had to accept the Northern version of history with all its condemnations and carping criticisms of Southern institutions and life with its chanting of "John Brown's Body," its

hanging of Jeff Davis on a sour-apple tree, its hosannas to factories and mines and the growth of populations as the only criterion of progress.[37]

Thus, the history of Wilson as the credible Southerner now exerted opinion leadership on behalf of the *same* industrial and economic prosperity to which the Agrarians were opposed. That rhetoric in history had to be countered, but Owsley the Agrarian was no match for Wilson the rhetor.

As a stylist, Wilson is known primarily for his presidential oratory.[38] Before entering politics, however, he was a prominent academician whose *Division and Reunion* held special appeal for Southerners. Yet rhetorical analysis of that volume of historical writing is predicated on the fact that "during his student and teaching careers," the future president's "interest in history was subordinate to his interest in political science."[39] Although he taught various history courses early in his academic career at Bryn Mawr and Wesleyan, his doctoral dissertation at Johns Hopkins University in 1886 was an unfootnoted if not polemical book, *Congressional Government,* published previously in 1885. By 1889, as a result of his lectures and other publications, Wilson's reputation was sufficiently secure for him to be invited to Princeton University as a professor of jurisprudence and political economy.[40] In 1889, Wilson received another invitation as well. Albert Bushnell Hart at Harvard asked him to write the third volume of *Epochs of American History,* to be published by Longmans, Green to make up for "the lack of textbooks for classes in United States history," and Wilson understood he would write "a sketch of causes, movements, and results," rather than "detailed history," covering the period "from 1829 to say 1889" in "200 to 256 pages of 320 words each."[41] Hart chose him as "a man who can impartially judge the South, and its degree of responsibility and its share in the restoration of the Union."[42] Regarding the beginning of a student's work in any subject as a "critical period" for which a textbook author must make "every effort to tell on young minds," Wilson nevertheless believed that the material he had on hand for his writing project was "so scanty that the work would necessarily be much retarded in its progress."[43] Finally agreeing with "great pleasure," though, he thanked Hart for "confidence in my impartiality." Then, admitting he was "born in the South and bred in its sympathies" with "full identification with the South," the prospective author hoped those "affectionate, reminiscent sympathies" would not hinder his "detachment" for "historical judgments."[44] Accepting Hart's suggested title of *"Division and Reunion,"* Wilson saw the period from 1829 to 1889 as one about "which I have some ideas of my own," including "the necessity of doing justice to those abolitionist rascals."[45] Also significant are Wilson's admissions that his being successful as a writer of history was "intrinsically unlikely" and that "the role of the historian would be a new one" for him.[46]

So *Division and Reunion* is the product of selectivity by an author who admitted both biases and shortcomings as an historian. Wilson's selectivity manifests itself in several ways. For example, the largest section of the book, eighty-eight pages, is about the Jacksonian period of 1829 through 1841. While social reform movements and the intellectual awakening therein are covered in less than four pages, banking controversies during this era receive twenty-five pages. The entire Civil War merits but twenty-five pages. Although the issues in "The Slavery Question, 1842–1856" receive seventy-seven pages, those in "Secession, 1856–1861" are treated in eighteen pages. The longest span of time, that covered in "Rehabilitation of the Union, 1865–1889," receives but forty-six pages of treatment. To a relatively detached reviewer abroad, the book was thus mainly about economic issues and the conversion of "the old simple agricultural States of the early century into the vast complex nation we know now": "Mr. Woodrow Wilson has shown with almost equal clearness the economic basis of the whole of American political controversy."[47] Despite what subsequent analysis identified as its "unbalanced" emphasis on economic matters, this textbook was widely used for several decades and in later editions was promoted on its title page as written by the "LATE PRESIDENT OF THE UNITED STATES, FORMERLY PRESIDENT OF PRINCETON UNIVERSITY, AUTHOR OF 'CONGRESSIONAL GOVERNMENT,' 'THE STATE: ELEMENTS OF HISTORICAL AND PRACTICAL POLITICS,'ETC."[48] Even the format of the text evinces the author's competence and and thereby contributes to his credible image: each chapter *begins* with an extensive list of "Bibliographies," "General Accounts," "Special Histories," and "Contemporary Accounts" upon which ensuing discussion presumably is based. Readers of the 1926 edition also might be swayed by the publisher's further efforts to project the author's credibility: "This volume was written by Woodrow Wilson twenty years before he became President of the United States. . . . That it is a sincere and vivid narrative of the period that it covers is proven by its remarkable success. It had been printed more than thirty-five times. . . . It stands for itself as an accepted authority.

. . . The volume seems to many historical critics to be the best historical work that ever proceeded from Woodrow Wilson's pen. Had he lived to revise it there is no reason to suppose that he would have substantially altered the conclusions here set forth." The book thereby had an advantage for securing a wide readership from the public schools as well as from that "general reader" at large "who is a pupil without a teacher."[49] From the outset, its author was extolled as a "brilliant writer" worthy of "prompt reception in literary circles and a quick reading among students young and old." And for any nation seeking "to gaze with cleansed and hopeful eyes upon the assured future of a stronger and statelier growth than had before more than dreamed of," *Division and Reunion* should be "studied by the thousands of our youth who are, under God, to make the country what it is yet to become."[50] Opinion leadership was within Wilson's capability as a writer of history.

The book admittedly received some mixed reactions. Categorizing it as but a "rapid synopsis" of the "larger features of public affairs in the crowded space of sixty years," the *Nation* lauded Wilson for "learning and literary skill," having "his subject well in hand," and proceeding with "a candor and a discrimination that are worthy of praise." Nevertheless, the work suffered from "contradictions which are self destructive" caused by the author's "obvious historical parallax, only the more misleading for being entirely unconscious" and capable of creating "much confusion of ideas so far as the average reader is concerned."[51] While praising its author for "unimpeachable honesty and undeviating singleness of purpose" to strive "as Ranke puts it—'simply to say how it was,'" Hermann von Holst characterized *Division and Reunion* as a "smooth-running narrative" in which "the bias of his Southern blood asserts itself to some extent, and casts a film over his eyes in regard to some persons and questions."[52] A Northerner who had served in the Union Army also saw Wilson's assertions as "wrong in principle," "dangerous in tendency," and worthy of being "challenged especially in view of the fact that your work is intended for use in schools and colleges."[53]

For many Southerners, though, Wilson upheld what a reviewer in the *North Carolina University Magazine* called "the high reputation acquired by his two previous works and makes us all the more proud that he is Southern born." In projecting Wilson's credibility as a "philosophic seeker of truth" who "has come as near to the Right as any writer has done," that reviewer also quoted and praised these "conclusions as to the treatment of slaves":

Scarcely any generalization that could be formed would be true for the whole South, or even for all periods alike in any one section of it. Slavery showed at its worst where it was most seen by observers from the North—upon its edges. . . . In the heart of the South conditions were different, were more normal. Domestic slaves were almost uniformly dealt with indulgently, even affectionately, by their masters. . . . The negroes suffered most upon the larger properties, where they were under the sole direction of hired overseers. . . . Books like Mrs. Stowe's "Uncle Tom's Cabin," which stirred the pity and deep indignation of Northern readers, certainly depicted possible cases of inhuman conduct towards slaves. Such cases there may have been; they may have been frequent, but they were in every sense exceptional, showing what the system could produce, rather than what it did produce as its characteristic spirit and method. For public opinion in the South, while it recognized the necessity for maintaining the discipline of subordination among the hosts of slaves, was as intolerant of the graver forms of cruelty as was the opinion of the best people in the North. . . . Even in the ruder communities public opinion demanded that when negroes were sold families should be kept together, particularly mothers and their children.

The reviewer then offered a final appraisal:

We know that these statements are true to North Carolina, and we venture the assertion with confidence that, judging from the reports of cruelty to wives and children by drunken husbands in the slums of great cities, there is as much physical suffering there as was inflicted by the worse of masters. Even such masters protected their dependents from cruelty to one another. We regret that we have not space for more quotations from this uncommonly strong, impartial, interesting book. . . . Dr. Wilson has earned the gratitude of seekers after truth by his masterly production.[54]

Wilson read that "warm praise" as evidence that he attained his objective "to write *a just* account of the great controversy. . . . Such praise as yours, therefore, coming from a Southerner who is recognized as a most competent judge, heartens me. . . . Some bitter things have been said about the book in the South (doubtless a great deal more than I have seen) but it has been welcomed, too."[55] Even those "bitter things" suggest potential rhetorical effectiveness, however. The New Orleans, the

Picayune of 28 May 1893 saw Wilson as not having gone far enough in praising Southern treatment of slaves!

> The author, in his preface, suggests a fear that he may be unable to handle the subject without prejudice, and presently justifies the fear by manifesting the most violent partisan bias. The ignorance that he displays of the real conditions of the slaves in the south is simply amazing, and the pictures that he draws of their miseries would be appalling if they were not ridiculous. Every one who knows anything about it understands that the slaves before '61 were far better off than the inhabitants of the slums and sweatshops of New York are today. The breaking up of the marriage relation among the slaves, which the author deplores, was nothing to compare with the looseness of that relation among the free negroes of today.[56]

On the whole, Wilson articulated what the South wanted to read about its racial values. If some Southerners found fault with *Division and Re-union*, it was that the textbook was not sufficiently lavish in its description of how well the white race treated slaves prior to the Civil War. Nevertheless, like Mahan, the historian who avoids being patently partisan on behalf of a cause may enhance an image of "scholarly" objectivity. For Wilson, a concomitant effect was a capability to emerge as an opinion leader to exert influence in favor of constancy and reinforcement of values *already* being read and heard in the South, particularly about a new economic base for the region.

An impoverished, rural South long looked to industrial growth for salvation. As early as the 1870s, Georgians, for example, often heard or read speeches extolling "material prosperity" and "glorious progress to wealth" coming from factories and industrialization. A substantial amount of discourse in Georgia was unified after 1872 by what Cal M. Logue identifies as the "common strategy" of advocating "economic prosperity and conciliation" founded upon what Southerners themselves saw as "the concomitants of wealth" and "manly efforts to regain and build up . . . broken fortunes." And John B. Gordon, addressing the Georgia Assembly in 1873, is offered as an exemplar of Southerners who "corrupted their own regional romanticism by preaching national prosperity":

> Get wealth—get wealth! Not only as a means of comfort, but of political power. Bring in population, for population is both capital

and power. Bring in your immigrants; educate your children to be artisans, and architects, and master mechanics. Build your factories, spin your cotton. The mountain has been going to Mohammed in the East long enough. Let us bring the Mohammed of manufactures to our Southern cotton mountain. . . . Soon the whirl of the spinning jenny shall join you in concert. And then musical spindles and murmuring waterfalls shall raise a hymn of gratitude to God until the very atmosphere shall revel and thrill and tremble with your triumph. . . . Do this my countrymen and, believe me, you shall in the new epoch, mount on wings of higher prosperity than ever before.[57]

Recounting that "love affair with middle class capitalism," Bruce Clayton observes that "economic changes that followed the Civil War exhilarated the Southerner, whose frame of reference was one of plantations and poverty. The promises of industrialism were heady"; or as Paul Gaston asserts, Henry Grady's "New South" slogan was a "description not of what ought to be or would be but of what already was."[58] By the 1920s, business progressives had won the governor's office in every state; their proposals for "real estate development, tourism, industrial development, and good roads were pervasive"; and thus as an "overt prescription for economic development" within this social climate, "the Agrarian myth was of little interest."[59] A more appealing view for readers of historians' writing in Owsley's generation was that of Woodrow Wilson, who, as a credible Southerner, reinforced or corroborated the merits of economic growth in a widely used textbook in the region for many years, *Division and Reunion 1829–1889*:

It has been but twenty-four years since the close of the war between the States; but these twenty-four years of steam and electricity had done more than any previous century. . . . The South had been changed as if by a marvel, into likeness to the rest of the country. Freed from the incubus of slavery, she had sprung into a new life; already she promised to become one of the chief industrial regions of the Union. . . . Manufactures sprang up on every hand. . . . The growth of wealth throughout the country was unprecedented, marvellous. Individual fortunes came almost suddenly into existence such as the country had not dreamed to see in former times, such as the world had seldom seen since the ancient days of Eastern luxury, or Roman plunder.[60]

Individuals who amass marvellous, individual fortunes constitute a formidable beckoning archetype in a vast "communication mosaic" of other stories of economic success against which Owsley competed.

That rhetorical second persona in *Division and Reunion* was perceived at subtle levels. In Frederick Jackson Turner's sanguine reaction, "it is your most attractive work. . . . Some of the chapters are destined to live with the classics of our literature and history." Yet his more pertinent reaction was that for Americans this "wonderful little book" had "a vitality—a flesh and blood *form*."[61] A Southerner's response to the textbook was that its essential message "is found in the word 'Americanism.'"[62] The most revealing insight about the volume, though, is from the *Political Science Quarterly* observation that while the work was designed to "interest the general reader, instruct and direct the student and aid the teacher" (with "extensive references"), Woodrow Wilson's "historical talent of an extraordinary quality . . . *is not so much in any originality of idea as in his frequently brilliant precision of expression*."[63] If indeed so unoriginal, *Division and Reunion* merely articulated well—as epideictic history, similar to Carl Becker's later efforts—what people heard and read already in their vast communication mosaic. By corroborating and reinforcing eloquently what was read or heard elsewhere, the credible Wilson could function rhetorically as an opinion leader.

Owsley took his stand, but he did not have credibility comparable to Wilson's. In the academic community, the feeling was that "no Southern historian produced a more balanced treatment of the sectional conflict than did Woodrow Wilson" and that *Division and Reunion* was his "first and best book on American history."[64] Indeed, the future president's "reputation as a historian would be higher if he had written only *Division and Reunion*," for "no textbook would today receive as much critical attention."[65] As noted earlier, Owsley had hoped his views might be passed on by "historians who teach history classes and write textbooks." But he was "regarded with suspicion by many for his excursions into the partisanship of agrarianism"; and although a young Cleanth Brooks could conclude optimistically, "I have no reason to believe that all his allegations can't be proved up to the hilt," the militant tone in "The Irrepressible Conflict" made it only another shrill cry in the mid-twentieth century on behalf of a return by the South to older ways.[66] Wilson as historian, however, retained (for the general public at least) that credibility evinced when his textbook appeared in 1893 as a model of "frankness and candor."[67] Moreover, Wilson's words from that volume *were* passed on by other historians "who teach history classes and write text-books."

In the 1930s through the 1950s, although *Division and Reunion* itself was no longer widely used in the public schools, some of its broad ideas and exact sentences still could be studied by young Southerners. Frances FitzGerald's analysis of American history texts lists among those most widely used in these three decades a book published under various titles by Harold Faulkner and Tyler Kepner.[68] In versions of their textbook called *America—Its History and People* (with editions in 1934, 1938, 1942, 1947, and 1950), the chapter on the Civil War epitomized the Southern cause with this quotation from chapter 10 of Woodrow Wilson's *Division and Reunion*: "The great struggle was maintained by sheer spirit and devotion, in spite of constantly diminishing resources and constantly waning hope. Her whole strength was put forth, her resources spent, exhausted, annihilated; and yet with such concentration of energy that for three years she seemed as fully equal to the contest as did the North itself. And all for a belated principle of government, an outgrown economy, an impossible purpose."[69] Amid page after page of undistin-guished prose by Faulkner and Kepner, a summary statement by an-other historian, ostensibly the expert, was set off or "foregrounded" not only by indentation and space but also by Wilson's epigrammatic style. Southern readers might have their pride emphasized anew by Wilson's antithesis which sets "diminishing resources" and "waning hope" in apposition to "sheer spirit and devotion." They might be moved favor-ably too when reminded through eloquent *klimax* and *asyndeton* about the resources of a lost cause "spent, exhausted, annihilated." Most important, though, they *still* could read Wilson during the 1930s through the 1950s in a credible history textbook arguing that agrarianism in the South was an "outgrown economy."

For Southerners reluctant to accept the inevitable change in their society, Woodrow Wilson's textbook offered an attractive rationaliza-tion. Immediately before and after the turn of the century, many South-erners' beliefs in the values of industrialism and capitalism were founded upon a faith in "scientific method" as a "needed way of thinking that promised objective truth, and not the mythology or boastful assertions that had been the bane of the South. . . . They had had enough of romance; they wanted realism—'candor,' as they put it." In an intellec-tual climate fostered in public schools and colleges, particularly in the teaching of history, educated Southerners by the first decade of the twentieth century regarded "sensible" and "candid" as "two of their favorite words." Moreover, having had a "long and quite un-American experience with poverty"—being "poor in a rich country" in a nation "that worshipped success"—they "were 'ready' for such a view."[70] So an American history textbook such as Wilson's *Division and Reunion* could be a subtle but pervasive "bit" of influential information in the communication mosaic of the South.

Division and Reunion also was attuned to what Brant Short calls "America's rhetorical vision of progress."[71] A wide range of commentary attests to the potency of prevailing American attitudes about "progress." Calling it a "god term" with the "greatest blessing" in contemporary society, Richard Weaver suggests "progress" is "probably the only term which gives to the average American or West European of today a concept of something bigger than himself, which he is socially impelled to accept and even to sacrifice for."[72] For, as Short goes on to say, "progress" is "one of the primary values used in American rhetoric of the mid-twentieth century," and faith in this cultural value is "an accepted truth."[73] Still other findings confirm that audiences of this generation believe widely that "the best is yet to be, and nothing is impossible. Early American experience taught that change was both necessary and beneficial; hence, the present is better than the past, and the future will be better than the present."[74] Thus, "progress" is an American cultural value that closely resembles what Michael McGee terms an "ideograph," one of those ordinary language terms which nevertheless connote commitment to a normative goal and become a warrant for attitudes and actions, and because of enduring values like "liberty" and "rule of law" within a social or political structure, people are "not permitted to question the fundamental logic of ideographs."[75] But additional rhetoric on behalf of "progress" in the form of industrialization and economic growth came from still other historians who, as opinion leaders, helped reinforce a myth nurturing Americans' imperatives to achieve financial success.

III

Americans are achievers. Characteristically, they strive to attain ever higher goals. And when striving for achievement is particularly arduous, ultimate successes somehow seem all the sweeter. Notions of "self-made" men and women appeal to Americans, for people who rise from proverbial "rags to riches" by their "bootstraps" demonstrate success derived not from inherited wealth or position but by harder, more admirable enterprises. Describing how "every culture has its own myths and sets of heroes who do things valued by that culture," a persuasion textbook identifies the "possibility of success" as one of this country's consistently used motivational appeals; for "you may be predisposed to persuasion that articulates the possibility of success if you follow the values prescribed by myth—work hard and honestly for your grades or job or pay and, if you have faith and stamina, you will succeed."[76] Attaining success—against odds and across the widest spectrum of endeavors—is an impelling motive of Americans, and for many people who so strive, a likely measure of their success often is an economic one.

   This national imperative derives force from several rhetorical vectors. For some people, religious dogma motivates desires for attainment. A Protestant work ethic has inspired New Englanders and many of their offspring to be industrious achievers. Another factor is our immigrant heritage. From lives of social and economic immobility—if not abject poverty and oppression in the Old World—many of those who entered the "Golden Door" believed firmly if not fervently that hard work would bring better lives in the New World. Children and grandchildren of those immigrants often grew up persuaded to outdo their ancestors in achievements, particularly economic ones. The frontier also is a complementary force in our heritage. Ray Billington epitomizes our pioneer experiences as "a Promethean struggle between man and the wilderness, with man emerging triumphant."[77] In messages of this country's popular culture, therefore, from early dime novels through later electronic media, frontier men and women are portrayed persistently as facing seemingly insurmountable odds—and succeeding. Surveying those early dime novels, whose numbers in circulation extended into hundreds of thousands and "almost baffle enumeration," Henry Nash Smith concludes that their literary characters became "fixtures of American mythology." And later, after the demise of the dime novel, "the movies . . . tidied up the morals, or at least the manners, of the genre, but plot construction and characterization follow an apparently unbreakable pattern."[78] Now, television programs and their advertising often repeat the motif, for although the time of action typically is the present, many of our favorite characters portray through their paraphernalia or manners or dress appealing links to our frontier past.

   Although Turner's essay "The Significance of the Frontier in American History" ostensibly would alter the thrust of historiography in this country, the general public overlooked that argument. Whether reacting to the Frontier Thesis in its various reprintings after the turn of the century or as the first chapter of his book published in 1920, *The Frontier in American History,* a popular readership perceived the statement as a paean to pioneer attributes, made salient in that oft-quoted single passage praising "coarseness and strength combined with acuteness and inquisitiveness; that practical, inventive turn of mind, quick to find expedients; that masterful grasp of material things, lacking in the artistic but powerful to effect great ends; that restless, nervous energy, that dominant individualism working for good and for evil, and withal that buoyancy and exuberance which comes from freedom." Of course, other opinion leaders praised the same personal attributes before 1893. In 1885, for example, while identifying "the closing years of the nineteenth century" as one of those "great focal points of history . . . from which have radiated the molding influences of the future," the Reverend Josiah Strong praised our typical Anglo-Saxon pioneer in particular for "his unequaled energy, his indomitable perseverance, and his personal independence" which are "peculiarly American."[79] But Turner's Frontier Thesis praise of pioneer attributes began coming to public attention at a more opportune time.

In 1888, Horatio Alger published a novel entitled *Struggling Upward: Or Luke Larkin's Luck.* Analyzing Americans' need to find "new heroes in new places," James Robertson uses this book to epitomize many stories in a popular culture which now "openly accepted" the new "urban and industrial world." *Luke Larkin's Luck* begins not in frontier wilderness but in a small town, and then is set largely in Chicago and New York, where "leading paternal characters are affluent *city* businessmen." Whereas the frontier *was* the place "where Americans sought opportunity and success," this novel says that "success and progress are to be found in the city." The story nevertheless has episodes about experiences in gold-mining camps in the Black Hills as well as scenes in which characters go west to redeem themselves, but frontier experiences in Alger's novel thereby strengthen personal attributes which afterwards are applied in urban environments to attain success.[80] In shifting locales to big cities as places to apply frontier attributes, these novels reflected new demographics. For instance, when the Civil War began, one American in four was a townsman, but by 1900, four in ten were. Similarly, the number of cities with more than 50,000 people had risen from sixteen to seventy-eight; the population of Chicago in 1900 was over 1,500,000 and that of New York had tripled to 3,500,000.[81] When Turner's thesis was first published in 1894, popular culture already had started substantially to reflect the new demographic profile. Therefore, his statement as an historian presumably writing "literature of actuality" seemed to corroborate authoritatively what our novelists were telling us in their fiction— and "seemed" is the appropriate word.

Perception is selective. People typically read or hear more of what they expect in a message rather than what is there as its discursive statement. That aforementioned reviewer in Milwaukee who quoted Turner's passage portraying the pioneer omitted one word, "coarseness" (feeling perhaps that this particular attribute was not one for emulation after the frontier had gone). And he was joined by a newspaper reporter who listened to Turner lecture on the Frontier Thesis, wrote a piece about the event, quoted in it the same passage, and included a reference to what he thought he had heard Turner praise as "calmness of purpose" (a misperception to which Turner responded with a question mark next to the phrase in his copy of the newspaper).[82] In similar ways, people also read into or out of Turner's thesis—or what has paraphrased for them by other opinion leaders—pragmatic inferences for their own lives after the frontier was replaced by an urban and industrialized society. In a significant segment of those responses, people perceived that the historian said pioneer attributes were pertinent for attaining personal economic success whether during financial crises of the 1890s, the boom of the 1920s, or the Great Depression and the "great national emergencies" of the 1930s.[83] Sometimes, reactions were as general as an expression of belief in the need to "apply the old spirit to modern life"; other interpretations were as specific as that in class notes of one of Turner's students at Harvard in 1910, who concluded that Daniel Boone in the twentieth century would have been a "great captain of industry."[84] After the turn of the century, with the frontier gone, the ways of frontiersmen still were pertinent.

Turner perceived that pertinence. Gathering materials and preparing a lecture to be entitled "The New Era," the historian cut out an excerpt from a 1904 issue of the *Portland Oregonian*:

We hear a great deal about the man who comes West to make his fortune, but we do not hear so much about the man who has made his fortune or his career in the west going east to become a great figure in the world of affairs. One movement is as real and vital as the other. Harriman left the Illinois central to go to New York; Hill went from St. Paul, Rockefeller from Ohio. The four biggest traffic men in Chicago are from the Pacific coast. The railroad world is run by men from the west. Ride along Fifth Avenue and listen to the guide as he tells off the names of the owners of the great palaces that line the richest residence street in the world. Take out a dozen old New York families, and what have you got left? Men who come from western oil fields or copper mines or steel plants or harvester works. . . . They grew up in the west, they made their pile, and now they are laying down the law to Wall Street.[85]

No wonder Turner's students at Harvard could conclude that Daniel Boone in the twentieth century would be a "great captain of industry," for the historian was teaching them that the "frontier" engendered attributes that facilitated financial success which, in turn, was a source of power anywhere in America.

   One other crucial "bit" of information was necessary for Americans at that time, however. In 1913, Charles A. Beard published his *Economic Interpretation of the Constitution of the United States*. This book caught the attention of Americans in a way perhaps unequaled by any previous book in American history. Just as Turner had many disciples, so did Beard. Commenting on Beard's "so powerful an influence," Cushing Strout notes that "when the *New Republic* ran a symposium in 1938 on 'Books That Changed Our Minds,' no writer was cited by other intellectuals more often than Beard, and the wide acceptance of his views on the making of the Constitution . . . in the great majority of college textbooks on American history made his impress vivid to thousands of students."[86] David Noble suggests that this book in 1913 "made Beard's reputation as a historian. From this moment on, most young men going into history looked, not to Turner, but to Beard as the intellectual leader of the profession."[87] Surely here was another opinion leader for the masses. But Beard's mode of historiography seemed unusual, for he largely incorporated demographic, primary-source information such as voting records by economic class and ethnic group or voting records in ratifying conventions organized by occupation or investments in securities and land. Furthermore, this empirical data supported a thesis that the framers of the Constitution were not a mythic yeomanry of farm and frontier but commercial men of wealth and property who designed a document to protect and further undemocratically their own personal economic interests.[88]

Many professional peers believed Beard had been neither original nor objective. In Thomas A. Bailey's view, "there can be no doubt that Beard's chief contribution to American history has been to stress economic motivation, which of course is not original except in the degree of emphasis. But he really went all out, as you know, and like every evangelist he overstates his case." In his efforts to prove "the interest of the 'Funding Fathers' in framing and ratifying the constitution," Beard "blows up the economic factors to an undue degree, thus getting the picture badly out of focus. . . . Beard I believe has rather overdone it" and in some cases "is guilty of suppressing facts, handpicking others, overstressing others, and misrepresenting still others—for all of which shysterism we would flunk the dissertation of a Ph.D. candidate in history."[89] So in 1956, Robert E. Brown published *Charles Beard and the Constitution: A Critical Analysis of "An Economic Interpretation of the Constitution."* Also acknowledging Beard's impact on the profession and adaptations of his theory into revisions of college textbooks by other historians, Brown utilized Beard's footnotes and examined the same statistical data. After summarizing Beard's thesis that (1) "the Constitution originated with and was carried through by personality interests—money, public securities, manufactures, and commerce"—and that (2) "the Constitution was put over undemocratically in an undemocratic society," Brown described that 1913 book as "anything but an arid catalogue of facts. Its pages are replete with interpretation, sometimes stated, sometimes implied." Furthermore, "if historical method means the gathering of data from primary sources, the critical evaluation of the evidence thus gathered, and the drawing of conclusions consistent with this evidence, then we must conclude that Beard has done great violation to such method in his book."[90]

Some contemporary historians offer explanations of why Beard portrayed framers of the Constitution as men motivated by economic self-interest. David Noble, for instance, saw Beard as a Jeremiah who would "begin the millennium" by leading a "major assault on that Constitution of the aristocrats, the Constitution of checks and balances which thwarted the will of the people," all to demonstrate that the framers of the document "were not inspired by God but only by their own greed," for if this historian could "conclusively prove the economic selfishness of the founding fathers, he would break the chains of ideology which tied the loyalty of the people to the Constitution and the Court."[91] Analyzing an ideology of progressive historians "so involved in showing that the Constitution did not measure up to their criteria of democracy," Richard Hofstadter similarly placed Beard among those who perceived "the limitations of the eighteenth-century federal Constitution" as an "archetype for everything that was wrong with American political society."[92] Nevertheless, Beard's motivations as perceived objectively by some subsequent historians are less pertinent here than are the impressions likely formed in his own time by readers in the general public.

Responding to Beard's mass of seemingly empirical support, many college students and other readers likely could agree with him and conclude that our founding fathers framed the Constitution not exclusively along mythic lines as an agrarian yeomanry of farm and frontier but in "actuality" as a commercial people of town and city who achieved economic success and wanted to protect the fruits of their achievements. In an analysis more attuned to the age in which *Economic Interpretation of the Constitution of the United States* was widely read, Vernon Parrington saw Beard's book bringing readers to "a sobering sense of reality." Parrington, an opinion leader in his own right, regarded Beard's argument as persuading Americans "to get back once more on the main traveled road, to put away all profitless romanticisms and turn realist."[93] Like Turner's reinforcement for pioneer attributes after popular culture shifted scenes of success stories to cities, Beard's analysis in 1913 of the motives of the framers of the Constitution was a crucial and credible "bit" within a communication mosaic of popular culture whose other salient "bits" provided a sordid interpretation of some mercenary imperatives. In the first decade of the twentieth century, America was preoccupied with the writings—published particularly in mass-circulation magazines—of novelists and journalists who sought to expose the underside of contemporary social, political, and economic conditions. Although Theodore Roosevelt called them "muckrakers," the general public was attentive enough and ultimately concerned enough to press for reform and government regulation of abuses in business practices and corruption in city, state, and national government. A prime example of this new platform for the voicing of social conscience is *McClure's Magazine* of January 1903, which contained Lincoln Steffens's lead article, "The Shame of Minneapolis: The Rescue and Redemption of a City that Was Sold Out"; an article by Ray Stannard Baker, "The Right to Work, the Story of Non-striking Miners"; and the third chapter of Ida Tarbell's *History of the Standard Oil Company,* portraying John D.

Rockefeller as a malignant force behind the growth of Standard Oil.[94] Popular culture for a decade was replete with images of unsavory achievers of economic success, but Beard's thesis in 1913 and his disciples in history contended (and apparently persuasively for many people) that framers of the Constitution *also* functioned with mercenary imperatives, and that this, therefore, was our true heritage. The Constitution might be changed to remedy abuses prevalent in Beard's time, but to strive for economic success was to conform to a custom of the frontier—as Turner seemed to say—as well as a basic value instilled by our founding fathers in the Constitution itself. In early twentieth-century America, that inference about our past would be a realistic conclusion because our credible historians said it was so.

The tarnished image of big business required brightening, however. Events themselves helped accomplish that goal. Many Americans believe we won World War I and World War II in part because of an industrial capacity whose foundations were established by the likes of Henry Ford and John D. Rockefeller. Nevertheless, historians also nurtured an appreciation for industrialists who helped make America an "arsenal of democracy," and Allan Nevins was a prime mover in that endeavor with his well-known biographies of Ford and Rockefeller as well as his formal, personal credo about "Business and the Historian."[95] In 1969, while serving as an advisor to a television documentary series, Nevins characterized his contributions: "These films I am convinced must not be merely a succession of historic episodes, but must have a basic conception or idea as a central theme, to give them satisfactory backbone, knit them together, and leave the viewer with a feeling that the film tries hard to hit an important mark and succeeds in doing so." Then, to project desired images about a "new economic order" which "lend themselves admirably to use in television or on the motion picture screen," Nevins recommended photographs from "the birth of mass production in the Ford factory on the River Rouge in 1911" as well as later Ford and General Motors assembly lines "for automobile frames turned out at the rate of 10,000-a-day." And for particular "visual eloquence," Nevins thought that "a general audience would be much more interested in a film showing how America tooled up for total war before 1945 than in speeches by war leaders or battle scenes of combat in the World War." Finally, the historian's rationale for using these images for the general public was for their appealing evidence of our "youthful vigor, daring and imagination."[96] Some attributes for success on the frontier were equally applicable, in this opinion leader's mind, for business and industry.

The persistence of that notion became evident in 1978, when Frederick Merk published his *History of the Westward Movement*. Turner's student at Wisconsin, Merk followed his mentor to Harvard University, ultimately succeeding him as the premier lecturer on the history of the West. ("Wagon Wheels" was the affectionate name given by students to Merk's course.) In one review of *History of the Westward Movement*, Gordon Wood singled out for praise its emphasis on portraying pioneers: "people—particularly individuals doing concrete things—are everywhere in Merk's story." Moreover, in Woods's view, those frontier character- izations provided a viable model for Americans to emulate when beset with problems of national magnitude, such as those of the environment, energy, the economy, mass transportation, the deteriorating quality of life in the cities, drugs and crime: "our heightened sense of limits and depleted resources" provides the "context that makes Merk's book on the Western Movement so timely. . . . this book based on a course that comes out of another time is in no way out of date. . . . its publication is more fitting to our times and our concerns than it would have been to those of two or three decades ago."[97] Indeed, Merk's "Afterward" reminded readers that some people in the past "misread" Turner's Fron- tier Thesis, thinking the essay said that "the frontier in all its aspects had ended." No, Merk countered, our frontier still persists but in different domains, and his last three sentences argue for applying pioneer attributes "to make things better" for the future: "Increasingly, however, the open frontier has become one in the realms of science and technology, of man's control over the environment and of the relations of man to his fellow man. This is the frontier now challenging the national energies. The hope of the future is that all the optimism, all the indomitable will to over- come obstacles, all the love of freedom and of democratic process, and all the determination to make things better for the future, which the old frontier nourished and symbolized, will remain part of American thought and aspirations."[98] Appropriately, Merk's peroration paraphrased the same passage from Frederick Jackson Turner that was often singled out so favorably. Also appropriately, the History Book Club's promotional statement for Merk's book ended by quoting from that very passage about pioneer qualities used successfully to promote Turner's book, *The Frontier in American History*, fifty-eight years earlier. The choice was apt. Many people who requested the July 1978 History Book Club selection received instead an apology: the organization was "doing everything possible to expedite delivery" of *History of the Westward Movement,* but shipments would be delayed "because of exceptional demand."[99]

Influential works of several historians in essence supported conclusions Americans learned previously from their popular culture. Or, as in the case of Beard, they provided a way to rationalize what was read or heard from other sources. Surely this was the case for our national imperative towards attaining economic successes, particularly as we might achieve them now by emulating the qualities of our frontiersmen and founding fathers. Americans first learned of these attributes—as well as a host of ethnic, societal, and religious values—from myriad other sources in popular culture. But during the twentieth century, those "bits" of information received reinforcement at particularly crucial times from particularly credible discourse such as the Frontier Thesis. Henry Nash Smith's conclusion is pertinent: Turner's writing basically "found an echo in ideas and attitudes already current . . . a massive and deeply held conviction . . . the image of themselves which many—perhaps most—Americans of the present day cherish, an image that defines what Americans think of their past, and therefore what they propose to make of themselves in the future."[100] So American youths "believe that people can actually live a Horatio Alger story," according to a Gallup Youth Survey: "nationally, 81 percent of the teen-agers interviewed . . . said they thought it was possible for someone in this country to start out poor and become rich by working hard."[101] American historians contributed to the formation of a formidable myth.

Yes, the South *is* receptive to myth. Even if "increasingly unrelated to reality," as Stephen Smith concludes, the fact that "the South's controlling mythology" has "endured for so long does have meaning for the rhetorical critic and communication scholar"; for as Dewey Grantham observes, "the emotional attachment to the idea of 'the South,' constantly reinforced by vague memories, family tales, and endless rhetoric in public places, produced what surely was one of the most remarkable loyalties in American history."[102] Nevertheless, to be a persuasive alternative to materialism and industrialism, Owsley's view in *I'll Take My Stand* required *some* grounding in vivid, specific supporting evidence that counteracted the "hard truths of external reality" apparent to most Southerners daily. Although ribbons of concrete increasingly crossed the rural South as forerunners of interstate highways, too many yeoman farmers lived on Tobacco Roads. Even on the matter of race, Owsley faced formidable opposition from our sense of historical consciousness. Many messages helped promote integration in the South. Prominent among them were that host of statements about "liberty" and "equality" which Gunnar Myrdal identified in a landmark study of 1944 as an "American Creed." Arguing that "America, relative to all the other branches of Western civilization, is moralistic and 'moral conscious,'" Myrdal saw the typical American as one who more often than not *"thinks, talks, and acts under the influence of high national and Christian precepts"* which have been "hammered" into our minds: "The schools teach them, the churches preach them. The courts pronounce their judicial decisions in their terms. They permeate editorials with a pattern of idealism so ingrained that the writers could scarcely free themselves from it even if they tried. They have fixed a custom of indulging high-sounding generalities in all written or spoken addresses to the American public, otherwise so splendidly gifted for the matter-of-fact approach to things and problems."[103] Yet those "principles which *ought* to rule" came in conflict with what Myrdal called in 1944 "the Negro problem" in which a group of people because of their race "had not yet been given the elemental civil and political right of formal democracy."[104] Competing attitudinal bases for racial discrimination found ample expression, of course, in messages advocating "white supremacy," "massive resistance," or what George Tindall called the "Southern Credo."[105] Writing in 1944, though, Myrdal was optimistic: "the American Creed is older and wider than America itself," evermore "gradually realizing itself," and "still growing" to the point where "no other norm could compete in authority over people's minds."[106]

In 1960, while assessing race relations in the South, Tindall perceived that "a gradual diminution in the force of the Southern Credo has been apparent for several decades." Then, with optimism equal to Myrdal's, Tindall epigrammatically concluded that "while the American as Southerner has been unable to shake off the pro-slavery argument, the Southerner as American has never abandoned the American Creed."[107] Although slavery and postbellum institutions of white supremacy by the twentieth century had evolved into "segregation as a general civil institution and as a hallowed social myth," the South was changing:

Looking back over the first half of the twentieth century, it becomes clear that a whole series of developments was beginning imperceptibly to undermine the ideological defense of white supremacy almost as soon as its new institutional patterns became established. The doctrine of biological inferiority was questioned by anthropologists and geneticists who could find no conclusive evidence for it, and their ideas seeped into the public consciousness. Tortured interpretations of the Scriptures were taken less and less seriously by literate Southerners. The need for a mudsill labor force was reduced by the development of mechanization in agriculture and industry. The argument for a separate Negro culture ran up against the manifest fact that Negroes could and did assimilate the general southern and American patterns, even in their separate institutions. The fear of race conflict with any relaxation of caste barriers eventually was found to be exaggerated as Negroes were re-enfranchised and segregation was ruled out in some areas without the predicted blood bath. And finally, these matters were opened up for discussion and debate in countless classrooms and organizations.[108]

For all their zeal, Agrarians who hoped to stem the tide of change in the South could not compete rhetorically against the wide range of communication arrayed against them. For their "view of progress could not counter the dual forces of an economic depression and culturally-ingrained belief in progress as a savior for the individual and society." Rhetorical "power inherent in that ideograph, and the related ideographs that composed the ideological foundations of American society in the 1930s, were too powerful for these advocates."[109] The position argued by Owsley in his attitude of diatribe necessarily would be ineffectual against the weight of myth.

Extent and effectiveness of his rhetorical opposition notwithstanding, Owsley ultimately was motivated to soften the vehemence evident in his essay for *I'll Take My Stand*. Upon returning from a trip abroad in 1932, "the temptation came upon him," in Donald Davidson's words, "to find good in what he had deplored in American life; he had never felt so patriotic as when he was in Europe."[110] In so doing, Owsley was like other historians who experienced similar changes of heart only after travel abroad. For example, despite the outspokenness with which Howard K. Beale had denounced some aspects of American life, a trip to Germany in 1936 caused him to admit, "I have come back to America feeling more than ever the importance of preserving democracy, feeling that America is perhaps the one place in the world where democracy can yet be reformed and made to work, where sanity can yet be maintained."[111] Nevertheless, Owsley's "vanity" still had him sensitive about adverse reactions to "The Irrepressible Conflict" and his "stepping out of his 'field,'" and he therefore seemed adamant, as Tate saw it, about "sticking to 'objective' history."[112] That imperative found fruition in 1949 with *Plain Folk of the Old South*. This book, which Owsley admitted could have been titled "The Forgotten Man of the Old South," supported a thesis that "volumes and shelves of history" were wrong in suggesting that antebellum society consisted of "only three important classes in the South—planters, Negro slaves, and poor whites."[113] With help from his wife, Harriet, Owsley examined "manuscript census reports and other neglected sources—wills, county-court minutes, marriage licenses, church records inventory of estates, trial records, mortgage books, deed books, tax records, as well as travel accounts and local histories—to recreate the society of the antebellum South." Covering Alabama, Florida, Georgia, Louisiana, Mississippi, South Carolina, and Tennessee, their research found that substantial numbers of white, yeoman farmers had lived a middle-class existence akin to that only asserted without sufficient support nearly two decades earlier in "The Irrepressible Conflict."[114] Admittedly, one reaction to the way data was used in *Plain Folk* was that its author was "much too innocent of the use and resources of modern statistical method" and his materials were "statistically unrepresentative."[115] Nevertheless, even as Owsley's preliminary findings appeared in a 1940 journal article, some historians finally began to notice his claims in the positive way he had hoped for. Sensing a similarity between Owsley's primary sources and methodology and those of his own in *Economic Interpretation*, Charles A. Beard wrote to Owsley urging such studies "be extended all over the country, for they alone can provide a solid base for discovering the status of agricultural economy at given periods."[116] A "solid base" can be a cornerstone of opinion leadership.

If a middle-class, good life of small farmers existed in the antebellum South, its imagery was not sufficiently vivid in Southerners' consciousness during the Great Depression of the 1930s and the years thereafter. If "vague memories" or "family tales" or other vestiges of "leisurely and unhurried" agrarian life indeed were salient in the 1930s, "The Irrepressible Conflict" could be epideictic discourse reinforcing values by articulating well certain sentiments with which its audience already agreed. Although Donald Davidson thought in 1929 that "concrete" data from the Agrarians would be sufficient to persuade readers to their point of view, by 1935 he rationalized why *I'll Take My Stand* was not as persuasive as hoped, saying in retrospect that the volume "was first of all a book for mature Southerners who, we trusted, were not so far gone in modern education as to require coloured charts, statistical tables, graphs, and journalistic monosyllables, but were prepared to use intelligence and memory."[117] But the "memory" that hopefully would be activated was superseded by scenes of Southern rural poverty during the Great Depression and afterward, all of which were readily apparent. Historian William Hesseltine only could react wryly in 1931: "the Young Confederates of Nashville make themselves a little ridiculous in apotheosizing agrarian culture, and elevating the yeoman farmer to a pedestal. Agrarian culture, as any one raised on a farm will tell them, is almost a contradiction in terms, and the average farmer of the south most certainly is undeserving of a pedestal. . . . At no time in history, from Jamestown to Dayton, has the American south been other than a horrible example of the spiritual failure of agrarianism."[118] We retain a sense of those conditions from the Farm Security Administration's starkly poignant photographs, such as the picture of despair taken in 1936 and entitled simply "Floyd Burroughs and Tengle children, Hale County, Alabama."[119]

To compete rhetorically with that imagery, Owsley should have eschewed his "rage to explain" and endowed his thirty-one pages with more than a few paragraphs of generalizations about middle-class farming as a life-style to which readers should return. Although it probably never could have exerted mass persuasion, his discourse nevertheless might have acquired lasting literary merit for individuals seeking reinforcement for their inclinations to go against the grain of imperatives toward materialism and economic success. Consider Henry David Thoreau and *Walden*, "the one golden book in any century of best books." This discourse articulated a beckoning archetype for iconoclasts who exerted some degree of cultural force in American society. In retrospect, *I'll Take My Stand* might be viewed (as some literary critics do) not as "a political tract seeking to change attitudes and behavior in the depression-era South" but as "a timeless statement affirming the importance of nature in human life."[120] Viewed this way, Owsley's essay is part of a collective effort in "the American pastoral tradition, a protest against the dehumanizing influence of urban society that can be compared most profitably with *Walden*."[121] On behalf of the Agrarian cause, however, Owsley did not write a *Walden* but only an essay whose length approximated that of a substantial public speech. Thus, what "The Irrepressible Conflict" *could* have done can be appreciated in that context of public speaking. Indeed, although Brant Short characterizes the Agrarians' effort as "a rhetorical failure in its first life," he also concludes "there is little doubt that *I'll Take My Stand* is a rhetorical response to a given exigency in a particular historical context."[122] Owsley's was, however, the wrong response.

During the Great Depression and thereafter, Owsley's attempt to persuade might have been more successful had he heeded Davidson's 1929 view that contributors to *I'll Take My Stand* must link their "Cause" to "something very concrete and of an importance that overwhelms all else—it can't be a mere intellectual issue or pure sentiment. It must be as important as Food, Money, Sex, before real work can be done." But a format different from diatribe was required. An instructive counterpoint is Russell H. Conwell's "Acres of Diamonds," a speech delivered between 1870 and 1925 "over 6000 times in lecture halls, churches, Chautauqua tents, and even over the radio" to nearly thirteen million people. The distinguishing rhetorical characteristic of "Acres of Diamonds" is its author's "telling of 'true' anecdotes . . . that . . . made the drama appear 'real,'" all "exhorting his audience to go out and get rich."[123] Yes, "Acres of Diamonds" complemented—and was complemented by— other discourse ranging from Horatio Alger success stories to our historians teaching us that pursuing financial success was the American way. But Conwell's audiences also were aware of extreme poverty in big cities and appalling working conditions for both child and adult laborers. So Conwell's beckoning archetype was embedded in "true life" stories with verisimilitude for many audiences because a "welter of concrete details made them believable."[124] Although Davidson had foreseen in 1929 that the Agrarians, similarly, should "accumulate data" and ground their appeal in "something very concrete," Owsley ignored that advice in both his content and form for "The Irrepressible Conflict." His rhetoric for *I'll Take My Stand* failed because it lacked in 1930 both the specificity of the supporting materials he accumulated later and published in 1949 in *Plain Folk* in a form more appealing than that based upon invective against the North. Evidence to establish firmly "hard truths of an external reality" could not be developed during "two or three months" Owsley spent in the spring of 1930 hurriedly composing "The Irrepressible Conflict." And for all his suasory aspirations, he failed in his efforts to compete rhetorically with other historians. He lost the hearts and minds of the South to the lure of progress and economic prosperity.

Perhaps a suggestive index of Owsley's rhetorical loss to the forces of economic imperative resides in the case of George Wallace and integration in the South. On 13 June 1963, Governor Wallace "stood in the schoolhouse door" at the University of Alabama. Personally barring two blacks from the university summer session, he would nullify a court ruling that they be admitted. After President Kennedy federalized part of the Alabama National Guard, George Wallace stepped aside.[125] Earlier in 1957, President Eisenhower ordered federal troops to enforce integration of Central High School in Little Rock, Arkansas. In 1962, President Kennedy also federalized National Guard troops to protect James Meredith and enforce his admission to the University of Mississippi, an event marred tragically by rioting, injuries to nearly 200 marshals and guardsmen, and two deaths. Even more tragic in 1963 were the murder of Medgar Evers in front of his home in Jackson, Mississippi, and the deaths of four girls in the bombing of the 16th Street Baptist Church in Birmingham, Alabama.[126] All were part of "massive resistance" to integration communicated vividly to America and the world by newspapers of 4 May 1963, with photographs of Eugene "Bull" Conner's police dog lunging at a black woman demonstrating to end discrimination in Birmingham shops, restaurants, and employment. Although fixed bayonets do have coercive eloquence, truly "massive resistance" surely would have resulted in greater bloodshed than that which tragically did occur in the South. What some voices predicted to be a movement of great scope turned out to have relatively minimal final proportions. After all, George Wallace's doorway stance was "a theatrical show for home consumption . . . a knowingly empty and foolish gesture"; and while publicly barring James Meredith from the University of Mississippi, Governor Ross Barnett privately agreed beforehand to "give in gracefully" if federal marshals drew their guns on him (and could be photographed so doing).[127] Other forces were operative, including Civil Rights orators generally and the eloquence of Martin Luther King, Jr., specifically. Without discounting the potency of those and other oratorical efforts (or fixed bayonets, for that matter), persuasion to integrate in the South was complex. A comprehensive view of what took place rhetorically must acknowledge the role of a moralistic "American Creed" which schoolchildren dutifully learned for decades as well as its complementary, pragmatic argument advanced in a particularly subtle but highly credible mode of rhetoric: American history textbooks.

For the South in the 1950s and 1960s, integration constituted a "time of widening uncertainty and chronic stress" during which some people might have been particularly receptive to recalling a lesson learned from a credible historian: racial values of an agrarian past were less important than commercial considerations for the future. For whether it is called "rioting" or, more euphemistically, "civil disturbance," unrest is bad for business. Looking in retrospect at race relations in the South, Tindall suggests that the cooperation between the races which developed over the decades invariably involved economic benefit—in dollars—to members of both groups: "During any period of southern history since the Civil War some instances of interracial action may be found in the labor movement, among craftsmen, longshoremen, miners, factory workers, and others. In the agrarian revolt of the eighties and nineties the 'wool hat boys' found themselves allied with Negro farmers in the struggle against their common economic grievances, and since the nineteen-thirties an indigenous organization of tenant farmers and agricultural laborers has existed without racial barriers."[128] But the American Creed is not about the dollar! In Myrdal's definition, this "moralistic attitude is founded upon high *national and Christian precepts.*" Although American history textbooks also played their part in reinforcing that particular outlook, people often require pragmatic, "logical" arguments to justify actions undertaken in fulfillment of needs more abstract in principle.

From this perspective, reconsider George Wallace. The man who in 1963 stood in the schoolhouse door to bar blacks from the University of Alabama returned as governor in 1982 with assistance from blacks. During his campaign to regain the governorship, the former spokesman for segregation in the South ran on a different platform, which said: "everywhere in Alabama the message is the same: folks are hurtin,'" and the candidate portrayed himself as the person who "can bring new industries and new jobs to the state."[129] Looking from detached distance at Wallace's victory, a Canadian journalist identified both the theme of the campaign as well as the importance of the black vote: Alabama is "in deep trouble. Steel mills are closing, tire factories have cut back. Per capita income is among the lowest in the country. During his campaign Wallace told supporters that he could help. . . . Bygones being bygones . . . Wallace received enormous support from Black voters."[130] When the proverbial chips are down, realistic dollars often count. The historian Owsley as rhetor misjudged his audience.

Notes

1. Frank L. Owsley, quoted in the introduction to *The South: Old and New Frontiers — Selected Essays of Frank Lawrence Owsley,* ed. with an introduction by Harriet C. Owsley (Athens: University of Georgia Press, 1969), xvii.

2. Frank Owsley to Allen Tate, 29 February 1932; cited in Michael O'Brien, *The Idea of the American South 1920–1941* (Baltimore: Johns Hopkins University Press, 1979), 168.

3. Cleanth Brooks to Donald Davidson, 18 March 1931; cited in *The Idea of the American South,* 170. See also John Shelton Reed, "For Dixieland: The Sectionalism of *I'll Take My Stand,*"in *A Band of Prophets: The Vanderbilt Agrarians after Fifty Years,* ed. William C. Harvard and Walter Sullivan (Baton Rouge: Louisiana State University Press, 1982), 44, 55; and Virginia Rock's biographical essay on Owsley in "The Twelve Southerners: Biographical Essays," in *I'll Take My Stand: The South and the Agrarian Tradition,* with an introduction by Louis D. Rubin, Jr. (Baton Rouge: Louisiana State University Press, 1962), 392.

4. Cited in Rock, "The Twelve Southerners: Biographical Essays," in *I'll Take My Stand,* 392.

5. Allen Tate to Donald Davidson, 9 November 1929, in *The Literary Correspondence of Donald Davidson and Allen Tate,* ed. John Tyree Fain and Thomas Daniel Young (Athens: University of Georgia Press, 1974), 240. Hereafter cited as *LCDT.*

6. Allen Tate to Andrew Lytle, 30 May 1932, in *The Lytle Tate Letters,* ed. Thomas Daniel Young and Elizabeth Sarcone (Jackson: University Press of Mississippi, 1987), 56. Hereafter cited as *LTL.*

7. John Crowe Ransom to Allen Tate, in *Selected Letters of John Crowe Ransom,* ed. Thomas Daniel Young and George Core (Baton Rouge: Louisiana State University Press, 1985), 217–18. Hereafter cited as *SLJCR.*

8. Ransom to Tate, 22 February 1930, in *SLJCR,* 195; Davidson to Tate, 26 October 1929, in *LCDT,* 237.

9. Tate to Davidson, 10 August 1929, in *LCDT,* 233.

10. Davidson to Tate, 26 October 1929, in *LCDT,* 236.

11. Tate to Davidson, 9 November 1929, in *LCDT,* 240.

12. Lyle H. Lanier, cited in *A Band of Prophets,* 160.

13. Tate to Davidson, 11 December 1929, in *LCDT,* 243.

14. Ransom to Tate, 22 February 1930, in *SLJCR,* 194–95. Davidson received a contract for the same project from Macmillan on 21 February 1930.

15. Ransom to Tate, 15 March 1930, in *SLJCR,* 197–99.

16. Davidson to Tate, 21 July 1930, in *LCDT,* 250.

17. O'Brien, *The Idea of the American South,* 222.

18. Wendell Holmes Stephenson, *Southern History in the Making: Pioneer Historians of the South* (Baton Rouge: Louisiana State University Press, 1964), 66, 139.

19. Frank L. Owsley, "The Irrepressible Conflict," in *I'll Take My Stand: The South and the Agrarian Tradition* (New York: Harper and Brothers, 1930), 91.

20. Alexander Karanikas, *Tillers of a Myth: Southern Agrarians as Social and Literary Critics* (Madison: University of Wisconsin Press, 1969), 35–36; H. L. Mencken, "Uprising in the Confederacy," *American Mercury* 22 (March 1931): 381.

21. Davidson to Tate, 26 October 1929, in *LCDT,* 237.

22. Fred Hobson, *Tell about the South: The Southern Rage to Explain* (Baton Rouge: Louisiana State University Press, 1983), 3–5. As Hobson also observes, "the Southern experience is now more than ever not only the South's but the nation's. Not only has the South long provided a mirror image for America's flaws and blemishes, but in post-Vietnam America those qualities we have identified as Southern—frustration, failure, defeat, guilt—can be shared by the rest of the nation. Dixie has to some extent become Americanized, but America has absorbed much of Dixie too. Country music, fried chicken, stock car racing, evangelical religion, and opposition to busing schoolchildren—all these have replaced cotton as Dixie's leading export, not to mention a general distrust of analysis, bureaucracy, big government, and impersonality in human affairs. To tell about the South, then, becomes increasingly to tell about America" (16).

23. Owsley, "The Irrepressible Conflict," in *I'll Take My Stand,* 62, 69, 73, 77–80.

24. Owsley, "The Fundamental Cause of the Civil War: Egocentric Sectionalism," address to the Southern Historical Association (1940), in *The South: Old and New Frontiers,* 51.

25. R. C. Beatty, "A Personal Memoir of the Agrarians," *Shenandoah* 3 (Summer 1952): 12–13.

26. Robert Penn Warren, "The Briar Patch," in *I'll Take My Stand: The South and the Agrarian Tradition* (New York: Harper and Brothers, 1930), 246–64.

27. Davidson to Tate, 21 July 1930, in *LCDT,* 251.

28. See Walter R. Fisher, "Narration as a Human Communication Paradigm: The Case of Public Moral Argument," *Communication Monographs* 51 (1984): 2, 6–8, 10, 14–15.

29. See Merton L. Dillon, *Ulrich Bonnell Phillips: Historian of the Old South* (Baton Rouge: Louisiana State University Press, 1985), 134–35, 164.

30. Donald Davidson, review of *Life and Labor in the Old South,* by Ulrich B. Phillips, reprinted in *The Spyglass: Views and Reviews, 1924–1930,* ed. John Tyree Fain (Nashville: Vanderbilt University Press, 1963): 216.

31. Tate to Davidson, 10 August 1929, in *LCDT,* 233.

32. See Edwin Black, "The Second Persona," *Quarterly Journal of Speech* 56 (April 1970): 109–19.

33. Owsley, "The Irrepressible Conflict," in *I'll Take My Stand,* 71–72, 89.

34. Charles W. Ramsdell, review of *States Rights in the Confederacy,* by Frank L. Owsley, *Mississippi Valley Historical Review* 14 (June 1927): 107–10. Ramsdell's cover letter to Milo M. Quaile, 2 January 1926, is cited in Stephenson, *Southern History in the Making,* 274.

35. See Stephenson, *Southern History in the Making*, 139–41. In 1944, after a lapse of half a century, Petrie himself still retained "vivid memories" of Woodrow Wilson as his own "dynamic teacher" at Johns Hopkins (see *Southern History in the Making*, 136).

36. Owsley, "The Irrepressible Conflict," in *I'll Take My Stand*, 74. For other historians who sensed that dichotomy, see Henry Wilkinson Bragdon, *Woodrow Wilson: The Academic Years* (Cambridge: Harvard University Press, 1967), 238–39; and C. E. Cauthen, "The Coming of the Civil War," in *Writing Southern History: Essays in Historiography in Honor of Fletcher M. Green*, ed. Arthur S. Link and Pembert W. Patrick (Baton Rouge: Louisiana State University Press, 1965), 231–32.

37. Owsley, "The Irrepressible Conflict," in *I'll Take My Stand*, 64–65. Italics are mine. I have elsewhere pointed out that Wilson's book was required reading for Owsley at Auburn, and part of Owsley's motivation for "The Irrepressible Conflict" came from a desire to refute Wilson—and other historians who quoted Wilson's textbook as representing what the South was all about. See my essay "On American History Textbooks and Integration in the South: Woodrow Wilson and the Rhetoric of *Division and Reunion 1829–1889*," *Southern Speech Communication Journal* 51 (Fall 1985): 1–23.

38. See, for instance, Dayton D. McKean, "Woodrow Wilson," in *A History and Criticism of American Public Address*, ed. William Norwood Brigance (New York: McGraw-Hill, 1943), 2:968–92; Howard Runion, "An Objective Study of the Speech Style of Woodrow Wilson," *Communication Monographs* 3 (1936): 75–94; Clair R. Henderlider, "Woodrow Wilson's Speeches on the League of Nations, September 4–25," *Communication Monographs* 8, no. 1 (1946): 23–34; George C. Osborn, "Woodrow Wilson as a Speaker," *Southern Speech Communication Journal* 12 (Fall 1956): 61–72; and Mary G. McEdwards, "Woodrow Wilson: His Stylistic Progression," *Western Journal of Speech Communication* 26 (Winter 1962): 28–38.

39. George C. Osborn, *Woodrow Wilson: The Early Years* (Baton Rouge: Louisiana State University Press, 1968), 260.

40. *Woodrow Wilson: The Early Years*, 154–55, 195–97.

41. Albert Bushnell Hart to Woodrow Wilson, 23 April 1889. This letter as well as all further citations from Wilson's correspondence and reviews of his work are taken from *The Papers of Woodrow Wilson*, 69 vols., ed. Arthur S. Link (Princeton: Princeton University Press, 1969), 6: 174. Hereafter cited as *PWW*.

42. Hart to Wilson, 1 June 1889, in *PWW* 6: 243.

43. Wilson to Hart, 1 May 1889, in *PWW* 6: 183. To appreciate the degree of Wilson's need for material, consider his correspondence to Frederick Jackson Turner requesting assistance, 23 August 1889, in *PWW* 6: 368–71.

44. Wilson to Hart, 3 June 1889, in *PWW* 6: 243.

45. Hart to Wilson, 5 June 1889; Wilson to Hart, 12 June 1889; Wilson to Herbert Baxter Adams, 27 June 1889; Wilson to Richard Heath Dabney, 31 October 1889, all in *PWW* 6: 311–12, 321, 327, 409.

46. Wilson to John Franklin Jameson, 12 June 1889; Wilson to Adams, 27 June 1889, in *PWW* 6: 322, 327.

47. Review of *Division and Reunion 1829–1889,* by Woodrow Wilson, *London Daily Chronicle,* 21 April 1893, in *PWW* 8: 196.

48. Woodrow Wilson, *Division and Reunion 1829–1889* (New York: Longmans, Green, 1929), vii. For further discussion of Wilson's "unbalanced" treatment, see Bragdon, *Woodrow Wilson: The Academic Years,* 235–36.

49. *Division and Reunion 1829–1889,* ix. For further assessment of this textbook's prominence, see Link's "Editorial Note," *PWW* 8:141–48.

50. Review of *Division and Reunion 1829–1889,* by Woodrow Wilson, *Church Union,* 15 April 1893, in *PWW* 8: 191. Link's note (*PWW* 8:192) suggests that Wilson's father was the author of this piece.

51. Review of *Division and Reunion 1829–1889,* by Woodrow Wilson, *Nation* 56 (13 April 1893): 278–79, in *PWW* 8: 185–90.

52. Hermann von Holst, review of *Division and Reunion 1829–1889,* by Woodrow Wilson, *Educational Review* 6 (June 1893): 87–90, in *PWW* 8: 222–24.

53. William Henry Bartlett to Wilson, 29 April 1893, in *PWW* 8: 200.

54. Kemp Plummer Battle, review of *Division and Reunion 1829–1889,* by Woodrow Wilson, *North Carolina University Magazine* 12 (May 1893): 283–85, in *PWW* 8: 203–5.

55. Wilson to Battle, 29 June 1893, in *PWW* 8: 274.

56. Review of *Division and Reunion 1829–1889,* by Woodrow Wilson, *Picayune,* 28 May 1893, in *PWW* 8: 218–19.

57. Cal M. Logue, "Restoration Strategies in Georgia, 1865–1880," in *Oratory in the New South,* ed. Waldo W. Braden (Baton Rouge: Louisiana State University Press, 1979), 61–64, 66–68.

58. Bruce Clayton, *The Savage Ideal: Intolerance and Intellectual Leadership in the South 1890–1914* (Baltimore: Johns Hopkins University Press, 1972), 17–20, 132; Paul M. Gaston, *The New South Creed* (New York: Alfred A. Knopf, 1970), 7. The Southern "love affair with middle class capitalism" is described in C. Vann Woodward, *Origins of the New South, 1877–1913* (Baton Rouge: Louisiana State University Press, 1951), 107–41.

59. Stephen A. Smith, *Myth, Media, and the Southern Mind* (Fayetteville: University of Arkansas Press, 1985), 30–33.

60. Wilson, *Division and Reunion 1829–1889,* 316–17.

61. Turner to Wilson, 16 July 1893 and 24 December 1894, in *PWW* 8: 279, 9: 118.

62. Review of *Division and Reunion 1829–1889,* by Woodrow Wilson, *Sewanee Review* 3 (February 1895): 172–88, in *PWW* 9: 162.

63. Frederick Bancroft, review of *Division and Reunion 1829–1889,* by Woodrow Wilson, *Political Science Quarterly* 8 (September 1893): 533–35, in *PWW* 8: 344. Italics are mine.

64. Cauthen, "The Coming of the Civil War," in *Writing Southern History,* 231–32; Bragdon, *Woodrow Wilson: The Academic Years,* 79.

65. Bragdon, *Woodrow Wilson: The Academic Years,* 239, 251.

66. For discussion of reactions to Owsley's "tone" of writing, see Michael

O'Brien, *The Idea of the American South 1920–1941* (Baltimore: Johns Hopkins University Press, 1979), 168–70.

67. George C. Osborn, *Woodrow Wilson: The Early Years*, 273.

68. See Frances FitzGerald, *America Revised: History Schoolbooks in the Twentieth Century* (Boston: Little, Brown, 1979), 229.

69. Harold Underwood Faulkner and Tyler Kepner, *America: Its History and People*, 5th ed. (New York: McGraw-Hill, 1950), 269. In the 1925 edition of *Division and Reunion*, Wilson's statement is on p. 239.

70. Clayton, *The Savage Ideal*, 35–39.

71. Brant Short, "'Reconstructed but Unregenerate': *I'll Take My Stand*'s Rhetorical Vision of Progress," *Southern Communication Journal* 29 (Winter 1994): 112–24.

72. Richard Weaver, *The Ethics of Rhetoric* (Chicago: Henry Regnery, 1953), 214.

73. Short, "'Reconstructed but Unregenerate,'" 113–14.

74. Edward Steele and Charles Redding, "The American Value System: Premises for Persuasion," *Western Speech* 26 (Spring 1962): 86.

75. Michael C. McGee, "The 'Ideograph': A Link Between Rhetoric and Ideology," *Quarterly Journal of Speech* 66 (February 1980): 5–6.

76. Charles U. Larson, *Persuasion: Reception and Responsibility* (Belmont, Calif.: Wadsworth, 1973), 140–43.

77. Ray A. Billington, *Frederick Jackson Turner: Historian, Scholar, Teacher* (New York: Oxford University Press, 1973) 185–86.

78. Henry Nash Smith, *Virgin Land: The American West as Symbol and Myth* (Cambridge: Harvard University Press, 1970), 12, 120.

79. Josiah Strong, *Our Country: Its Possible Future and Its Present Crisis* (New York: Baker and Taylor, 1885), 1, 173; see also 144–53 and 159–80.

80. James Oliver Robertson, *American Myth, American Reality* (New York: Hill and Wang, 1980), 165–70.

81. See, for instance, David Chalmers, *The Muckrake Years* (New York: D. Van Nostrand, 1974), 5.

82. *Milwaukee Sentinal*, 30 January 1921; *Minnesota Daily*, 7 June 1900. Turner's marked copy of the latter item is in Box 54 of the Frederick Jackson Turner Collection, Henry E. Huntington Library, San Marino, Calif.

83. See chapter 2 above, or my "Frederick Jackson Turner and the Rhetorical Impact of the Frontier Thesis," *Quarterly Journal of Speech* 63 (April 1977): 117–29, esp. 125–28.

84. Guy Emerson to Turner, 23 June 1920, in Box 30; George W. Bell's notebook, in File Drawer 14D. Both in the Turner Collection, Huntington Library.

85. *Portland Oregonian*, 1904 issue, in File Drawer 15D, Turner Collection, Huntington Library.

86. Cushing Strout, *The Pragmatic Revolt in American History: Carl Becker and Charles Beard* (New Haven: Yale University Press, 1958), 86.

87. David Noble, *Historians against History: The Frontier Thesis and the National Covenant in American Historical Writing since 1830* (Minneapolis: University of

Minnesota Press, 1965), 65–66.

88. For another summary of Beard's thesis, as well as a critique of his handling of evidence, see Lee Benson, *Turner and Beard: American Historical Writing Reconsidered* (New York: Free Press, 1960), 107–213.

89. Thomas A. Bailey to Merle Curti, 17 March 1948, in Box 3, File 3, Merle Curti Papers, State Historical Society of Wisconsin, Madison, Wis.

90. Robert E. Brown, *Charles Beard and the Constitution: A Critical Analysis of "An Economic Interpretation of the Constitution"* (Princeton: Princeton University Press, 1956), 8–9, 22–23, 194.

91. Noble, *Historians against History*, 65–66.

92. Richard Hofstadter, *The Progressive Historians* (New York: Alfred A. Knopf, 1969), 268.

93. Vernon L. Parrington, *Main Currents in American Thought*, 3 vols. (New York: Harcourt, Brace, 1927), 3:409.

94. See in particular lda Tarbell, "John D. Rockefeller, A Character Study, I," *McClure's Magazine* 25 (July 1905): 249. Examples of the muckrakers' essays are reprinted in Chalmers, *The Muckrake Years*, 77–151.

95. See *Allan Nevins on History*, ed. Ray A. Billington (New York: Scribner's Sons, 1975), xxiii and 68–81.

96. Allan Nevins to Walter Schwimmer, 10 April 1969, in Box 45, Allan Nevins Collection, Henry E. Huntington Library, San Marino, Calif.

97. Gordon S. Wood, review of *History of the Westward Movement*, by Frederick Merk, *History Book Club Review*, July 1978, 3–7.

98. Frederick Merk, *History of the Westward Movement* (New York: Alfred A. Knopf, 1978), 616–17.

99. As a fairly regular purchaser of History Book Club selections over the years, I do not recall receiving such a notification about another book.

100. Henry Nash Smith, *Virgin Land*, 4.

101. Gallup Youth Survey, in *St. Petersburg Times*, 4 July 1982. See also my "America's Opinion Leader Historians on Behalf of Success," *Quarterly Journal of Speech* 69 (May 1983): 111–26.

102. Stephen A. Smith, *Myth, Media, and the Southern Mind*, 45; Dewey W. Grantham, *The South and the Sectional Image* (New York: Harper and Row, 1967), 39–40. For a discussion of the "legend of the Old South" as "fantasy," see T. Harry Williams, *Romance and Realism in Southern Politics* (Athens: University of Georgia Press, 1961), 6–7.

103. Gunnar Myrdal, *An American Dilemma: The Negro Problem and Modern Democracy* (New York: Harper and Brothers, 1944), xlvi–xlvii, 4.

104. *An American Dilemma*, 1, 23–25; for an overview of the development of this creed in America, see 8–17.

105. See George B. Tindall, "The Central Theme Revisited," in *The Southerner as American*, ed. Charles Grier Sellers, Jr. (Chapel Hill: University of North Carolina Press, 1960), 104–29.

106. Myrdal, *An American Dilemma*, 23–25.

107. Tindall, "The Central Theme Revisited," in *The Southerner as American*, 116.

108. "The Central Theme Revisited," in *The Southerner as American*, 109, 115.

109. Short, "'Reconstructed but Unregenerate,'" 122–23.

110. Davidson to Tate, 29 October 1932, in *LCDT*, 275.

111. Howard K. Beale to Merle Curti, 6 October 1936, in Box 4, File 11, Curti Papers.

112. Tate to Lytle, 28 September 1935, in *LTL*, 97.

113. Frank L. Owsley, *Plain Folk of the Old South* (Baton Rouge: Louisiana State University Press, 1982), xix–xxi.

114. See Grady McWhiney, introduction to *Plain Folk of the Old South*, vii–xvii.

115. See Rupert Vance, review of *Plain Folk of the Old South*, by Frank L. Owsley, *Journal of Southern History* 16 (November 1950): 545–47.

116. Charles A. Beard, cited in McWhiney, introduction to *Plain Folk of the Old South*, x.

117. See Donald Davidson, "*I'll Take My Stand*: A History," *American Review* 5 (1935): 304.

118. William B. Hesseltine, "Look Away, Dixie," *Sewanee Review* 39 (1931): 101.

119. This particular photograph has been widely reprinted. See, for instance, *Time*'s special collector's issue (fall 1989) entitled *150 Years of Photo Journalism*, p. 37.

120. See Short, "'Reconstructed but Unregenerate,'" 116.

121. Richard Gray, *Writing the South: Ideas of an American Culture* (Cambridge: Cambridge University Press, 1986), 133.

122. Short, "'Reconstructed but Unregenerate,'" 116, 123.

123. A. Cheree Carlson, "Narrative as the Philosopher's Stone: How Russell H. Conwell Changed Lead into Diamonds," *Western Journal of Speech Communication* 53 (Fall 1989): 343–44.

124. Carlson, "Narrative as the Philosopher's Stone," 353.

125. Arthur M. Schlesinger, Jr., *A Thousand Days: John F. Kennedy in the White House* (Boston: Houghton Mifflin, 1965), 964.

126. See *A Thousand Days*, 966; Stefan Lorant, *The Glorious Burden: The American Presidency* (New York: Harper and Row, 1968), 814; Harold Faber, *The Kennedy Years* (New York: Viking, 1964), 284–85; James D. Barber, *The Presidential Character: Predicting Performance in the White House* (Englewood Cliffs, N.J.: Prentice-Hall, 1972), 340.

127. Theodore Sorensen, *Kennedy* (New York: Harper and Row, 1965), 492–93; and Barber, *The Presidential Character*, 340.

128. Tindall, "The Central Theme Revisited," in *The Southerner as American*, 121.

129. "George Wallace Overcomes: Running for Governor with New Black Friends," *Time*, 11 October 1982, 15–16.

130. Fred Bruning, "A Governor Snookers a Nation," *Macleans*, 7 February 1983, 9.

Chapter Seven

Barbara Tuchman, John Kennedy, and Why "The Missiles of October" Did Not Become *The Guns of August*: Narrative Fidelity from Archetypal Story Form

On 26 October 1962, during the Cuban Missile Crisis, President John Kennedy told his brother Robert, "I am not going to follow a course which will allow anyone to write a comparable book about this time, *The Missiles of October*. . . . If anybody is around to write after this, they are going to understand that we made every effort to find peace and every effort to give our adversary room to move." That "comparable book" was Barbara Tuchman's history of the onset of World War I, *The Guns of August*. Tuchman "made a great impression on the President," who expressed his perception of her moral to his brother Robert, Ted Sorensen, and Kenny O'Donnell that night by saying that "miscalculations of the Germans, the Russians, the Austrians, the French, and the British" caused World War I, and thus, with regard to the Cuban Missile Crisis, that "the great danger and risk in all of this is a miscalculation—a mistake in judgment."[1] As O'Donnell recalls: "Bobby, Ted Sorensen, and I sat with the President in his office and talked about the rash and impulsive actions . . . that can start wars. The President had recently read . . . *The Guns of August* . . . and was greatly impressed."[2] Sorensen remembers that John Kennedy restated then "the 1914 conversation between two German leaders on the origins and expansion of that war, a former chancellor asking 'How did it all happen?' and his successor saying, 'Ah, if one only knew.' 'If this planet,' said President Kennedy, 'is ever ravaged by nuclear war—if the survivors of that devastation can then endure the fire, poison, chaos and catastrophe—I do not want one of those survivors to ask another, 'How did it all happen?' and to receive the incredible reply: 'Ah, if only one knew.'"[3] Other commentaries acknowledge that when "the Kennedy brothers sat talking together of the crisis," the president "mentioned Barbara Tuchman's book, *The Guns of August,* and the miscalculations that had led the Great Powers to stumble into the 1914 war."[4] Now, when Richard Neustadt and Ernest May advocate in their *Thinking in Time: The Uses of History for Decision Makers* the application of the past in the making of present choices, their "Success Story" is the Cuban Missile Crisis and Tuchman's "sobering reference point" for Kennedy.[5] So discourse approached and read as history can be examined fruitfully in terms of its rhetorical influence upon one person at a precise, pivotal point in time.

Tuchman's impress upon Kennedy in October 1962 is not explained primarily as a result of the recency of his having read her book. Yes, Robert Kennedy said his brother read it "a short time before" 26 October 1962, and Neustadt and May describe Kennedy as "having just read" Tuchman's book.[6] Nevertheless, on 2 May 1962, Tuchman had Secretary of Defense Robert McNamara (her skiing acquaintance) "ask Mr. Kennedy on my behalf if we could quote him": her publishers had "heard via a rather circuitous grapevine that the President has also read the book and has said . . . *The Guns of August* should be required reading for everybody in the Army and Air Force over the rank of major."[7] Her letter was referred to Presidential Press Secretary Pierre Salinger, who confirmed that Kennedy "read your book with the greatest interest and felt that it would be extremely valuable for top officers in the Armed Services to read as well. He instructed General Chester V. Clifton, his Military Aide, to make arrangements for the book to be stocked in Armed Forces Libraries. This has been done." (But, Salinger added, "it would be better" if this fact "were not used either in connection with the further printing of your book or with any advertising.")[8] After reading Tuchman's book, Kennedy also telephoned Secretary of the Army Elvis Stahr, Jr., and requested he come to get a copy of the book, saying, "I want you to read this. And I want every officer in the Army to read it" (Stahr ordered the book be placed in officers' day rooms on army bases around the world, and commanders were informed that their commander-in-chief wanted them and their men to read it).[9] An earlier reading of Tuchman by Kennedy also is suggested in General Maxwell Taylor's recollection that the president "often quoted" *The Guns of August.*[10] We thus can say with reasonable certainty that Kennedy read the book at least six months before the Cuban Missile Crisis, a relatively long time for its message about "miscalculation" to be remembered and recited in October 1962 as pertinent to his presidential decision of monumental significance.

In October 1962, Kennedy's memory of the moral advanced by Tuchman's book functioned in an occurrence of that aforementioned phenomenon whereby one message must be evaluated critically in the context of other messages amid that "large and complex communication environment or 'mosaic' . . . of fragments or bits of information scattered over time and space and modes of communication."[11] Prominent among these were recommendations carefully considered and forcefully articulated by the executive committee of the National Security Council, "Excom," convened then to advise the president. For instance, Air Force Chief of Staff Curtis LeMay urged a "first strike" against the Soviet Union. Joint Chiefs of Staff General Maxwell Taylor's early recommendation was to "shoot them out" (although a "surgical" air strike was ruled out on 21 October when Tactical Air Command General Walter Sweeney "readily conceded" to Kennedy that "any such attack could not guarantee the destruction or neutralization of all the missiles"). For both the president and Excom members, another persuasive argument against an air strike was Bobby Kennedy's likening it to the Japanese sneak attack on Pearl Harbor.[12] President Kennedy ultimately decided to make Russia an offer: in return for the Soviets' not putting missiles in Cuba, the United States would remove Jupiter missiles from Turkey and guarantee not to mount military action against Fidel Castro, and while Russia considered that offer, a U.S. Navy blockade would interdict Soviet ships en route bringing the missiles to set upon already constructed launch pads. That decision reflected a lesson emergent from *The Guns of August* because (1) Tuchman's conscious intentions and compositional concerns to achieve a credible and interesting narrative yielded (2) persuasive emplotment metaphors, including (3) a synecdoche promoting a "conservative" solution to the crisis, (4) a metonymy heightening an alternative "tragic" outcome, and (5) an ultimate *allegoresis* achieved when her narrative made salient an analogy between the Cuban Missile Crisis and the outbreak of World War I.

I

Kennedy's concerns about "miscalculations" leading to nuclear war—the "great danger and risk" in October 1962—were consonant with Tuchman's conscious intentions for her book as well as her compositional choices on behalf of those objectives. Unlike other inquiries wherein critics' conclusions about discourse are derived largely from readings of texts under examination, this analysis is predicated upon Tuchman's compositional concerns as they are revealed in her correspondence with Denning Miller. During two years Tuchman was writing *The Guns of August*, Miller served editorially to "bring your publisher's scheme into possibly better focus" and "act as your sounding board." While viewing the book as "partially my brain child," Miller acknowledged to Tuchman that "our relationship . . . was much more on the level of a collaboration in creation, in which it was understood from the beginning that yours would be the travail and yours the credit therefrom."[13] These letters show Tuchman to be what Roderick Hart and Don Burks have described as a *"rhetorically sensitive person . . . willing to undergo the strain of adaptation"* in order "to deal better with the very different perceptual world of the Other." For while someone might "tell it like it is" from a "determination of which ideas are to be made known," that particular "it" does not necessarily prescribe the specific *"rhetorical configurations which can make 'it' social fare."* For a person to be "rhetorical means to have a kind of communicative humility, a realization that the idea as first constituted in my head may not be worth a damn when it confronts an unknown quantity—the Other." Moreover, *"because ideas themselves do not prescribe forms of verbalization, the rhetorically sensitive person tries to understand that an idea can be rendered in multi-form ways,"* and that person will "attempt to process and to choose among all possible verbal strategies *before* giving utterance to an idea."[14] Therein resides a rationale for writers of history to engage in that rhetorical process of adjusting ideas to people.

Tuchman's conception of her focus was delineated early when Miller recommended her book be "the single incident or thread" type, with this advice: "The canvas is indeed large and from your point of view overly formidable, perhaps, but I would submit that you might exercise a degree of exclusion to avoid writing simple history. I can suggest selecting those calculations and miscalculations of the statesmen and the General Staffs that led in due course to an almost perfect stalemate which persisted for some thirty-six months, with of course enormous slaughter."[15] Admittedly, some readers missed her moral about miscalculation. In retrospect, she lamented that "fifty percent at least of the critics of *The Guns of August* commented on what they said was my exposé of the stupidity of generals. Nothing of the kind was in my mind when I wrote.

What I meant to convey was that the generals were in the trap of circumstances, training, ideas, and national impulses of their time and their individual countries. I was not trying to convey stupidity but tragedy, fatality. Many reviewers understood this . . . but too many kept coming up with that word 'stupidity' to my increasing dismay."[16] For the Cuban Missile Crisis, however, Kennedy's closure as reader reflected an intended goal for the book—and discrete compositional preferences to achieve that impress by consciously striving for corroborative detail yielding credibility, engaging and maintaining interest, and identification with intellectual readers.

Tuchman believed that "corroborative detail" makes history "vivid and memorable" because (borrowing from Pooh-Bah in Gilbert and Sullivan's *The Mikado*) such particulars give "artistic verisimilitude to an otherwise bald and unconvincing" narrative.[17] But deciding what detail to include or discard for *The Guns of August* was difficult. Miller cautioned, "you love what you call the irrelevancies: they are the jewels; the history is only the thread in which they're hung. But like all jewels, there must be a setting, and this is what you must most carefully supply."[18] So he told her to visit France—which she did in August 1959—to experience the weather at that time of year and gain "the exact and proper meteorological frame for your enormous picture, and this will add depth and perceptiveness to the final story."[19] Indeed, Miller suggested a return to Flanders later that autumn to "see the kind of weather and the other conditions resulting from events in August."[20] As drafts progressed, Tuchman's editorial advisor lauded her methodology: "when you are dealing with incidents and people and closely coupled events, you string them together like jewels on a thread or embellish them beautifully with an effective style. This praise is justified and carried through over the vast majority of the work."[21] In Miller's assessment, "main issues" and "dramatic, climactic points to be stressed in your outlandish job of compression" were not obscured by overabundant details, and "the order and balance between the background material and the actual events is to me completely satisfactory."[22] Indeed, her ultimate book was praised as "military history at its clearest" reflecting a "real gift for military exposition" as well as "accurate emphasis of complete knowledge of what you are saying."[23]

The resultant credibility is evident in reactions to *The Guns of August*. One reader called it "the best book of war I have read." And, recognizing that Tuchman's "research must have been tremendous," a former

Army officer proclaimed that the book "sounds as if it were written by a graduate of the Command and General Staff School and a high ranking graduate at that." "I do not," he continued in well-intentioned praise, "see how a woman and civilian could have written this book."[24] Tuchman's residual ethos led to her being asked to write a chapter on the World War I battle of Tannenberg for a volume titled *Great Battles* as well as one about World War I "for a new series in the history of the United States."[25] If these sanguine reactions are any index, that credibility was apparent to John Kennedy, too.

During the Cuban Missile Crisis, many voices articulated advice, warnings, and suggested courses of action. Each voice, however, evinced varying degrees of credibility. In a situation when military intervention was considered seriously as an option, President Kennedy was wary of recommendations from several members of the Joint Chiefs of Staff. For example, after listening to Air Force Chief of Staff General Curtis LeMay present bombing plans to an Excom meeting, Kennedy asked, "How will the Russians respond?" LeMay said, "They'll do nothing." "Are you trying to tell me," retorted the president, "that they'll let us bomb their missiles, and kill a lot of Russians and then do nothing?" Back in his office, Kennedy observed that the Chiefs of Staff had one thing going for them: "If we listen to them, and do what they want us to do, none of us will be alive later to tell them that they were wrong."[26] Actually, LeMay was the least credible of Kennedy's chiefs of staff. The president often walked out of meetings in which LeMay conducted briefings, and a White House staffer said that Kennedy often had "a kind of fit" if LeMay were mentioned.[27] Richard Reeves concludes that Kennedy "distrusted the military, at least its commanders" because the Joint Chiefs of Staff "had mislead him, even betrayed him, in the weeks leading up to the Bay of Pigs." In the spring of 1962, Kennedy also read *Seven Days in May* by Fletcher Knebel and Charles Bailey, a novel about an attempted military coup against an American president. To a confidant, Red Fay, Kennedy admitted, "It's possible" but "conditions would have to be right. If the country had a young president, and he had a Bay of Pigs, there would be a certain uneasiness. Maybe the military would do a little criticizing behind his back. Then if there were another Bay of Pigs, the reaction of the country would be 'Is he too young and inexperienced?' The military would almost feel that it was their patriotic obligation to stand ready to preserve the integrity of the nation and only God know just what segment of Democracy they would be defending."

A military man Kennedy did respect, however, was Army General Maxwell Taylor, who during the Missile Crisis served him as chairman of the Joint Chiefs. Taylor was credible because he was, as Richard Reeves concludes, an "intellectual," and Kennedy "liked to make the point that his chief military advisor spoke French and German and Spanish. The official White House line, repeated often to reporters, was that if you asked Taylor about a problem in the Middle East, he wanted to know how Xerxes had handled it."[28] Whether he was reacting to Tuchman the writer of history or to Taylor the reader of that discourse, Kennedy was impressed favorably by a person's historical knowledge; and the more someone's sense of history was evident, the more that source may have influenced the president's thinking during the Cuban Missile Crisis.

Tuchman also was concerned about reader interest when heretofore unknown "miscalculations" caused ultimate horror *already* known. Although she had considered using "the sand-bag technique" which described French miscalculations first followed by German planning which was unanticipated and thereby successful, Tuchman preferred what she called a "Look out!" approach that described von Schlieffen's plan before discussing France's incorrect assumptions:

> That is, if Schlieffen is first and the reader knows the Germans are coming through in a wide right wing sweep across the whole of Belgium and THEN we show the French making all their plans for offense and defense to the east and north-east and turning their backs to the Belgian frontier, the reader will (I hopefully conceive) get into the state of the play—or movie-goer watching in agony as the heroine all unaware is stalked by the villain about to bash her dead in until he—the play-goer—cannot contain himself any longer and screams "Look out!" . . . The French plan seems to REQUIRE the reader to know the German plan first."[29]

Yet she admitted a "problem that has been bothering me for some time":

> I find myself constantly—well, not constantly, but here and there—putting in those signposts to doom and disaster of which you disapprove as "anticipating," when, as you say, the story should be allowed to tell itself. . . . I ask myself why do I feel the need to put those things in; there must be some reason. I have come up with two

possible answers. 1) What does the average reader know about the early part of the war? Generally speaking, I should think, strictly from nothing. He knows the Allies won in the end but I am sure he has little idea how close a shave it was in August or how disastrous were the German successes (occupation of Belgium and northern France) in creating the conditions for a prolonged war with all its casualties and consequences for Europe and the world. 2) Many of the dooms and disasters did not take place or were not evident until after the period which my book covers and therefore the reader will not have them in mind or remember them unless I suggest them. 3) If the reader does not know that such-and-such a decision is going to lead to disaster, then such-and-such lacks drama, no? Or, to put it another way: does it not heighten the drama to hint or suggest that around that next turn disaster waits in ambush? Or do you not think so? Or what do you think about all this?[30]

Miller affirmed the "serious technical problem" of "letting your reader have a signpost to disaster" but deemed her "pace and timing" such that "interest is supported and stimulated, and the matter which you select to recount dramatic, intimate and full of splendid personalized action."[31] Readers agreed. A mother "couldn't resist reading page after page out loud" to her daughter, who "listened spellbound." Another reader said The Guns of August "has been so engrossing . . . that I haven't wanted to put it down, which is strange for a story where the plot is known."[32] But for a reader like Kennedy, Miller's advice had implications in addition to interest.

While commenting about a "signpost to disaster," Miller described "disadvantages of asserting superiority, or using hindsight, of making an active participant sound or look like a fool."[33] He warned Tuchman against being "portentous or confidential . . . superficial, flip or—worst of all—to any degree partisan" and against "the subconsciously egotistical pleasure you might be feeling about stressing the follies, the mistakes, the errors in judgment that so copiously appear in the events you have set out to recount." Moreover, he told her, "you mustn't tell your reader what you're going to tell him. Tell him when you come to it and tell it ardently and dramatically. . . . I would like you to guide your reader a little less. He is bound to make the correct inferences if you give him the facts one by one." (And in this fifteen-page letter, Miller suggested that Tuchman delete passages that were making her writing portentous)[34] Wary of anything which "slightly insults the intelligent reader," Miller also explained why she must be "more indirect, more thoughtful, less quick, less hindsighted, less superior, less critical":

> As to "signposts," let me set myself straight with you. There are, of course, places where they are needed, notably where you are pointing ahead—way ahead—to things that are to occur after the close of your book. These, I suggest, are of one class—large, big lettering and clear. Then there are those others that refer to the account which you are telling. These are to heighten suspense, to alert a sluggish reader or to titillate a sophisticated one.
>
> In both cases the technical means should be carefully examined, I think. "Did any of the other boys playing with that blond-haired child think that one day . . . ?" "If she had only known that this chance decision. . . ." "Who would have thought . . . ?" "If the future were known, would anyone . . . ?"
>
> Such devices as these have all been used and indeed delighted readers when they were new and in fashion, but such techniques have become increasingly subtle and refined as readers have become more experienced and sophisticated.[35]

As a Harvard history and government major, John Kennedy studied the origins of World War I and later read British historian A. J. P. Taylor's writings about World War II.[36] Indeed, history, specifically, may have been Kennedy's favorite academic subject as early as the sixth grade at Riverdale Private School. Later, in boarding school at Choate, he "blossomed" and "realized his high potential in History." And at Harvard, as young Jack proclaimed it to his isolationist father, his goal in his senior honors thesis was "the explanation of why England was so badly prepared for the present war."[37] After publication of that thesis in 1940 as *Why England Slept,* the Harvard undergraduate received "an extraordinary letter of congratulation" from Liddell Hart, then among prominent British military historians; young Kennedy was sufficiently familiar with Hart's writings subsequently to defend that military historian when he was criticized by a "misguided editor" in the American press.[38] With these historical perspectives brought to his presidency, John Kennedy was among those more "sophisticated" and "intelligent" readers Miller had in mind.

Reader reactions to *The Guns of August* suggest that Tuchman's "superb vignettes" made 1914 leaders "come alive" by showing "roots and the very knots of human behavior." Because of Tuchman's "extraordinary" ability "to bring alive the men who played parts in the drama," another reader likened her to Herodotus, who believed "proper study of history is men. . . . People are always to the fore in this book."[39] Tuchman had heard Miller's advice to avoid "making an active participant sound or look like a fool" and to avoid suggesting that "people were puppets of fate and intelligence was not human and apt to reason incompletely or erroneously." And as Miller further explained to her, "making people out fools doesn't seem to me to be either interesting or attractive history."[40] Thus, in *The Guns of August,* those leaders who made the human "miscalculations" in August 1914 that lead to world war were people with whom Kennedy could identify in October 1962. All adaptations described in Tuchman's correspondence are indices of her *conscious* compositional efforts; but the effect of those efforts upon the resultant emplotment undergirding her narrative suggests other, more subtle sources of rhetorical impress by *The Guns of August.*

II

Narration is a primary mode of communication deriving rhetorical potency overtly through fidelity (corroborating what people know already as true) or probability (revealing a patent, discursive logic of good reasons).[41] Yet within broader elements of narrative, subtle cues of form may reside and appeal to "the psychology of the audience." Kenneth Burke further expounds on this principle of persuasion: "*Form* . . . is an arousing and fulfillment of desires. A work has form insofar as one part of it leads a reader to anticipate another part, to be gratified by the experience." Moreover, that "form, having to do with the creation and gratification of needs, is 'correct' in so far as it gratifies the needs which it creates."[42] Current theory of history offers an intriguing paradigm of potential affect derived from form: capabilities of narrative to embody emplotment metaphors conducing to readers' perceptions of emergent persuasive, archetypal story formulae. For Hayden White, "historical narratives are not only models of past events and processes, but also metaphorical statements which suggest a relation of similitude between such events and processes and the story types that we conventionally use to endow the events of our lives with culturally sanctioned meanings."[43] White's paradigm is useful not only to describe historical texts but also to make informed speculation about how narrative form in its most subtle dimensions rhetorically may affect readers—including a president of the United States engaged in making a decision pivotal to world peace.

Explication of the rhetoric of emplotment metaphors presumes, however, that White does not define metaphor in the traditional sense, as current communication studies do—i.e., as a word or phrase used nonliterally whereby a communicator strives to have us understand "something in terms of something else. . . . the thisness of a that, or the thatness of a this."[44] Literally, no curtain made of iron descended across the continent of Europe at the close of World War II, yet to view the fortified boundary between Communist east and democratic west as being strong and impenetrable, excluding any view of what was happening on the other side, is partially a result of Winston Churchill's use of "Iron Curtain" as a metaphor to represent those new geopolitical conditions. Moreover, for any mode of metaphor, figuration is archetypal when it evokes imagery "grounded in prominent features of conditions which are inescapably salient in human consciousness." Universally understood across cultures or communities, such figurations include those of light and darkness, high and low (as in the 23rd Psalm reference to "the valley of the shadow of death"), as well as the sea (as in Martin Luther King's reference to "the Negro lives on a lonely island of poverty in the midst of a vast ocean of material prosperity").[45]

Foregoing an impulse to regard figuration in the traditional sense of a linguistic manipulation whereby a word or phrase *per se* is used nonliterally, metaphor is regarded profitably here as a way of thinking that is widely pervasive among humans. George Lakoff and Mark Johnson offer the emphatic reminder that "human *thought processes* are largely metaphorical":

> Metaphor is for most people a device of the poetic imagination and the rhetorical flourish—a matter of extraordinary rather than ordinary language. Moreover, metaphor is typically viewed as a characteristic of language alone, a matter of words rather than thought or action. For this reason, most people think they can get along perfectly well without metaphor. We have found, on the contrary, that metaphor is pervasive in everyday life, not just in language but in thought and action. Our ordinary conceptual system, in terms of which we both think and act, is fundamentally metaphorical in nature. . . . the way we think, what we experience, and what we do every day is very much a matter of metaphor.

Furthermore, because "*the essence of metaphor is understanding and experiencing one kind of thing in terms of another*," an appropriate frame of reference for the remainder of this chapter is the fact "that *metaphor* means
metaphorical concept."[46] Thus, to support their assertion that "*no metaphor
can ever be comprehended or even adequately represented independently of its
experiential basis*," Lakoff and Johnson demonstrate in great detail how
"our thoughts, attitudes, and actions" are "grounded in our experience"
so that our perception of the world about us is often a synecdoche, i.e.,
the part is apprehended for the whole; or a metonymy, i.e., the tangible
entity is apprehended for the less tangible one.[47] What remains here is
to illustrate with *The Guns of August* how history may embody
emplotments to affect readers such as John Kennedy during the Cuban
Missile Crisis.

In White's view, any emplotment "metaphor" implicit in historical
writing evolves from selectivity during the process of creating that narrative, for what is included (however meticulously) or deleted in narration achieves only an incomplete "representation" of events as literal
fact—and therefore constitutes metaphor. Unlike the chronicler who
"simply describes what happens in the order in which it happens," the
historian as "narrator . . . picks out the most important events, traces the
causal and motivational connections between them, and gives us an organized, coherent account." The resultant "good story" is one where
"all the extraneous noise or static is cut out" and "we the audience are
told . . . just what is necessary to 'further the plot.' . . . selection is made
of all the events and actions the characters may engage in, and only a
small minority finds its way into the story."[48] Or, in another view from
historians describing the philosophy of their discourse, attaining "historical truth" poses a problem for its writers. On the one hand, "historical narratives are clearly not arbitrary compositions. They are anchored
in reality in all sorts of ways." Yet a historical narrative is not a "mechanical reproduction of what happened . . . not a photographic portrait
of a sequence of events . . . its truth or truthfulness cannot be tested by
looking at the actual events." When creating their discourse, historians
of necessity exercise selectivity so that in their final products, "history is
not the totality of events, but only what people think happened."[49] Stated
another way, the "only ordering relation of chronicles" is that by which
writers proceed "and then . . . and then . . . and then. . . ." Narratives,
however, "contain indefinitely many ordering relations, and indefinitely

many ways of *combining* these relations. It is such combination that we mean when we speak of the coherence of a narrative, or lack of it. . . . So narrative form in history, as in fiction, is an artifice, the product of individual imagination. Yet at the same time it is accepted as claiming truth—that is, as representing a real ensemble of interrelationships in past actuality."[50] Selectivity has rhetorical implications.

Tuchman's readers told her they were impressed by "the brilliant manner in which you organized and presented this staggering array of material" and "your great skill in manipulating such a vast amount of material with the utmost clarity and economy of style."[51] Creative selectivity also may impose upon historians' narratives "a deep structural content," however. Hayden White describes this "essentially *poetic* act" as one whereby the historian "*pre*figures . . . a domain upon which to . . . explain 'what was *really* happening,'" and the "deep level of consciousness on which a historical thinker chooses conceptual strategies" manifests itself in one of several "tropes of poetic language." Furthermore, these "*unique* structural elements" attain "explanatory affect" derived from "archetypal story forms" with which "the historian emplots his narrative account of 'what happened' . . . to explicate 'the point of it all' or 'what it all adds up to' in the end." This emplotment metaphor "is *poetic* inasmuch as it is precognitive and precritical in the economy of the historian's own consciousness."[52] Yet the "verbal model offered by the historian as a representation and explanation of 'what *really* happened' in the past" also is rhetorical. For White in the *Content of the Form,* "historical discourse directs the reader's attention to a secondary referent, namely, the plot structures of the various story types cultivated in a given culture. When the reader recognizes the story being told in a historical narrative as a specific kind of story—for example, as an epic, romance, tragedy, comedy, or farce,—he can be said to have comprehended the meaning produced by the discourse. This comprehension is nothing other than the recognition of the form of the narrative."[53] And for archetypal plot structures "more serious, more authoritative, more educational and closer to fact and truth than the rest," the most pertinent and appealing narrative form for a world leader at a time of apocalyptic crisis may reflect either of "two main tendencies, a 'comic' tendency to integrate the hero with his society, and a 'tragic' tendency to isolate him"—particularly when those "traditional tales and myths and histories have a strong tendency to stick together and form encyclopaedic aggregates."[54] However subtle their impress, those aggregates are rhetorically generated.

III

For *The Guns of August,* Tuchman at the outset decided to depict "a kind of madness arising out of those first 30 days that to realize is to shiver for mankind"—a decision which made Miller "extremely happy."[55] Her "single thread or incident" book attributes the four years of horror of World War I to events that took place in one month. The narrative thereby is emplotted with synecdoche—a part signifying the whole. For although the leaders' miscalculations are the products of several years of planning (also explained by Tuchman), her story essentially takes place in August, a time span with easily perceived parameters. Synecdoche has its counterpart in verbal behavior at the sentence level when a word or phrase signifying a prominent part stands for or represents the whole. For example, a sailor may be called a "hand." Or a group of ships may be referred to in the manner of the Roman historian who wrote, "They saw a fleet of ten sails on the horizon." Or as Winston Churchill epitomized Dunkirk in World War II, where—from 29 May to 4 June 1940—338,226 British and French troops (with some Dutch and Belgians as well) were evacuated off an open beach under constant shelling and aerial attack: "If the British Empire and its Commonwealth last for a thousand years, men will say: 'This was their finest hour.'" To Kenneth Burke, synecdoche conduces to "realism" in discourse because

> sensory representation is, of course, synecdochic in that the senses abstract certain qualities from some bundle of electro-chemical activities we call, say, a tree, and these qualities (such as size, shape, color, texture, weight, *etc.*) can be said "truly to represent" a tree. Similarly, artistic representation is synecdochic, in that certain relations within the medium "stand for" corresponding relations outside it. There is also a sense in which the well-formed work of art is internally synecdochic, as the beginning of a drama contains its close or the close sums up the beginning, the parts all thus being consubstantially related.[56]

Although "critical selection and compression" constituted a problem for Tuchman— "one of the hardest parts" of her writing"—synecdoche allowed her "to stick closely to the calendar," a technique which Miller deemed the "correct solution" for the organization of the book.[57] That solution also might be 'correct" for readers who mentally might mark off days in the progression toward doom.

For Kennedy in October 1962, Tuchman's day-by-day unfolding of momentous events could have been realistically poignant. The word "August," specifically, could have special poignancy for the president because of his own earlier experiences. During August 1939, on the eve of the outbreak of World War II, while his father, Joseph P. Kennedy, was ambassador to Great Britain, young Jack Kennedy was traveling extensively and sending reports to his father from Paris, Munich, Berlin, Russia, Rumania, German-occupied Prague, and Vienna. In those last days of peace, the Harvard undergraduate witnessed "a level of brinksmanship that would not be repeated until he himself became commander-in-chief of the most powerful armed forces in the world." In Germany, Jack listened to Adolf Hitler's speech in the Reichstag demanding that Poland return the free city of Danzig. He also was present on 3 September 1939 in the Strangers' Gallery of the House of Commons to hear Prime Minister Neville Chamberlain announce the British declaration of war (a day on which he heard the air raid sirens in London).[58] In the president's experiences as a college student, "August" could easily have connoted the eve of a catastrophic war whose antecedents could be traced to events and preparations that had taken place years if not decades earlier. Yet Kennedy's decision about the blockade could have been affected in another way—by synecdochic compression, if indeed this particular mode of emplotment heightens a reader's appreciation of conservative solutions to problems at hand.

In White's paradigm of emplotment metaphors, synecdoche evolves from historians' abilities "to concentrate on the individual details of the scenes" being narrated after proceeding "through the flood of documents to the sure selection of those that were significant and those that were insignificant as evidence"; these historians thereby "grasp the essence of an 'idea' at the heart of the process of development which it was their purpose first to ensnare in narrative prose."[59] One acknowledged epitome of this mode of historiography is Leopold von Ranke, who believed a significant way "of acquiring knowledge about human affairs" is through "perception of the particular." Although "particulars" might give a "harsh, disconnected, colorless, and tiring" aspect to narrative, "the study of particulars, even of a single detail, has its value, if it is done well," and historians thus must distinguish between significant and insignificant historical evidence to achieve "penetration of details."[60] Selected materials then become sequential bases of historians' narratives. Such synecdochic "representation" can establish (implicitly or explicitly) what Kenneth Burke calls "a *relationship* or *connectedness* between" the elements. In White's paradigm, however, that process likely yields an archetypal story cast in the mode of "Comedy" which is "a plot form that has as its central theme the notion of *reconciliation*." The resultant "feeling engendered in the audience" is "specifically Conservative" because "the tone of voice is accommodationist, the mood is optimistic"; for "Conservatives are inclined to imagine historical evolution as a progressive elaboration of the institutional structure that *currently* prevails . . . that is, the best form of society that men can 'realistically' hope for, or legitimately aspire to, for the time being."[61] Furthermore, "reconciliations which occur at the end of Comedy are reconciliations of men with men, of men with their world and their society; the condition of society is represented as being purer, saner, and healthier as a result of the conflict among seemingly inalterably opposed elements in the world."[62] More significantly, in emplotments of this particular narrative mode (often set forth in some "calendar arrangement" suggestive of a "natural cycle"), the archetypal "central figure" in what Northrup Frye labels the comic mode eventually achieves "a heroic triumph . . . in the teeth of strong opposition."[63] What role would be more appropriate as a beckoning archetype with which Kennedy might identify?

When perceived as "characteristically more competent" with "wider sources of information," historians in specific contexts can be those "opinion leaders" corroborating authoritatively what people read or hear from other sources and already are inclined to believe. Such reinforcement from Tuchman likely would help cause Kennedy to seek a "conservative" solution to the Missile Crisis in order to avoid making his own "miscalculation." Sorensen attests that "a favorite Kennedy word from my earliest association with him was 'miscalculation,'" for the president's Harvard course on origins of World War I taught him "how quickly countries which were comparatively uninvolved were taken, in the space of a few days, into war."[64] Kennedy's preoccupation with that word irritated Russian Premier Nikita Khrushchev during their 1961 meeting in Vienna to discuss Germany, disarmament, and nuclear testing. During the first day of talks, Kennedy referred to "the danger that a Russian miscalculation might trigger a war." Use of that word triggered an angry retort from Khrushchev: "All I ever hear from you people and your news correspondents and your friends in Europe and every place else is that damned word miscalculation! You ought to take that word and bury

it in cold storage and never use it again! I'm sick of it."[65] In Arthur
Schlesinger's characterization of Kennedy during the Missile Crisis, the
president's decision-making capability in the face of nuclear war was
influenced by "fear, not of Khruschev's intentions, but of error, of something going terribly wrong down the line."[66] From the standpoint of fidelity and probability, a narrative structure embodying at some level of
perception a conservative approach would appeal to a reader adamant
about avoiding "miscalculation."

Tuchman also complemented the more direct, impassioned plea
(with heavily underscored words) that Adlai Stevenson made to
Kennedy, urging him to avoid "rash" or "impetuous" action: "I know
your dilemma is to strike before the Cuban sites are operational. . . . The
national security must come first. *But the means adopted have such incalcu-
lable consequences that I feel you should have made it clear that the existence of
nuclear missile bases anywhere is* NEGOTIABLE before we start anything.
. . . So I will only repeat that it should be clear as a pikestaff that the U.S.
was, is, and will be ready to negotiate the elimination of bases and anything else. . . . blackmail and intimidation *never,* negotiation and sanity
always."[67] Believing that Khrushchev was "testing his toughness,"
Kennedy was "annoyed" at first by Stevenson's inclinations toward "negotiation and sanity," for he initially regarded them as evidence of the
U.N. Ambassador's favoring appeasement.[68] Nevertheless, an indirect
index of consonance between Tuchman's "conservative" moral and
Kennedy's ultimate closure then comes from another of her readers in
1962: "What sticks in my mind a few weeks after an admittedly quick
reading, concentrated on the political rather than the purely military
story": Tuchman "put across some points of vital importance—points
which in view of the audience your book will reach may even make a
shred of difference." Hers was "compounded evidence that for non-to-
talitarian man there are no grand solutions—only immediate problems
calling for an endless search for the lesser evil, the minor loss, the outcome that will in the long run be less harmful to humanity in both senses
of the word, to human beings and to human values. If more of us realized that, our leaders might have a better chance to bring mankind
through the Sixties."[69] But if synecdochic emplotment as archetype "even-
tuates in a vision of the ultimate *reconciliation* of opposed forces," tragedy is an archetypal story in metonymical form conducing to "*revelation*
of the nature of forces opposing man."[70] In Tuchman's book, the "Guns"
of the title constitutes a metonymy and a complementary emplotment

mode with the potential to heighten for readers the tragic outcome of any decision that is radical rather than conservative.

IV

Whereas "August" is a synecdochic part representing a whole of events leading to World War I, "Guns" epitomizes scrupulous, long-term German planning for the war and thus constituted metonymy. This figure of "reduction" from intangibles like mental thought processes and decisions to a "corresponding" tangible object "so material that it can be reproduced, bought, and sold," thereby creates an "*embodiment*" capable of producing "a corresponding state of *consciousness*" in readers. More-over, metonymy as a device of "poetic realism" is the concomitant of that process of reduction which yields "scientific realism." For as Burke also suggests, "language develops by metaphorical extension, in bor-rowing words from the realm of the corporeal, visible, tangible and applying them by analogy to the realm of the incorporeal, invisible, intangible." Therefore, from the standpoint of meaning evoked by dis-course, "any attempt to deal with human relationships . . . becomes nec-essarily the *reduction* of some higher or more complex realm of being to the terms of a lower or less complex realm of being."[71] For instance, to express metonymically the superiority of what can be achieved with the mind, an intangible, over what is achieved through the very tangible force of arms, one might say, "The pen is mightier than the sword"—using two objects, the both of which are tangible and touchable. Emplotment with metonymy can be compatible with synecdoche within the same dis-course, for as Mink suggests, two narratives might "be combined (un-der suitable restrictions on chronology and coincidence of characters and events) to form a single more complex narrative." Furthermore, because "there are different ways of emplotting the same chronicle of events," a likelihood exists that "historical narratives *should* aggregate; insofar as they make truth-claims about a selected segment of past ac-tuality, they must be compatible with and complement other narratives which overlap or are continuous with them."[72] Tuchman's metonymy and synecdoche could complement each other in Kennedy's mind.

Tuchman's metonymy to represent intangible German planning became "Guns"—"gigantic siege cannon of such size and destructive power that it had not been thought possible that such guns could be made mobile." Engineered, built, and tested by Germany in 1909 and

1910 to be ready at precisely the right time to reduce Belgian forts, particularly at Liege, in 1914, they are described by Tuchman in *The Guns of August*:

> One, built by Skoda, the Austrian munitions firm, was a 12-inch (305 mm.) mortar; the other built by Krupp's at Essen, was a monster of 16.5 inches (420 mm.) which together with its gun carriage was 24 feet long, weighed 98 tons, fired a shell a yard long weighing 1,800 pounds at a range of 9 miles and required a crew of 200 attendants. . . . Krupp's, working in iron secrecy, was ready with a model of the 420 in 1909. The sawed-off bloated giant . . . had to be transported by rail in two sections each requiring a locomotive to pull it. Spur tracks had to be laid to bring the gun to its emplacement pit which, owing to the tremendous downward thrust of the recoil, had to be dug several yards deep and filled with concrete in which the gun was embedded and from which it could only be released by blasting. The emplacement process required 6 hours. . . . The Austrian Skoda 305s, completed in 1910, had the advantage of superior mobility. Motor-drawn in three sections consisting of gun, mount, and portable foundation, they could travel 15 to 20 miles in a day. Instead of tires, their wheels were continuous belts of what was then awesomely described as "iron feet." At the point of emplacement, the portable steel foundation was set down, the mount bolted to it, and the gun fitted to the mount, the whole process requiring 40 minutes.[73]

While writing about those guns, Tuchman corresponded with Miller about accuracy of detail (whether they were mortars or howitzers, if their barrels were rifled, if the barrel was a "section," if there were three or four sections, and what was a "traction engine" to pull sections).[74] Miller proclaimed that "the stuff about the guns is wonderful" because "we all expected the great Belgian fortresses to be impregnable. Thus the great shock of August 1914 was their reduction in as short a time. . . . The figures you quote seem almost unbelievable. The German railways that brought them to the border must have been, I would guess, entirely rebuilt for this purpose. . . . All you tell me about the crew, *etc.* is to me stimulating and exciting. It is—I agree—indeed great!" And while concluding "the idea of the Big Guns is perfect," Miller articulated a *literary* rationale which may reflect his appreciation for the "objective correlative" whereby an external object represents an inner condition not readily perceived: "Up to this chapter you have sought out people to illustrate and inspirit your tale. To switch to objects here makes, I think, for a good, dramatic contrast, since the switch is so historically right."[75]

For *rhetorical* impress, however, Tuchman's "switch to objects," deemed by Miller "so historically right," had other implications. Again, Kennedy's earlier experiences at the outbreak of World War II would have endowed German "guns" of 1914 with poignancy for him. After Britain declared war against Germany, Ambassador Joseph Kennedy was "panic stricken" for the safety of his family and immediately booked passage for his wife, Rose, all the children, and their nanny back to New York. Sensitive, though, "to possible charges that the members of his own family were, like proverbial rats, deserting the sinking ship" ahead of other American citizens in England, Joe Kennedy staggered the departures of his family members. Young Jack was among the last to leave England and before going was pressed into service by the American Embassy. On the first full day of the war, the British passenger liner *Athenia*, bound from Liverpool to New York, was torpedoed and sunk by the U-30, one of 39 German submarines already on station in the area. Of 1,400 passengers aboard, over 300 were Americans; and of more than 100 people who died, 28 were U.S. citizens. Most of the American survivors, picked up by a British destroyer, were landed in Scotland. On the evening of 6 September 1939, as newspapers reported, "Jack Kennedy was sent up to Glasgow to represent his father because the Embassy staff in London was so rushed with work that no regular member could be spared." In Glasgow, the "schoolboy diplomat," as he was called in the press, had the task of reassuring American survivors who were demanding a return to America either on a U.S. Navy battleship or in a convoy escorted by American destroyers. Often shouting, young Kennedy as a twenty-two-year-old college student explained how in the face of a German naval blockade "we are still neutral, and the neutrality law still holds. . . . You will be safe in a ship flying the American flag under international law; a neutral ship is safe" (an appeal by which most of the survivors were "unimpressed").[76] In his first, direct experience with a wartime event, Kennedy dealt with effects of an attack in 1939 by a German submarine, a tangible object whose being already in the area at the outset of the war was the direct result of prior planning and long-term preparation—just as German "guns" were ready in August 1914.

Tuchman's "switch to objects" had additional implications. In retrospect, we know Kennedy did not fear the likelihood that atomic warheads would be affixed to Russian missiles en route by sea for launchpads in Cuba. In 1987, scholars of the early 1960s convened at the Hawk's Cay Conference with surviving "Excom" members (including Robert McNamara, Arthur Schlesinger, Jr., and Theodore Sorensen) to reassess the event. Thomas Shelling observed that "Given the fact that the Soviets had never deployed any nuclear missiles outside the Soviet Union before, and that they do not even trust their own military with custody of warheads in the Soviet Union . . . it seems almost inconceivable . . . they would then have trusted the warheads with anybody outside their borders." Secretary of Defense McNamara, who had no "hard evidence" about Russia's putting atomic warheads in Cuba, later explained why they had not been the crux of the problem: "I believe we had 5,000 nuclear warheads at that time and the Soviets had 300. . . . Did putting 40 launchers in Cuba change the military balance of power? I didn't believe it then and I don't believe it today. I asked in 1962: What difference did it make if we were killed by a missile from Moscow or a missile from Cuba? I don't think it makes any difference. When you try to understand something like this, you have to begin with an understanding of what the problem is." Conference participants agreed a "subtext dancing just beneath the surface" of Excom's discussions in 1962 was "whether the Soviet challenge was primarily military or political." Hindsight says Kennedy deemed the challenge political; missiles in Cuba were tangible objects signifying intangible Russian influence in the Caribbean.[77] According to Arthur Schlesinger's observations of Kennedy during the events of October, the president perceived the purpose of Russian missiles in Cuba as dealing America "a tremendous political blow."[78] Subsequently at the Hawk's Cay Conference, Schlesinger epitomized his view:

> while the missiles might not have had much effect on the overall U.S.-Soviet military balance, they had a considerable effect on the world *political* balance. The emplacement of nuclear missiles in Cuba would prove the Soviet ability to act with impunity in the very heart of the American zone of vital interest—a victory of great significance for the Kremlin. . . . It was a bold move into the American political sphere which, had it worked, would have dealt a severe blow to the American position world-wide. The simple calculus of military power wasn't the only thing that mattered.[79]

Or in White's words, man may have "a tendency toward Metonymical reductions of *events* into *agencies*, or of 'phenomena' into 'manifestations' of imagined 'noumenal' substances."[80]

So at one level, Tuchman's metonymy about tangible phenomena in 1914 complemented Kennedy's intuition about Soviet intentions in 1962 as intangibly political. For as White also explains, "by metonymy, then, one can simultaneously distinguish between two phenomena and reduce one to the status of a manifestation of the other."[81] Further corroboration for the likelihood of such a closure on Kennedy's part emerged during the 1987 Hawk's Cay Conference when former Excom members met with historians to reassess what they referred to several times as "the *Guns of August* scenario" of the Cuban Missile Crisis and the lesson that "seems to hold as clearly today as it did then." When elaborating about "the First World War or *Guns of August* analogy," Theodore Sorensen clarified his point by speculating about "whether your loss of control problem was with a howitzer or with a nuclear missile."[82] The metonymy of Tuchman's "Guns" persisted as a potent frame of reference!

At another level, the metonymic analog of the "Guns of August" and the "Missiles of October" made more salient in Kennedy's consciousness the dire outcome of "miscalculation" then: his expressed fear of resultant nuclear war using all missiles. For emplotment purposes, metonymy offered a "dramatic contrast" (in Miller's phrase, as Tuchman's editorial advisor) between a conservative, reconciliatory crisis outcome and a radical one of the "tragedy" and "enormous slaughter" of total war Tuchman hoped to make vivid. Tragedy as an archetypal story form has "no festive occasions, except false or illusory ones; rather, there are intimations of states of division among men more terrible than that which incited the tragic agon at the beginning of the drama." Moreover, metonymy is a "fundamental trope of 'realistic' prose," for "the fundamental problem of 'realistic' representation of those areas of experience not terminologically disciplined in the way that physics is, is to provide an adequate schema of words for representing the schema of thoughts which it takes to be the truth *about* reality."[83] From the standpoint of the capability to communicate effectively an archetype, narrative should embody some element of "realism" which "evokes the response 'How like that is to what we know'!" Furthermore, narratives also often rely on "the introduction of an omen or portent, or the device of making a whole story the fulfillment of a prophecy given at the beginning"[84] (and Tuchman's "Guns" are the omen or portent present to the reader from the moment of reading her title). Finally, for the reality of nuclear war resulting from "miscalculation," narrative invariably suggests the other inescapable outcome of archetypal tragedy, the downfall of the hero (often a person of youth and courage) from a position "typically on top of the wheel of fortune": whether "in the central or high mimetic sense," tragedy is about "the fall of a leader."[85] Kennedy would not want that.

As a hallmark of his new leadership, Kennedy's inaugural address proclaimed: "the torch has been passed to a new generation of Americans—born in this century, tempered by war, disciplined by a hard and bitter peace." Governmental decisions now would result from intellect and cool, analytical judgment in world affairs of "the best and the brightest."[86] Not only did a "radical" Khruschev take umbrage at their desire to avoid the "miscalculation" characterizing the old order, but umbrage was evident as well in the response evoked then from General Curtis LeMay: "Gobbledygook has become the union card of defense intellectuals. At a White House meeting with President John F. Kennedy in 1962, I recall being lectured by an articulate defense intellectual. . . . For the listening President's benefit he told me how 'provocative' Strategic Air Command bombers were, how their 'first strike' characteristics were 'destabilizing' and liable to result in a '*miscalculated*' or 'spasm' war. . . . A lifetime of study and practice of the military art had not prepared me for the pretentious language of the new breed of military philosophers."[87] After the crisis was over, Kennedy invited the Joint Chiefs of Staff to the White House so he could thank them for their support, and a still-bitter LeMay came out saying, "We lost! We ought to just go in there today and knock 'em off!"[88] But LeMay's more radical stance and recommendation to Excom were not incorporated in Kennedy's final decision, a fact reflecting still another metaphorical aspect of Tuchman's narrative: the effect of her discussion of "blockade" as an ultimate *allegoresis*.

V

Tuchman's chapter entitled "Blue Water, Blockade, and the Great Neutral" has a forceful opening sentence: "Risk was the least favorite concept of the British Admiralty in 1914."[89] Miller made her read about the British Navy in the sixteenth century, about "the care, the caution . . . of Howard, Drake, Frobisher . . . in dealing with the Spanish fleet . . . a careful testing of means and an ability to use the experience obtained after each day of the running battle up the Straits of Dover."[90] He also had her read historians describing British Admiral Jellicoe in 1914 as prudent but "in no sense an old woman or overly cautious."[91] Although Miller wanted the book to give details about how naval vessels were built, Tuchman said, "I couldn't do this in a million years—it scares me to think of it." And she "deliberately" decided to omit details about ship-building because "it would take pages and divert attention" from one of the "key issues . . . the distant vs the close blockade, and when and how the British decided upon this."[92] For a chapter about "the nature of the blockade," she decided that "the less extraneous matter, however valid, I bring in, the clearer (one hopes) the main picture will be for the reader."[93] Miller accepted "entirely your way of telling the story" but cautioned Tuchman *again* about "talking down to your reader, as if you were offer-ing him simple food because you felt sure he wouldn't understand or appreciate a more sophisticated diet."[94]

To create compositionally a "main picture" about blockade which was "clearer" for her readers, Tuchman often resorts to language whose nuances of meaning favor figurative connotations moreso than literal denotations. Her style thereby gives foregrounding to ideas. For instance, when discussing "the legality of arrest under the rules of blockade," Tuchman says: "the problem bristled like a floating mine with spikes of trouble." Similarly, phraseology of maritime law about blockade and its "immense train of results" poses an issue that is "alive, spitting, and sharp of claw." Again, the focus of this chapter in *The Guns of August* could have been consonant with Kennedy's earlier experiences in 1939 when the *Athenia* was sunk. We have heard Lakoff and Johnson insist: metaphor is "grounded in our experience." Upon his return to Harvard, Jack wrote a case study about blockades and neutrality for Dr. Payson Wild's course in international law (in which he received a B+), and in the paper he subsequently wrote, Kennedy dealt specifically with rights of a nation "to attack neutral ships carrying munitions to an enemy power in a so-called war zone" (its summary stated, "There is a question even whether the war zone is legal"). "Blockade" and its implications were not new topics for John Kennedy when he read Tuchman's book or when he ordered "a naval blockade off Cuba that would bring the United States and Russia to the brink of nuclear war."[95]

In addition to using figurative language to heighten the sense of potential dangers in the situation in *The Guns of August*, Tuchman uses a simile to describe how a blockade is implemented to minimize risk. To clarify how the British naval blockade of Germany in 1914 posed a "very

real danger" to favorable relations with the America and its preoccupation with strict neutrality and freedom of the seas, Tuchman focuses on
how "this was a problem that had occurred to Sir Edward Grey, and
required careful handling." Portraying an identificand after whom
Kennedy might model his own behavior in the Cuban Missile Crisis,
Tuchman describes how "with instinctive English dislike of absolutes,
Sir Edward Grey was able to pick his way from incident to incident,
avoiding large principles as a helmsman avoids rocks and being careful
not to allow discussion to reach a clear-cut issue that would require either side to take a position from which it could not climb down." Or as
Kennedy on the evening of 26 October 1962 phrased his own position
concerning the blockade: "If anybody is around to write after this, they
are going to understand that we made every effort to find peace and
every effort to give our adversary room to move." After all, as Tuchman
writes in the book, Grey's prudence and caution were able "to secure
the maximum blockade that could be enforced without a rupture with
the United States."[96] By the spring of 1940, young Jack Kennedy had
forsaken his father's isolationism and come out in the Harvard *Crimson*
on behalf of Americans' rearming: "failure to build up her armaments
has not saved England from a war, and may cost her one. Are we in
America to let that lesson go unlearned?" In so saying, he quoted Sir
Edward Grey, who had declared in 1914 that "the enormous growth of
armaments in Europe, the sense of insecurity and fear caused by them,
it was these that made war inevitable."[97] Kennedy felt that setting up a
blockade some distance from Russian ships carrying missiles to Cuba
was an option for the fall of 1962 which gave him the advantage of being "careful not to allow discussion to reach a clear-cut issue that would
require either side to take a position from which it could not climb down."
Grey—as depicted by Tuchman—provided Kennedy with a persona
whose behavior one could emulate.

Kennedy's desire for caution was not unnoticed by his rhetorical
alter ego, speech writer Ted Sorensen. Well before the final recommendation of Excom and the final decision of the president were reached,
Sorensen was at work drafting a speech Kennedy planned to deliver on
the Monday evening of 22 October. Sorensen presented a draft of that
speech to Kennedy on Sunday the 21st, along with a memo summarizing four days of secret meetings of Excom which the president had not
attended. Sorensen sensed the advantages of blockade as "prudent"
course of action:

I. There are 2 fundamental objections to air strike which have never been answered:

1) Inasmuch as no one has been able to devise a satisfactory message to Khrushchev to which his reply could not outmaneuver us, an air strike means a US-initiated "Pearl Harbor" on a small nation which history could neither understand nor forget.

2) Inasmuch as the concept of a clean, swift strike has been abandoned as militarily impractical, it is generally agreed that the more widespread air attack will inevitably lead to an invasion with all of its consequences.

II. There are 2 fundamental advantages to a blockade which have never been answered:

1) It is a more prudent and flexible step which enables us to move to an air strike, invasion or any other step at any time it proves necessary, without the "Pearl Harbor" posture.

2) It is the step least likely to precipitate general war while still causing the Soviets—unwilling to engage our Navy in our own waters—to back down and abandon Castro.[98]

Even in his prediction of Soviet naval inclinations, Sorensen's conclusion was consonant with Tuchman's. According to the conclusion of her chapter "Blue Water, Blockade, and the Great Neutral," this British action at the outset of the war did *not* lure the Imperial German North Sea Fleet out to do battle in an effort to break that blockade, and by that "default" of the Kaiser's surface navy, Britain achieved—without undue risk—"complete destruction of German sea-borne trade, the fullest practical blockade."[99] Implicit as another analogic aspect of the situation was the likelihood that the Russian fleet in 1962 also would not do battle to break the blockade of Soviet ships en route to Cuba.

With a chapter whose "main picture" portrays a leader successfully employing blockade as a prudent means of reducing risk, Tuchman likely achieved for Kennedy what White perceives as the *allegoresis* which fulfills another role of content in the form of history as "the discourse of the real":

The historical narrative does not, as narrative, dispel false beliefs about the past, human life, the nature of the community, and so on; what it does is test the capacity of a culture's fictions to endow real events with the kinds of meaning that literature displays to consciousness through its fashioning of patterns of "imaginary" events. Precisely insofar as the historical narrative endows sets of real events with the kinds of meaning found otherwise only in myth and literature, we are justified in regarding it as a product of *allegoresis*. . . . Thus envisioned, the narrative figurates the body of events that serves as its primary referent and transforms these events into intimations of patterns of meaning that any literal representation of them as facts could never produce.[100]

By opting for blockade and stating his analog between *The Guns of August* and a possible book called *The Missiles of October*, Kennedy demonstrated the ability of metaphor to epitomize the "truth of things" and to provide a "prescription for action" that answers the question, "What shall we do about this?" For, behaving in a way that supports the anthropological view of human beings as "time binders . . . framed between the remembered past and the imagined future with the need to fill the inchoate present with activity," we often rely upon metaphorical meaning that provides "a futureness to the past and a pastness to the future that is fundamentally reassuring."[101] Kennedy did not retain the word "blockade," however, to designate his chosen course of action, for Excom was concerned that in international law, any blockade is an act of war.[102] Reacting to General Maxwell Taylor's concerns that a blockade would constitute "the violation of international law we were indulging in," Dean Acheson offered his view: "The hell with international law. International law gets made, it's just a series of precedents and decisions that have been made in the past. But this is a unique situation and this is one in which one can, and should, make international law rather than follow past precedents. There aren't any real precedents for this. And if you're troubled with what the books say about the blockade, then change the name."[103] Perhaps recalling Franklin Roosevelt's potent metaphorical call at the advent of World War II to "quarantine the aggressors," Kennedy chose to refer publicly to the blockade as a quarantine.

Admittedly, Kennedy likely would have opted for his course of action without reading Tuchman. After all, during Excom deliberations, the idea of some form of naval blockade was "initially mentioned in passing by General Taylor" as a measure to be considered before the launching of a military attack. The possibility of taking that course of action came up again on Tuesday, 16 October, and by Wednesday,

McNamara was its "strongest advocate."[104] Potent arguments also were presented against an air strike upon the missile sites in Cuba. Foremost among these were statements by Excom members, such as George Ball's likening an air action to the Japanese attack on Pearl Harbor. Indeed, as Bobby Kennedy said in a note passed to his brother during one of the group meetings, "I now know how Tojo felt when he was planning Pearl Harbor."[105] That "Pearl Harbor analogy" was countered, however, by former Secretary of State Dean Acheson, who had been invited into Excom for their deliberations and who "told the President that there were no points of similarity and many points of difference": "At Pearl Harbor the Japanese without provocation or warning attacked our fleet thousands of miles from their shores. In the present situation, the Soviet Union had installed missiles ninety miles from our coast—while denying they were doing so—offensive weapons that were capable of lethal injury to the United States. This they were doing a hundred and forty years after the warning given in [the Monroe Doctrine]. How much warning was necessary to avoid the stigma of 'Pearl Harbor in reverse.'"[106] Kennedy at several points during the Cuban Missile Crisis seemed personally to favor an air strike against the sites, but Air Force leaders (particularly the commanding general of the Tactical Air Command) were not able to assure him that the facilities could be destroyed with "one blow."[107] As General Walter Sweeney frankly declared, "you can't expect me to get 'em all; some of the missiles would get away."[108] Chairman of the Joint Chiefs, General Maxwell Taylor agreed that complete success of a military strike was unlikely: "the best we can offer you, Mr. President, is to destroy 90 percent of the known missiles."[109] Although a firm advocate of strong military action throughout Excom deliberations, Taylor "never wavered until my Commander-in-Chief took another decision" (although Taylor later characterized himself as a "double hawk" at the time, Defense Secretary McNamara regarded him then as "a *dove* among the military people").[110]

For the most part, forceful recommendations from the generals and admirals favored some form of military intervention as a solution to the problem, and even if such action entailed risk, major participants from the military establishment would be inclined by professional nature to adhere to that mode of intervention. In an attempt to explain why military decision-makers "do what they should not do," an analysis of deliberations leading to the disastrous Dieppe amphibious raid by Britain in World War II is helpful in its suggestion as to why commanders "try to avoid an impression of negativism." Major participants in the Dieppe raid confided afterwards how "even in the best of times it was difficult ... for a soldier to advise against a bold offensive plan. One lays himself open to charges of defeatism, or inertia, or even of 'cold feet.' Human nature being what it is, there is a natural tendency to acquiesce in an offensive plan of doubtful merit rather than face such charges."[111] Admittedly, some military advice to Kennedy with respect to Cuba favored restraint. In one briefing, "when talk of invading Cuba was becoming fashionable," the Commandant of the Marine Corps, General David M. Shoup, made his point vividly with "a remarkable display of maps" prepared by Brigadier General Edwin Simmons (retired and currently director of U.S. Marine Corps Museum and Archives):

> First he took an overlay of Cuba and placed it over the map of the United States. To everybody's surprise, Cuba was not a small island along the lines of, say, Long Island at best. It was about 800 miles long and seemed to stretch from New York to Chicago. Then he took another overlay, with a red dot, and placed it over the map of Cuba. "What's that?" someone asked him. "That, gentlemen, represents the size of the island of Tarawa," said Shoup, who had won a Medal of Honor there, "and it took us three days and eighteen thousand Marines to take." He eventually became Kennedy's favorite general.[112]

Being a naval officer himself during World War II, Kennedy likely knew of "Terrible Tarawa" and the inordinately high casualties suffered by the Marines (1,027 killed and 2,292 wounded) in their seventy-six-hour fight to take an island whose area was less than half the size of New York City's Central Park. As America moved inexorably closer to the Cuban Missile Crisis, Kennedy retained his appreciation for the way Shoup made his arguments cogent, later commending the marine for his "lucid and incisive" statements: "as usual, your views went to the heart of the issue involved, and were praiseworthy for their direct and unequivocal manner of expression."[113] Thus, whether cautiously cogent or brashly bellicose, a wide range of arguments from the military were part of the communication mosaic confronting Kennedy in October 1962. But the president opted for caution.

The president's ultimate decision favoring blockade instead of more direct military action probably was undertaken with greater confidence, however, because of his reading Tuchman's book and appreciating what he felt was its moral. Moreover, that historical discourse well could have retained some salience in Kennedy's mind simply because it did not compete directly with many of the arguments brought up during Excom deliberations. As Robert Kennedy described the crucial period during October 1962, his brother did not attend some of the Excom sessions "to keep the discussions from being inhibited": "personalities change when the President is present, and frequently even strong men make recommendations on the basis of what they believe the President wishes to hear. He instructed our group to come forward with recommendations for one course or possibly several alternative courses of action." Although preparations to attack Cuba continued, "by Thursday night, there was a majority opinion in our group for a blockade." Having been told of their decision, "the President, not at all satisfied, sent us back to our deliberations" because proponents of military action still made forceful arguments; and he directed Excom "split into groups to write up our respective recommendations." Between 2:30 and 5:10 P.M. on 26 October, the president heard a final overview of all options considered by Excom and only decided "that afternoon in favor of the blockade" despite his uncertainties about "unanticipated things happening out there." For when asked what would happen when a Russian ship reached the blockade line, Admiral George Anderson, Chief of Naval Operations, boasted that "the Navy has been running blockades since the days of John Paul Jones" and declared, "We'll hail it." And in answer to Defense Secretary McNamara's next question—"In what language—English or Russian?"—Anderson's response was "How the hell do I know?"[114] Yet Anderson was one of those Joint Chiefs who believed that the only plan that could succeed was "complete destruction of Soviet power" in Cuba.[115] Additional evidence exists that Kennedy understood the pertinence of *The Guns of August* for the issue of the blockade: "I wish we could send a copy of that book to every Navy officer on every ship right now," he said to his brother Robert, Sorensen, and O'Donnell—"but they probably wouldn't read it," he added regretfully.[116]

In the final analysis, Tuchman's historical discourse was no "magic bullet," no message in and of itself persuading Kennedy to decide on blockade during the Cuban Missile Crisis. After all, despite forceful arguments by the Joint Chiefs of Staff, the final recommendation of Excom endorsed blockade or "quarantine" rather than the more bellicose air strikes against the missile sites or even the "first strike" against the Soviet Union suggested at one point by General LeMay. What *The Guns of*

August did provide was the potent imprimatur of "history" for Kennedy's decision about a blockade. Tuchman's writing interacted conceptually with what a younger Jack Kennedy had written about in October 1939 at Harvard as a case study for his course in international law: "the rights of submarines to attack neutral ships carrying munitions to an enemy power in a so-called war zone."[117]

To rely on Tuchman's book was consonant with Kennedy's personal sense of historical consciousness as well as, perhaps, to some extent, a "self-fulfilling prophecy" on his part. Although the New Frontier campaign slogan conjured up imagery of earlier Western rustics and their ways, this presidency was characterized by efforts to flaunt the intellectual prowess of its leading participants. The choices of so many "Harvards" for Kennedy's cabinet (to the consternation of House Speaker Samuel Rayburn and Vice President Lyndon Johnson) "revealed his desire to be among men with highly respected intellectual credentials. One magazine counted sixteen Phi Beta Kappas, four Rhodes scholars, and a Nobel Prizewinner." Also consonant with projecting that "Kennedy image" of intellect, historian Arthur Schlesinger, Jr., was named special assistant to the president, although, as Thomas Reeves suggests, Kennedy "had no intention of giving Schlesinger any serious authority in the administration."[118] Kennedy's own book, *Profiles in Courage,* suggests his motivation to view himself—and to be perceived by others—as a student of history who would bring a sense of historical consciousness to a forthcoming presidency. Recognizing Theodore Sorensen for lending "invaluable assistance in the assembly and preparation of the material upon which this book is based" and Allan Nevins for making "criticisms" by which "the entire manuscript was greatly improved," Kennedy also acknowledges that "Chapters 2 through 10 were greatly improved by the criticisms" of Arthur Schlesinger and others. Indeed, Nevins's foreword to the book lauds Kennedy's account of "the courage of intelligent, farsighted, reasonable men anxious to hold the ship of state to its true course." Discussing the book in terms of attributes which suggest its author's sense of historical consciousness, Nevens continues: "His examples, chosen from the history of the American Congress and mainly the Senate, are striking, varied and memorable; he puts into his narration a fine mastery of the psychology of the different periods described, as well as of the facts in each drama; and he makes his whole book so absorbing that most readers will race through it, fully comprehending at the end the lesson in civic virtue which it reinforces. Indeed, this volume teaches so much in history, in practical politics and in sound morals, all bound together, that it constitutes a real public service."[119] In addition to the direction his education had taken and to this image he desired to create for himself, Kennedy in October 1962 was sufficiently aware of the event's historical significance to have a photographer present during Excom meetings to record for posterity their deliberations.[120] History impressed Kennedy.

And Tuchman appealed subtly to that sense of, and appreciation for, history in Kennedy in still another way. Although her book is about August 1914, its opening chapter describes "the May morning of 1910 when nine kings rode in the funeral of Edward VII of England," when "the sun of the old world was setting in a dying blaze of splendor never to be seen again." That funeral of a man called "Peacemaker" prompts the diary entry by Lord Esher that concludes the chapter: "There never was such a break-up. All the old buoys which have marked the channel of our lives seem to have been swept away."[121] Readers who actually witnessed the 1910 event lauded her "excellent description," saying "your opening chapter is splendid" and "the dramatic opening scene is an inspiration."[122] Indeed, Tuchman's publishers said her account of Edward VII's funeral was "a flash of inspiration" and such an "essential part" of *The Guns of August* that *Life* could not use it as a prologue in a proposed publication for the fiftieth anniversary of the beginning of World War I (although *Life* and Tuchman ultimately agreed upon a quotation from her book).[123] That funeral scene could be poignant to a president whose new leadership desiring to avoid miscalculation might end an old order just as Edward VII's funeral had (because of opening paragraphs about the funeral of Edward VII in *The Guns of August*, the *St. Louis Post-Dispatch* asked Tuchman to write an account of John Kennedy's funeral).[124]

After concluding that the Cuban Missile Crisis constituted a "success story" of how knowledge of history affected a crucial decision, Neustadt and May characterize John Kennedy then as a president who "came to see such issues in a stream of time" which included learning from "stories about real people" more so than from "abstract constructions from philosophy or social sciences." And to qualify further their opinion "that reading history *may* help" in that learning process typical of "the majority of humankind, ourselves included," they also aver that "we are not confident that anyone who reads can gain proficiency, if what he reads is history and what he does is govern, but we cannot think of a better way."[125] Thus, amid a communication mosaic during the Cuban Missile Crisis, including both recommendations to be cautious as well as strident, "radical" voices urging military action, *The Guns of August* was a compelling narrative including "stories about real people" making the miscalculations in 1914 leading to the carnage of World War I. In so doing, that discourse acquired an advantage to become prominent and persuasive for a president opting for a "conservative" solution to the "Missiles of October" in 1962.

In 1966, Tuchman called history "the literature of actuality" and crystallized for the American Historical Association what may have been her rhetorical role for John Kennedy: "it may be that in a time of widening uncertainty and chronic stress the historian's voice is most needed, the more so as the others seem inadequate, often absurd. . . . the opportunity, I think, is plain for the historian to become the major interpreter in literary experience of man's role in society."[126] For all his youth and sometimes apparent rashness, Kennedy consistently sought advice and reinforcement from various people who might be regarded as opinion leaders, including his father Joseph P. Kennedy: "as always, when in trouble, Jack turned to his father" (the senior Kennedy was continually telephoned or visited by the president for "consultations," advice to which "he paid special attention," and for substantial "private discussion" before making final decisions).[127] Being an Anglophile, John Kennedy also showed photographs of the missile sites to and sought advice from "his friend David Ormsby-Gore" about the "bombing or blockade choice"; the British ambassador promptly endorsed "blockade" (and immediately sent a telegram to his prime minister, Harold Macmillan, warning of "an impending crisis").[128] A decision which echoed advice or reinforcement from an opinion leader historian would not be out of character for John Kennedy during the Cuban Missile Crisis.

Although persuasiveness of *The Guns of August* can be explained as but another instance in the functioning of credibility or corroboration, Kennedy's precise, stated analog of "The Missiles of October" suggests as well the rhetorical role of what Hayden White labels as metaphors of emplotment evolving from—and complementing—Tuchman's conscious rhetorical choices while developing her narrative. For a reader such as Kennedy, Tuchman's historical discourse embodied form capable of achieving "an arousing and fulfillment of desires. A work has form insofar as one part of it leads a reader to anticipate another part, to be gratified by the experience." Moreover, that "form, having to do with the creation and gratification of needs, is 'correct' in so far as it gratifies the needs which it creates." At the most subtle levels of responses to narrative, readers reacting to historians' discourse may yield to archetypal story forms implicit therein as well as more overt sources of persuasion. The final task herein is to suggest what happens rhetorically when historians' prowess with style and narrative on behalf of a metaphor interacts with other sources of the same ideas and images in a communication mosaic over a span of decades for people who "see issues in a stream of time."

Notes

1. John F. Kennedy, quoted in Robert Kennedy, *Thirteen Days: A Memoir of the Cuban Missile Crisis* (New York: W. W. Norton, 1969), 62, 127.

2. Kenneth O'Donnell, David Powers, and Joe McCarthy, *Johnny, We Hardly Knew Ye* (Boston: Little, Brown, 1972), 330–31.

3. Theodore Sorensen, *Kennedy* (New York: Harper and Row, 1965), 513. See also Arthur M. Schlesinger, Jr., *A Thousand Days: John F. Kennedy in the White House* (Boston: Houghton Mifflin, 1965), 832.

4. Hugh Sidey, "Getting Gorby on the Line," *Time*, 9 April 1990, 39; Elie Abel, *The Missile Crisis* (Philadelphia: Lippincott, 1966), 207.

5. Richard Neustadt and Ernest May, *Thinking in Time: The Uses of History for Decision Makers* (New York: Free Press, 1986), 15, 244. For further discussion of the Cuban Missile Crisis as a "Success Story" of presidential decisions founded upon knowledge and applications of history, see 1–33.

6. Robert Kennedy, *Thirteen Days*, 62; Neustadt and May, *Thinking in Time*, 244.

7. Barbara Tuchman to Robert McNamara, 2 May 1962. Tuchman correspondence cited herein is in Boxes 1 and 9, both labeled "Correspondence 1959–64. Of special significance in Box 9 is File Folder 182, "Correspondence with D. Miller, 1959–62." Also useful is Box 14, "Newspaper Reactions and Reviews of TGOA," in the Barbara Wertheim Tuchman Papers, MS Collection No. 574, Yale University Library, New Haven, Conn. Unless otherwise noted, all references to correspondence are as specified here.

8. Pierre Salinger to Tuchman, 1 June 1962. The Kennedy Library in Boston offers no evidence, however, that the president himself ever wrote to Tuchman.

9. Cited in Richard Reeves, *President Kennedy: Profile of Power* (New York: Simon and Schuster, 1993), 306.

10. Maxwell Taylor, *Swords into Plowshares* (New York: W. W. Norton, 1972), 205.

11. Samuel Becker, "Rhetorical Studies for the Contemporary World," in *The*

Prospect of Rhetoric, ed. Lloyd Bitzer and Edwin Black (Englewood Cliffs, N.J.: Prentice-Hall, 1971), 33.

12. Taylor, *Swords into Plowshares*, 271; J. Anthony Lukas, "Class Reunion: Kennedy's Men Relive the Cuban Missile Crisis," *New York Times Magazine*, 30 August 1987, 27, 58; James Blight and David Welch, *On the Brink: Americans and Soviets Reexamine the Cuban Missile Crisis* (New York: Hill and Wang, 1989), 50, 78, 152, 167, 215; Robert Kennedy, *Thirteen Days*, 31.

13. Denning Miller to Barbara Tuchman, 14 January 1959, 22 March 1960, 13 August 1959, and 5 October 1961.

14. Roderick Hart and Don Burks, "Rhetorical Sensitivity and Social Interaction," *Speech Monographs* 39 (June 1972): 75–91.

15. Miller to Tuchman, 14 January 1959.

16. Barbara Tuchman, *Practicing History: Selected Essays* (New York: Alfred A. Knopf, 1981), 38.

17. *Practicing History*, 33.

18. Miller to Tuchman, 4 February 1960.

19. Miller to Tuchman, 3 August 1959.

20. Miller to Tuchman, 18 August 1959.

21. Miller to Tuchman, 16 April 1961.

22. Miller to Tuchman, 22 March 1960.

23. Miller to Tuchman, 20 October 1960, 29 November 1960, and 16 March 1961.

24. Kenneth Ross to Tuchman, 1 February 1962; Lt. Col. S. G. Brady (U.S. Army, Retired) to Tuchman, 19 May 1962.

25. Cecil Falls to Tuchman, 18 May 1962; Eric Goldman to Tuchman, 8 April 1962.

26. This exchange is cited in Richard Reeves, *President Kennedy*, 378–79.

27. Although Kennedy at one point had said, "I don't want that man near me again," he nevertheless appointed LeMay to the position of Air Force chief of staff, saying, "LeMay's like Babe Ruth. Personally he's a bum, but he's got talent and the people love him" (cited in Richard Reeves, *President Kennedy*, 182–83). The "kind of fit" remark is attributed to Deputy Secretary of Defense Roswell Gilpatric.

28. See Richard Reeves, *President Kennedy*, 305–7. After the Bay of Pigs fiasco, Kennedy complained bitterly about his "generals and admirals with tiers of service ribbons": "Those sons of bitches with all the fruit salad just sat there nodding, saying it would work" (cited in *President Kennedy*, 103).

29. Tuchman to Miller, 18 February 1960.

30. Tuchman to Miller, 24 April 1960.

31. Miller to Tuchman, 2 May 1960 and 3 March 1960.

32. Margaret Cruikshank to Tuchman, 3 November 1963; "Helen" (Weston, Mass.) to Tuchman, 22 February 1962.

33. Miller to Tuchman, 2 May 1960.

34. Miller to Tuchman, 25 May 1960.

35. Miller to Tuchman, 1 June 1961 and 3 June 1960.

36. Sorensen, *Kennedy*, 513.

37. For details about Kennedy's early predilection for study of history, see Nigel Hamilton, *JFK: Reckless Youth* (New York: Random House, 1992), 75, 103, 134, 227, 249, 298, 317–19; Kennedy's characterization of his book to his father is cited on p. 328.

38. See Hamilton, *JFK: Reckless Youth*, 377–78, 485–87.

39. Ernest Gruening to Tuchman, 1 May 1963; "Jane" (52 East 92nd Street, N.Y.C.) to Tuchman, 18 January 1962; G. Sauerwein to Tuchman, 12 September 1963; Bernice Cronkhite to Tuchman, 16 March 1962.

40. Miller to Tuchman, 2 May 1960 and 21 April 1960.

41. See Walter R. Fisher, *Human Communication as Narration: Toward a Philosophy of Reason, Value, and Action* (Columbia: University of South Carolina Press, 1987).

42. Kenneth Burke, "Psychology and Form" and "Lexicon Rhetoricae," in *Counter-Statement* (Los Altos, Calif.: Hermes Publications, 1931), 30–31, 124, 138.

43. Hayden White, "The Historical Text as Literary Artifact," in *The Writing of History: Literary Form and Historical Understanding*, ed. Robert H. Canary and Henry Kozicki (Madison: University of Wisconsin Press, 1978), 51.

44. Kenneth Burke, *A Grammar of Motives* (New York: Prentice-Hall, 1945), 503.

45. See Michael Osborn, "Archetypal Metaphor in Rhetoric: The Light-Dark Family," *Quarterly Journal of Speech* 53 (April 1967): 115–26; and Osborn, "The Evolution of the Archetypal Sea in Rhetoric and Poetic," *Quarterly Journal of Speech* 63 (December 1977): 347–63.

46. George Lakoff and Mark Johnson, *Metaphors We Live By* (Chicago: University of Chicago Press, 1980), 3–6.

47. *Metaphors We Live By*, 19, 39–40.

48. David Carr, *Time, Narrative, and History* (Bloomington: Indiana University Press, 1986), 57–59.

49. Peter Munz, *The Shapes of Time: A New Look at the Philosophy of History* (Middletown, Conn.: Wesleyan University Press, 1977), 230–31.

50. Louis O. Mink, "Narrative Form as a Cognitive Instrument," in *The Writing of History: Literary Form and Historical Understanding*, ed. Robert H. Canary and Henry Kozicki (Madison: University of Wisconsin Press, 1978), 144–45.

51. Alfred de Liagre to Tuchman, 10 May 1962; Frederick Gutheim to Tuchman, 14 May 1963.

52. Hayden White, *Metahistory: The Historical Imagination in Nineteenth-Century Europe* (Baltimore: Johns Hopkins University Press, 1973), ix–xi, 5, 10–11, 31.

53. Hayden White, *The Content of the Form* (Baltimore: Johns Hopkins University Press, 1987), 43.

54. Northrop Frye, *Anatomy of Criticism* (Princeton: Princeton University Press, 1957), 54–56.

55. Miller to Tuchman, 15 May 1959. Tuchman originally made the statement in a letter to Miller; he in turn quoted it to her in responding that he was "extremely happy" about her choice of focus.

56. Burke, *A Grammar of Motives*, 508–9.

57. Miller to Tuchman, 23 September 1959 and 9 June 1960.

58. Hamilton, *JFK: Reckless Youth*, 261, 270–72, 280.

59. White, *Metahistory*, 167, 190.

60. Leopold von Ranke, cited in White, *Metahistory*, 165–66.

61. *Metahistory*, 25, 27–28. White developed his theory of emplotment metaphors originally to demonstrate how historical writings are "consonant" with "ideological positions of the times in which they were written."

62. *Metahistory*, 9.

63. Frye, *Anatomy of Criticism* 43, 203.

64. Sorensen, *Kennedy*, 513.

65. Cited in Thomas C. Reeves, *A Question of Character: A Life of John F. Kennedy* (New York: Free Press, 1991), 299.

66. Arthur M. Schlesinger, Jr., *Robert Kennedy and His Times* (Boston: Houghton Mifflin, 1978), 528–29.

67. Adlai Stevenson to Kennedy, 17 October 1962, in *The Papers of Adlai Stevenson*, 8 vols., ed. Walter Johnson (Boston: Little, Brown, 1979), 8:300.

68. Thomas Reeves, *A Question of Character*, 370, 374–76; Sorensen, *Kennedy*, 695.

69. "Ernst" (102 Woodhull Road, Huntington, L.I., N.Y.) to Tuchman, 16 February 1962.

70. White, *Metahistory*, 10.

71. Burke, *A Grammar of Motives*, 503, 506, and 509.

72. Mink, "Narrative Form as a Cognitive Instrument," in *The Writing of History*, 142.

73. Barbara Tuchman, *The Guns of August* (New York: Macmillan, 1962), 166–67.

74. Tuchman to Miller, 24 April 1960; Miller to Tuchman, 21 April and 2 May 1960.

75. Miller to Tuchman, 16 May 1960 and 21 April 1960.

76. Cited in Hamilton, *JFK: Reckless Youth*, 284–85.

77. Cited in Lukas, "Class Reunion: Kennedy's Men Relive the Cuban Missile Crisis," *New York Times Magazine*, 30 August 1987, 24–27, 51. Comprehensive discussion of this conference is in Blight and Welch, *On the Brink*. For other indices that Kennedy deemed the missiles as a political threat more than a military one, see Pierre Salinger, *With Kennedy* (Garden City: Doubleday, 1966), 262–63.

78. Schlesinger, cited in Richard Reeves, *President Kennedy*, 427.

79. Schlesinger, cited in Blight and Welch, *On the Brink*, 28.

80. White, *Metahistory,* 335.

81. *Metahistory,* 35.

82. Cited in Blight and Welch, *On the Brink,* 91–92, 95–96.

83. White, *Metahistory,* 9, 31, 33.

84. Frye, *Anatomy of Criticism,* 136–39.

85. *Anatomy of Criticism,* 37, 207, 219–20.

86. See David Halberstam's analysis of the people in leadership roles during the Kennedy presidency, *The Best and the Brightest* (New York: Random House, 1969).

87. Curtis LeMay, *America Is in Danger* (New York: Funk and Wagnalls, 1968), xii. Italics are mine.

88. Curtis LeMay, cited in Blight and Welch, *On the Brink,* 51.

89. Tuchman, *The Guns of August,* 325.

90. Miller to Tuchman, 17 and 23 November 1960.

91. Miller to Tuchman, 7 April 1961.

92. Tuchman, comments handwritten on Miller's letter to her of 16 April 1961.

93. Miller, quoting Tuchman back to her in a letter of 24 April 1961.

94. Miller to Tuchman, 28 April 1961.

95. Hamilton, *JFK: Reckless Youth,* 298–99.

96. Tuchman, *The Guns of August,* 334–36.

97. Cited in Hamilton, *JFK: Reckless Youth,* 328.

98. Sorensen, cited in Richard Reeves, *President Kennedy,* 387–88.

99. Tuchman, *The Guns of August,* 340.

100. White, *Content of the Form,* 20, 45.

101. J. Christopher Crocker, "The Social Function of Rhetorical Forms," and James W. Fernandez, "The Performance of Ritual Metaphor," both in *The Social Uses of Metaphor: Essays on the Anthropology of Rhetoric,* ed. J. David Sapir and J. Christopher Crocker (Philadelphia: University of Pennsylvania Press, 1977), 37–39, 46–47, 118.

102. Thomas Reeves, *A Question of Character,* 374; Richard Reeves, *President Kennedy,* 385; and Sorensen, *Kennedy,* 693–94.

103. Blight and Welch, *On the Brink,* 79 and 143.

104. Neustadt and May, *Thinking in Time,* 5–6.

105. Robert Kennedy, cited in Thomas Reeves, *A Question of Character,* 371. See also Robert Kennedy, *Thirteen Days,* 12.

106. Cited in Neustadt and May, *Thinking in Time,* 7. See also Dean G. Acheson, "Dean Acheson's Version of Robert Kennedy's Version of the Cuban Missile Crisis: Homage to Plain Dumb Luck," *Esquire* 71 (February 1969): 76ff.

107. Thomas Reeves, *A Question of Character,* 374–77.

108. Walter Sweeney, cited in Blight and Welch, *On the Brink,* 79–80.

109. Maxwell Taylor, cited in Richard Reeves, *President Kennedy,* 384.

110. Cited in Blight and Welch, *On the Brink,* 50–51, 78–79.

111. Brian Loring Villa, *Unauthorized Action: Montbatten and the Dieppe Raid* (Toronto: Oxford University Press, 1989), 93.

112. Cited in Halberstam, *The Best and the Brightest*, 67. At the 1993 Speech Communication Association Convention in Miami, General Edmund H. Simmons presented the critic-response to a panel of papers on "Rhetoric among the Military." During his presentation, he affirmed his role in preparing those maps.

113. John F. Kennedy to General David M. Shoup, 3 February 1962, in Box 31, Shoup Papers, Hoover Institution on War, Revolution, and Peace, Stanford University, Stanford, Calif.

114. Cited in Robert Kennedy, *Thirteen Days*, 33–34, 37, 43–45, 47–48; and in Blight and Welch, *On the Brink*, 64–65, 71–72.

115. Richard Reeves, *President Kennedy*, 384.

116. John F. Kennedy, cited in O'Donnell, *Johnny, We Hardly Knew Ye*, 330–31. See also Richard Reeves, *President Kennedy*, 379.

117. John F. Kennedy, cited in Hamilton, *JFK: Reckless Youth*, 298–99.

118. Thomas Reeves, *A Question of Character*, 228–29.

119. See John F. Kennedy, *Profiles in Courage* (New York: Harper and Brothers, 1955), ix–xi, xvii–xviii.

120. See Robert Kennedy, *Thirteen Days*, 133; and Jacques Lowe's photographs in Harold Faber, *The Kennedy Years* (New York: Viking, 1964), 272.

121. See Tuchman, "A Funeral," in *The Guns of August*, 1–14.

122. R. Leslie to Tuchman, 18 February 1963; Roger Ward to Tuchman, 19 October 1962; Lewis Gannett to Tuchman, 18 January 1963.

123. Gerald Goss to Edward Thompson of *Life*, 3 April 1963; Thompson to Tuchman, 22 April 1963.

124. See Tuchman, *Practicing History*, 3.

125. Neustadt and May, *Thinking in Time*, 15, 263–64.

126. Barbara Tuchman, "The Historian's Opportunity," address to the American Historical Association, December 1966; repr. in *Saturday Review*, 25 February 1967, 27–31; and in Tuchman, *Practicing History*, 51–64. See in particular p. 51.

127. Thomas Reeves, *A Question of Character*, 218, 222, 224, 265, 272.

128. Richard Reeves, *President Kennedy*, 384.

Part III

Historians in a Stream of Time

The majority of humankind . . . learn to think in streams of time as we learn to think mathematically—if we do either or at all—from teachers and books. It probably also follows that the learning comes through pieced-together stories about real people better than through abstract constructions from philosophy or social sciences, or even through invented characters in fiction (a close question).

Richard Neustadt and Ernest May,
Thinking in Time: The Uses of History for Decision Makers

Chapter Eight

History and the Frontier Metaphor
for War in American Society:
From Syntax through Archetype

In 1918, French High Commissioner to the United States, Louis Aubert, reminisced about World War I for Illinois readers: "I will remember when I was in the trenches over there how in order to find an analogy to the strange existence I was thrown into, I who had always lived in cities and whom war had surprised in a study, had to go back to a chapter of your historian F. J. Turner in 'The Significance of the Frontier in American History.' Those trenches marked the farthest line of our civilization—trails—paths—wagon roads—RRs—so in our turn we passed through the different stages of your frontier life." Aubert thus would "safely predict that the qualities of your frontiersmen will come out in the sons of Illinois who are to fight in France."[1] Literally, World War I was twentieth-century technology serving slaughter. What was further from Americans' pioneer past than trench warfare with artillery barrages, poison gas, flame throwers, tanks, and emerging uses of air power? Yet many Americans and some of their historians saw that combat metaphorically as an extension of frontier experience fighting Indians and their "savagery" in antithetical juxtaposition with "civilization" in Turner's alliterative syntax.

After World War I, a frontier analogy often characterized subsequent combat in World War II and then, tragically, in Vietnam.[2] Persistence of that metaphorical figuration for twentieth-century combat is a function of many messages, including discourse read as history corroborating popular culture, which make an impact only after successive exposures over long periods of time. For as Richard Neustadt and Ernest May conclude, "the majority of humankind . . . learn to think in streams of time as we learn to think mathematically—if we do either or at all—from teachers and books. It probably also follows that the learning comes through pieced-together stories about real people better than through abstract constructions from philosophy or social sciences, or even through invented characters in fiction (a close question)."[3] What remains here is to indicate how the rhetoric of some historians has functioned as but one, albeit influential, aspect of opinion leadership reinforcing the metaphorical analogy within that "stream of time"—and then to suggest how America now requires a differing, more ethically responsible perspective on whose behalf rhetorical prowess in writing history might be fruitfully applied.

Scholarship in rhetoric and communication offers exemplary explications of metaphor as tenor-vehicle interaction evoking meaning, complemented by comprehensive analyses of recurring metaphors such as the archetypal sea, light-dark figurations, or metaphorical clusters revealing inventional *topoi* in discourse.[4] That rich rhetorical theory nevertheless often skirts "*moral*" judgments because scholars seeking "facts" more than "values" typically favor "safer territory, showing how individual metaphors 'work' in themselves" or "how they function in given contexts. . . . We find today hardly any serious appraisal of how particular metaphors might be good or bad for those who embrace them." Moreover, while including metaphors among the "most powerful" modes of "narrative" working good or ill in the world, Wayne Booth singles out as particularly dangerous those about weaponry "designed to win by destroying an opponent": "the worst distortions occur when we think we have arrived at absolute truth through univocal, simple, economical clarities."[5] After all, "social functions" of metaphors reflect how well they aptly crystallize a "truth of things" and a "prescription for action" answering the question, "What shall we do about this?" Even if false, that analogy "does not just *express* the pertinence of certain cultural axioms to given social conditions, it provides *the semantic conditions through which* actors deal with that reality." And to people as "time binders . . . framed between the remembered past and the imagined future with the need to fill the inchoate present with activity," those metaphors can give "a futureness to the past and a pastness to the future that is fundamentally reassuring."[6] For Americans' frontier metaphor for twentieth-century combat, reinforcement (1) began with the Spanish-American War and its immediate aftermath of armed conflict in the Philippines, (2) continued through both world wars as well as the Cold War with communism, (3) was seriously questioned during the Vietnam War, and (4) now, reemergent, may require modification.

Methodologically, this effort draws together "disparate scraps of discourse which, when constructed as an argument, serve to illuminate otherwise hidden or taken for granted social practices," and in "composing a text from a vast profusion of utterances, images, and narratives, inventing a mosaic that is larger and truer than any of its parts . . . the critic must argue for their coherence and substance."[7] For the frontier metaphor of Americans in twentieth-century war, that "text" is drawn from decades of "disparate" materials including speeches, films, propaganda pamphlets, television advertising and programming, theater, song, photographs, and personal correspondence or reminiscences of American troops in the field—all as reinforced briefly but credibly by historians in a "stream of time." Those materials are synthesized here because, as Booth suggests, "to *describe* or *summarize* any myth is almost inevitably to reduce its power, or even to destroy it." Moreover, the tragedy of this metaphor is made manifest herein by demonstrating not only its lack of "truth" but also its "comparative worth" to "rival narratives" that conduce to "more plausible or fruitful myth"; for "ethical evaluation of grand metaphors, like all other evaluation, depends on comparison."[8] After all, nearly three centuries of experience with a frontier created a rich lode of *other* figurative analogies for rhetorical applications ethically more responsible now.

I

In 1893, Turner's timing was fortuitous for his Frontier Thesis address to the American Historical Association. Citing the 1890 U.S. Census Report, his oratorical proem established that as unsettled area our frontier ceased to exist. Population density had attained levels whereby, with attendant ease of transportation and communication, America no longer had a vast and dangerous wilderness on this continent to be confronted and conquered, particularly in combat with Indians (the 1890 massacre of Sioux at Wounded Knee suggested to many Americans that our Indian menace was ended). Although advocating scholarly research about past westward expansion, Turner nevertheless often was interpreted as calling upon Americans to apply frontier attributes in other, future endeavors. For, as demonstrated in earlier chapters here, many people perceived his peroration as embodying the moral of Turner's famous statement:

To the frontier the American intellect owes its striking characteristics. That coarseness and strength combined with acuteness and inquisitiveness; that practical, inventive turn of mind, quick to find expedients; that masterful grasp of material things, lacking in the artistic but powerful to effect great ends; that restless, nervous energy, that dominant individualism, working for good and evil, and withal that buoyancy and exuberance which comes with freedom— these are traits of the frontier, or traits called out elsewhere because of the existence of the frontier.[9]

Asking "when and how did the United States become a land of the past, a culture with a discernible memory or with a configuration of recognized pasts," Michael Kammen identifies the closing of the frontier as pivotal. Prior to this time, when Americans sought guidance from the record of the past, they read histories of Europe. Publishers in this country then knew that Americans "enjoyed reading European history" because "it contained utilitarian lessons for them." Many Americans had the attitude of "who ever wants to read American history?" Or, as it was widely believed near the beginning of the twentieth century, "the truth is that in many respects . . . the story which the Old World historian has to tell is a better story to tell than ours."[10] Indeed, the Alamo had relatively little significance for Texans until the 1890s—after the frontier closed. Only in 1891 were concerted efforts made to restore the building, "which had been allowed to deteriorate and had been commercially exploited as a wholesale-retail liquor emporium," as a shrine. Then once again, in 1901, the building had to be saved from a venture to raze it and build a hotel on the site (Clara Driscoll, who initiated the fund-raising campaign in 1901, became known in Texas as "the savior of the Alamo").[11] Absence makes hearts grow fonder. Frontier experiences loomed larger and seemed more valuable when they were no longer available. Americans needed other arenas in which to exercise such behavior.

In 1894, Theodore Roosevelt decided that Turner "put into definite shape a good deal of thought which has been floating around rather loosely."[12] That "thought" in 1885 included Reverend Josiah Strong's *Our Country: Its Possible Future and Its Present Crisis*, which identified the "closing years of the nineteenth century" as "second in importance to that only which must remain first . . . the birth of Christ." He also praised Anglo-Saxon pioneers who made America that "principal seat of his power" by which "the destinies of mankind, for centuries to come, can be seriously affected, much less determined, by the men of this generation in the United States."[13] By 1898, Theodore Roosevelt and other in-

fluential people (such as Henry Cabot Lodge and John Hay of the "Pleas-
ant Gang" in Washington, D.C.) decided "everything good in America
was a result of the frontier" and Americans needed a new one "even if
they had to go overseas to find it" fighting Spain.[14] For Turner's Frontier
Thesis peroration also proclaimed "America has been another name for
opportunity, and the people of the United States have taken their tone
from the incessant expansion which has not only been open but has been
forced upon them. He would be a rash prophet who should assert that
the expansive character of American life has now entirely ceased. . . .
American energy will continually demand a wider field for its exercise."
War with Spain—and its bloody aftermath in the newly acquired Philippine Islands—offered just that "wider field."

The outcome of the Spanish-American War of 113 days' duration
was determined largely by two decisive sea battles: Admiral Dewey's
victory at Manila Bay in the Philippines, and Admiral Sampson's at
Santiago, Cuba. At sea, these impressively easy triumphs assured
victory by cutting off Spanish colonial possessions from supplies and
reinforcements. Moreover, both victories were attained with but one
American sailor killed (thus vividly confirming the potency of sea
power espoused by Alfred Thayer Mahan).[15] On land in Cuba, however, military ineptness made our effort less than John Hay's "splendid
little war." With inadequate transportation and communication, U.S.
troops in the tropics wore winter uniforms; many of them still used black-
powder rifles; and in several engagements they displayed disorder if
not panic. The land war, "which America entered upon as lightheart-
edly as if it were with a tribe of Indians," had one bright spot: a presumed charge at San Juan Hill by Teddy Roosevelt's "Rough Riders,"
whose ranks ostensibly were filled with cowboys and other Westerners.
Also including eastern playboys and other adventuresome spirits, this
volunteer regiment fought not on horseback but as infantry; their objective in several engagements around El Caney and the San Juan heights
was Kettle Hill. With black troopers of the Tenth Cavalry (now dis-
mounted) under Lieutenant John J. Pershing, the Rough Riders advanced
up Kettle Hill in less a formal "charge" and more a slow, disorganized
approach against a Spanish position.[16] Ever since 1886 and the "pleas-
ing possibility of 'trouble with Mexico,'" the idea "of riding into battle
at the head of a command of cowboy cavalry had long been a dream of
Mr. Roosevelt's . . . martial mind." He proposed then to "raise some
companies of horse riflemen" from among the "harum-scarum rough

riders of the West," and in 1898, the group evolved from "Teddy's Terrors" through "Rocky Mountain Rustlers" to "Roosevelt's Rough Riders" in Cuba.[17] Embellished newspaper accounts of their "charge" and a widely reproduced painting by famed Western illustrator Frederic Remington bestowed mythic stature upon the event and thrust Roosevelt to political prominence.[18] By consistently omitting the important role of Pershing's black cavalrymen in securing the objective, those portrayals suggested that Americans at war abroad succeeded as they emulated stereotypical frontier forebears.

Americans accepted that view of combat in 1898 because their heritage, as reinforced by American-history textbooks, nurtured unshakable faith in frontiersmen's marksmanship and martial prowess. Mythic antecedents were minutemen with muskets at Lexington and Concord as well as "untrained rabble" at Bunker Hill holding their fire against British troops until they saw "the whites of their eyes." Crystallization came at the Battle of New Orleans on 8 January 1815, when British troops suffered 2,000 killed and wounded from Andrew Jackson's ill-organized, ill-equipped, and outnumbered body of men hastily assembled from Louisiana, Mississippi, Tennessee, and Kentucky—who themselves suffered only eight killed and thirteen wounded. Despite "available records as to what did happen at New Orleans," the legend arose that "the British were slaughtered because of the sharpshooting skill of the American frontiersman." Anecdotes reprinted in many newspapers headlined "Sharp Shooting"; widely published poetry extolled these "sun-burnt men, in simple garb of foresters" and proclaimed "the fatal aim of the western marksmen was never so terribly exemplified"; and one of the most popular songs in America for decades was "The Hunters of Kentucky," whose eight verses included these lines:

> I s'pose you've read it in the prints.
> How Packenham attempted
> To make old Hickory Jackson wince,
> But soon his scheme repented
> For we with rifles ready cock'd,
> Thought such occasion lucky,
> And soon around the gen'ral flock'd
> The Hunters of Kentucky.
> . . . .
> For well he knew what aim we take

With our Kentucky rifles.
. . . .
We did not choose to waste our fire,
    So snugly kept our places.
But when so near we saw them wink,
    We thought it time to stop 'em
And 'twould have done you good I think,
    To see Kentuckians drop 'em.[19]

Actually, the 2,250 Kentuckians arriving on 4 January 1815 were, in Jackson's words, "the worst provided body of men, perhaps, that ever went 1,500 miles from home to help a sister state." Only a few had fire-arms; Jackson got rifles for about 500 others. By 7 January, only 250 of them had reached the assigned position (behind two ranks of Tennesseeans), and at a crucial point in the battle, those Kentuckians "ran full speed to the rear." Memoirs and correspondence show British casualties were primarily from American cannons and grapeshot; wounds from small arms were superficial because they were from buck-shot (hardly ammunition of "sharpshooting" riflemen).[20] But the West-ern film *The Man Who Shot Liberty Valance* (1962, directed by John Ford and starring John Wayne and James Stewart) suggests that when choos-ing between fact and fiction about the frontier, Americans "print the legend." So children learned from American-history textbooks that at New Orleans, for "the bloodiest battle of the war," Jackson gathered "militia from the frontier of the Southwest," and 2,000 British troops "fell before the crack rifle fire of the despised frontiersmen."[21] Thus, the Rough Riders' success was a "story" with "narrative probability and fidelity" complementing "self-conceptions that people hold of them-selves."[22] Many American historians helped reinforce an image that success in combat came from applying frontier attributes—even if the frontier was no longer literally in existence.

One instance of metaphorical analogy from Cuba in 1898, however, was insufficient to establish firmly a figurative frontier "truth of things" for twentieth-century war. Corroboration also came during bloody com-bat in the Philippine Islands newly acquired from Spain. Seeking inde-pendence from a new colonial master, Filipinos under Emilio Aguinaldo fought American troops including Regular Army cavalry regiments re-cently from the frontier, whose officers including then-Captain Pershing had vivid "memories of Geronimo, of the Sioux at Wounded Knee, or the ragged, hapless Cree." Pershing himself could not resist describing an encounter with Moro tribesman who were surrendering as "a display to beggar the 'greatest Wild West Show.'"[23] In correspondence and speeches reaching wider audiences through newspapers in Chicago, Detroit, New York, and various western cities, President Theodore Roosevelt compared Filipinos in arms to "the Sioux, the Comanche, and the Apache Indians" and declared that Emilio Aguinaldo was "the typical representative of savagery, the typical foe of civilization and the American people."[24] Racist overtones of combat against Filipinos also were evident among U.S. Marine officers who, "despite upper middle-class prerogatives and ongoing social ties," resorted to "lower-class military mores—roughneck values descended from the frontier which survived in popular culture," including continual reference to their enemy as "niggers" (admittedly, this term at the turn of the century may have been a more neutral colloquialism than now).[25] For Americans asking "what shall we do about this?" and seeking a "prescription for action" in the Far East, fighting Filipinos provided "a pastness to the future that is fundamentally reassuring" although fortification palisades were made of bamboo instead of American timbers. After all, "the need to bind past and future together in the present is even more pressing in rapidly transitional societies."[26]

American troops in the Philippines did view their combat as analogous to frontier experiences. In an officer's report of operations against Aguinaldo's "hostile tribesmen" typically "lying in wait for small detachments" and mounting "treacherous" attacks, the U.S. Army *still* fought savages who "burned a number of towns and killed men, women, and children . . . in the most ruthless and brutal manner."[27] More revealing are recollections of an enlisted man from Boston serving in the 34th U.S. Volunteer Infantry. After Parkmanesque descriptions of Army wagon trains proceeding through "jungles" or "rolling country" where "rivers were sparkling," he lauded "sheer American nerve and dogged determination" enabling their advance "over the mountains, diving into valleys, with rushing streams, through the country of the savage." The scenic analog of mythic westward expansion across a continent to achieve Manifest Destiny now was being played out abroad. Then, that soldier described enemies "armed with steel hatchets, steel-pointed spears, bows and arrows, with wooden shields," whose "savage cruelty" included subjecting prisoners to "unprintable indignities" or "burying a man to his neck in the ground, with water just beyond his lips." Most pertinent, however, is the Bostonian's prescient conclusion about soldiers' conversations in the field: "The boys from the Middle West could tell some tall tales of the exploits of Davy Crockett, from the canebrakes of Tennessee to the Alamo; of Daniel Boone, from the forests and clearings of Kentucky to the Missouri. I listened to these stories with avidity. I saw in them a part of the folklore of the future. In my turn, I feebly tried to imitate them, with similar stories of Down East; but with indifferent success." So troops in the Philippines conversed about exploits of frontiersmen; easterners' folklore was unimportant. And to gain the acceptance of his peers, that Bostonian admitted, he purchased and carried a bowie knife, a weapon of frontier fame.[28] Furthermore, a figurative "truth of things" persists in historical writing when Vandiver's account of combat in the Philippines lapses easily into metaphor about "Emilio Aguinaldo's maintenance of the *warpath* against his benefactors."[29] Americans still see years of combat against Filipinos as another Indian war.

II

In the advent of World War I, imagery of American soldiers as frontiersmen was reinforced in 1916 when General Pershing's troops pursued Pancho Villa into Mexico after his raids across the border. Opponents were not Indians but Mexican "bandits" who qualified as frontier foes. During the U.S. military buildup on the border between 1909 and 1912 (in response to unrest in Mexico), an officer perceived the "value" of sending "cavalry units from the north to the border, a country well suited for cavalry training throughout the years": "the necessity imposed upon the mounted arms to patrol the border, gave much opportunity for the proper training of cavalry on *frontier* work."[30] Although Pershing had machine-gun platoons, some motorized transport, and the Curtis Jenny for observers aloft (the First Aero Squadron JN-2s were ineffective in the mountains of Mexico), newspaper photographs showed horse- or mule-drawn supply wagons easily reminiscent of Western wagon trains. In a widely published picture, Pershing wore the wide-brimmed campaign hat of frontier cavalry and forded a stream on horseback, with Lieutenant George S. Patton riding at his side. As on the frontier, mounted cavalry were prominent. At Ojos Azules on 5 May 1916, Eleventh Cavalry troopers (with Apache scouts) heard their bugler sound "Charge," wheeled from a column of fours into line abreast, and at the bugle call

"Gallop," conducted the U.S. Army's last combat cavalry charge. The Villistas' position was taken; no American was wounded; the action, in Pershing's word, was "brilliant."[31] Although Pershing arrived in France for World War I in more modern garb, his first troops in the American Expeditionary Force landed wearing wide-brimmed campaign hats of earlier combat on the frontier and in Cuba. When an advance A.E.F. unit paraded through Paris on 4 July 1917, a battalion of the 16th Infantry Regiment, First Division, reminded French people sufficiently of Rough Riders to prompt ecstatic cheers: "*Vive les Teddies*" (Americans soon wore steel helmets *de rigueur* for modern armies).[32]

A.E.F. troops as well as the American public *were* indoctrinated by propaganda portraying combat in France as further frontier experience. American historians encouraged that analogy. Frederick Jackson Turner helped create a National Board for Historical Service to persuade Americans about their righteous cause. And as Edgar Robinson of Stanford explained the need for "adequate and accurate information" about the "meaning of the struggle," our troops should understand "the way in which this continent was peopled" and thereby carry "the torch of the American frontiersman."[33] Other influential propaganda came from Turner's student Carl Becker, who wrote pamphlets for the Committee on Public Information because his earlier essay entitled "Kansas" argued eloquently that Kansans' pioneer attributes were those of Americans generally and that our "mission in the world" was to promulgate them abroad: "They have solved great problems hitherto unsolved, have realized utopias dreamed of but never realized by Europe. They are therefore in the van of civilization, quite sure of the direction, triumphantly leading the march towards the ultimate goal."[34] To emphasize Prussian brutality, government speakers were taught in a handbook written by historian Albert Bushnell Hart and Arthur O. Lovejoy to suggest continuity of earlier experiences by telling audiences that now "captured soldiers are tortured, not *a la* Iroquois, but *a la* Junker."[35] All of this could constitute a "truth of things" for troops led by career officers whose combat experience was, as Captain Thomas Shipley wrote from France, in "tropical and semi-tropical campaigns against semi-civilized tribes in wild unbroken country."[36] America had an experienced, professional army officer corps for World War I primarily because of the perceived need to protect frontier settlers from "savage" Indians. Without the "frontier myth" of "Indians as agents of the Devil," the United States at the close of the nineteenth century "probably would not have had a regular army" in which those officers could gain leadership experience.[37]

Between the two world wars, Americans had further opportunities to perceive twentieth-century combat as extensions of frontier experience. Locales for that analog often were in Central America and islands of the Caribbean Sea. After the turn of the century, the U.S. Marine Corps began a series of military campaigns of substantial length in Nicaragua, from 1909 through 1913 and from 1926 through 1933, as well as in Haiti and the Dominican Republic, off and on from 1905 to 1934.[38] These governments often were characterized by political and resultant financial instability, and other nations such as France, Germany, and Great Britain were tempted to intervene militarily for purposes of collecting debts. To estop those interventions, America consistently invoked the Roosevelt corollary of the Monroe Doctrine, whereby in cases of "chronic wrongdoing or impotence" on the part of Latin American states, the United States was bound, "however reluctantly," to "exercise an international police power."[39] Military means for wielding such power was the branch of service whose World War I "recruiting effort had made 'Marine Corps' virtually a household word throughout the United States and had captivated the public not only for the length of the war but afterward."[40]

The Marines' image of prowess as marksmen with the 1903 Springfield rifle also had been complemented in popular culture after World War I by the popularity of the Marine characters in *What Price Glory?* (in both the successful Broadway play by Maxwell Anderson and Lawrence Stallings as well as the movie with Victor McLaglen and Wallace Beery). Imaging of the lengthy Marine military endeavors in Latin America reached an apogee in popular culture through the numerous short stories and illustrations of Captain John W. Thomason, Jr., in the *Saturday Evening Post, Harper's* and the *New Yorker*.[41] Photographs, as well as Thomason's drawings, often show marines in combat garb with holsters low on their hips, frontier style. Indeed, "the public image of the United States Marine was taking shape: lean, sunburnt, in faded khaki and rakish field hat . . . an '03 rifle in one hand and a bottle in the other."[42] The image was nostalgic, however, for reality revealed in archival photographs shows those marines often armed with enhanced firepower of a preferred Thompson submachine gun and Browning automatic rifle (BAR).[43] As on the frontier with Indians, a racist tendency also existed. In their correspondence, for example, officers referred to their Latin American opponents in such terms as "nigger" and "bad niggers" and made such generalizations as "you can never trust a nigger with a gun."[44]

The characterization of them as "savage" occurred frequently as well.[45] Another frontier motif was present when for two decades *all* of the Marines' "caco" opponents in Haiti—whether reformers, revolutionaries, mercenaries, or criminals—simply were called "bandits."[46] The same epithet often was applied in Nicaragua where Marines were developing their forte of using aircraft in support of ground forces but still utilized mounted cavalry.[47] As a Marine Corps historian concludes metaphorically, the Caribbean, Central America, and new possessions in the Pacific "represented a *frontier* for American idealism and commercial expansion."[48] The metaphorical analogy for combat persisted.

Another anachronism of frontier imagery between the world wars came from the "Horse Marines" in Asia, where for "forty years the Marine Corps and service in exotic China were to be synonymous in the public mind."[49] After the Boxer Rebellion and ensuing treaty protocols, Marines were stationed in China to protect American civilians and business interests, the most sizable unit being the 4th Marine Regiment at Tientsin with its detached Legation Guard in Peking. In 1907, the Legation Guard created a mounted detachment for "use in crowd control and for warning the Americans living in the hinterlands," and these "Horse Marines" became an "elite unit noted for their smart appearance, elan in mounted drill, and arrogance."[50] Initially "trained and equipped like cavalry to protect Americans," the Horse Marines on their Mongolian ponies "in truth . . . were used mostly to climax Marine parades with a galloping dash, their sabers flashing."[51] Although Marines often had armed confrontations both with Japanese troops between the wars and various factions in Chinese civil wars, the China Expeditionary Force soon earned the nickname (in some quarters) of "exhibition force," by virtue of its "nickel plated" machine guns and light artillery as well as helmets "refinished in glistening paint" to look "like some German Guard regiment with silver helmets on."[52] But for purposes of his Marines' public image, Brigadier General Smedley Butler characterized for the press in 1927 their mission in China as one with a "sense of chivalry" to "protect the lives of American women and children out here," including those American civilians in Peking "who would be rescued from their homes by the legation guard's 'suicide squad,' forty men riding Mongolian ponies."[53] The Marine Legation Guard soon acquired sufficient motorized transport, however; and as the commanding officer of the Horse Marines unit in 1933, then Captain "Chesty" Puller questioned his orders: "our evacuation plans call for taking our people out on horseback. You know we couldn't do that in time. We have about thirty big trucks, and they would carry thirty or forty people each. Why do we have to keep up this nonsense?" Puller's request in writing to his headquarters to change the evacuation plans was ignored (although he subsequently received unofficial, oral approval to use trucks), for the Horse Marines were deemed "the colorful symbol of American influence in North China."[54] In the 1930s, cavalry still could come to the rescue and evince "the venerable frontier ethos of rescuing innocent women and children from menacing savages."[55]

As America came closer to entering World War II, Hollywood helped persuade isolationists with several pro-British films, including those depicting "Indians" of India being pacified by Cary Grant, Douglas Fairbanks, Jr., and Victor McLaglen in *Gunga Din* (1939). Britain also provided technicolor films about fighting "Indians" of India in *Drums* (1938), or more epically, the Sudanese Mahdi's Fuzzy-Wuzzy "Indians" in *Four Feathers* (1939). Most pertinent for pre-war propaganda about American soldiers as frontiersmen was *Sergeant York*, starring Gary Cooper, whose earlier roles included *The Virginian* (1929) and *The Plainsman* (1936). Released before Pearl Harbor in 1941, *Sergeant York* has Cooper as a Tennessee mountaineer and marksman with stereotypically pioneer speech and manners. Unwilling at first to fight in World War I, York finally accepts his righteous mission and becomes a hero in the trenches of France with a hunter-woodsman's canny ways and marksmanship with a bolt-action 1903 Springfield rifle, an epitome of the mythic sharpshooter from our past. Early in that film, York as a civilian wins a shooting match with characteristic behavior of wetting his thumb with his tongue and then cleaning off the front sight of his rifle. In the trenches of France, he does the same thing; and making turkey sounds which get German soldiers to look up from their trenches to reveal their positions, he then picks them off one by one as the frontier sharpshooter par excellence. *Sergeant York* exemplified World War II films as allegorical Westerns wherein "strong, silent, lonely men ride in from the prairie, conquer their aversion to the use of weapons and, without profit to themselves, defend freedom-loving farmers against gangs bent on grabbing land and power." The persuasiveness of that imagery was revealed in September 1941 during a Senate investigation of Hollywood for making propaganda films, when isolationist Senator Gerald Nye singled out *Sergeant York* as having been "designed to create war hysteria."[56] The film's lingering appeal is indicated by the fact that it is now available in a colorized version for rental on videotape.

Although wartime cinema infantry squads and bomber or submarine crews usually were cross sections of America—including a big city
"wise-guy," such as John Garfield's character in *Air Force* (1943) or *Des-
tination Tokyo* (1943)—their steadying force or modest hero often was
from a farm, ranch, or small town not far removed from its frontier roots,
roles such as Robert Walker's as the sailor who finds himself stranded
in an infantry squad on *Bataan* (1943) and Harry Carey's veteran crew
chief of the B-17 *Mary Ann* in the film *Air Force* (1943).[57] That those portrayals were plausible is supported by reality: a boyishly bucolic Texan,
Audie Murphy, made the cover of *Life*, 16 July 1945, as our "most decorated soldier," and after coming to Hollywood to act in *Beyond Glory*
and *To Hell and Back*, the story of his wartime exploits, Murphy in turn
was featured in numerous Western films during the 1950s and 1960s.

In American films during World War II and years thereafter, the
quintessential cowboy-*cum*-combatant was John Wayne. Although in
many Westerns during the 1930s, Wayne attained prominence in *Stagecoach* (1939) as the loner fleeing the law who nevertheless defends innocent travelers from Indians. In his easy transition to war films, Wayne
wore almost every possible uniform: airman in *Flying Tigers*; naval officer in *They Were Expendable, The Fighting Seabees, Wings of Eagles* and *In
Harm's Way*; army officer in *Back to Bataan* and *The Longest Day*; and
marine in *Flying Leathernecks* and *Sands of Iwo Jima*. That last film is salient because as Marine Sergeant Stryker, for which he received an Academy Award nomination, Wayne was seen as having "merged his own
personality with a character . . . who personified the ideal soldier, sailor,
or Marine." This "Stryker-Wayne characterization," Lawrence H. Suid
has asserted, "will be the one people remember, the one that forever
established Wayne as the fighting man who remains ever ready to fight
for and defend his country."[58] But Wayne continued as cowboy in numerous films and, more importantly, as frontier U.S. Cavalry officer in
John Ford's films *Fort Apache, Rio Grande*, and *She Wore a Yellow Ribbon*—
all complementary to what Robert Ray calls the "masterplot" of real or
"disguised" Westerns dominating classic Hollywood films from 1930 to
1980: a tendency to portray American cinema heroes as embodying traits
of frontiersmen.[59]

America at war also had other opportunities to perceive contemporary combatants as former frontiersmen. Fighting the Japanese on
Guadalcanal in the early part of the war in the Pacific, U.S. Marine pa-

trols often got lost in the dense jungle. A call went out to all units of the First Marine Division for men with "special aptitude" to serve in an ad hoc unit of guides that became known officially as the "Scout-Snipers." Although the Regimental Commander of the 5th Marines, Colonel Gerald Thomas, at one point referred to these men as "the weirdest characters you've ever seen," he attributed their combat contribution to their being "real Daniel Boone types."[60] On the home front, while addressing the U.S. House of Representatives in 1943, Madame Chiang Kai-shek asked Americans to continue "the pioneer work of your ancestors, beyond the frontiers of physical and geographical limitations."[61] In 1942, at the request of "the U.S. Army Air Forces," John Steinbeck wrote *Bombs Away: The Story of a Bomber Team*. The acclaimed chronicler of dustbowl "Okies" in *The Grapes of Wrath* reconciled "past and present" for civilian readers by depicting those crewmen as springing from frontier traditions of "Kentucky hunter and the Western Indian-fighter," for when exchanging rifle for turret machine gun, "the American boy simply changes the nature of his game. Instead of raiding Sioux or Apache, instead of buffalo or antelope, he lays his sights on Zero or Heinkel, on Stuka or Messerschmitt."[62] So in *Thirty Seconds over Tokyo* (1944), the turret gunner on the B-25 named *Ruptured Duck* was Robert Walker, in a reprise of his role as the modest hero from a farm, ranch, or small town not far removed from its frontier roots. Against that backdrop of German and Japanese pilots portrayed as but savage Indians of frontier days, Wayne's roles were a montage of past pioneers indistinguishable from martial models for the present.

In depictions of World War II, melding military and frontier imagery was easy because of historical circumstance. For his general reading public, military historian John Keegan describes the highest leadership in the U.S. Army at the outbreak of the war as coming from an environment of "old Army" and "real soldiering" when "Indian wars had been the private concern of 'a homogeneous class—straight, lean, squarejawed, clear eyed, mustachioed soldiers, professionally going about their business without a flicker of fear or a moment of self-doubt.'" Whether he saw John Wayne as *precisely* that U.S. Cavalry Captain Nathan Brittles in *She Wore a Yellow Ribbon*, Keegan observes that many prominent World War II officers revered the chapel at Fort Leavenworth, Kansas, that is a memorial to "the regiments which fought for the frontier in the Indian Wars of the 1860s and 1870s" (and kept Indians contained on reservations thereafter).[63] The impact of fiction about frontier cavalry clearly was greater than that of the facts, however. Despite what John Ford's epic Westerns depicted as the adventurous combat of frontier cavalry life, a participant then could write in his diary—as did Second Lieutenant John G. Bourke—about only "sickness, heat, bad water, flies, sandstorms, and utter isolation," to the conclusion that "the humdrum life of any post in Arizona in those days was enough to drive one crazy."[64] Nevertheless, American generals who caught the public's fancy during World War II displayed artifacts from earlier experiences on the frontier: Douglas MacArthur's corncob pipe, "Vinegar Joe" Stillwell's cavalry campaign hat in Burma, and—perhaps most vividly—George S. Patton's two ivory-handled Colt .45 revolvers holstered at each side of his waist.

History books and their reviewers subsequently reinforced metaphorical analogies of American combatants in World War II as frontiersmen. Keegan, for instance, says that on D-Day, a 505th Parachute Infantry detachment fought a "minor Alamo" at la Fiere. Troops of the 82nd Airborne Division in Normandy he speaks of as "pioneers" who "in an unknown land, ignorant of its language and landmarks, uncertain of what danger the next thicket or stream-bottom might hold, confident only in themselves and the mastery of the weapons in their hands . . . marched forth and planted the roots of settlement in the soil that was there for the taking."[65] To review and promote Keegan's book, military historian Russell Weigley restates the metaphor: "The Americans became the pioneers, the first natural explorers of dangerous unknown ground, the pioneer spirit of the American West embodied, in 1944, in the parachute and glider assaults of the 82nd and 101st Airborne Divisions that opened the battle of Normandy."[66] In actual military terminology, the paratrooper who jumps first to mark landing zones for those who follow is called "Pathfinder," the mythic character out of James Fenimore Cooper's Leatherstocking Tales. So in his office at Fort Benning, Georgia, an airborne officer recently displayed a "picture of John Wayne as a cavalry officer on the shelf behind him."[67] After all, in *The Longest Day*, Wayne—formerly of *Fort Apache*—played Lieutenant Colonel Benjamin Vandevoort commanding the 2nd Battalion of 505th Parachute Infantry, which secured Ste. Mere-Eglise on D-Day.

Hot war of the 1940s evolved into the Cold War of the 1950s. Aptness of frontier metaphors for combat likely should have diminished because of the distance in time from our pioneer past as well as the emergence of the imagery of electronic, avionic, and atomic technology of war. But metaphorical analogies from the past frontier for present military endeavors endured. During the Korean War, Marines in combat reminisced about enlisting because of "John Wayne movies," and they often compared their personal hygienic behavior in the field and their physical appearance with depictions in "a Duke Wayne war movie."[68] The John Wayne analogy also persisted at higher command echelons in the Korean War—making an appearance, for example, during a heated deliberation on 23 August 1950 in Tokyo. Upon learning that General Douglas MacArthur was planning an audacious landing of Marines at Inchon—clearly one of the most unlikely sites because of unfavorable geographic and hydrographic conditions—Joint Chiefs of Staff members General Lawton Collins and Admiral Forest Sherman flew to Tokyo to dissuade him. After hearing an extensive briefing by amphibious landing experts about why Inchon was unsuitable, Admiral Sherman proclaimed, "I wouldn't hesitate to take a ship up there," prompting MacArthur's exclamation, "Spoken like a Farragut!" In turn, the Navy's Far East expert on such operations, Admiral James H. Doyle, muttered to be heard by those around him, "Spoken like a John Wayne."[69] Whether the military endeavor was truly heroic or brash bravado, the icon of the cowboy *cum* cavalryman *cum* twentieth-century combatant had become deeply ingrained in American culture. And this continued "truth of things" may be attributed to still other rhetorical forces, metaphorical in themselves.

American cold-war rhetoric and its historical antecedents relied consistently upon images of our enemies' "savagery," and those justifications for war occur from the time of the colonists' arguments for combat against Great Britain through that of the presidential rhetoric supporting war in Vietnam. Some of that discourse is explicit. Franklin Roosevelt condemned German "forces of savagery and of barbarism" and "savage and brutal forces seeking to subjugate the world." But "images of savagery" also are derived, as Robert Ivie asserts, from "metaphorical terms rich with depersonalizing and decivilizing connotations."[70] More recently, Ronald Reagan as president favored "the metaphor of savagery" and "decivilizing vehicles" to characterize Soviets as "untamed," "barbarous," "evil," "cruel," and "murderous."[71] Other rhetorical justification for military endeavors or preparedness included one historian's call for a "counter-ideology" against "Soviet tyranny" during the Cold War: "our military forces and their civilian springboards must have ideals to fight for if they are to combat the *savage* fanaticism of thoroughly indoctrinated Communist troops."[72] Nevertheless, the cultural counterpoint of "savagery" is the frontiersman's victorious combat—as pioneer, cowboy, or cavalryman—in the struggle to settle this continent.

In the American psyche, "savage" was synonymous with Indian. Frederick Jackson Turner alliteratively defined the frontier as "the meeting point between savagery and civilization." Because of this persistent foe during colonization and westward expansion, popular culture was replete with lurid tales of Indians scalping, torturing, and burning prisoners at the stake, taking women and children into captivity, ambushing wagon trains, and massacring settlers and soldiers. In James Fenimore Cooper's Leatherstocking Tales, Indians typically are "devils," "miscreants," or "riptyles" (yet Allan Nevins calls Uncas and Chingachgook "men of nearly every virtue, few limitations, and no vices").[73] Although Pershing in Mexico had friendly Apache scouts and the Lone Ranger on radio later had his "faithful Indian companion" Tonto, frontiersmen's triumphs over Indian "savagery" remained salient in American popular culture when Cold War leaders were younger. For instance, *Northwest Passage* was a technicolor epic in 1940 about Major Rogers's Rangers during the French and Indian War. Like the later Green Berets, they conducted daring operations with physical stamina, exceptional mobility, and unorthodox methods, and the film epically depicts their 1759 mission against St. Francis, from which Indians ravaged frontier settlements. To reach their objective undetected, Rangers trek into wilderness, wade through swamps, and ford a raging river. Briefing his men at the outset, Rogers (Spencer Tracy) has another Ranger describe what happened to others of their unit captured earlier by Indians: "Phillips had a strip of skin torn upwards from his stomach. They hung him from a tree by it. . . . They tore my brother's arms out of him. They chopped the ends of his ribs away from his backbone and pried them out through his skin one by one." Rogers says the same atrocities happened to "your folks on the border farms. They weren't fighting anybody. They were clearing woods and plowing and raising children . . . trying to make a home of it. And then one night . . . tomahawks hit the door. If it was over quick they were lucky." Then, just before the attack, Rogers issues a final order: "Now pay attention. Now we're under orders to wipe out this town. So see that we do it. Kill every fighting Indian. Kill 'em quick. And kill 'em dead."[74] Rangers comply, clad in buckskins dyed green to blend in with the woods and jaunty green caps (perhaps remembered by viewers over two decades later when worn by U.S. Special Forces troops, the Green Berets).

Nearly three centuries of experience and popular culture bestowed credibility on this frontier adage: "The only good Indian is a dead Indian." So they were killed or contained on reservations (as "containment" later was foreign policy toward Communists) by pioneers with muskets, U.S. Cavalry with Sharps carbines, and cowboys with Colt .45 revolvers dubbed "Peacemakers." If formidable enemies defeated before the turn of the century were literal savages in the popular mind, twentieth-century frontiersmen might have similar success against subsequent "Red" savages. Indeed, so potent are negative connotations of "savage" in American culture that an attorney representing a murder suspect named James Hudson Savage believed it could cost his client a fair trial. Accordingly, he filed a motion to have the defendant identified by a "less-violent sounding alias during the trial" because when jurors "hear 'savage,' they see Indians attacking and all that."[75] Such is the semantic heritage of the frontier in our national "stream of time."

In Korea, a frontier analogy for combat was obscure, however. Korean climate and topography admittedly were as inhospitable as any confronted during westward expansion and contributed to what military historian S. L. A. Marshall called "the century's nastiest little war."[76] For American troops soft from occupation duty in Japan, early "bug outs" (leaving equipment and fleeing before enemy envelopment) led to almost the complete rout of the Eighth Army before it stiffened at the Pusan Perimeter. Discipline improved after MacArthur's masterful Inchon landing, the Marines' swift advance to the "Frozen Chosin" Reservoir near the Yalu River, and their epochal retreat described by General O. P. Smith as "We are not retreating. We are merely advancing in another direction." But the final, negotiated stalemate at the 38th Parallel did not resemble earlier martial triumphs.[77] This atypical war also displayed disturbing contradictions for Americans. On one hand, David Douglas Duncan's memorable photographs of Marines in combat there included a widely published one of a muddy, grimly determined marine rifleman charging past a dead body—to evoke memories of Sergeant York or "Hunters of Kentucky." Yet a Defense Department photograph showed U.S. Air Force Captain John Gosnell taxiing for takeoff from Japan in an F-82 for an interdiction mission over Korea—while his wife and two children, standing by the family sedan, wave goodbye as he leaves for "work."[78] Korea was less a war than it was a brief interruption of civilian lives—as in the case of the U.S. Navy pilot portrayed by

William Holden in *The Bridges at Toko-Ri,* a successful attorney who as a reservist was activated to fly against North Korea. The resultant incongruity is clear in *M*A*S*H** and the subsequent television series: the Mobile Army Surgical Hospital is commanded by Colonel Henry Potter, a career man from the days of horse cavalry, and the central-character doctors have such hunter-woodsman names as "Hawkeye" and "Trapper John"—but behave like Tom Sawyer, Huck Finn, confidence men from earlier American mythology, or "Joe College and Fred Premed" demonstrating the best (or worst) of *Animal House* activities.[79] For civilians at heart who maintain urbanity and provoke laughter during war in Korea, frontier names are appealing parodies. Less popular was the black humor in *Dr. Strangelove* (1964), when Slim Pickens as Strategic Air Command pilot Major King Kong—with cowboy boots, Stetson hat, and wide Western drawl—rode an atomic bomb astride as it hurled toward its Russian target.[80] Despite that persistent tendency of combatants to characterize themselves as John Wayne, our metaphorical "truth of things" for war briefly was less apt for Americans.

III

John Kennedy's rhetoric fostered a clearer connection between armed confrontation with communism and combat roles of earlier cowboys, cavalry, and hunter-woodsmen. Following his "New Frontier" call to "explore the stars, conquer the deserts, eradicate disease," we penetrated outer space. Popular culture soon depicted the New Frontier of space as Hollywood's Old West. *Outland,* for instance, is "essentially a remake of *High Noon,* replacing Gary Cooper with Sean Connery" as a marshal in a space-moon mining outpost. When the cowardly "townspeople" fail to support him against a murderous company "boss," Connery faces a bloody showdown alone. Similarly, in *The Right Stuff,* Chuck Yeager frequents Pancho's Fly Inn, "the saloon in any classic western," and rides a horse to the X-1 in which he will scout the perimeter of space. And although Ronald Reagan's 1983 Strategic Defense Initiative was called "Star Wars" by its critics, a rhetorical appraisal sees S.D.I. controlling the "high ground" as applying "Old Frontier values onto the New Frontier of space."[81] Moreover, to complement numerous Western film allusions in *Star Wars,* Han Solo, with laser gun holstered low on the hip, visits an outer-space version of the classic cowboy-movie saloon, with his faithful Wookie companion, Chewbacca. Kennedy's "New Frontier" also appealed to Peace Corps members who in the Third World applied text-books and stethoscopes instead of axes and muskets. *The Ugly American* profoundly affected America in general and Senator John Kennedy in particular, who in 1959 sent a copy of the novel to every U.S. Senate member. Instead of affluent ambassadors dispensing economic largess from air-conditioned offices, our better effort at foreign aid was to be made in the fields and villages of underdeveloped nations, a scene perceived by John Hellmann as "a frontier where Americans could return to the remembered virtues of their heritage . . . to find progress and virtue in the rigors and basic values of nature."[82] A significant scene for this new pioneer was Southeast Asia, where events prompted Kennedy's intervention with troops.

In May 1954, France capitulated at the siege of Dien Bien Phu, colonialism ended in Indochina, and Communist North Vietnam became a nation threatening South Vietnam. As president, Kennedy feared being perceived as too weak to deter Red expansion. After all, a Democratic president, Truman, seemingly "lost" China to communism and caused stalemate in Korea.[83] With martial metaphors about a "beachhead of cooperation" and "now the trumpet summons us," Kennedy's inaugural address was tough talk: "we shall pay any price, bear any burden, meet any hardship, support any friend or oppose any foe to assure the survival and the success of liberty." So in 1961, he sent the first 400 troops to Vietnam jungles—Special Forces, known as the Green Berets. A literal precedent for their success lay in British Prime Minister Harold Macmillan's reports about the triumph of the elite S.A.S. (Special Air Service) over Communists in Malayan jungles. S.A.S. lineage included World War II British Commandos (who wore green berets), the First Airborne Division (the "Red Devils" of Arnhem), the Long Range Desert Group of North African exploits, the Special Boat Squadron of other extraordinary raids, and General Orde Wingate's "Chindits," who operated behind Japanese lines in Burma with daring deeds—all taking part in historical events that an Anglophile would appreciate. In 1948, when Communists arose against colonial rule in Malaya, regular troops were unsuccessful at suppression, so new jungle tactics came from an expert in irregular warfare, former "Chindit" Michael Calvert. Landing by helicopter or parachute deep in the jungle, small S.A.S. teams knew the local language and won "hearts and minds" of villagers, who then helped track and ambush "C.T.'s" (Communist Terrorists), and populations of outlying villages were relocated to easily protected "strategic hamlets." By 1956, S.A.S. success led Macmillan to visit Johore and observe their skills; in 1957, the Malayan Emergency was declared ended.[84] Although that literal comparison was available, Kennedy preferred tapping our frontier nostalgia. After all, from 1957 to 1961, the highest-rated television show was "Gunsmoke," followed in 1958–59 by "Wagon Train," "Have Gun, Will Travel," and "The Rifleman." The top ten also included "Maverick," "Tales of Wells Fargo," and "The Life and Legend of Wyatt Earp." "Wagon Train" was number one in 1961–62, and from 1964 to 1967, "Bonanza" topped the ratings.[85] Although Kennedy's FCC Chairman, Newton Minnow, characterized television as a "vast wasteland," Americans clearly cherished their Old West.

Under the chapter title "The Return of the Frontier Hero," Hellmann argues that "Kennedy's well-publicized interest in the Special Forces made them extensions of the commander-in-chief, just as the Hunters of Kentucky and the Rough Riders had once magnified the respective images of Andrew Jackson and Theodore Roosevelt." By 1962, media images "crystallized into a portrayal of the Green Beret as a contemporary reincarnation of the western hero" with "wilderness skills" for any environment and superb physical conditioning. In a publicity photograph, Special Forces troops paddling a rubber raft was said to resemble "a canoe full of Rogers' Rangers emerging from the forest streams of the American past." And by studying Mao Tse-tung and Che Guevara on guerrilla warfare, Green Berets were said to have acquired a "fused image of sophisticated contemporary professional and rough Indian fighter . . . squarely in the American tradition of skill in irregular fighting 'from the French and Indian wars through Marion in the Revolution, Mosby's Rangers in the Civil War and Merrill's Marauders in World War II." Also bringing "medical care and all the other arts of progress" to Southeast Asia, Special Forces were called an "ideal answer of the New Frontier . . . hunter at the wooded edge of civilization, builder and teacher in the pastoral landscapes behind"; as "successors to the standard band of frontiersmen accompanied by an Indian scout, they had entered a wilderness that, in the global context of the Cold War, was a meeting point between savagery and civilization."[86] Again, the alliterative syntax of Turner's antithesis between savagery and civilization reappears. Admittedly, the Special Forces, or Green Berets, evolved in part from the U.S. Army Rangers, an elite group in World War II so named by General Lucian Truscott "after Colonial guerrillas who had fought the French and the Indians in the French and Indian War of 1755–1763."[87] To sum-

marize Kennedy's rhetorical use of the Green Beret myth, one commen-
tator concludes that through "a public relations image of the frontier
hero, and more traditional public speaking, the President and his advi-
sors tried to communicate to America and the world the idea that the
Special Forces were the answer to Communist wars of national liberation."[88] America accepted Green Berets that way—for a while.

During our most active military role in Vietnam, Hollywood made
one major film about U.S. combat there: *The Green Berets* (1968), starring
John Wayne and made by his own Batjac company.[89] Wayne's son,
Michael, as producer announced to *Variety* that "we're not making a
political picture; we're making a picture about a bunch of right guys . . .
Cowboys and Indians. . . . Americans are the good guys and the Viet
Cong are the bad guys. . . . Maybe we shouldn't have destroyed all those
Indians, but when you are making a picture, the Indians are the bad
guys." And that Western motif is expressed further, as Julian Smith writes,
in "Wayne's line to the effect that 'out here, due process is a bullet,' the
Dodge City sign over the main gate to the Green Beret outpost, the crossbow toting 'native' scouts—and Wayne himself" in a film that "isn't so
much about winning the war against the Vietcong as it is about winning
the hearts and minds of the American public."[90] The quintessential cowboy or archetypal cavalryman in blue uniform and campaign hat was
equally at home as Special Forces Colonel in jungle fatigues, for *The
Green Berets* provided continuity to obligatory combat against savagery.
Trying to be convinced of our righteous cause in Vietnam, a cynical reporter (David Janssen) views the body of a Montagnard girl raped and
killed by five Vietcong guerrillas and listens to Wayne's speech beginning "It's pretty hard to talk to anyone about this country till they've
come over here and seen it," followed by more discourse about "murder, mutilation, torture, disembowelment, bonecrushing, and the 'abuse'
of a chieftain's wife by no less than *forty* Vietcong." After all, in many
propagandistic movies before and during the two world wars, "rape
was a convenient device for making the 'enemy' hateful figures who
could be disposed of with dispatch."[91] The "briefing" in *Northwest Passage* also has its counterpart in *The Green Berets,* with the opening scene
in Fort Bragg, North Carolina, at the John K. Kennedy Center for Special
Warfare. Sergeant Muldoon (Aldo Ray) tells skeptical reporters about
Green Berets in Vietnam, and the unit's black member (Raymond St.
Jacques) testifies about Vietcong "extermination of the civilian leadership, the intentional murder and torture of innocent women and chil-

dren." *The Green Berets* seems to reflect "our hankering after lost frontiers" and a likelihood that "for lack of a West to conquer, we have gone
east" to Asia.[92]

"Savagery" also prevailed in presidential discourse about Vietnam.
At Johns Hopkins University on 7 April 1965, Lyndon Johnson said:
"Simple farmers are the targets of assassination and kidnapping. Women
and children are strangled in the night because their men are loyal to
their government. And helpless villages are ravaged by sneak attacks."
Richard Nixon later decried "Communist massacres," a "bloody Reign
of Terror," a "nightmare" of "atrocities" and "murder," civilians' being
"clubbed, shot to death and buried in mass graves."[93] For Johnson, however, Vietcong "savagery" may have reflected less the conventions of
presidential justifications for war and more the Texan's sense of his own
past. Analogies to the Alamo were prominent in his statements about
the Vietnam War and consistent with repeated but often embellished
and exaggerated accounts of his familial forebears as Indian fighters.[94]
For Johnson, an adage about "the only good Indian" required but slight
emendation: "The only good Vietcong is a dead Vietcong." Nevertheless, metaphors of Green Berets or any G.I.'s in Vietnam as twentieth-
century frontiersmen soon were to be no longer "the truth of things."

Although Kennedy considered withdrawal, Johnson resorted to
massive troop increases as well as different tactics and technology which
General William Westmoreland summarized in 1969: "The Army has
undergone in Vietnam a quiet revolution in ground warfare," and this
new "automated battlefield" required "an Army built into and around
an integrated area control system that exploits the advanced technology
of communications, sensors, fire direction, and the required automatic
data processing."[95] Initially, however, many Americans went to Vietnam
with John Wayne as their model for emulation in combat, and marine
recruits at Camp Pendleton often said his portrayals influenced their
decisions to enlist; a Marine Corps pilot was photographed wearing a
non-issue six-shooter in a cowboy holster low on his hip *à la* hero in a
Hollywood Western; and dangerous areas were called "Indian country," Vietnamese scouts were "Kit Carsons," and many G.I. flak jackets
proclaimed "THE ONLY GOOD GOOK IS A DEAD GOOK."[96] Indeed, our warfare
in Vietnam seemed to parallel earlier combat against Filipinos, with history repeating itself, as newspaper accounts of the Philippines insurrection suggest. Under a Manila dateline of 22 August 1900, this story could
have been read in the 1960s with only place names changed:

In Manila talk of ending the war deals no longer with weeks but with months, and even years. Whether the end comes after a few months or after two or three years, depends on whether the same sort of tactics which dragged through five months and resulted in the conquest of three square inches on the two-foot map of Luzon be continued or methods of striking the enemy fast and repeatedly and holding the country gained be substituted. . . . The whole effort of the insurgents for three months was to hold off the Americans until their ally, the rains, arrived. . . . They read the American newspapers and think the home sentiment against war is growing. Their policy after the rains will be as it was before, a campaign of gaining time and wearing out their opponents. They profess to imagine that Congress will declare against annexation. If Congress fails them they will try to prolong the struggle until the presidential campaign, with the expectation that one of the political parties will declare against imperialism, and the hope that such a party may win.[97]

As that Boston trooper described the war—and apathy at home toward it—Filipinos hid "sharp pointed bamboo sticks" in trails to puncture troops' shoes "entirely through the foot," and "these men could go through all of that, and grin. We have read for one hundred and fifty years of the bleeding feet of the troops at Valley Forge. The sufferings of these men in the Philippines are never mentioned. Why ?"[98] Later in *The Green Berets*, Americans in Vietnam were shown also being impaled by cunningly hidden "sharp pointed bamboo sticks," a fate also suffered by Nat King Cole playing an American in the French Foreign Legion fighting the Vietcong in *China Gate*. For Vietnam, the past was prologue.

But the war changed. Combat "by the numbers" entailed alternatives evaluated as statistical probabilities, tonnage of bombs dropped per square mile, or as an accounting of officers rotated through in ratios reflecting sound career management.[99] American armed forces personnel also relied on an ultimate low in "How to Lie with Statistics"—high body counts. This was "a terrible, long war without the tangible elements of myth" about our frontier.[100] Vietnam was no place for Sergeant York's 1903 Springfield rifle of World War I nor Audie Murphy's M1 Garand rifle of World War II. As a beleaguered marine position at Khe Sanh began to resemble Dien Bien Phu with uncanny fidelity, Americans needed no "sharpshooters" with M16s on automatic fire but the massively increased killing power of weaponry like the AC-47 aircraft called "Puff the Magic Dragon," whose three General Electric Gatling guns sprayed a "rain of fire" of 7.62-mm bullets at the rate of 18,000 per minute.[101] For this war was unlike other conflicts: we watched it nightly on television, with unsurpassed news coverage. Southeast Asia was not more westward expansion after all.

Popular culture soon showed deterioration or distortion in the aptness of frontier analogies. In *Apocalypse Now* (1979), Colonel Kilgore (Robert Duvall) leads an Air Cavalry unit in Vietnam wearing a frontier-army campaign hat, blue uniform shirt, and yellow neckerchief. The sarcasm is obvious. Although Rushing and Frentz see *The Deer Hunter* (1978) as depicting rituals of war generally, Hellmann finds a "western formula" and "the relation of the hero to the frontier."[102] But Michael Vronsky (Robert De Niro) and his friends are of European immigrant stock—men who practice Russian Orthodox Church rituals, work in a Pennsylvania steel town, and ultimately play unpioneerlike Russian roulette. So as Hellmann also admits about our "dominant American historical-mythic tradition," this film "turns the genre upside down" and "stands the western myth on its head."[103] Consider also Sylvester Stallone's popular *Rambo* character. This "winner" in Vietnam is less a frontiersman and more his Indian enemy. Sinewy, stoic in demeanor, laconic in speech, and adept with knife or crossbow and arrows, Rambo "bare-chested, with a band of cloth about his head and shoulder-length hair" is "an avenging Apache": "the frontier hero has returned not as Shane but as Geronimo."[104] Yet before Vietnam, resorting to savages' ways—as did John Wayne's character, Ethan, in *The Searchers* (1956), scalping Indians in racial hatred—seemed disquieting to Americans. More compelling indices of the deterioration of frontier metaphors are in the films *Platoon* and *Full Metal Jacket*. For the latter, in particular, sets viscerally affective scenes of combat and death in counterpoint with marines' imitations of John Wayne as objects of derision and sardonic humor. Reminiscing about a "mythic quality" of Hollywood's Marine Sergeant Stryker, producer Dore Shary in 1975 still saw Wayne as "a representation of the American image . . . of the frontiersman, of the American . . . willing to pick up the gun and fight." [105] Combat heroism often was, metaphorically, "pulling a John Wayne" for young men who imitated his characteristic swagger. But in Stanley Kubrick's *Full Metal Jacket*, marines sneer about one another's John Wayne mannerisms and their ability to "talk the talk and walk the walk."

Popular culture reflects another, inescapable fact: America did not win in Vietnam. In Oliver Stone's *Platoon*, Sergeant Elias (Willem Dafoe) admits "We're gonna lose this war. . . . We've been kickin' other people's asses for so long I figure it's time we got ours kicked." Yet frontier tradition promised success. After surviving adversities of nature and Indian attacks, pioneers often won farms or ranches or ultimately triumphed in other ventures, including commerce and industry. With military success in Southeast Asia, our frontier metaphor might have been reinforced anew. But victory eluded us. In 1952, in "The Irony of Southern History," C. Vann Woodward described "the American legend of success and victory, a legend not shared by any other people of the civilized world. The collective will of this country has simply never known what it means to be confronted by complete frustration. Whether by luck, by abundant resources, by ingenuity, by technology, by organizing cleverness, or by sheer force of arms, American has been able to overcome every major crisis—economic, political, or foreign—with which it had to cope." At that point in time, Woodward could say that "the legend has been supported by an unbroken succession of victorious wars."[106] In his "A Second Look" in 1968, however, Woodward voiced his perception that the legend of an "unbroken succession of victorious wars"—or, more accurately, "what Americans had been taught to think of as victories"—was now less sound: "history has begun to catch up with Americans. . . . we have found that all our power and fabulous weaponry can be ineffective in a war with a weak and undeveloped nation torn by a civil war of its own."[107] The future of this figurative analogy is uncertain.

Two vectors of cultural force still influence Americans, though. First, we remain fascinated with the frontier, although its scene often is changed from land to outer space. The 1980s and later could be characterized as "the era of the urban cowboy" for favoring Western clothing and music, emulating frontier customs, and electing "a 'cowboy President' by a landslide."[108] Television ads persistently use frontier appeals. Although the "Marlboro man" is gone because the F.C.C. banned cigarette ads, cowboys around a campfire laud a steak sauce whose British name they cannot pronounce. Add Americans' fascination with pickup trucks, particularly those with off-the-road capability such as Ford "Broncos," Dodge "Dakotas," and Chevrolet "Blazers" (pioneers "blazed" or marked forest trails by hatchet slashes on trees). Beginning about 1978, American automobile manufacturers responded to a developing preference for rugged, off-the-road vehicles, for "in many sections of the country

. . . lightweight trucks are outselling passenger cars by a country mile" and their popularity "surged to the point that the two dominant truck makers, General Motors Chevrolet Division and Ford Motor's Ford Division, are now selling more trucks than automobiles in numerous regions where car sales traditionally outpaced truck sales."[109] In television ads, these vehicles ford streams, climb rugged hills, cross barren deserts, and, in the case of Dodge Dakotas, pull a pioneer family's covered wagon out of a river and win approving stares from Plains Indians stoically watching on horseback. Yet only 6 percent of their owners are ranchers or farmers.[110]

Consider also current interest in Australia, where settlers overcame aborigines and an "outback" as environmentally inhospitable as many frontier areas. Although recent Australian films about military endeavors, *Gallipoli* and *Breaker Morant*, received critical acclaim in America, they did not have much box-office appeal. The former depicts an ill-planned landing against Turks at the Dardanelles in World War I, with terrible toll of lives; the latter is about the trial and execution of Australian troopers for "excesses" against irregular forces in South Africa during the Boer War. Both had morals relevant but disquieting for the post-Vietnam era. Conversely, Paul Hogan as the Australian Crocodile Dundee entranced us with his marksmanship, hunting prowess, wilderness survival skills, barroom brawling, and preference for a knife resembling Jim Bowie's of frontier folklore—and more than a match for a mugger's switchblade when Dundee visits New York City. (In *Crocodile Dundee II*, his woodsy ways allow him to overwhelm well-armed drug dealers who pursue him to the rugged Australian outback). Here was an upbeat analog for American frontier experiences. To account for the fact that its wine cooler sold better as Australian "Matilda Bay" than as "Tropical Islands," a Miller Brewing Company spokesperson admitted, "Americans are intrigued by Australians. They are perceived as being where Americans were 100 years ago, the whole Western mystique."[111] The frontier remains a viable, cultural force in America.

The second vector of cultural force is more ominous: Americans' predilection for violence. H. "Rap" Brown said, "Violence is as American as cherry pie." Proliferation of firearms in American households—and, tragically, in our public schools—is as staggering as the willingness to use them—even to vent frustrations on Los Angeles freeways. Our popular spectator sport is football, vicarious war in which quarterbacks throw "bombs" on "offense" and linebackers "blitz" on "defense." In basket-

ball, spectators cheer slam dunks, apogees of offensive power and sometimes sufficient violence, in the guise of grace, to shatter opponents'
morale as well as backboard glass.

Unfortunately, violence and the frontier have an affinity in the American experience because metaphors seem to have potentially greater "social function" to express "the truth of things" as they depict "such diverse manifestations of power as thunder, gunpowder, the police, ancestral spirits, atomic fission."[112] For decades, American popular culture
praised pioneers' power over enemies with tales of marksmanship by
the likes of Daniel Boone, Davy Crockett, Kit Carson, Calamity Jane,
and Buffalo Bill Cody. After surveying myriad dime novels and other
publications whose numbers in circulation "almost baffle enumeration,"
Henry Nash Smith proclaims those personae to be "fixtures of American mythology."[113] Or as Richard White recently observed about our
"glutinous consumption," those fictions about the frontier continue to
intrude "constantly on everyday American life," and the West and its
heroes constitute a story that "explains who . . . Americans . . . are and
how they should act," despite the fact that "in its everyday colloquial
sense, myth means falsehood."[114] Frontier violence and current marksmanship meld easily in Clint Eastwood's popular Dirty Harry films,
where the detective's revolver with an 8-inch barrel is "the central icon
of the myth"—and a central character is sufficiently appealing that many
viewers (including Ronald Reagan as president) adopted his verbal
"make my day" mode of confrontation with others.[115] But before portraying the detective with a frontier-like revolver successfully combat-
ing contemporary crime, Eastwood achieved cinematographic fame as a
Western gunfighter, notably in *A Fistful of Dollars*. To view modern American combatants as reincarnated, sharp-shooting frontiersmen, "no additional, previously unknown elements are added to the listener's knowledge of the empirical characteristics of things; rather he is led to see
their *natures* through their *relationships*" which provide "futureness to
the past and a pastness to the future that is fundamentally reassuring."[116]

However subtle in their mode of reinforcement, historians such as
Allan Nevins, for instance, contributed to our predilection for conflict
and violence. Consistently, Nevins discarded some words in favor of
others for shades of meaning which heightened readers' impressions of
physical struggle, if not warfare, between people even when martial
endeavor was not literal. For the U.S. Capitol Historical Society, he advised that "brief narrative" should include "some account of the oppo-

sition you met, and of the support you received, in very personal terms," and "if you can put in an account of a fist fight with some antagonist among the members of Congress, so much the better!"[117] Nevins's emendations in successive drafts of his own sentences display that predilection in both figurative and literal language choices which he displays in volumes 3 and 4 of *The Ordeal of the Union* (*The Organized War 1863–1864* and *The Organized War to Victory 1864–1865*). For Nevens, someone had not "criticized" Lincoln and Blair in speeches but "attacked" them. Southerners were not a "vanquished people" but a "vanquished enemy." And Charles Sumner's "excitement and belligerence" became "vehemence and belligerence."[118] Later, handwritten revisions (now in an unsteady penmanship) show a leader "growled" instead of "said" something, "troubles" in Europe became "conflicts," "uncertain of the outcome" became "apprehensive of defeat," and Prussian "violence" became a viscerally affective "bayonets."[119] Preference for language more vividly descriptive of conflict clearly was a vector of Nevens's form and style in discourse, but what about content and substance of the resultant narrative?

Nevins did not believe that impulses toward combat necessarily were preeminent in the American ethos. While analyzing the appeal of James Fenimore Cooper's Leatherstocking, he acknowledged that American popular culture was replete with tales of frontier men and women engaged in conflict but that Natty Bumppo embodied as well, from youth to age, "a quiet, ruminative, philosophical cast of mind—a natural creation . . . of wilderness solitude." Daniel Boone and Kit Carson also were capable of "placid temperament" and being "patient, unaggressive, reflective" men, and "history bears evidence that Cooper's depiction of the quiet contemplative type of frontiersman is just as valid as Turner's emphasis on the combative, uncontrolled, and grasping type."[120] So with rhetorical inclinations at the level of style toward lexical choices descriptive of combat, Nevens's revisions to *The Ordeal of the Union* yield a resultant, broader narrative emphasizing conflict. Why?

For two decades as a journalist and contributor to magazines, Nevins wrote for people who read his discourse if its content interested them, and interest value remained salient in his thoughts about writing history. In correspondence to Merle Curti, he eschewed attempts "to stuff historical work with a jargon or lingo" and "uncouth terminology that has been given education by the professional pedagogues," for "historical writing ought to be kept fresh, simple, literary, and unpedantic."[121] Sometimes, desired effects evolved from "a lively account of . . . personal traits and character," for someone's "quality of writing" improved with "a telling combination of description, narration, and personal portraiture."[122] But if history was "so much the better!" when the writer included "an account of a fist fight with some antagonist among the members of Congress," its purpose ia that of creating "as much human interest as possible."[123] As persuasion theorists attest, conflict is a factor of interest to focus and sustain attention.[124] And Nevins displayed his rhetorical sensitivity another way. Conflict between unimposing parties is uninteresting. Football games between inept teams do not sustain interest as well as vicarious wars between powerful teams for championships. Nevins knew this; his style shows it when revisions emphasize epic scope and grandeur of conflict between imposing foes. For examples, in the chapter "Toward a New Nation" in *The Ordeal of the Union,* the United States did not simply "raise an army" but plural "armies East and West," and a "huge industrial effort" became a "colossal" one. Similarly, a "contest in endurance" became one of "spartan endurance," a hero catching up a battle flag from "dead bodies of predecessors" did so from "preceding martyrs," and a mere "wonderful impulse" became the "titanic impulse" given to all enterprise in America by rapid extension of railroads and the telegraph throughout the nation.

The Ordeal of the Union thereby reflects traditional rhetorical theory on style. Word choices heightening conflict and endeavors of epic scope correspond to Cicero's notion of grand style, whereby "majesty of diction" on behalf of "grave" issues could "arouse and sway the emotions" as it "rushes along with the roar of a mighty stream."[125] To the Greeks, such "impressive style" was congruent with the "grandeur" of such subject matter as "a great and notable battle on land or sea, or when there is talk of the heavens, or of the earth."[126] Indeed, when style evolves from "grandeur of thought . . . spirited treatment of the passions . . . dignified expression . . . majesty and elevation of structure," discourse approaches the Longinian sublime.[127] In Nevins's history, congruity between content and form confirms the Ciceronian dictum that the "proper topics" expressed by rhetoric are linked inextricably with "the proper method of embellishing them," for the historian's writing had not "separated from one another things that cannot readily stand apart."[128] Nevins's narrative content of history was shaped subtly in part by its style.

In World War II, frontier metaphors for combat helped sustain Americans' morale in the fight against Nazis as well as perpetrators of the

Pearl Harbor attack and the Bataan Death March. For all-out war against totalitarian evil, those figurative analogies were righteous. But Hitler's Holocaust was one thing, and armed support to protect oil tankers in the Persian Gulf is another. As Americans should have realized in 1815 after the Battle of New Orleans, frontier analogies for combat are false. War is not merely marksmen killing only other combatant's with single shots. Nor is war a "smart bomb" directed with unerring accuracy down an air duct of an Iraqi command post during the Persian Gulf War (although some editorial cartoons about that combat depicted American troops as Western lawmen with sheriffs' badges and six-guns strapped at their waists). Our weaponry is increasingly more capable of inflicting widespread suffering and death. Firebombs devastating German and Japanese cities, as well as atomic bombs at Hiroshima and Nagasaki, only preview an ultimate disaster looming from armed conflict between nations: nuclear war. Yet Americans "confounded modern warfare with their nostalgia for the frontier" and "therefore invested a barbarous reality" with "fantasy." And, in Michael Osborn's words, this "confusion of war and progress" is a "cultural tragedy." Whereas the medieval mind favored verticality as an archetypal figuration, with significant markers of progress being "the heights of heaven and the depths of hell," Renaissance "interest and faith in materialism" shifted the spatial vision: "Just as 'up' represented a preferred direction in the older mindset, 'forward' became the direction of choice in his new consciousness of horizontal space. . . . So one can see the grounds for confusion and confounding between war and progress."[129] That "cultural tragedy" resulting from confusing war with progress is more readily apparent when it is contrasted with other, more ethically responsible metaphors from frontier experiences of Americans.

Westward expansion and pioneers' struggles against a wilderness taught virtues to emulate—and thus gave rise to analogies to apply—in peaceful endeavors, too. Economic matters, for example, were often the object of such analogies drawn by people reacting to the Frontier Thesis of Frederick Jackson Turner. Pioneer idealism or a "new frontiersman" was appealing amid "agitation and ferment of the silver problem before us" in the 1890s, for "cooperation in economic enterprises" and "concerted political and economic action" in "legislation against monopolies" during the 1920s, or "to secure social regulation of business enterprises" during "great national emergencies . . . we have been going through" in the Great Depression of the 1930s.[130] Although that Harvard undergraduate who heard Turner lecture in 1910 saw Daniel Boone in the twentieth century as a "great captain of industry," students today might think of Boone as another J. R. Ewing on the television show "Dallas."[131] Moreover, some contemporary Yuppies, Yumpies, or Dink couples (dual income, no kids) might appreciate in more reflective moments the reaction of one of Turner's readers in 1910: "Our boys and girls are growing up possessing wealth which their fathers and mothers did not. With this wealth has come false ideals. Your great work, it seems to me, has been to impress upon our young people here the great work which their fathers accomplished. You gave them an insight into the true greatness of America."[132] More recently, in the hiatus between the Vietnam War and combat in the Persian Gulf, historians suggested still other frontier analogies. For people believing "the frontier in all its aspects had ended," Frederick Merk reminded readers in a *History of the Westward Movement* that "the open frontier has become one in the realms of science and technology, of man's control over the environment, and of relations of man to his fellow man."[133] A reviewer deemed Merk's book "so timely" because with our "heightened sense of limits and resources . . . its publication now is more fitting to our times and our concerns than it would have been to those of two or three decades ago"—or, as it was articulated in another recent commentary, "adaptation" is "America's next frontier."[134]

Many Americans sense those other uses of frontier metaphors. Close in time to publication of Merk's book, the musical *Oklahoma!* reopened in New York and toured with a national company. Originally opening on Broadway in 1943 during World War II, the show ran for five years and over two thousand performances before touring. Its love story of Laurey and Curly, set against a feud between ranchers and farmers, poignantly reminded us of our earlier national experience. In its revival and tour, audiences again were stirred not only by rousing optimism of the title song in the last scene of the show—and its obligatory reprise—but also by dialogue that follows. After Curly kills Jud and may be convicted for murder, Laurey in a moment of despair seeks solace from her Aunt Eller on their Oklahoma farmhouse porch. And the loving advice that the aunt offers is an American maxim for life: "'At's all right, Laurey baby. If you cain't fergit, jist don't try to, honey. Oh, lots of things happens to folks. Sickness, er bein' pore and hungry even—bein' old and afeared to die. That's the way it is—cradle to grave. And you can stand it. They's one way. You gotta be hearty, you got to be. You cain't deserve the sweet and tender things in life less'n you're tough."[135] Audiences often seemed to hold their breath, momentarily, as that "truth" hit home. When another national company was formed for the "50th Anniversary Celebration Tour of *Oklahoma!*" during the 1993–94 theater season, its director perceived the lasting popularity of the show as a tribute not only to the artistry of composer Richard Rodgers and lyricist Oscar Hammerstein II but also to a narrative which in any period of "grim reality" might be "very current . . . harkening back to the values that I think the country is trying to harken back to—honor, the importance of keeping your word, hope, the idea that if we can all pull together we can become what we want to become."[136] The show often played to sell-out audiences.

Substantially more people viewed on television the "highest-rated multi-part movie of the 1988–89 season," the eight-hour CBS Western miniseries based on Larry McMurtry's Pulitzer Prize novel, *Lonesome Dove.* In some respects, historical writing is now being supplanted by television programming. Many Americans who do not read about the Civil War can be entranced by a Public Broadcasting System documentary about the conflict. While Alex Haley's *Roots* surely derived some of its appeal simply from the historical sweep of events spanning several generations in the life of a black family, *Lonesome Dove* capitalized as well on its historical tone—despite the likelihood that the show would be considered anomalous for television as the decade of the 1980s came to a close— for the television Westerns in the late 1950s and early 1960s that former F.C.C. Chairman Newton Minnow deplored as "vast wasteland" had now been displaced by sports, situation comedies, and "soap opera" drama. Yet in a rental videotape documentary entitled *Lonesome Dove: The Making of an Epic,* the producers articulated an accurate perception of why the show would be a success: realism. Although the novel was written with the idea that the major characters would be played on screen by John Wayne, James Stewart, and Henry Fonda, the show—promoted as being about "a nation coming of age"—was cast instead with actors who were not linked with the unauthentic Western films of the past. Moreover, production staff members themselves extolled "authenticity" of their efforts. Director Simon Wincer—an Australian—asserted that *Lonesome Dove* was not a "Hollywood" Western but instead "absolutely right . . . accurate" because an American director could not look back objectively. Costume Designer William Ramsy did "staggering research" with "diaries" and "photographs" to assure clothing looked "beat up" as rightfully so before permanent press attire and handy washing machines. *Male* characters in the show—with torn, badly worn, and poorly fitting attire—were among the seediest looking heroes yet seen in American Westerns (this did not apply, however, to heroine Angelica Huston, for the show's producers admittedly "wanted women as an audience"). Production Designer Carey White exerted "tremendous effort" to find landscapes as "bleak and barren as possible." Stunt Coordinator Bill Burton proclaimed, "it's real." And for viewers relatively knowledgeable about firearms, the cast's diverse weaponry was, for the period depicted, among the most authentic ever seen on television. In a description for potential purchasers of the boxed set of the *Lonesome Dove* videotapes, a Public Radio catalogue calls the series "a powerful journey back through time to the *real* American West—vivid, inspiring, and unforgettable."[137] To fulfill a "sense of yearning" created by *Lonesome Dove* and its depiction of "how life must have been," ABC developed "The Kid," a series about youngsters riding for the Pony Express, and CBS came out with "Paradise," about a Western gunfighter who forsakes former ways to raise his late sister's four children.[138]

Clint Eastwood also aptly redefined his Western character for the film *Unforgiven*, which received immediate and widespread critical acclaim upon its release in the summer of 1992. In a "revisionist" Western with 1990s overtones," Eastwood as "one of Hollywood's few icons" directed and acted in the film, which was "the talk of Hollywood for months" and identified early as having "the potential for Academy Awards" (it did win an Oscar for Best Picture).[139] Unlike other epic Westerns such as *Shane, Stagecoach,* or *High Noon,* Eastwood's *Unforgiven* "seems to have a compulsion to de-romanticize Western gunfighters and gunfighting," for as one reviewer wrote, "There are no heroes, and there is little courage." And to suggest further how "it's not the movie Gary Cooper would have made," the reviewer pointed out how Eastwood's character in the film, a retired gunman who takes up his weapons one more time, "is nearly unable to pull the trigger. . . . The senselessness of his past killings has come back to haunt him."[140] To appreciate how Americans viewed their current combat metaphorically as an extension of the former frontier—but in a more realistic way—we may conceptualize the visual imagery and the dialogue of *Unforgiven* as the "vehicle" by which an essential, prevailing meaning or "tenor" is evoked, one consonant with a more contemporary narrative having fidelity and probability.[141]

Film Vehicle	Audience Tenor
William Munny (Clint Eastwood) is a Western gunfighter whose earlier violence has done "terrible things" to women and children.	In Vietnam, American combatants did "terrible things" at My Lai and elsewhere with napalm and bombs against women and children.
Now a widowed farmer having forsaken violent ways, Munny is shown as unable to shoot straight anymore.	America having been unable to win in Vietnam, its prowess in arms is now in doubt.
The formerly feared gunfighter is now shown having fallen face down in the mud of a pig pen as he struggled to control those animals.	So too are many Americans mired in their doubts or guilt about the righteousness (or lack thereof) of the war in Vietnam.
Munny gets another chance as gunfighter: this time, although he also will receive needed money from a reward, he could be clearly on the side of "good"against "evil" as he goes forth to kill two cowboys who cruelly cut and scarred a prostitute.	America gets another opportunity for combat: this time, although we also will help insure control of the world's oil supply, war in the Persian Gulf to free Kuwait has us on the side of "good" against the clearly "evil" ruler of Iraq, Saddam Hussein.
Munny is assisted by a friend, a former gunfighter who is black and sometimes acts as the voice of Munny's conscience.	Increasing numbers of Americans are heeding the voices of blacks on matters of the national conscience.
At several points in the film, a writer of pulp Westerns is corrected and told what gunfighters really did and how they did it.	What we did in Vietnam and how we did it is the subject of closer scrutiny in numerous books and documentaries.
In a final Western showdown (in a saloon, after his black friend has been killed by a sadistic sheriff),	Against Iraq and Saddam Hussein, American arms were the epitome of lethal efficiency, dropping "smart"

Munny becomes again his cold, efficient, totally lethal self on behalf of "good," killing not only the evil, arrogant sheriff but also all other evil personae.

bombs into the air ducts of command posts and decimating the vaunted Iraqi army at will in a short war without the "mother of battles" Saddam predicted.

After resorting once again to lethal violence, Munny returns to obscurity, leaving his farm and moving to a city where he runs a dry goods store—and all that remains as evidence of what he was is a tombstone with only his wife's name and no other explanation.

After still other combat of good against evil, America has only the most poignant of reminders of that former combat whose merit is still dubious in many minds: a vividly stark Vietnam War Memorial with only names and no other explanation.

Unforgiven may be a metaphorical analog not only for military intervention in the Persian Gulf but also for a national conscience about police beating Rodney King in Los Angeles, the way a "sheriff" reacted to the violence of the ensuing riots there, and a moral indignation subsequently felt in other parts of the country. Eastwood himself admitted that "numerous elements of the new movie had contemporary overtones, including the passivity of the deputies who are impervious to the sheriff's brutality. . . . I purposely cast his deputies as guys somewhat in shock who find his violence distasteful. . . . It's kind of like what it must have been like for a rookie cop to be involved in the Rodney King thing. How does a rookie cop feel when his superiors are condoning that kind of behavior?"[142] Even in its more realistic imagery, the frontier as metaphor still has relevance for Americans, and they *are* supplementing their viewing of films and television with more reading about the West, both fiction and nonfiction.[143] But how should our frontier metaphor be applied most fruitfully in contemporary society?

In 1983, Janice Rushing concluded that "It is hard to predict whether the Western myth will return to older forms, stagnate and die, re-work itself into an appropriate philosophy for an urbanized society, or translate itself into a more cosmological form. Whatever lies ahead needs myths and heroes. Perhaps the time is ripe for a hero who will transcend the dialectic altogether. In order to guide and revitalize America, the defining myth must provide fitting challenges for its heroes."[144] At the conclusion of *Platoon*, while wounded and being evacuated by helicopter, Chris (Charlie Sheen) poignantly articulates a complementary sentiment over the mournful music of Samuel Barber's *Adagio for Strings*: "I think now, looking back, we did not fight the enemy. We fought ourselves. And the enemy wasn't us. The war is over. . . . Those of us who did make it have an obligation to teach others what we know and try with what's left of our lives to find goodness and meaning to this life." Americans faced a crossroads after Vietnam. Although "a public's understanding of itself, of its identity, in history" can constitute *doxa* constraining capabilities "to break the present off from the past, to see what is happening to us and our world," cultural memory also can "recall words and deeds of the past " and "reassemble the bits and fragments of visions that have been forgotten in history"; for "history is open" and other "aspects of our heritage that have been forgotten can be retrieved"—a *dynamis* whose potential is "what we can make from it."[145] And as Michael Kammen forcefully reminded Americans in *The Mystic Chords of Memory*, we *do* "arouse and arrange our memories to suit our psychic needs."[146]

One index of those arousals and arrangements may be in the way certain motion pictures, including *Unforgiven*, seem so "right" in the timing of their releases to the viewing public. Lead time to produce *Patton* allowed its release during the Vietnam War as if to be aimed at President Richard Nixon and his "Great Silent Majority" then "like a space missile seemingly headed nowhere that gradually zeros in more and more accurately on its target."[147] Nixon saw this film at least five or six times in 1970—and twice during the month he was considering the incursion of American troops into Cambodia, "steeling himself for a major decision."[148] The film generally and particularly the introductory speech of General Patton (George C. Scott) standing before a giant American flag were perceived by audiences as relevant to war in Vietnam— from a general noteworthy for flaunting his two ivory-handled Colt revolvers of frontier days. That film about how Americans "love a winner and will not tolerate a loser" had many audiences staying through an intermission between showings to view again and applaud Patton's opening speech about "That's why we've never lost a war."[149] On 30 April 1970, to justify the Cambodian incursion, Nixon said, "I would rather be a one-term President and do what I believe is right than to be a two-term President at the cost of seeing America become a second-rate power and to see this nation accept the first defeat in the proud 190-year history."[150] So Pattonesque!

After *Lonesome Dove* appeared on television, another Hollywood film

about the frontier caused mystic chords of Americans' memory to reso-
nate in a different but nevertheless complementary way. With passing
of time, scars on our national psyche over Vietnam were healing. And if
viewed as "metaphorical vehicle," *Dances with Wolves* may evoke a
"tenor" justifying combat in Vietnam by poignantly depicting an American cavalry officer on the frontier who aids racially different people
warring among themselves. Although this film shows military "bad
apples" inflicting atrocities against Indians as well as their own men
(like lethal "fragging" with grenades of American officers by their own
troops in Vietnam), Lieutenant Dunbar (Kevin Costner) helps "good"
Indians in their righteous struggle against "bad" Indians, who easily in
audiences' minds are Vietcong of the frontier. Thus, as Vietnam combat
receded into peripheries of memory and after America readied itself for
other war under President Reagan, still later conflict under President
George Bush ostensibly on behalf of another race in the Persian Gulf
might be accepted not as an endeavor to insure our source of oil but
instead as portrayed starkly in traditional Western films—good versus
evil. When viewed literally, *Dances with Wolves* could strike other responsive chords in an increasingly diverse, multicultural society. Bill
Cosby's Huxtable family of television today has many of the trials and
tribulations of June and Ward Cleaver in "Leave it to Beaver" yesterday.
In *Dances with Wolves*, formerly despised Indians now are seen as mainstream families with similar trials, tribulations, humor, and—most significantly—not "savagery" but humanity. By extension, then, perhaps
any heretofore excluded minority or cultural entity might be seen as
more mainstream American. But therein resides a factor portending
potential demise of frontier mythology prominent in our psyche.

Much of the "history" reflected in frontier mythology is about white,
Anglo-Saxon heroes from Boone to Bowie, Cody to Crockett, and
Deerslayer to Deadwood Dick, with occasional acknowledgment of
Calamity Jane. In the early twentieth century, children of immigrants
from eastern and southern Europe became playground cowboys as one
way of leaving cultural confines of their ethnic ghettos and assimilating
into a mainstream American ethos depicted in countless dime novels
and numerous films. Even subsequent immigrants were drawn to such
emulation. As chairman of the Joint Chiefs of Staff in 1994, U.S. Army
General John M. Shalikashvili reminisced about emigrating to America
at age sixteen from Bavaria; his being turned "into an early John Wayne
fan" was a defining experience in his new home in Peoria, Illinois: "There

302 Historians in a Stream of Time

was a movie theater on Main Street, not far from where I lived, and that's where I'd go right after school, and sit there through the movie over and over again. It was the only way that I found to help me with the English language. To come to the United States was an adventure. We all had a vision of America that was greater than life. Perhaps cowboys and John Wayne more than anyone else personified that for my generations."[151] That avenue of assimilation is less smooth for newly arriving Asian immigrants and for blacks—here since the beginning of the seventeenth century and long denied their frontier role in pages of discourse projecting American mythology. After all, few children learned that during the Spanish-American War, the disciplined troops substantially responsible for success at what is known as San Juan Hill were not the Caucasian cowboys of Teddy Roosevelt's "Rough Riders" but the black troopers of the Tenth Cavalry, led by Lieutenant John J. "Black Jack" Pershing. So should frontier mythology, nurtured now for well over a century in popular culture—and reinforced by some historians—serve a diverse, multicultural society? If so, how?

Nations need a sense of their histories, however mythic in overtones, for "public memory, which contains a slowly shifting configuration of traditions, is ideologically important" to help sustain people in unity during times of adversity.[152] Myth is integral to that memory, and for Americans, no other mythic factor has been more pervasive and persuasive than that of the frontier. Other nations, of course, tend to ground their myths in tangible objects, places, and monuments. But that impulse is only a relatively recent phenomenon in America, largely coinciding in time (as pointed out earlier) with the closing of the frontier.[153] For the frontier experience was less one persistent in a single, fixed place over a long span of time than it was an intangible *process* of settlement and civilizing, proceeding across a continent, continually moving onward to new locales. As Frederick Jackson Turner himself proclaimed about our "continually advancing frontier line" and "new" development for each successive locale, "American social development has been continually beginning over again on the frontier. This perennial rebirth, this fluidity of American life, this expansion westward with its new opportunities . . . furnish the forces dominating American character." But what aspect of that process currently deserves emphasis?

In an *American Heritage* interview, Arthur Schlesinger deplored current impulses on the part of distinct cultural factions in American society to require that only their own versions of history be taught in the public schools—often excluding elements conducive to an accurate, larger view. Several groups today are concerned that the teaching of American history embodies "Eurocentric" approaches whereby "Afro-Americans, Asian-Americans, Puerto Ricans/Latinos and Native Americans have all been the victims of an intellectual and educational oppression that has characterized the culture and institutions of the United States and the European American world for centuries." In response to a task-force conclusion in 1989 (after New York state public schools already had revised their curriculum in 1987), a subsequent commission recommended in 1991 that 2.5 million schoolchildren of New York needed still "greater emphasis on the role of nonwhite cultures." Nor is New York alone in this controversy, for "multiculturalism has become a national movement, leading to controversies in California and other states and to the imposition of Afrocentric curriculums on the public schools in a number of cities across the land." Responding to that trend, Schlesinger admitted that "the impact of feminism and of the civil rights revolution on the rewriting of American history has been extraordinary and hugely productive," for "we all look back into the past in terms of our current preoccupations and find 'new' things in the past, things that previous generations were not concerned about." Yet impulses to correct past sins of history textbooks have produced "absurdities like the current New York State curriculum's stress on the Iroquois contribution to the American Constitution." Moreover, when "the plight of inner-city Americans is indeed appalling," the tendency has been to teach "a series of therapeutic absurdities" in lieu of "the best education we can deliver them." And "bad history" is the result of depicting the slave trade as a "white conspiracy" when black Africans delivered slaves to Arab traders who in turn forced those peoples to white ships at the ports—and when the slave trade was abolished not by Africans but by Europeans. A viable alternative to such "corruption of history" might be taught more consistently.

For Schlesinger, who sees the teaching of American history as a force to unify this nation, a solution to our curricular problem may reside in the premise that "the United States is the only large-scale multiethnic society that has really worked." The reason that society did work is that America really has "been multicultural from the beginning, but we have countered the diversity of cultural backgrounds by aspiring from the start to create a new American nationality and a new American identify." Although first-generation immigrants kept their native cultures in language, foods, and neighborhoods delimited by ethnic boundaries, "the pull of the host culture was immensely strong for their children," and "schools were the prime mechanism for assimilation" (Mario Cuomo never spoke English until he was enrolled in the public schools). Moreover, those "unifying forces are still in the ascendancy." Almost all first-generation Hispanics born here speak English fluently, and Spanish is less and less likely the preferred language for second-generation Hispanics. According to a poll of Anglophone Hispanics, "their most admired historical figures were—in this order—Washington, Lincoln, and Teddy Roosevelt. Benito Juarez was fourth, and Eleanor Roosevelt and Martin Luther King tied for fifth." The "new unmeltable ethnics are proving less unmeltable than the multiculturalists would have us think" because "for most Americans ethnicity is not the defining experience."[154]

Other voices echo such sentiments. Reacting against school systems that adopt "therapeutic" or "feel good history" whereby inspiration "only comes from studying people of one's own ethnicity," George Will argues that "a black American and the grandson of Polish immigrants have more in common than the former has with a Nigerian or the latter with a resident of Warsaw. This is because American nationality has always been creedal rather than racial or ancestral."[155] Noting how Robert Penn Warren believed that "to be an American is not . . . a matter of blood; it is a matter of idea," Michael Kammen agrees that "newcomers (the ceaseless flow of immigrants and their children) can have an imaginative and meaningful relationship to the determinative aspects of American history."[156] Theirs is a story on whose behalf the eloquent syntax and archetypal metaphors of historians also might achieve persuasive narratives. For as much as violence was integral to frontier experiences, so too was immigration.

Incontrovertibly, America is a nation of immigrants. With exception of their Indian foes, peoples involved in the frontier experience had immigrant roots, some of them coming to America precisely to be part of that westward expansion and its opportunities. The common as well as the extraordinary aspects of their lives—other than warfare against savages—surely can be emphasized as variations on the frontier myth that might serve to unify disparate peoples in a society more acutely aware than before of its multicultural identities. Popular culture currently provides an inkling that Americans might be receptive to reinforcement of that dimension of frontier experience, for the film *Far and Away* dramatized struggles of an Irish immigrant (Tom Cruise) whose trials and tribulations newly arrived in America culminate in his participation in an epic version of the Oklahoma Land Rush. Not only does this immigrant find in the New World the ability to gain the economic success and independence derived from free land of the frontier, but he also can overcome the class differences that constrained him in the Old World.

If recent motion pictures are a meaningful index of frontier factors potentially resonant in the mystic chords of our national memory, "land" with its spaciousness is poignant, particularly as the scene in which dispirited or disadvantaged peoples overcome adversities in their lives as well as differences that divide them. In *Far and Away* (filmed in Montana), the Oklahoma landscape is sunlit and bright in stark contrast to the bleak Irish countryside, which invariably appears on screen during dark, overcast days or foggy nights. Yet dramatic action of the Oklahoma Land Rush was filmed to emphasize wagon loads of settlers and horsemen racing to stake their claims; and although some panoramic views of the land are used, its enormity is not as prominent as in *Dances with Wolves*. After the horror of his experiences in the Civil War, Lieutenant Dunbar begins the trek to his new outpost in the West, facing a broad, empty horizon with no seeming end. Unlike John Ford Westerns—which typically were filmed in Monument Valley, with prominent visual landmarks easily located—*Dances with Wolves* makes the land seem virtually limitless, an endless avenue to success or serenity or both.

For many Americans, though, "land" is out of the question now as their scene for links to the past (except for outdoor recreation). Just as other cultural groups are finding and evincing their "roots" in various activities, many "Eurocentric" Americans are turning to country and Western dancing. An instructional videotape host proclaims, "It's really kind of America and I think that's what we're back to—back to basics and the foundation on which this country was established." A dance instructor then explains: "the whole country is infested with Western fever. Disco is out and the two-step is in as the country gets back to its roots, with a desire for things more basic, more real."[157] From a somewhat unique perspective, a workshop instructor recently referred to Western dancing, with its traditional format of a strong male lead for a female partner, as "the last frontier." Although they may arrive at places of dance in their B.M.W.'s or Mercedes, those Americans (including medical doctors whose roots are distinctly eastern) share an impulse to find a link to the frontier with brethren who arrived in pickup trucks.

Yet America still may have cause for concern. In *Lonesome Dove*, the cattle drive from Texas to Montana Territory, against the elements and wilderness, has epic grandeur; central characters played by Robert Duvall and Tommy Lee Jones display noble virtues of loyalty, hardiness, courage, and compassion. Being retired Texas Rangers, though, they also revert quickly to type and dispense instant justice as violent death to lawbreakers. As Tommy Lee Jones proclaimed about his character in the videotape documentary about the production, Woodrow Call has been a "law enforcement officer all his life . . . good against evil." And as Robert Duvall asserted about his character, Augustus McCrae, he and other Texas Rangers "had the vigilante thing about them. . . . they had to be killers." Television fiction about the past mirrors present fact. Americans lapsed easily into a frontier frame of mind when resurrecting Western terminology to characterize Bernhard Goetz metaphorically as a "vigilante" for shooting four black youths threatening him on a New York subway car. To what wider extent, however, can former frontier language influence present-day behavior?

"Semantic conditions" can affect physical action. Current research in physiological psychology suggests that physically impaired people who ostensibly no longer can perform specific motor functions are able to do so when given verbal commands to perform *other*, strongly associated motor functions. For example, when some Parkinson's disease patients are told only to "walk," their neural deficiencies allow only slow, short steps and minimal movement of their arms. When told to "swing your arms," they have quicker steps with longer strides. In terminology of physiological psychology, the improved walk is the result of "self-initiated *re*afferent recruitment of allied reflexes" whereby strongly associated movements and their verbal commands "learned in the past" trigger heretofore impossible acts. Similarly, heretofore impossible physical movements also can be evoked by "indirect triggering" of "allied reflexes." Patients who cannot rise voluntarily from a sitting position nevertheless do so when told to catch the ball being thrown to them. And a Parkinson's victim who is "frozen" and cannot "walk" voluntarily nevertheless can do so if told to "step over the wad of paper on the floor." Some victims of the disease carry wads of paper or other small objects to place on the floor in front of them to trigger indirectly the formerly impossible motor activity to walk.[158] In all these instances, action results from *nonliteral* commands that tap what was "learned in the past." So ponder the possibility of the ultimate tragedy of nuclear war between nations, when American weaponry includes missiles named metaphorically after mythic, sharp-shooting riflemen from our earlier national experience. Now in versions II and III, a mainstay of the American missile arsenal is "Minuteman." For one way to make "increasingly sophisticated" defense weaponry more appreciated is to coin their "names metaphorically to make the unknown comprehensible and familiar." And "Minuteman," specifically, prompts recall of "ways and weapons of the early frontier" and thereby a persuasive, figurative view of "missiles as muskets." (President Ronald Reagan in 1982 wanted to name the MX missile "Peacemaker," after the Colt .45 revolver of frontier fame, but, sensitive to a likelihood of political cartoons of him "with a six-shooter in my hand," Reagan advocated the name "Peacekeeper" instead, a name still is close enough to remind us of Samuel Colt's contribution to Americana.)[159]

In the aftermath of rioting in Los Angeles and other cities, as well as staggering crime rates in many other locales, more Americans are arming themselves with personal weapons to be twentieth-century minutemen or Boones or Codys or Crocketts on behalf of their homes, possessions, and personal safety. Yet at some point, an armed citizenry can cross a line into lawlessness. On the Western frontier, a newspaper of that earlier time lauded the armed violence of outlaws such as the Doolin-Dalton gang: "Their life is made up of daring. Their courage is always with them and their rifles as well. They are kind to the benighted traveler. . . . Bill Doolin, at present the reigning highway man is friendly to the people in one neighborhood, bestowing all sorts of presents upon the children. . . . This is fully a romantic figure as Robin Hood ever cut."[160] The possibility now for such emulation is suggested in 1992 by a formal group (including a family of wife, husband, and sons) in Texas known as the "Gunfighters of the Chisolm Trail": although the "Wild, Wild West is a thing of the past, they get their kicks reliving those days through choreographed gunfights, fake bank robberies and mock public hangings" performed at fairs, fund-raisers for charity, and demonstrations of gun safety in the schools. Admitting he wishes he "had lived a century ago," the leader of the group articulated a reason for his fascination: "I self-appointed myself as the sheriff. But playing a bad guy is more fun. I get more attention from the women. Ladies love outlaws. . . . I feel like I was born too late."[161]

America has ethically more responsible uses for frontier metaphors and mythology shaped in part by people who produced the books portraying our past as "history" to be learned. Complementing popular culture for decades, a particularly credible mode of reinforcement about the myth of the frontier was the writing of many American historians. The eloquent syntax of Frederick Jackson Turner, for instance, may exemplify that rhetorical vehicle by which a portrayal of frontiersmen to be emulated was foregrounded and corroborated by a credible historian, and in a "stream of time," complementary metaphors of other historians helped bestow virtual archetypal, enduring meaningfulness for Americans' twentieth-century combat as but extensions of frontier endeavors against other "savages." That discourse can reinforce *other* valuable perspectives on our past, however. Residing in their prowess with style and narrative on behalf of able historiography is a capability to redirect the course of a significant metaphorical concept in the American "stream of time." For the rhetoric of discourse approached and appreciated as history is persuasive.

Notes

1. Frederick Jackson Turner's longhand copy of this passage from Louis Aubert's recollections as published in *Transactions of the Illinois Historical Society* 24 (1918): 84. Turner marked the reference to the trenches in red ink. See File Drawer 15D, Frederick Jackson Turner Collection, Henry E. Huntington Library, San Marino, Calif., hereafter cited as HEH, TU.

2. For my earlier treatment of this subject, see "America's Tragic Metaphor: Our Twentieth-Century Combatants as Frontiersmen," *Quarterly Journal of Speech* 76 (February 1990): 1–22.

3. Richard Neustadt and Ernest May, *Thinking in Time: The Uses of History for Decision Makers* (New York: Free Press, 1986), 263–64.

4. See Michael Osborn and Douglas Ehninger, "The Metaphor in Public Address," *Speech Monographs* 29 (August 1962): 223–34; William Jordan, "Toward a Psychological Theory of Metaphor," *Western Speech* 35 (Summer 1971): 169–75, and "A Reinforcement Model of Metaphor," *Speech Monographs* 34 (August 1972): 223–26; Michael Osborn, "The Evolution of the Archetypal Sea in Rhetoric and Poetic," *Quarterly Journal of Speech* 63 (December 1977): 347–63, and "Archetypal Metaphor in Rhetoric: The Light-Dark Family," *Quarterly Journal of Speech* 53 (April 1967): 115–26; and Robert L. Ivie, "Images of Savagery in American Justifications for War," *Communication Monographs* 47 (November 1980): 279–94, and "Metaphor and the Rhetorical Invention of Cold War 'Idealists,'" *Communication Monographs* 54 (June 1987): 165–82.

5. Wayne C. Booth, *The Company We Keep: An Ethics of Fiction* (Berkeley: University of California Press, 1988), 4, 10, 18–19, 25–28, 302, 300ff. In Ivie's essays (see note 4 above), Booth's "ethical" judgments do tend to emerge.

6. J. Christopher Crocker, "The Social Function of Rhetorical Forms," and James W. Fernandez, "The Performance of Ritual Metaphor," both in *The Social Use of Metaphor: Essays on the Anthropology of Rhetoric*, ed. J. David Sapir and J. Christopher Crocker (Philadelphia: University of Pennsylvania Press, 1977), 37–39, 46–47, 118.

7. Raymie E. McKerrow, "Critical Rhetoric: Theory and Praxis," *Communication Monographs* 56 (June 1989): 101.

8. Booth, *The Company We Keep*, 325, 338, 347, 354.

9. For my earlier discussions of this point, see chapter 2 above, as well as my "Frederick Jackson Turner and the Rhetorical Impact of the Frontier Thesis," "America's Opinion Leader Historian's on Behalf of Success," and *The Eloquence of Frederick Jackson Turner.*

10. Michael Kammen, *The Mystic Chords of Memory* (New York: Alfred A. Knopf, 1991), 7, 178–79.

11. *The Mystic Chords of Memory*, 240–42.

12. Theodore Roosevelt to Turner, 10 February 1894, in Box 1, HEH, TU.

13. See Josiah Strong, *Our Country: Its Possible Future and Its Present Crisis* (New York: Baker and Taylor Company, 1885), 1, 144–53, 159–80; or see the discussion of Reverend Strong in my *Eloquence of Frederick Jackson Turner*, 72–73.

14. G. J. A. O'Toole, *The Spanish War: An American Epic—1898* (New York: W. W. Norton, 1984), 91–92. See also Howard K. Beale, *Theodore Roosevelt and the Rise of America to World Power* (Baltimore: Johns Hopkins University Press, 1956).

15. See chapter 5 above.

16. O'Toole, *The Spanish War*, 310–20; Samuel Eliot Morison, *The Oxford History of the American People* (New York: Oxford University Press, 1965), 801–4. Pershing's nickname, "Black Jack," came from his commanding black cavalrymen on the frontier.

17. Walter Millis, *The Martial Spirit* (New York: Houghton Mifflin, 1959), 171, 217.

18. James Barber, *The Pulse of Politics: Electing Presidents in the Media Age* (New York: W. W. Norton, 1980), 38–44. See also Louise E. Levahese, "Frederic Remington—The Man and the Myth," *National Geographic* 174 (August 1988): 200–231.

19. See John William Ward, *Andrew Jackson: Symbol for an Age* (New York: Oxford University Press, 1955), 13–17; the complete lyrics of "The Hunters of Kentucky" are on 217–19. The British at New Orleans were led by General Sir Edward Packenham.

20. John Mahon, *The War of 1812* (Gainesville: University of Florida Press, 1972), 362–69. See also Ward, *Andrew Jackson*, 21–26.

21. See, for example, Harold Underwood Faulkner and Tyler Kepner, *America: Its History and People*, 5th ed. (New York: McGraw-Hill, 1950), 192. Earlier editions were 1934, 1938, 1942, and 1947.

22. See Walter R. Fisher, "Narration as a Human Communication Paradigm,"

Communication Monographs 51 (March 1984): 1–22.

23. Frank E. Vandiver, *Black Jack: The Life and Times of John J. Pershing,* 2 vols. (College Station: Texas A and M University Press, 1977), 1:249, 512. Pershing served in the Philippines from 1899 to 1913; Vandiver devotes over 300 pages to his duty there.

24. See Beale, *Theodore Roosevelt,* 72; and Thomas G. Dyer, *Theodore Roosevelt and the Idea of Race* (Baton Rouge: Louisiana State University Press, 1980), 69–88, 140.

25. See Hans Schmidt, *Maverick Marine: General Smedley D. Butler and the Contradictions of American Military History* (Lexington: University of Kentucky Press, 1987), 10.

26. Fernandez, "The Performance of Ritual Metaphor," in *The Social Use of Metaphor,* 118.

27. Robert C. Cotton, "Military Operations in the Philippines, 1904–1910: Notes," Robert C. Cotton Collection, Henry E. Huntington Library, San Marino, Calif.

28. Leslie E. Dennison, "Reminiscences," in File Folder "34th U.S.V. Infantry—ms, meetings, reminiscences, etc.," in Box 2, Charles F. Manahan Collection, Henry E. Huntington Library, San Marino, Calif.

29. Vandiver, *Black Jack,* 1, 225. Italics are mine.

30. Robert C. Cotton, "Notes on U.S.-Mexican Conditions along the Border, 1909–1912," in Cotton Collection. Italics are mine.

31. For an account of Pershing and the Punitive Expedition in Mexico, see Vandiver, *Black Jack,* 11 and 595–668; for the Pershing-Patton photograph, see 806–7; concerning the cavalry at Ojos Azules, see 642. In another view, the last U.S. Cavalry charge was on Bataan, 16 January 1942. Under Lt. Edwin Ramsey, twenty-eight Filipinos of the 26th Cavalry Regiment, Philippine Scouts charged a Japanese column of about seventy-five men. The Philippine Scouts had American officers. See *Time,* 23 November 1987, 13.

32. S. L. A. Marshall, *American Heritage History of World War I* (New York: American Heritage/Bonanza Books 1964), 212. Theodore Roosevelt wanted to form a unit for France, and a cavalry officer who served on the Mexican border requested duty in it. Roosevelt's office informed the officer that "President Wilson has refused to take advantage of the provisions in the recent act passed by Congress, and will not allow Colonel Roosevelt to organize one or more divisions of troops for service in France" (W. E. Dame to Captain Robert C. Cotton, 6 June 1917, in Cotton Collection).

33. Edgar E. Robinson to Frederick Jackson Turner, 27 April 1918, in Box 28, HEH, TU. See also my *Eloquence of Frederick Jackson Turner,* 66–67, and George T. Blakey, *Historians on the Homefront: American Propagandists for the Great War* (Lexington: University of Kentucky Press, 1971).

34. See chapter 3 above.

35. Albert Bushnell Hart and Arthur O. Lovejoy, *Handbook of the War for Public*

Speakers (New York: National Security League and the Committee on Patriotism Through Education, 1917), 54–55.

36. Thomas Shipley, cited in S. L. A. Marshall, *American Heritage History of World War I*, 250.

37. This is the point of view of military historian John K. Mahon, which he expressed in a letter to the author, 13 May 1990.

38. See, for instance, J. Robert Moskin, *The U.S. Marine Corps Story*, 2d ed. (New York: McGraw-Hill, 1987), 150.

39. Edwin H. Simmons, *The United States Marines 1775–1975* (New York: Viking, 1976), 100–101.

40. Allan R. Millett, *Semper Fidelis: The History of the United States Marine Corps*, in *The Macmillan Wars of the United States*, ed. Louis Morton (New York: Macmillan, 1980), 317. Popular histories, which also contributed heavily to the image, included John W. Leonard and Fred F. Chitty, *The Story of the United States Marines* (New York: U.S. Marine Corps Publicity Bureau, 1919), and Willis J. Abbot, *Soldiers of the Sea* (New York: Dodd, Mead, 1918). See also Millet, *Semper Fidelis*, 686, n. 72.

41. *Semper Fidelis*, 230.

42. See Simmons, *The United States Marines*, 126; as well as the photograph in Millett, *Semper Fidelis*, 238–39.

43. See *Semper Fidelis*, 238–39; and Burke Davis, *Marine! The Life of Lt. General Lewis B. (Chesty) Puller, USMC (Ret.)* (Boston: Little, Brown, 1962), 212–13.

44. Smedley Butler, cited in Schmidt, *Maverick Marine*, 31, 75; Col. Littleton Waller, cited in Millett, *Semper Fidelis*, 187.

45. Schmidt, *Maverick Marine*, 75.

46. See *Maverick Marine*, 75; and Moskin, *The U.S. Marine Corps Story*, 150, 176. Haitian insurgents called themselves "cacos," after a red-plummed bird of prey, and typically wore something red on their clothing as a badge. See Simmons, *The United States Marines*, 102.

47. See the photograph in Moskin, *The U.S. Marine Corps Story*, 146.

48. Millett, *Semper Fidelis*, 267. Italics are mine.

49. *Semper Fidelis*, 163.

50. *Semper Fidelis*, 229.

51. Moskin, *The U.S. Marine Corps Story*, 213. "Horse Marines" were "armed, along with their '03s, with heavy, straight-bladed swords designed by a U.S. Army cavalryman named George S. Patton" (Simmons, *The United States Marines*, 134). See also the photograph in Moskin, *The U.S. Marine Corps Story*, 119.

52. Schmidt, *Maverick Marine*, 173, 177.

53. *Maverick Marine*, 188.

54. Davis, *Marine! The Life of Lt. General Lewis B. (Chesty) Puller*, 87–91.

55. Schmidt, *Maverick Marine*, 175.

56. Julian Smith, *Looking Away: Hollywood and Vietnam* (New York: Charles Scribner's Sons, 1975), 2–3, 24, 27. See also Lawrence H. Suid, *Guts and Glory:*

Great American War Movies (Reading, Mass.: Addison-Wesley, 1978), 38. Cooper also had British Army duty fighting "Indians" of India in *Lives of a Bengal Lancer* (1935).

57. Suid, *Guts and Glory*, 40–44, 54–56.

58. *Guts and Glory*, 92, 102–4.

59. See Robert B. Ray, *A Certain Tendency of the Hollywood Cinema, 1930–1980* (Princeton: Princeton University Press, 1985).

60. Gerald Thomas, cited in Richard B. Frank, *Guadalcanal* (New York: Random House, 1990), 264.

61. Madame Chiang Kai-shek, quoted in *New York Times*, 19 February 1943, 4.

62. John Steinbeck, *Bombs Away: The Story of a Bomber Team* (New York: Viking, 1942), 45, 72.

63. John Keegan, *Six Armies in Normandy: From D-Day to the Liberation of Paris* (New York: Viking, 1982), 24. For discussion of MacArthur's childhood on a frontier Army post, including Fort Leavenworth, see William Manchester, *American Caesar: Douglas MacArthur 1880–1964* (Boston: Little, Brown, 1978), 39–44.

64. John G. Bourke, cited in Geoffrey O'Brien, "Killing Time," *New York Book Review* 39 (5 March 1992): 38–42.

65. Keegan, *Six Armies in Normandy*, 99, 114.

66. Russell F. Weigley, promotional flyer for *Six Armies in Normandy*, by John Keegan, *History Book Club Review*, January 1983, .

67. *St. Petersburg Times*, 7 April 1985.

68. James Brady, *The Coldest War: A Memoir of Korea* (New York: Simon and Schuster, 1990), 9, 135, 155.

69. Cited in Victor H. Krulak, *First To Fight: An Inside View of the U.S. Marine Corps* (Annapolis: U.S. Naval Institute Press, 1984), 131. See also my "General Douglas MacArthur's Oratory on Behalf of Inchon: Discourse that Altered the Course of History," *Southern Communication Journal* 58 (Fall 1992): 1–12.

70. See Robert L. Ivie, "Images of Savagery in American Justifications for War," *Communication Monographs* 47 (November 1980): 279–94; Ivie, "Metaphor and the Rhetorical Invention of Cold War 'Idealists,'" *Communication Monographs* 54 (June 1987): 165–82; and Ivie, "Literalizing the Metaphor of Soviet Savagery: President Truman's Plain Style," *Southern Speech Communication Journal* 51 (Winter 1986): 91–105.

71. See Robert L. Ivie, "Speaking 'Common Sense' about the Soviet Threat: Reagan's Rhetorical Stance," *Western Journal of Speech Communication* 48 (Winter 1984): 39–50.

72. John J. Harter, University of Southern California, to Merle Curti, 12 February 1951, in Box 18, File 15, Merle Curti Papers, State Historical Society of Wisconsin, Madison, Wis.

73. Allan Nevins, *The Leatherstocking Saga* (New York: Pantheon Books, 1954), 32.

74. *Northwest Passage*, 1940.

75. *Gainesville Sun*, 8 November 1989, 7A.

76. S. L. A. Marshall, cited in Max Hastings, *The Korean War* (New York: Simon and Schuster, 1987), 329.

77. My discussion here reflects Hastings, *The Korean War*, as well as Donald Knox, *The Korean War Pusan to Chosin: An Oral History* (Orlando: Harcourt Brace Jovanovich, 1985). Our Korean enemy was racially different from us—as had been the Japanese in World War II, against whom hatred was as easily aroused as against Indians. See John W. Dower, *War without Mercy: Race and Power in the Pacific War* (New York: Pantheon Books, 1986).

78. Marine photographs to which I refer are David Douglas Duncan's in *Life*, 18 September 1950. That of the rifleman charging past a body (p. 43) has been widely reprinted and is the cover photograph for Duncan's book *This Is War: A Photo-Narrative of the Korean War* (Boston: Little, Brown, 1990). For reprintings of this particular picture, see Jorge Lewinski, *The Camera at War: War Photography from 1848 to the Present Day* (New York: Simon and Schuster, 1978), 138; and Duncan's *Yankee Nomad: A Photographic Essay* (New York: Holt, Rinehart and Winston, 1966), 299. The air-force family picture to which I refer is in the *Pictorial History of the Korean War* (Veterans' Historical Book Service, 1951), 243; or in *The Complete Encyclopedia of the World's Aircraft*, ed. David Mondey (New York: A & W Publishers, 1978), 47.

79. For similar reading of *M*A*S*H*, see Suid, *Guts and Glory*, 267–69; the bon mot about *Animal House* comes from film critic and my departmental colleague Julian Smith.

80. While serving as a U.S. Air Force officer in the 1950s, I knew pilots who favored cowboy boots as flight gear.

81. Janice Hocker Rushing, "Mythic Evolution of 'the New Frontier' in Mass Mediated Rhetoric," *Critical Studies in Mass Communication* 3 (September 1986): 265–96.

82. John Hellmann, *American Myth and the Legacy of Vietnam* (New York: Columbia University Press, 1986), 3–5, 15–35.

83. For discussion of the origins of America's propensity to intervene in Asia, see Robert P. Newman, "Lethal Rhetoric: The Selling of the China Myths," *Quarterly Journal of Speech* 61 (April 1975): 113–28.

84. The Kennedy-Macmillan relationship is discussed in Theodore Sorensen, *Kennedy* (New York: Harper and Row, 1965), 558–59, 642–43. My source on the S.A.S. is James G. Shortt, *The Special Air Service* (London: Osprey, 1981); on Macmillan's observing the S.A.S. in Malaya, see 18–20. As "strategic hamlets" were implemented in Vietnam during 1961–62, British personnel advised Ngo Dinh Diem's government and the U.S. Military Assistance Command; see Frances FitzGerald, *Fire in the Lake: The Vietnamese and the Americans in Vietnam* (Boston: Little, Brown, 1972), 123. One of my departmental colleagues served with British forces in Malaya during the emergency and went to Vietnam as such an advisor.

85. Jerry Buck, "Westerns Gallop Back onto the TV Screen," *Gainesville Sun*, 21 June 1989, 5D.

86. See Hellmann, *American Myth*, 41–69, particularly 44–49. Hellmann surveys mass media publicity about Special Forces, including Robin Moore's *Green Berets* (New York: Crown, 1965).

87. See Russell Miller, *The Commandos* (Chicago: Time-Life Books, 1981), 28, 35, 64–65.

88. J. Justin Gustainis, "John F. Kennedy and the Green Berets: The Rhetorical Use of the Hero Myth" (Paper presented at the Central States Speech Association-Southern States Communication Association Joint Convention, St. Louis, 1987). Gustainis traced the deterioration of the Green Beret's image to that of "damaged hero," in "From Savior to Psycho and Back Again: The Changing Role of Green Berets in Vietnam Films" (Paper presented at the Eastern Communication Association Convention, Baltimore, 1988).

89. Americans did have opportunities to see motion pictures about combat in Vietnam, however. Films about the French at Dien Bien Phu included *Jump into Hell* in 1955 and *The Lost Command* in 1966. Americans had earlier cinema baptisms of fire in Southeast Asia, such as those of Alan Ladd in *Saigon* (1948), Dick Powell in *Rogues Regiment* (1948), and Gene Barry and Nat King Cole in *China Gate* (1957). Hollywood also made *A Yank in Viet Nam* (1963) and *To the Shores of Hell* (1965), both low-budget films with minimal box-office success. *Go Tell the Spartans* (with Burt Lancaster) told a story of the war that Americans were not ready to accept. Clearly, the film capturing public attention was *The Green Berets*. See Julian Smith, *Looking Away*, 3, 104–10 and 122–26.

90. Michael Wayne, cited in Julian Smith, *Looking Away*, 129. Smith also notes that the U.S. Information Agency made a documentary "presenting a view of the war favorable to American interests." *Vietnam! Vietnam!* was directed by John Ford, who was responsible for John Wayne's emergence as Western hero. See *Looking Away*, 133–34.

91. *Looking Away*, 134–35, 168.

92. See *Looking Away*, 128–32. Smith observes that *The Green Berets* is a recycled *Back to Bataan*, where Wayne as an American colonel leads Filipino guerrillas against Japan with similar dialogue. In *She Wore a Yellow Ribbon*, Captain Nathan Brittles (John Wayne) faces retirement after frontier soldiering and announces a decision to "move on West."

93. Cited in Ivie, "Images of Savagery," 285, 293–94.

94. Ronnie Dugger, *The Politician: The Drive for Power, from the Frontier to Master of the Senate* (New York: W. W. Norton, 1982), 30–45. Dugger suggests that in Johnson's mind an analogy was forming whereby "the Alamo became Khe Sanh." See 34–35 in particular.

95. General William Westmoreland, cited in Loren Baritz, *Backfire: A History of How American Culture Led Us into Vietnam and Made Us Fight the Way We Did* (New York: William Morrow, 1985), 50; for the evolution of Kennedy's thinking on Vietnam, see 102–43.

96. See Baritz, 51–52; see also Suid, *Guts and Glory,* 106–9. The photograph to which I refer is in John Morrocco, *The Vietnam Experience—Rain of Fire: Air War, 1969–1973* (Boston: Boston Publishing Company, 1985), 173.

97. See File Folder marked "Ephemera" related to the 34th Infantry Regiment during the Philippine Insurrection, in Box 2, Charles F. Manahan Collection.

98. Leslie E. Dennison, "Reminiscences," in File Folder "34th U.S.V. Infantry—ms, meetings, reminiscences, etc.," in Box 2, Charles F. Manahan Collection.

99. Baritz, *Backfire,* 144–87.

100. Hellmann, *American Myth,* 93.

101. Morrocco, *Rain of Fire,* 17 and 127. For a vivid photograph of how that "rain of fire" looked at night, see John Morrocco, *The Vietnam Experience—Thunder from Above: Air War, 1941–1968* (Boston: Boston Publishing Company, 1984), 80; for the comparison of Khe Sanh to Dien Bien Phu, see 177.

102. See Janice Hocker Rushing and Thomas S. Frentz, "*The Deer Hunter*: Rhetoric of the Warrior," *Quarterly Journal of Speech* 66 (December 1980): 392–406; and Hellmann, *American Myth,* 174–77;

103. *American Myth,* 175, 202. In *Apocalypse Now,* as Hellman explains, the mission of Captain Willard (Martin Sheen) to kill Colonel Kurtz (Marlon Brando) parallels a pioneer's wilderness trek "on a continuum with American historical myth," although Willard resembles a detective such as Raymond Chandler's Philip Marlowe, a frontiersman in twentieth-century urban America (see *American Myth,* 188–204).

104. In "Rambo: The Frontier Hero with a Cross" (Paper presented at the American Studies Association Convention, New York, 1987), Hellman also argued that "the Kennedy-inspired hyperbole with which the media originally created the Green Beret legend" led to "expectations for the involvement in Vietnam as a reaffirmation and improving revision of America's frontier character." Rambo's appeal as a combat "winner" also is suggested by Stallone's having planned at the time a fourth such film, to be set in Central America (*Tampa Times-Tribune,* 30 April 1989, 2I). For discussion of Wayne as anti-hero in *The Searchers,* see Ray, *A Certain Tendency of the Hollywood Cinema,* 171; and Jon Tuska, *The American West In Film* (Westport, Conn.: Greenwood Press, 1985), 56–57.

105. Dore Shary, cited in Suid, *Guts and Glory,* 104–7. In accounts of the Persian Gulf War against Iraq, the more bellicose leaders in Washington often were characterized as "John Wayne" types.

106. C. Vann Woodward, "The Irony of Southern History," *Journal of Southern History* 19 (1953): 3–19; repr. in *The Burden of Southern History,* 2d ed. (Baton Rouge: Louisiana State University Press, 1986), 187–211, esp. 188.

107. C. Vann Woodward, "A Second Look at the Theme of Irony," in *The Burden of Southern History,* 2d ed. (Baton Rouge: Louisiana State University Press, 1986), 213–15.

108. For further discussion of this trend, see Rushing, "Mythic Evolution of

'The New Frontier' in Mass Mediated Rhetoric," 265–96; and Rushing, "The Rhetoric of the American Western Myth," *Communication Monographs* 50 (March 1983): 14–32.

109. *Jacksonville Times-Union and Journal*, 5 August 1978, C6.

110. *Orlando Sentinel*, 18 February 1988, F3.

111. "Miller Decides Its New Wine Cooler Is Australian," *Gainesville Sun*, 5 September 1987, 1, Section 2A.

112. Crocker, "The Social Function of Rhetorical Forms," in *The Social Use of Metaphor*, 57. Wayne Booth laments at length the "venality" of such weapon metaphors; see *The Company We Keep*, 304–18.

113. Henry Nash Smith, *Virgin Land: The American West as Symbol and Myth* (Cambridge: Harvard University Press, 1970), 12, 120.

114. Richard White, *"It's Your Misfortune and None of My Own": A New History of the American West* (Norman: University of Oklahoma Press, 1991), 612–14.

115. Stephen Hunter, "Movies Blow Up Firearms to Mythic Proportions," *Gainesville Sun*, 7 August 1988, F1, 4. The tragic proliferation of guns in America received poignant treatment in *Time*, 17 July 1989, 30–61, with portraits of the 464 people killed thereby, just during the first week of May of that year.

116. Crocker, "The Social Function of Rhetorical Forms," in *The Social Use of Metaphor*, 42; Fernandez, "The Performance of Ritual Metaphor," in *The Social Use of Metaphor*, 118.

117. Nevins to Fred Schwengel, U.S. House of Representatives, 19 October 1965, in Box 45, Allan Nevins Collection, Henry E. Huntington Library, San Marino, Calif.

118. See handwritten revisions to chapter 3, "Cement of the Union," for *The Organized War to Victory 1864–1865*, in Box 37, Nevins Collection.

119. See handwritten revisions of chapter 13, "New Crises in Foreign Relations," for *The Organized War 1863–1864*, in Box 37, Nevins Collection.

120. Allan Nevins, *Leatherstocking* (New York: Pantheon Books, 1954), 20–21.

121. Nevins to Merle Curti, 7 March 1947 and 4 April 1947, in Box 27, File 37, Merle Curti Papers.

122. Nevins to William Q. Maxwell, 8 October 1969, in Box 45, Nevins Collection.

123. Nevins to Fred Schwengel, U.S. House of Representatives, 19 October 1965, in Box 45, Nevins Collection.

124. See, for instance, Kenneth Andersen, *Persuasion: Theory and Practice* (Boston: Allyn and Bacon, 1971), 101–2.

125. Cicero, *Orator* 5.20, 28.97, trans. H. M. Hubbell, Loeb Classical Library (Cambridge: Harvard University Press, 1971), 319, 377.

126. Demetrius, *On Style* 75, trans. G. M. A. Grube (Toronto: Toronto University Press, 1961), 80.

127. Longinus, *On the Sublime* 8; in *The Art of the Writer*, ed. Lane Cooper (Ithaca: Cornell University Press, 1952), 91.

128. Cicero, *De Oratore* 3.5.19, trans. H. Rackham, Loeb Classical Library (Cambridge: Harvard University Press, 1948), 17.

129. Michael Osborn, "Responses to Metaphors of War" (Paper presented at the Speech Communication Association Convention, New Orleans, 1988).

130. See citations to these of Turner's respondents in chapters 2 and 6 above.

131. George W. Bell's 1910 lecture notes, in File Drawer 14D, HEH, TU.

132. Charles McCarthy to Turner, 23 June 1910, in "Vol. 1, Red Book," HEH, TU. See also chapter 2 above about the same reaction.

133. Frederick Merk, *History of the Westward Movement* (New York: Alfred A. Knopf, 1978), 616–17.

134. Gordon S. Wood, review of *History of the Westward Movement,* by Frederick Merk, *History Book Club Review,* July 1978, 3–7; Robert B. Reich, *The Next American Frontier* (New York: Times Books, 1983), 21.

135. *Oklahoma!* act 2, sc. 3, in Richard Rodgers and Oscar Hammerstein II, *6 Plays by Rodgers and Hammerstein* (New York: Modern Library, 1959), 81.

136. Cited in Ann Hyman, "*Oklahoma!* Sweeps into Town," *Jacksonville Times-Union,* 9 November 1993, D1.

137. *Wireless: A Catalogue for Fans and Friends of Public Radio* (St. Paul: Minnesota Public Radio, 1992), 11.

138. Buck, "Westerns Gallop Back onto the TV Screen," *Gainesville Sun,* 21 June 1989, 5D; *Parade Magazine,* 5 February 1989, 16. The popularity of *Lonesome Dove* led to litigation between the publisher Simon and Schuster, who held the rights to an audio version of the novel, and Dove Books-on-Tape, who owned the miniseries videotape and expected 6 million dollars in sales that year (*St. Petersburg Times,* 21 May 1989, 3F). "The Kid" became "The Young Riders."

139. Bernard Weinraub, "Eastwood: New Film May Be the Best One Ever," *Gainesville Sun,* 25 August 1992, D1.

140. David Crumpler, "Unforgiven Rewrites Legend of Old West," *Jacksonville Florida Times-Union,* 16 August 1992, G1.

141. For discussion of metaphor as interaction of tenor and vehicle, see Michael Osborn and Douglas Ehninger, "The Metaphor in Public Address," *Speech Monographs* 29 (August 1962): 223–34; and William Jordan and W. Clifton Adams, "I. A. Richards' Concept of Tenor-Vehicle Interactions," *Central States Speech Journal* 27 (Summer 1976): 136–43.

142. Clint Eastwood, cited in Weinraub, "Eastwood: New Film May Be the Best One Ever," *Gainesville Sun,* 25 August 1992, 2D.

143. The "Books" section of the *St. Petersburg Times* for 16 August 1992 was devoted to reviews of several of those volumes about "Way Out West."

144. Rushing, "The Rhetoric of the Western Myth," 32.

145. J. Robert Cox, *Cultural Memory and Public Moral Argument,* Van Zelst Lecture in Communication, Northwestern University (Evanston: Northwestern University, 1987), 5, 7, 10, 12, 14.

146. Kammen, *The Mystic Chords of Memory,* 9.

147. "Stanley Kauffmann on Films," *New Republic* 162 (7 March 1970): 24.

148. Rowland Evans and Robert Novak, *Nixon in the White House: The Frustration of Power* (New York: Random House, 1971), 252.

149. Ronald H. Carpenter and Robert V. Seltzer, "Nixon, *Patton,* and a Silent Majority Sentiment about the Vietnam War: The Cinematographic Bases of a Rhetorical Stance," *Central States Speech Journal* 25 (Summer 1974): 105–10.

150. Richard M. Nixon, "The Situation in Southeast Asia: The President's Address to the Nation, April 30, 1970," *Weekly Compilation of Presidential Documents* 6 (4 May 1970): 596–601.

151. John M. Shalikashvili, cited in Tad Szulc, "What We Need To Do: A Profile of JCS Chairman, General John M. Shalikashvili," *Parade Magazine,* 1 May 1994, 4–5.

152. Kammen, *The Mystic Chords of Memory,* 13.

153. See also Richard Stengel, "American Myth 101," review of *The Mystic Chords of Memory,* by Michael Kammen, *Time,* 22 December 1991, 78–80.

154. Frederic Smoler, "An Interview with Arthur Schlesinger, Jr.: What Should We Teach Our Children about American History?" *American Heritage* 43 (February/March 1992): 45–52.

155. George Will, "Feel-good History Distorts Reality," *Gainesville Sun,* 15 July 1991, 6A.

156. Kammen, *The Mystic Chords of Memory,* 15.

157. *Texas Honky-Tonk Dancin'* (Texas International Films, 1982).

158. For these insights and terminology, I am deeply indebted to Phillip Teitelbaum, Graduate Research Professor of Psychology, University of Florida.

159. See Charles Kauffman, "Names and Weapons," *Communication Monographs* 56 (September 1989): 277–81.

160. Cited in White, *"It's Your Misfortune and None of My Own,"* 336–37.

161. Cited in Monica Stavish, "Latter-day Cowpokes Hold Shoot-'em-ups," *Tampa Tribune,* 25 September 1992, B3.

Bibliography

Unpublished manuscript collections constitute my major source of evidence in explicating the rhetoric of style and narrative in historical writing. The Frederick Jackson Turner Collection at the Huntington Library offers insights into Turner's development as a rhetorical stylist, and these materials include his winning orations as a student in high school and college as well as his Commonplace Book. The Turner Collection also contains letters to the historian which reveal reactions of his readers over the years, all of which help confirm the rhetorical impress of his style in discourse. The chapter on Carl L. Becker relies extensively on his collected papers at the Olin Library of Cornell University. These materials reveal Becker's emergent sense of rhetorical goals in historical writing as well as demonstrate the persuasive nature of his style in discourse. Again, pertinent evidence exists in letters to Becker from readers in the general public. Both of the chapters on Alfred Thayer Mahan utilize his collected papers in the Library of Congress as well as the letters from his fellow naval officers in the Naval Historical Foundation Collection—correspondence that importantly suggests the sources of Mahan rhetorical effectiveness as a stylist. Also significant in the Mahan Papers is his personal file of reviews of *The Influence of Sea Power upon History* published in newspapers and periodicals in the United States and abroad (all are cited in the footnotes but are not included individually in this bibliography). For the chapter on *The Guns of August,* the Barbara Wertheim Tuchman Papers at Yale University yielded letters between Tuchman and Denning Miller, her editor at Macmillan while she was writing that historical account of the beginning of World War I. Their contrapuntal views on the development of her chapters suggest how Tuchman's rhetoric in narrative likely helped influence John F. Kennedy during the Cuban Missile Crisis. Other unpublished primary-source collections used in several chapters herein include the Merle Curti Papers at the State Historical Society of Wisconsin and the Allan Nevins Collection at the Huntington Library. Other Huntington collections (see below) were helpful for the chapter explicating how historians helped reinforce Americans' use of frontier metaphors to characterize their twentieth-century combat.

Published manuscript collections also were helpful for this book. For both of the chapters on the naval historian, the three-volume set of *Letters and Papers of Alfred Thayer Mahan*, edited by Robert Seager II and Doris Maguire, was supplemented by letters published in Richard W. Turk, *The Ambiguous Relationship: Theodore Roosevelt and Alfred Thayer Mahan*. Especially significant for explicating Mahan's influence on Japanese planning for the Pearl Harbor attack were numerous primary-source documents (including battle orders, war diaries, and post-war testimony) translated in *The Pearl Harbor Papers: Inside the Japanese Plans*, edited by Donald M. Goldstein and Katherine V. Dillon. Similar materials are translated in Gordon W. Prange, *At Dawn We Slept: The Untold Story of Pearl Harbor*. Analyses of the historical writings of Frank Owsley and Woodrow Wilson drew upon several volumes of *The Papers of Woodrow Wilson*, edited by Arthur S. Link, as well as collections of the letters of Owsley's Agrarian peers, including *The Literary Correspondence of Donald Davidson and Allen Tate*, edited by John Tyree Fain and Thomas Daniel Young; *The Lytle Tate Letters*, edited by Thomas Daniel Young and Elizabeth Sarcone; and *Selected Letters of John Crowe Ransom*, edited by Thomas Daniel Young and George Core.

Unpublished Manuscript Collections

Carl L. Becker Papers, Cornell University, Ithaca, New York.
Robert C. Cotton, "Military Operations in the Philippines, 1904–1910: Notes," and "Notes on U.S.-Mexican Conditions along the Border, 1909–1912." Cotton Collection, Henry E. Huntington Library, San Marino, California.
George Creel Papers, Library of Congress, Washington, D.C.
Merle Curti Papers, State Historical Society of Wisconsin, Madison, Wisconsin.
Leslie E. Dennison, "Reminiscences," in File Folder "34th U.S.V. Infantry—ms, meetings, reminiscences, etc." Charles F. Manahan Collection, Henry E. Huntington Library, San Marino, California.
Admiral Stephen B. Luce Papers, Library of Congress, Washington, D.C.
Alfred Thayer Mahan Papers, Library of Congress, Washington, D.C.
Naval Historical Foundation Collection, Library of Congress, Washington, D.C.
Allan Nevins Collection, Huntington Library, Washington, D.C..
General David M. Shoup (U.S.M.C.) Papers, Hoover Institution on War, Revolution, and Peace.
Barbara Wertheim Tuchman Papers, MS Collection No. 574, Yale University Library, New Haven, Connecticut.

Frederick Jackson Turner Collection, Henry E. Huntington Library, San Marino, California.
Frederick Jackson Turner Collection, State Historical Society of Wisconsin, Madison, Wisconsin.

Books, Chapters, and Published Collections

Abel, Elie. *The Missile Crisis*. Philadelphia: Lippincott, 1966.
Andersen, Kenneth E. *Persuasion: Theory and Practice*. Boston: Allyn and Bacon, 1971.
Aristotle. *Rhetoric*. Translated by Lane Cooper. New York: Appleton-Century-Crofts, 1932.
Baird, A. Craig. *American Public Address 1740–1952*. New York: McGraw-Hill, 1956.
Barber, James D. *The Presidential Character: Predicting Performance in the White House*. Englewood Cliffs, N.J.: Prentice-Hall, 1972.
———. *The Pulse of Politics: Electing Presidents in the Media Age*. New York: W. W. Norton, 1980.
Baritz, Loren. *Backfire: A History of How American Culture Led Us into Vietnam and Made Us Fight the Way We Did*. New York: William Morrow, 1985.
Barnett, Correlli. *Engage the Enemy More Closely: The Royal Navy in the Second World War*. New York: W. W. Norton, 1991.
Beale, Howard K. *Theodore Roosevelt and the Rise of America to World Power*. Baltimore: Johns Hopkins University Press, 1956.
Becker, Carl L. *Everyman His Own Historian: Essays on History and Politics*. New York: Appleton-Century-Crofts, 1935.
———. "Frederick Jackson Turner." In *American Masters of Social Science*, edited by Howard W. Odum. New York: Henry Holt, 1927.
———. "Kansas." In *Everyman His Own Historian: Essays on History and Politics*. New York: Appleton-Century-Crofts, 1935.
———. *Modern History*. Morristown, N.J.: Silver Burdett, 1958.
———. *The History of Political Parties in the Province of New York 1760–1776*. Madison: University of Wisconsin Press, 1960. Published originally as Bulletin No. 286, *University of Wisconsin History Series*, Vol. 2, No. 1.
Becker, Samuel. "Rhetorical Studies for the Contemporary World." In *The Prospect of Rhetoric*, edited by Lloyd Bitzer and Edwin Black. Englewood Cliffs, N.J.: Prentice-Hall, 1971.
Benson, Lee. *Turner and Beard: American Historical Writing Reconsidered*. New York: Free Press, 1960.
Berelson, Bernard, and Gary A. Steiner. *Human Behavior: An Inventory of Scientific Findings*. New York: Harcourt, Brace, and World, 1964.
Billington, Ray A. *The Genesis of the Frontier Thesis*. San Marino, Calif.: Huntington Library, 1971.

———. *Frederick Jackson Turner: Historian, Scholar, Teacher.* New York: Oxford University Press, 1973.

———, ed. *Allan Nevins on History.* New York: Scribner's Sons, 1975.

———. *Billington on Nevins: A Talk Given before the Zamorano Club.* San Marino, Calif.: n.p., 1980.

Blair, Hugh. *Lectures on Rhetoric and Belles Lettres.* London, 1787.

Blakey, George T. *Historians on the Homefront: American Propagandists for the Great War.* Lexington: University Press of Kentucky, 1970.

Blight, James, and David Welch. *On the Brink: Americans and Soviets Reexamine the Cuban Missile Crisis.* New York: Hill and Wang, 1989.

Boorstin, Daniel J. *The Genius of American Politics.* Chicago: University of Chicago Press, 1953.

Booth, Wayne C. *The Company We Keep: An Ethics of Fiction.* Berkeley: University of California Press, 1988.

Brady, James. *The Coldest War: A Memoir of Korea.* New York: Simon and Schuster, 1990.

Bragdon, Henry Wilkinson. *Woodrow Wilson: The Academic Years.* Cambridge: Harvard University Press, 1967.

Broadbent, Donald E. *Perception and Communication.* London: Pergamon Press, 1958.

Brown, Judson S. *The Motivation of Behavior.* New York: McGraw-Hill, 1961.

Brown, Robert E. *Carl Becker in History and the American Revolution.* East Lansing: Spartan Press, 1970.

———. *Charles Beard and the Constitution: A Critical Analysis of "An Economic Interpretation of the Constitution."* Princeton: Princeton University Press, 1956.

Bryant, Donald C. *Rhetorical Dimensions in Criticism.* Baton Rouge: Louisiana State University Press, 1973.

Buffon, Georges-Louis. "Discours sur le Style." In *The Art of the Writer,* edited by Lane Cooper. Ithaca: Cornell University Press, 1952.

Burke, Kenneth. *A Grammar of Motives.* New York: Prentice-Hall, 1945.

———. *A Rhetoric of Motives.* New York: George Braziller, 1955.

———. *Counter-Statement.* Los Altos, Calif.: Hermes Publications, 1931.

Caiden, Martin. *Air Force: A Pictorial History of American Air Power.* New York: Bramhall House, 1957.

Campbell, George. *The Philosophy of Rhetoric* (1776). Edited by Lloyd F. Bitzer. Carbondale: Southern Illinois University Press, 1963.

Carpenter, Ronald H. "Admiral Mahan, 'Narrative Fidelity,' and the Japanese Attack on Pearl Harbor." In *Naval History: The Seventh Symposium of the U.S. Naval Academy,* edited by William B. Cogar. Wilmington, Del.: Scholarly Resources, 1988.

———. *The Eloquence of Frederick Jackson Turner.* San Marino, Calif.: Huntington Library, 1983.

———. "The Historical Jeremiad as Rhetorical Genre." In *Form and Genre: Shaping Rhetorical Action,* edited by Karlyn Campbell and Kathleen Jamieson. Falls Church, Va.: Speech Communication Association, 1977.

———. "The Statistical Profile of Language Behavior with Machiavellian Intent or While Experiencing Caution and Avoiding Self-Incrimination." In *The Language Scientist as Expert in the Legal Setting,* edited by Robert W. Rieber and William A. Stewart. New York: New York Academy of Sciences, 1990.

Carr, David. *Time, Narrative, and History.* Bloomington: Indiana University Press, 1986.

Castex, Raoul Victor. *Théories Stratégiques,* Vol. 1. Paris: Société d'Editions Géographiques, Maritimes et Coloniales, 1929.

Cauthen, C. E. "The Coming of the Civil War." In *Writing Southern History: Essays in Historiography in Honor of Fletcher M. Green,* edited by Arthur S. Link and Pembert W. Patrick. Baton Rouge: Louisiana State University Press, 1965.

Chalmers, David. *The Muckrake Years.* New York: D. Van Nostrand, 1974.

Chigusa, Sadao. "Conquer the Pacific Ocean aboard Destroyer *Akigumo:* War Diary of the Hawaiian Battle." In *The Pearl Harbor Papers: Inside the Japanese Plans,* edited by Donald M. Goldstein and Katherine V. Dillon. Washington, D.C.: Brassey's, 1993.

Chihaya, Masataka. "An Intimate Look at the Japanese Navy." In *The Pearl Harbor Papers: Inside the Japanese Plans,* edited by Donald M. Goldstein and Katherine V. Dillon. Washington, D.C.: Brassey's, 1993.

Chomsky, Noam. *Aspects of the Theory of Syntax.* Cambridge: M.I.T. Press, 1965.

———. "On the Notion 'Rule of Grammar.'" In *Structure of Language and Its Mathematical Aspects,* edited by Roman Jakobson. Vol. 12 of *Proceedings of Symposia in Applied Mathematics.* Providence, R.I.: American Mathematical Society, 1961.

Cicero. *Brutus.* In *Cicero on Oratory and Orators,* translated and edited by J. S. Watson. London: George Bell and Sons, 1909.

———. *De Oratore.* Translated by H. Rackham. Loeb Classical Library. Cambridge: Harvard University Press, 1948.

———. *Orator.* Translated by H. M. Hubbell. Loeb Classical Library. Cambridge: Harvard University Press, 1971.

Clark, E. Culpepper. "Argument and Historical Analysis." In *Advances in Argumentation Theory and Research,* edited by J. Robert Cox and Charles A. Willard. Carbondale: University of Southern Illinois Press, 1982.

Clayton, Bruce. *The Savage Ideal: Intolerance and Intellectual Leadership in the South 1890–1914.* Baltimore: Johns Hopkins University Press, 1972.

Clive, John. *Not by Fact Alone: Essays on the Writing and Reading of History.* New York: Alfred A. Knopf, 1989.

Cope, E. M. *An Introduction to Aristotle's "Rhetoric."* London: Macmillan, 1867.

Crocker, J. Christopher. "The Social Function of Rhetorical Forms." In *The Social Use of Metaphor: Essays on the Anthropology of Rhetoric*, edited by J. David Sapir and J. Christopher Crocker. Philadelphia: University of Pennsylvania Press, 1977.

Davidson, Donald. *The Spyglass: Views and Reviews, 1924–1930*. Edited by John Tyree Fain. Nashville: Vanderbilt University Press, 1963.

Davis, Burke. *Marine! The Life of Lt. General Lewis B. (Chesty) Puller, USMC (Ret.)* Boston: Little, Brown, 1962.

Dember, William N. *The Psychology of Perception*. New York: Holt, Rinehart and Winston, 1960.

Demetrius. *On Style*. Translated by G. M. A. Grube. Toronto: Toronto University Press, 1961.

Dillon, Merton L. *Ulrich Bonnell Phillips: Historian of the Old South*. Baton Rouge: Louisiana State University Press, 1985.

Dionysius of Halicarnassus. *On Literary Composition*. Translated by W. Rhys Roberts. London: Macmillan, 1910.

Dower, John W. *War without Mercy: Race and Power in the Pacific War*. New York: Pantheon Books, 1986.

Dugger, Ronnie. *The Politician: The Drive for Power, from the Frontier to Master of the Senate*. New York: W. W. Norton, 1982.

Duncan, David Douglas. *This Is War: A Photo-Narrative of the Korean War*. Boston: Little, Brown, 1990.

———. *Yankee Nomad: A Photographic Essay*. New York: Holt, Rinehart and Winston, 1966.

Dyer, Thomas G. *Theodore Roosevelt and the Idea of Race*. Baton Rouge: Louisiana State University Press, 1980.

Eisenson, Jon, J. Jeffery Auer, and John Irwin. *The Psychology of Communication*. New York: Appleton-Century-Crofts, 1963.

Evans, Rowland, and Robert Novak. *Nixon in the White House: The Frustration of Power*. New York: Random House, 1971.

Faber, Harold. *The Kennedy Years*. New York: Viking, 1964.

Fain, John Tyree, and Thomas Daniel Young, eds. *The Literary Correspondence of Donald Davidson and Allen Tate*. Athens: University of Georgia Press, 1974.

Faulkner, Harold Underwood, and Tyler Kepner. *America: Its History and People*. 5th ed. New York: McGraw-Hill, 1950.

Fernandez, James W. "The Performance of Ritual Metaphor." In *The Social Use of Metaphor: Essays on the Anthropology of Rhetoric*, edited by J. David Sapir and J. Christopher Crocker. Philadelphia: University of Pennsylvania Press, 1977.

Fisher, Walter R. *Human Communication as Narration: Toward a Philosophy of Reason, Value, and Action*. Columbia: University of South Carolina Press, 1987.

FitzGerald, Frances. *America Revised: History Schoolbooks in the Twentieth Century.* Boston: Little, Brown, 1979.

————. *Fire in the Lake: The Vietnamese and the Americans in Vietnam.* Boston: Little, Brown, 1972.

Frank, Richard B. *Guadalcanal: The Definitive Account of the Landmark Battle.* New York: Random House, 1990.

Frye, Northrop. *Anatomy of Criticism.* Princeton: Princeton University Press, 1957.

Fuchida, Mitsuo. "The Attack on Pearl Harbor." In *The Japanese Navy in World War Two: An Anthology of Articles by Former Officers of the Imperial Japanese Navy and Air Defense Force.* Annapolis: United States Naval Institute, 1971.

Fukudome, Shigeru. "Hawaii Operation." In *The Japanese Navy in World War Two: An Anthology of Articles by Former Officers of the Imperial Japanese Navy and Air Defense Force.* Annapolis: United States Naval Institute, 1971.

Gaston, Paul M. *The New South Creed.* New York: Alfred A. Knopf, 1970.

Gay, Peter. *Style in History.* New York: Basic Books, 1974.

Genda, Minoru. "Affidavit, 15 March 1948." In *The Pearl Harbor Papers: Inside the Japanese Plans,* edited by Donald M. Goldstein and Katherine V. Dillon. Washington, D.C.: Brassey's, 1993.

————. "Analysis No. 1 of the Pearl Harbor Attack, Operation AI." In *The Pearl Harbor Papers: Inside the Japanese Plans.*

————. "Analysis No. 2 of the Pearl Harbor Attack." In *The Pearl Harbor Papers: Inside the Japanese Plans.*

————. "How the Japanese Task Force Idea Materialized." In *The Pearl Harbor Papers: Inside the Japanese Plans.*

Genung, John F. *The Practical Elements of Rhetoric.* Boston: Ginn, 1896.

Gossman, Lionel. "History and Literature," In *The Writing of History: Literary Form and Historical Understanding,* edited by Robert Canary and Henry Kozicki. Madison: University of Wisconsin Press, 1978.

Gottschalk, Louis. "The Evaluation of Historical Writings." In *The Practice of Book Selection,* edited by Louis R. Wilson. Chicago: University of Chicago Press, 1940.

Grantham, Dewey W. *The South and the Sectional Image.* New York: Harper and Row, 1967.

Gray, Giles W., and Claude M. Wise. *The Bases of Speech.* 3d ed. New York: Harper and Row, 1959.

Gray, Richard. *Writing the South: Ideas of an American Culture.* Cambridge: Cambridge University Press, 1986.

Gruber, Carol S. *Mars and Minerva: World War I and the Uses of the Higher Learning in America.* Baton Rouge: Louisiana State University Press, 1975.

Gurney, Gene. *The War in the Air.* New York: Bonanza Books, 1962.

Halberstam, David. *The Best and the Brightest.* New York: Random House, 1969.

Hamilton, Nigel. *JFK: Reckless Youth.* New York: Random House, 1992.

Hart, Albert Bushnell, and Arthur O. Lovejoy. *Handbook of the War for Public Speakers.* New York: National Security League and the Committee on Patriotism Through Education, 1917.

Hastings, Max. *The Korean War.* New York: Simon and Schuster, 1987.

Hebb, D. O. *The Organization of Behavior.* New York: Science Editions, 1961.

Hellmann, John. *American Myth and the Legacy of Vietnam.* New York: Columbia University Press, 1986.

Hill, Adams Sherman. *The Principles of Rhetoric.* New York: Harper and Brothers, 1878.

Hobson, Fred. *Tell about the South: The Southern Rage to Explain.* Baton Rouge: Louisiana State University Press, 1983.

Hofstadter, Richard. *The Progressive Historians.* New York: Alfred A. Knopf, 1969.

Hoshor, John P. "American Contributions to Rhetorical Theory and Homiletics." In *A History of Speech Education in America,* edited by Karl R. Wallace. New York: Appleton-Century-Crofts, 1954.

Hostettler, Gordon F. "The Political Speaking of Robert M. La Follette." In *American Public Address: Studies in Honor of Albert Craig Baird,* edited by Loren Reid. Columbia: University of Missouri Press, 1961.

Howarth, Stephen. "Admiral of the Fleet Isoroku Yamamoto." In *Men of War: Great Naval Leaders of World War II,* edited by Stephen Howarth. New York: St. Martin's Press, 1992.

Howell, Wilbur Samuel. *Logic and Rhetoric in England, 1500–1700.* New York: Russell and Russell Reprints, 1961.

Ikeda, Kyoshi. "Vice Admiral Chuichi Nagumo." In *Men of War: Great Naval Leaders of World War II,* edited by Stephen Howarth. New York: St. Martin's Press, 1992.

Jacobs, Wilbur R. *The Historical World of Frederick Jackson Turner.* New Haven: Yale University Press, 1968.

Janis, Irving L. *Groupthink: Psychological Studies of Policy Decisions and Fiascos.* 2d ed. Boston: Houghton Mifflin, 1983.

Janis, Irving L., and Leon Mann. *Decision Making: A Psychological Analysis of Conflict, Choice, and Commitment.* New York: Free Press, 1977.

Johnson, Walter, ed. *The Papers of Adlai Stevenson.* 8 vols. Boston: Little, Brown, 1979.

Joseph, Sister Miriam. *Shakespeare's Use of the Arts of Language.* New York: Columbia University Press, 1947.

Kammen, Michael. *The Mystic Chords of Memory.* New York: Alfred A. Knopf, 1991.

———, ed. *What Is the Good of History?: Selected Letters of Carl L. Becker 1900–1945.* Ithaca: Cornell University Press, 1973.

Karanikas, Alexander. *Tillers of a Myth: Southern Agrarians as Social and Literary Critics.* Madison: University of Wisconsin Press, 1969.

Katz, Elihu, and Paul F. Lazarsfeld. *Personal Influence: The Part Played by People in the Flow of Mass Communication.* Glencoe: Free Press, 1955.

Keegan, John. *Six Armies in Normandy: From D-Day to the Liberation of Paris.* New York: Viking, 1982.

Kennedy, George A., *Aristotle on Rhetoric: A Theory of Civic Discourse.* New York: Oxford University Press, 1991.

Kennedy, John F. *Profiles in Courage.* New York: Harper and Brothers, 1955.

Kennedy, Robert. *Thirteen Days: A Memoir of the Cuban Missile Crisis.* New York: W. W. Norton, 1969.

Klapper, Joseph T. *The Effects of Mass Communication.* New York: Free Press, 1960.

Knox, Donald. *The Korean War: Pusan to Chosin: An Oral History.* Orlando: Harcourt Brace Jovanovich, 1985.

Krulak, Victor H. *First To Fight: An Inside View of the U.S. Marine Corps.* Annapolis: U.S. Naval Institute Press, 1984.

Kusaka, Ryunosuke. "*Rengo Kantai* (Combined Fleet), Extracts." In *The Pearl Harbor Papers: Inside the Japanese Plans,* edited by Donald M. Goldstein and Katherine V. Dillon. Washington, D.C.: Brassey's, 1993.

Lahman, Carroll P. "Robert M. La Follette." In *A History and Criticism of American Public Address,* edited by William Norwood Brigance, vol. 2. New York: McGraw-Hill, 1943.

Lakoff, George, and Mark Johnson. *Metaphors We Live By.* Chicago: University of Chicago Press, 1980.

Larson, Charles U. *Persuasion: Reception and Responsibility.* Belmont, Calif.: Wadsworth, 1973.

LeMay, Curtis. *America Is in Danger.* New York: Funk and Wagnalls, 1968.

Lerner, Max. *America as a Civilization.* New York: Simon and Schuster, 1957.

Lewinski, Jorge. *The Camera at War: War Photography from 1848 to the Present Day.* New York: Simon and Shuster, 1978.

Lines of Tribute to Allan Nevins from Several of His Friends on the Occasion of His Retirement from the Faculty of Columbia University in the City of New York. San Francisco: Peregrine Press, 1958.

Link, Arthur S., ed. *The Papers of Woodrow Wilson.* 69 vols. Princeton: Princeton University Press, 1969.

Livezey, William. *Mahan on Sea Power.* Norman: University of Oklahoma Press, 1947.

Logue, Cal M. "Restoration Strategies in Georgia, 1865–1880." In *Oratory in the New South,* edited by Waldo W. Braden. Baton Rouge: Louisiana State University Press, 1979.

Longinus. *On the Sublime.* In *The Art of the Writer,* edited by Lane Cooper. Ithaca: Cornell University Press, 1952.

Lorant, Stefan. *The Glorious Burden: The American Presidency*. New York: Harper and Row, 1968.

Lottinville, Savoie. *The Rhetoric of History: A Critical Examination of the Structures and Writing Techniques Essential to Successful Publication in the Field of History*. Norman: University of Oklahoma Press, 1976.

MacArthur, Douglas. *Reminiscences*. New York: McGraw-Hill, 1964.

Mahan, Alfred Thayer. "Fleet in Being and Fortress Fleet: The Port Arthur Squadron in the Russo-Japanese War." In *Mahan on Naval Warfare: Selections from the Writings of Rear Admiral Alfred T. Mahan*, edited by Allan Westcott. Boston: Little, Brown, 1920.

———. *From Sail to Steam*. New York: Harper and Brothers, 1907.

———. *The Influence of Sea Power upon History 1660–1783*. New York: Hill and Wang, 1957.

———. *Lessons of the War with Spain*. Boston: Little, Brown, 1899.

Mahon, John. *The War of 1812*. Gainesville: University of Florida Press, 1972.

Manchester, William. *American Caesar: Douglas MacArthur 1880–1964*. Boston: Little, Brown, 1978.

Marshall, S. L. A. *American Heritage History of World War I*. New York: American Heritage/Bonanza Books, 1964.

McGuire, William J. "The Nature of Attitudes and Attitude Change." In *Handbook of Social Psychology*, 2d ed., edited by Gardner Lindzey and Elliot Aronson, vol. 3. Reading, Mass.: Addison-Wesley, 1969.

McKean, Dayton D. "Woodrow Wilson." In *A History and Criticism of American Public Address*, edited by William Norwood Brigance, vol. 2. New York: McGraw-Hill, 1943.

Merk, Frederick. *History of the Westward Movement*. New York: Alfred A. Knopf, 1978.

Mikawa, Gunichi. "War Diary of the 3rd Battleship Division, 4–25 December 1941." In *The Pearl Harbor Papers: Inside the Japanese Plans*, edited by Donald M. Goldstein and Katherine V. Dillon. Washington, D.C.: Brassey's, 1993.

Miller, George A. *Psychology: The Science of Mental Life*. New York: Harper and Row, 1962.

Miller, George A., and Noam Chomsky. "Finitary Models of Language Users." In *Handbook of Mathematical Psychology*, edited by Robert D. Luce, Robert R. Bush, and Eugene Galanter, vol. 2. New York: John Wiley and Sons, 1963.

Miller, Russell. *The Commandos*. Chicago: Time-Life Books, 1981.

Millett, Allan R. *Semper Fidelis: The History of the United States Marine Corps*. In *The Macmillan Wars of the United States*, edited by Louis Morton. New York: Macmillan, 1980.

Millis, Walter. *The Martial Spirit*. New York: Houghton Mifflin, 1959.

Mink, Louis O. "Narrative Form as a Cognitive Instrument." In *The Writing of History: Literary Form and Historical Understanding*, edited by Robert H. Canary and Henry Kozicki. Madison: University of Wisconsin Press, 1978.

Mood, Fulmer, ed. *The Early Writings of Frederick Jackson Turner*. Freeport, N.Y.: Books for Libraries Press, 1969.

Moore, Robin. *The Green Berets.* New York: Crown, 1965.

Morison, Samuel Eliot. *The Rising Sun in the Pacific 1931–April 1942.* Vol. 3 of *History of United States Naval Operations in World War II.* Boston: Little, Brown, 1948.

———. *The Oxford History of the American People.* New York: Oxford University Press, 1965.

Morris, Edmund. *The Rise of Theodore Roosevelt.* New York: Coward, McCann and Geohegan, 1979.

Morrocco, John. *The Vietnam Experience—Rain of Fire: Air War, 1969–1973.* Boston: Boston Publishing Company, 1985.

———. *The Vietnam Experience—Thunder from Above: Air War, 1941–1968.* Boston: Boston Publishing Company, 1984.

Moskin, J. Robert. *The U.S. Marine Corps Story.* 2d ed. New York: McGraw-Hill, 1987.

Munz, Peter. *The Shapes of Time: A New Look at the Philosophy of History.* Middletown, Conn.: Wesleyan University Press, 1977.

Myrdal, Gunnar. *An American Dilemma: The Negro Problem and Modern Democracy.* New York: Harper and Brothers, 1944.

Nakahara, Giichi. "Diary Extracts, 11 August 1941–1 January 1942." In *The Pearl Harbor Papers: Inside the Japanese Plans,* edited by Donald M. Goldstein and Katherine V. Dillon. Washington, D.C.: Brassey's, 1993.

Neustadt, Richard, and Ernest May. *Thinking in Time: The Uses of History for Decision Makers.* New York: Free Press, 1986.

Nevins, Allan. *The Leatherstocking Saga.* New York: Pantheon Books, 1954.

Noble, David. *Historians against History: The Frontier Thesis and the National Covenant in American Historical Writing since 1830.* Minneapolis: University of Minnesota Press, 1965.

Novick, Peter. *That Noble Dream: The "Objectivity Question" and the American Historical Profession.* Cambridge: Cambridge University Press, 1988.

O'Brien, Michael. *The Idea of the American South 1920–1941.* Baltimore: Johns Hopkins University Press, 1979.

O'Conner, Raymond. "Commentary." In *The Japanese Navy in World War Two: An Anthology of Articles by Former Officers of the Imperial Japanese Navy and Air Defense Force.* Annapolis: United States Naval Institute, 1971.

O'Donnell, Kenneth, David Powers, and Joe McCarthy. *Johnny, We Hardly Knew Ye.* Boston: Little, Brown, 1972.

O'Toole, G. J. A. *The Spanish War: An American Epic—1898.* New York: W. W. Norton, 1984.

Ogden, C. K., and I. A. Richards. *The Meaning of Meaning.* New York: Harcourt Brace, 1923.

Osborn, George C. *Woodrow Wilson: The Early Years.* Baton Rouge: Louisiana State University Press, 1968.

Osgood, Charles E. "Some Effects of Motivation on Style of Encoding." In *Style in Language,* edited by Thomas A. Sebeok. Cambridge: M.I.T. Press, 1960.

Owsley, Frank L. "The Irrepressible Conflict." In *I'll Take My Stand: The South and the Agrarian Tradition.* New York: Harper and Brothers, 1930.

———. *Plain Folk of the Old South.* Baton Rouge: Louisiana State University Press, 1982.

Owsley, Harriet C., ed. *The South: Old and New Frontiers — Selected Essays of Frank Lawrence Owsley.* Athens: University of Georgia Press, 1969.

Parrington, Vernon L. *Main Currents in American Thought.* New York: Harcourt, Brace, 1927.

Parrish, Wayland Maxfield, and Marie Hochmuth, eds. *American Speeches.* New York: Longmans, Green, 1954.

Parrish, Wayland Maxfield, and Alfred Dwight Huston. "Robert G. Ingersoll." In *History and Criticism of American Public Address,* edited by William Norwood Brigance, vol. 1. New York: McGraw-Hill, 1943.

Peacham, Henry. *The Garden of Eloquence* (1593). Edited by William G. Crane. Gainesville, Fla.: Scholars' Facsimiles and Reprints, 1954.

"Pearl Harbor Operations: General Outline of Orders and Plans." In *The Pearl Harbor Papers: Inside the Japanese Plans,* edited by Donald M. Goldstein and Katherine V. Dillon. Washington, D.C.: Brassey's, 1993.

Pictorial History of the Korean War. N.p.: Veterans' Historical Book Service, 1951.

Potter, John Deane. *Yamamoto: The Man Who Menaced America.* New York: Viking, 1965.

Prange, Gordon W. *At Dawn We Slept: The Untold Story of Pearl Harbor.* New York: McGraw-Hill, 1981.

———. *Miracle at Midway.* New York: McGraw-Hill, 1982.

Pratt, Julius W. "Alfred Thayer Mahan." In *The Marcus W. Jernigan Essays in American Historiography,* edited by William T. Hutchinson. Chicago: University of Chicago Press, 1937.

Puleston, W. D. *Mahan.* New Haven: Yale University Press, 1939.

Puttenham, George. *The Arte of English Poesie* (1589). Edited by Gladys Dodge Willcock and Alice Walker. Cambridge: Cambridge University Press, 1936.

Ray, Robert B. *A Certain Tendency of the Hollywood Cinema, 1930–1980.* Princeton: Princeton University Press, 1985.

Reeves, Richard. *President Kennedy: Profile of Power.* New York: Simon and Schuster, 1993.

Reeves, Thomas C. *A Question of Character: A Life of John F. Kennedy.* New York: Free Press, 1991.

Reich, Robert B. *The Next American Frontier.* New York: Times Books, 1983.

Richards, I. A. *Speculative Instruments.* Chicago: University of Chicago Press, 1955.

Robertson, James Oliver. *American Myth, American Reality.* New York: Hill and Wang, 1980.

Rock, Virginia. "The Twelve Southerners: Biographical Essays." In *I'll Take My Stand: The South and the Agrarian Tradition,* introduction by Louis D. Rubin, Jr. Baton Rouge: Louisiana State University Press, 1962

Rodgers, Richard, and Oscar Hammerstein II. *6 Plays by Rodgers and Hammerstein.* New York: Modern Library, 1959.

Sadao, Asada. "The Japanese Navy and the United States." In *Pearl Harbor as History: Japanese-American Relations 1931–1941,* edited by Dorothy Borg and Shumpei Okamoto. New York: Columbia University Press, 1973.

Sakamaki, Kazuo. *I Attacked Pearl Harbor.* New York: Association Press, 1949.

Salinger, Pierre. *With Kennedy.* Garden City: Doubleday, 1966.

Sanagi, Sadamu. "Extracts from Diary and Papers." In *The Pearl Harbor Papers: Inside the Japanese Plans,* edited by Donald M. Goldstein and Katherine V. Dillon. Washington, D.C.: Brassey's, 1993.

Schlesinger, Arthur M., Jr. *A Thousand Days: John F. Kennedy in the White House.* Boston: Houghton Mifflin, 1965.

———. *Robert Kennedy and His Times.* Boston: Houghton Mifflin, 1978.

Schmidt, Hans. *Maverick Marine: General Smedley D. Butler and the Contradictions of American Military History.* Lexington: University of Kentucky Press, 1987.

Seager, Robert, II. *Alfred Thayer Mahan: The Man and His Letters.* Annapolis, Maryland: Naval Institute Press, 1977.

Seager, Robert, II, and Doris D. Maguire, eds. *Letters and Papers of Alfred Thayer Mahan.* 3 vols. Annapolis: Naval Institute Press, 1975.

Sherry, Michael S. *The Rise of American Air Power: The Creation of Armageddon.* New Haven: Yale University Press, 1987.

Sherry, Richard. *A Treatise of Schemes and Tropes* (1550). Edited by Herbert Hildebrandt. Gainesville, Fla.: Scholars' Facsimiles and Reprints, 1961.

Shortt, James G. *The Special Air Service.* London: Osprey, 1981.

Simmons, Edwin H. *The United States Marines 1775–1975.* New York: Viking, 1976.

Smith, Charlotte Watkins. *Carl Becker: On History and the Climate of Opinion.* Carbondale: Southern Illinois University Press, 1956.

Smith, Henry Nash. *Virgin Land: The American West as Symbol and Myth.* Cambridge: Harvard University Press, 1970.

Smith, Julian. *Looking Away: Hollywood and Vietnam.* New York: Charles Scribner's Sons, 1975.

Smith, Stephen A. *Myth, Media, and the Southern Mind.* Fayetteville: University of Arkansas Press, 1985.

Snyder, Phil L., ed. *Detachment and the Writing of History: Essays and Letters of Carl L. Becker.* Ithaca: Cornell University Press, 1958.

Sorensen, Theodore. *Kennedy.* New York: Harper and Row, 1965.

Spector, Ronald H. *Eagle against the Sun: The American War with Japan.* New York: Free Press, 1985.

Steinbeck, John. *Bombs Away: The Story of a Bomber Team.* New York: Paragon, 1942.

Stephenson, Wendell Holmes. *Southern History in the Making: Pioneer Historians of the South.* Baton Rouge: Louisiana State University Press, 1964.

Stott, Ian G. *The Fairey Swordfish Mks. I–IV, Profile #212.* Windsor, England: Profile Publications, n.d.

Strong, Josiah. *Our Country: Its Possible Future and Its Present Crisis.* New York: Baker and Taylor, 1885.

Strout, Cushing. *The Pragmatic Revolt in American History: Carl Becker and Charles Beard.* New Haven: Yale University Press, 1958.

Suid, Lawrence H. *Guts and Glory: Great American War Movies.* Reading, Mass.: Addison-Wesley, 1978.

Taylor, Maxwell. *Swords into Plowshares.* New York: W. W. Norton, 1972.

Tindall, George B. "The Central Theme Revisited." In *The Southerner as American,* edited by Charles Grier Sellers, Jr. Chapel Hill: University of North Carolina Press, 1960.

Toland, John. *The Rising Sun: The Decline and Fall of the Japanese Empire 1936–1945.* New York: Random House, 1970.

Trani, Eugene P. *The Treaty of Portsmouth: An Adventure in American Diplomacy.* Lexington: University of Kentucky Press, 1969.

Trefousse, Hans Louis, ed. *What Happened at Pearl Harbor: Documents Pertaining to the Japanese Attack of December 7, 1941, and Its Background.* New York: Twayne, 1958.

Tuchman, Barbara. *The Guns of August.* New York: Macmillan, 1962.

———. *Practicing History: Selected Essays.* New York: Alfred A. Knopf, 1981.

———. *The Proud Tower: A Portrait of the World before the War 1890–1914.* New York: Macmillan, 1962.

Turk, Richard W. *The Ambiguous Relationship: Theodore Roosevelt and Alfred Thayer Mahan.* New York: Greenwood Press, 1987.

Turner, Frederick Jackson. *Reuben Gold Thwaites: A Memorial Address.* Madison: State Historical Society of Wisconsin, 1914.

Tuska, Jon. *The American West in Film.* Westport, Conn.: Greenwood Press, 1985.

Uchida, Shigeshi. "Extracts from Diary and Duty Book." In *The Pearl Harbor Papers: Inside the Japanese Plans,* edited by Donald M. Goldstein and Katherine V. Dillon. Washington, D.C.: Brassey's, 1993.

Vandiver, Frank E. *Black Jack: The Life and Times of John J. Pershing.* 2 vols. College Station: Texas A and M University Press, 1977.

Villa, Brian L. *Unauthorized Action: Mountbatten and the Dieppe Raid.* Toronto: Oxford University Press, 1989.

Ward, John William. *Andrew Jackson: Symbol for an Age.* New York: Oxford University Press, 1955.

Warner, Denis, and Peggy Warner. *The Tide at Sunrise: A History of the Russo-Japanese War 1904–1905.* New York: Charterhouse, 1974.

Warren, Robert Penn. "The Briar Patch." In *I'll Take My Stand: The South and the Agrarian Tradition.* New York; Harper and Brothers, 1930.

Weaver, Richard. *The Ethics of Rhetoric.* Chicago: Henry Regnery, 1953.

Weiss, Walter. "Effects of the Mass Media of Communication" In *Handbook of Social Psychology,* 2d ed., edited by Gardner Lindzey and Elliot Aronson, vol. 5. Reading, Mass.: Addison-Wesley, 1969.

Wells, Rulon. "Nominal and Verbal Style." In *Style in Language,* edited by Thomas A. Sebeok. Cambridge: M.I.T. Press, 1960.

Whipple, A. B. C. *The Mediterranean.* Chicago: Time-Life Books, 1981.

White, Hayden. *Metahistory: The Historical Imagination in Nineteenth-Century Europe.* Baltimore: Johns Hopkins University Press, 1973.

———. *The Content of the Form.* Baltimore: Johns Hopkins University Press, 1987.

———. "The Historical Text as Literary Artifact." In *The Writing of History: Literary Form and Historical Understanding,* edited by Robert H. Canary and Henry Kozicki. Madison: University of Wisconsin Press, 1978.

White, Richard. *"It's Your Misfortune and None of My Own": A New History of the American West.* Norman: University of Oklahoma Press, 1991.

Whitney, Frederick C. *Mass Media and Mass Communication in Society.* Dubuque: William C. Brown, 1975.

Wilkins, Burleigh Taylor. *Carl Becker: A Biographical Study in American Intellectual History.* Cambridge: M.I.T. Press, 1961.

Williams, T. Harry. *Romance and Realism in Southern Politics.* Athens: University of Georgia Press, 1964.

Wilson, Woodrow. *Division and Reunion 1829–1889.* New York: Longmans Green, 1929.

Wish, Harvey. *Contemporary America.* 2d ed. New York: Harper, 1955.

Wohlstetter, Roberta. *Pearl Harbor: Warning and Decision.* Stanford: Stanford University Press, 1962.

Woodward, C. Vann. *Origins of the New South, 1877–1913.* Baton Rouge: Louisiana State University Press, 1951.

———. "The Irony of Southern History." *Journal of Southern History* 19 (1953): 3–19. Repr. in *The Burden of Southern History.* 2d ed. Baton Rouge: Louisiana State University Press, 1986.

———. "A Second Look at the Theme of Irony." In *The Burden of Southern History.* 2d ed.

Woodworth, Robert, and Harold Schlosberg. *Experimental Psychology.* 2d ed. New York: Holt, Rinehart, and Winston, 1954.

Yngve, Victor H. "The Depth Hypothesis." In *Structure of Language and Its Mathematical Aspects,* edited by Roman Jakobson. Vol. 12 of *Proceedings of Symposia in Applied Mathematics.* Providence, R.I.: American Mathematical Society, 1961.

Yokosuka Naval Air Corps Air Branch Committee, Battle-lessons Investigating Committee, "Lessons [air operations] of the Sea Battle off Hawaii, Vol. I." In *The Pearl Harbor Papers: Inside the Japanese Plans,* edited by Donald M. Goldstein and Katherine V. Dillon. Washington, D.C.: Brassey's, 1993.

Young, Thomas Daniel, and Elizabeth Sarcone, eds. *The Lytle Tate Letters.* Jackson: University Press of Mississippi, 1987.

Young, Thomas Daniel, and George Core, eds. *Selected Letters of John Crowe Ransom.* Baton Rouge: Louisiana State University Press, 1985.

Zich, Arthur. *The Rising Sun*. Chicago: Time-Life Books, 1977.
Zipf, George Kingsley. *Human Behavior and the Principle of Least Effort*. Cambridge: Addison Wesley Press, 1949.
———. *The Psycho-Biology of Language*. Cambridge: M.I.T. Press, 1965.

Essays, Reviews, Pamphlets, and Newspaper Articles

Acheson, Dean G. "Dean Acheson's Version of Robert Kennedy's Version of the Cuban Missile Crisis: Homage to Plain Dumb Luck." *Esquire*, February 1969, 76ff.
Bandura, Albert, and Althea Huston. "Identification as a Process of Incidental Learning." *Journal of Abnormal and Social Psychology* 63 (1961): 311–18.
Beard, Charles A. "A Review of *The Frontier in American History*." *New Republic*, 16 February 1921, 349.
Beatty, R. C. "A Personal Memoir of the Agrarians." *Shenandoah* 3 (Summer 1952): 12–13.
Becker, Carl L. *America's War Aims and Peace Program*. War Information Series, No. 21. Washington, D.C.: Committee on Public Information, 1918.
———. "Detachment and the Writing of History." *Atlantic Monthly*, October 1910, 524–36.
———. *German Attempts to Divide Belgium*. Bostion: World Peace Foundation, 1917.
———. Review of *Modern Germany and Her Historians*, by Antoine Guilland, and *History of Germany in the Nineteenth Century*, by Heinrich von Treitschke. *Dial* 60 (17 February 1916): 160
———. Review of *Berlin Diary*, by William Shirer. *Time*, 27 October 1941, 103.
———. Review of *The Life and Times of Thomas Smith*, by Burton Alva Konkle. *Nation* 79 (18 August 1904): 146
———. Review of *The Rise of American Civilization*, by Charles A. Beard and Mary R. Beard. *Nation* 120 (18 May 1927): 559.
———. Review of *The Loyalists in the American Revolution*, by Claude H. Van Tyne. *Nation* 76 (4 June 1903): 461.
———. Review of *German Social Democracy during the War*, by Edward Bevan. *Nation* 109 (13 December 1919): 768.
———. Review of *A History of the United States, Vol. I, 1000–1600*, by Edward Channing. *Nation* 81 (13 July 1905): 40.
———. Review *A History of the United States, Vol. II, 1660–1760*, by Edward Channing. *Nation* 87 (5 November 1908): 440.
———. Review of *American History and its Geographic Conditions*, by Ellen Churchill Semple. *Nation* 77 (31 Dec. 1903): 534.
———. Review of *Republican France 1870–1912*, by Ernest A. Vizetelly. *Nation* 96 (24 April 1913): 416.

————. Review of *The Black Hawk War,* by Frank E. Stevens. *Nation* 77 (8 October 1903): 289.

————. Review of *The Fall of the Dutch Republic,* by Hendrik W. Van Loon. *Nation* 97 (14 August 1913): 145.

————. Review of *France in the American Revolution,* by James Breck Perkins. *Nation* 92 (15 June 1911): 604.

————. Review of *The Second Empire,* by Phillip Guedalla. *New Republic* 33 (27 December 1922): 125.

————. Review of *The Life of Nathaniel Macon,* by William E. Dodd. *Nation* 78 (12 May 1904): 378.

————. Review of *Jacksonian Democracy 1829–1837,* by William MacDonald. *Nation* 83 (26 July 1906): 81.

————. Review of *The Life and Times of Cavour,* by William R. Thayer. *Dial* 51 (16 November 1911): 389.

————. Review of *A History of France from the Earliest Times to the Treaty of Versailles,* by William S. Davis. *New Republic* 22 (14 July 1920): 207.

————. Review of *Iowa: The First Free State in the Louisiana Purchase,* by William Salter. *Nation* 81 (20 July 1905): 64.

————. "The Monroe Doctrine and the War." *Minnesota Historical Society Bulletin* 2 (1917): 61–68.

————. "The Way of a War." Review of *Before the War,* by Viscount Haldane. *Nation* 110 (22 May 1920): 693.

————. Review of *A Brief History of Europe from 1789–1815,* by Lucius Henry Holt and Alexander Wheeler Chilton. *New Republic* 22 (5 May 1920): 322.

Bennett, James R., Ronald H. Carpenter, Samuel Hornsby, and Ann Garbett. "History as Art: An Annotated Bibliography." *Style* 13 (Winter 1979): 5–36.

Berlyne, D. E. "Novelty and Curiosity as Determinants of Exploratory Behavior." *British Journal of Psychology* 40 (1949): 68–80.

Berquist, Goodwin R., Jr. "The Rhetorical Heritage of Frederick Jackson Turner." *Transactions of the Wisconsin Academy of Sciences, Arts and Letters* 59 (1971): 23–32.

Billington, Ray A. "Frederick Jackson Turner: Non-Western Historian." *Transactions of the Wisconsin Academy of Sciences, Arts and Letters* 59 (1971): 7–21.

Bitzer, Lloyd F. "The Rhetorical Situation." *Philosophy and Rhetoric* 1 (Winter 1968): 1–14.

Black, Edwin. "The Second Persona." *Quarterly Journal of Speech* 56 (April 1970): 109–19.

Bormann, Ernest G. "Fantasy and Rhetorical Vision: The Rhetorical Criticism of Social Reality." *Quarterly Journal of Speech* 58 (December 1972): 396–407.

Brookhiser, Richard. "Deerslayer Helped Define Us All." *Time,* 9 November 1992, 92.

Bryant, Donald C. "Rhetoric: Its Functions and Its Scope." *Quarterly Journal of Speech* 39 (December 1953): 401–24.

Buck, Jerry. "Westerns Gallop Back onto the TV Screen." *Gainesville Sun,* 21 June 1989, 5D.

Carlson, A. Cheree. "Narrative as the Philosopher's Stone: How Russell H. Conwell Changed Lead into Diamonds." *Western Journal of Speech Communication* 53 (Fall 1989): 343–44.

Carpenter, Ronald H. "Admiral Mahan, 'Narrative Fidelity,' and the Japanese Attack on Pearl Harbor." *Quarterly Journal of Speech* 72 (August 1986): 290–305.

———. "Alfred Thayer Mahan's Style on Sea Power: A Paramessage Conducing to *Ethos.*" *Speech Monographs* 42 (August 1975): 190–202.

———. "America's Opinion Leader Historians on Behalf of Success." *Quarterly Journal of Speech* 69 (May 1983): 111–26.

———. "America's Tragic Metaphor: Our Twentieth-Century Combatants as Frontiersmen." *Quarterly Journal of Speech* 76 (February 1990): 1–22.

———. "Carl Becker and the Epigrammatic Force of Style in History." *Communication Monographs* 48 (December 1981): 318–39.

———. "Frederick Jackson Turner and the Rhetorical Impact of the Frontier Thesis." *Quarterly Journal of Speech* 63 (April 1977): 117–29.

———. "General Douglas MacArthur's Oratory on Behalf of Inchon: Discourse That Altered the Course of History." *Southern Communication Journal* 58 (Fall 1992): 1–12.

———. "On American History Textbooks and Integration in the South: Woodrow Wilson and the Rhetoric of *Division and Reunion 1829–1889.*" *Southern Speech Communication Journal* 51 (Fall 1985): 1–23.

———. "Rhetorical Genesis of Style in the 'Frontier Hypothesis' of Frederick Jackson Turner." *Southern Speech Journal* 36 (Spring 1972): 233–48.

———. "Style and Emphasis in Debate." *Journal of the American Forensic Association* 6 (Winter 1969): 27–31.

———. "Style in Discourse as an Index of Frederick Jackson Turner's Historical Creativity: Conceptual Antecedents of the Frontier Thesis in His 'American Colonization.'" *Huntington Library Quarterly* 40 (May 1977): 269–77.

———. "Stylistic Redundancy and Function in Discourse." *Language and Style* 3 (Winter 1970): 62–68.

———. "The Essential Schemes of Syntax: An Analysis of Rhetorical Theory's Recommendations for Uncommon Syntax." *Quarterly Journal of Speech* 55 (April 1969): 161–68.

———. "The Impotent Style of Ronald Reagan." *Speaker and Gavel* 24 (Spring 1987): 53–59.

———. "The Stylistic Basis of Burkeian Identification." *Communication Quarterly* 20 (Winter 1972): 19–23.

———. "The Stylistic Identification of Frederick Jackson Turner with Robert M. La Follette: A Psychologically Oriented Analysis of Language Behavior." *Transactions of the Wisconsin Academy of Sciences, Arts and Letters* 63 (1975): 102–15.

———. "The Symbolic Substance of Style in Presidential Discourse." *Style* 16 (Winter 1982): 38–49.

———. "The Ubiquitous Antithesis: A Functional Source of Style in Political Discourse." *Style* 10 (Fall 1976): 426–41.

———. "Woodrow Wilson as Speechwriter for George Creel: Presidential Style in Discourse as an Index of Personality." *Presidential Studies Quarterly* 19 (Winter 1989): 117–26.

Carpenter, Ronald H., and Robert V. Seltzer. "Nixon, *Patton,* and a Silent Majority Sentiment about the Vietnam War: The Cinematographic Bases of a Rhetorical Stance." *Central States Speech Journal* 25 (Summer 1974): 105–10.

Coleman, William. "Science and Symbol in the Turner Frontier Hypothesis." *American Historical Review* 72 (1966): 22–49.

Cox, Robert. *Cultural Memory and Public Moral Argument.* Van Zelst Lecture in Communication, Northwestern University. Evanston: Northwestern University, 1987.

Crumpler, David. "Unforgiven Rewrites Legend of Old West." *Jacksonville Florida Times-Union,* 16 August 1992, G1.

Curti, Merle. Review of *Allan Nevins on History,* edited by Ray A. Billington. *Pacific Historical Review* 45 (1976): 278.

Davidson, Donald. "*I'll Take My Stand:* A History." *American Review* 5 (1935): 304.

Fairley, Irene R. "Syntactic Deviation and Cohesion." *Language and Style* 6 (Summer 1973): 216–29.

Fisher, Walter R. "Narration as a Human Communication Paradigm: The Case of Public Moral Argument." *Communication Monographs* 51 (March 1984): 1–22.

Frentz, Thomas S. *Mass Media as Rhetorical Narration.* Van Zelst Lecture in Communication, Northwestern University. Evanston: Northwestern University, 1985.

Hart, Roderick, and Don Burks. "Rhetorical Sensitivity and Social Interaction." *Speech Monographs* 39 (June 1972): 75–91.

Henderlider, Clair R. "Woodrow Wilson's Speeches on the League of Nations, September 4–25." *Communication Monographs* 8 (1946): 23–34.

Hesseltine, William B. "Look Away, Dixie." *Sewanee Review* 39 (1931): 101.

Howes, Davis, and Solomon, Richard L. "Visual Duration Threshold as a Function of Word-Probability." *Journal of Experimental Psychology* 41 (1951): 401–410.

Hunter, Stephen. "Movies Blow Up Firearms to Mythic Proportions." *Gainesville Sun,* 7 August 1988, F1, 4.

Hyman, Ann. "*Oklahoma!* Sweeps into Town." *Jacksonville Times-Union,* 9 November 1993, D1.

Ivie, Robert L. "Images of Savagery in American Justifications for War." *Communication Monographs* 47 (November 1980): 279–94.

———. "Literalizing the Metaphor of Soviet Savagery: President Truman's Plain Style." *Southern Speech Communication Journal* 51 (Winter 1986): 91–105.

———. "Metaphor and the Rhetorical Invention of Cold War 'Idealists.'" *Communication Monographs* 54 (June 1987): 165–82.

———. "Speaking 'Common Sense' about the Soviet Threat: Reagan's Rhetorical Stance." *Western Journal of Speech Communication* 48 (Winter 1984): 39–50.

Ivie, Robert L., and W. Clifton Adams. "I. A. Richards' Concept of Tenor-Vehicle Interactions." *Central States Speech Journal* 27 (Summer 1976): 136–43.

Jordan, William. "A Reinforcement Model of Metaphor." *Speech Monographs* 34 (August 1972): 223–26.

———. "Toward a Psychological Theory of Metaphor." *Western Speech* 35 (Summer 1971): 169–75.

Kagan, Jerome. "The Concept of Identification." *Psychological Review* 65 (1958): 296–305.

Katz, Elihu. "The Two-Step Flow of Communication: An Up-To-Date Report on an Hypothesis." *Public Opinion Quarterly* 21 (1957): 63–77.

Kauffman, Charles. "Names and Weapons." *Communication Monographs* 56 (September 1989): 277–81.

Kauffmann, Stanley. "On Films." *New Republic* 162 (7 March 1970): 24.

Levahese, Louise E. "Frederic Remington—The Man and the Myth." *National Geographic* 174 (August 1988): 200–31.

Lukas, J. Anthony. "Class Reunion: Kennedy's Men Relive the Cuban Missile Crisis." *New York Times Magazine*, 30 August 1987, 22ff.

MacCoby, Eleanor E., and William C. Wilson. "Identification and Observational Learning from Films." *Journal of Abnormal and Social Psychology* 55 (1957): 76–87.

Mahan, Alfred Thayer. "The Writing of History." *Atlantic Monthly* 91 (1903): 289–97.

McEdwards, Mary G. "Woodrow Wilson: His Stylistic Progression." *Western Journal of Speech Communication* 26 (Winter 1962): 28–38.

McGee, Michael C. "The 'Ideograph': A Link Between Rhetoric and Ideology." *Quarterly Journal of Speech* 66 (February 1980): 1–16.

———. "In Search of 'The People': A Rhetorical Alternative." *Quarterly Journal of Speech* 61 (October 1975): 235–49.

McKerrow, Raymie E. "Critical Rhetoric: Theory and Praxis." *Communication Monographs* 56 (June 1989): 91–111.

Meissner, W. W. "Notes on Identification." *Psychoanalytic Quarterly* 39 (1970): 563–89.

Mencken, H. L. "Uprising in the Confederacy." *American Mercury* 22 (March 1931): 381.

Newman, Robert P. "Lethal Rhetoric: The Selling of the China Myths." *Quarterly Journal of Speech* 61 (April 1975): 113–28.

Nixon, Richard M. "The Situation in Southeast Asia: The President's Address to the Nation, April 30, 1970." *Weekly Compilation of Presidential Documents* 6 (4 May 1970): 596–601.

Nute, Grace Lee. "Frederick Jackson Turner." *Minnesota History* 13 (June 1932): 159–61.

O'Brien, Geoffrey. "Killing Time." *New York Book Review* 39 (5 March 1992): 38–42.

Osborn, George C. "Woodrow Wilson as a Speaker." *Southern Speech Communication Journal* 12 (Fall 1956): 61–72.

Osborn, Michael. "Archetypal Metaphor in Rhetoric: The Light-Dark Family." *Quarterly Journal of Speech* 53 (April 1967): 115–26.

———. "The Evolution of the Archetypal Sea in Rhetoric and Poetic." *Quarterly Journal of Speech* 63 (December 1977): 347–63.

Osborn, Michael, and Douglas Ehninger. "The Metaphor in Public Address." *Speech Monographs* 29 (August 1962): 223–34.

Peattie, Mark R. "Akiyama Saneyuki and the Emergence of Modern Japanese Naval Doctrine." *U.S. Naval Institute Proceedings* 103 (January 1977): 60–69.

Postal, Paul M. "Underlying and Superficial Linguistic Structure." *Harvard Educational Review* 34 (1964): 246–66.

Ramsdell, Charles W. Review of *States Rights in the Confederacy*, by Frank L. Owsley. *Mississippi Valley Historical Review* 14 (June 1927): 107–10.

"Reaching for Supremacy at Sea." *Time*, 31 January 1972, 29.

Reid, Ronald F. "The Boylston Professorship of Rhetoric and Oratory, 1806–1904: A Case Study of Changing Concepts of Rhetoric and Pedagogy." *Quarterly Journal of Speech* 45 (October 1959): 239–57.

Rosenthal, Paul I. "The Concept of the Paramessage in Persuasive Communication." *Quarterly Journal of Speech* 58 (February 1972): 15–30.

Runion, Howard. "An Objective Study of the Speech Style of Woodrow Wilson." *Communication Monographs* 3 (1936): 75–94.

Rushing, Janice Hocker. "Mythic Evolution of 'the New Frontier' in Mass Mediated Rhetoric." *Critical Studies in Mass Communication* 3 (September 1986): 265–96.

———. "The Rhetoric of the American Western Myth." *Communication Monographs* 50 (March 1983): 14–32.

Rushing, Janice Hocker, and Thomas S. Frentz. "*The Deer Hunter*: Rhetoric of the Warrior." *Quarterly Journal of Speech* 66 (December 1980): 392–406.

Schaefer, Joseph. "The Author of the 'Frontier Thesis.'" *Wisconsin Magazine of History* 15 (1931): 86–89.

Short, Brant. "'Reconstructed but Unregenerate': *I'll Take My Stand*'s Rhetorical Vision of Progress." *Southern Communication Journal* 29 (Winter 1994): 112–24.

Short, M. H. "Some Thoughts on Foregrounding and Interpretation." *Language and Style* 6 (Spring 1973): 97–108.

Sidey, Hugh. "Getting Gorby on the Line." *Time,* 9 April 1990, 39.

Smith, Charlotte Watkins. "Carl Becker: The Historian as Literary Craftsman." *William and Mary Quarterly* 9 (1952): 291–316.

Smoler, Frederic. "An Interview with Arthur Schlesinger, Jr.: What Should We Teach Our Children about American History?" *American Heritage* 43 (February/March 1992): 45–52.

Snyder, Phil L. "Carl L. Becker and the Great War: A Crisis for a Humane Intelligence." *Western Political Quarterly* 9 (1956): 1–10.

Solomon, Richard L., and Leo Postman. "Frequency of Usage as a Determinant of Recognition Threshold for Words." *Journal of Experimental Psychology* 43 (1952): 195–201.

Stavish, Monica. "Latter-day Cowpokes Hold Shoot-'em-ups." *Tampa Tribune,* 25 September 1992, B3.

Stengel, Richard. "American Myth 101." *Time,* 22 December 1991, 78–80.

Szulc, Tad. "What We Need To Do: A Profile of JCS Chairman, General John M. Shalikashvili." *Parade Magazine,* 1 May 1994, 4–5.

Tompkins, Phillip K. "The Rhetorical Criticism of Non-Oratorical Works." *Quarterly Journal of Speech* 55 (December 1969): 432–38.

Tuchman, Barbara. "The Historian's Opportunity." *Saturday Review,* 25 February 1967, 27–31.

Vance, Rupert. Review of *Plain Folk of the Old South,* by Frank L. Owsley. *Journal of Southern History* 16 (November 1950): 545–47.

Waugh, Nancy C. "Immediate Memory as a Function of Repetition." *Journal of Verbal Learning and Verbal Behavior* 2 (1963): 107–12.

Weinraub, Bernard. "Eastwood: New Film May Be the Best One Ever." *Gainesville Sun,* 25 August 1992, D1.

White, Theodore H. "The Danger from Japan." *New York Times Magazine,* 28 July 1985, 19.

Will, George. "Feel-good History Distorts Reality." *Gainesville Sun,* 15 July 1991, 6A.

Wood, Gordon S. Review of *History of the Westward Movement,* by Frederick Merk. *History Book Club Review,* July 1978, 3–7.

Unpublished Papers

Gustainis, J. Justin. "From Savior to Psycho and Back Again: The Changing Role of Green Berets in Vietnam Films." Paper presented at the Eastern Communication Association Convention, Baltimore, 1988.

Gustainis, J. Justin. "John F. Kennedy and the Green Berets: The Rhetorical Use of the Hero Myth." Paper presented at the Central States Speech

Association-Southern States Communication Association Joint Convention, St. Louis, 1987.

Osborn, Michael. "Response to Papers on Metaphors of War." Paper presented at the Speech Communication Association Convention, New Orleans, 1988.

Simmons, Edwin. H. "Response to Papers on Rhetoric among the Military." Paper presented at the Speech Communication Association Convention, Miami, 1993.

Index